Vic

Palgrave Sourcebooks

Series Editor: Steven Matthews

Published

Simon Bainbridge: **Romanticism**

Carolyn Collette and Harold Garrett-Goodyear: **The Later Middle Ages**

Lena Cowen Orlin: **The Renaissance**

Steven Matthews: **Modernism**

John Plunkett, Ana Vadillo, Regenia Gagnier, Angelique Richardson,
  Rick Rylance and Paul Young: **Victorian Literature**

Forthcoming

Nigel Wood: **The 'Long' Eighteenth Century**

Palgrave Sourcebooks
Series Standing order
ISBN 978–1–4039–4277–7 hardcover
ISBN 978–1–4039–4278–4 paperback
(outside North America only)

You can receive future titles in this series as they are published by placing a standing
order. Please contact your bookseller or, in the case of difficulty, write to us at the address
below with your name and address, the title of the series, and the ISBN quoted above.

Customer Services Department, Macmillan Distribution Ltd
Houndmills, Basingstoke, Hampshire, RG21 6XS, England

Victorian Literature

A Sourcebook

Edited by

John Plunkett

Ana Parejo Vadillo

Regenia Gagnier

Angelique Richardson

Rick Rylance

Paul Young

First published 2012 by
PALGRAVE MACMILLAN

Palgrave Macmillan in the UK is an imprint of Macmillan Publishers Limited,
registered in England, company number 785998, of Houndmills, Basingstoke,
Hampshire RG21 6XS.

Palgrave Macmillan in the US is a division of St Martin's Press LLC,
175 Fifth Avenue, New York, NY 10010.

Palgrave Macmillan is the global academic imprint of the above companies
and has companies and representatives throughout the world.

Palgrave® and Macmillan® are registered trademarks in the United States,
the United Kingdom, Europe and other countries

ISBN-13: 978-0-230-55174-9   hardback
ISBN-13: 978-0-230-55175-6   paperback

This book is printed on paper suitable for recycling and made from fully
managed and sustained forest sources. Logging, pulping and manufacturing
processes are expected to conform to the environmental regulations of the
country of origin.

A catalogue record for this book is available from the British Library.

A catalog record for this book is available from the Library of Congress.

10 9 8 7 6 5 4 3
21 20 19 18 17 16 15 14 1

Printed in China

In Memory of Sally Ledger,
colleague and friend:
1961–2009

Short Contents

Detailed Contents

List of Illustrations

Acknowledgements

The editors and publishers wish to thank the following for permission to reproduce copyright material:

The Literary Estate of Arthur Symons for an extract from Arthur Symons, 'The Decadent Movement in Literature', *Harper's New Monthly Magazine* (November 1893), 858–9.

University of Exeter Library Special Collections for Figure 1.1, 'Specimens from Mr. Punch's Industrial Exhibition', *Punch* 18 (1850); Figure 1.2, 'The Exterior', *Dickinson's Comprehensive Pictures of the Great Exhibition of 1851* (London: Dickinson, 1854); Figure 1.3, 'For Queen and Empire!!', *Punch* 112 (1897); Figure 2.1 [John Tenniel], 'Cartoon No. V. Capital and Labour', *Punch* 5 (July–December 1843); Figure 2.2, After a daguerreotype by Beard, 'The Wallpaper Girl', from Henry Mayhew, *London Labour and the London Poor*, vol. 1 (London: Griffin, Bohn and Co, 1861); Figure 3.1 [John Tenniel], 'An "Ugly Rush!" Mr. Bull. "Not if I know it!"', *Punch* 58 (January–June 1870); Figure 6.1, Alexander Pugin, 'Contrasted Residences for the Poor', *Contrasts: or, a parallel between the noble edifices of the Middle Ages, and corresponding buildings of the present day, shewing the present decay of taste* (1838; London: Charles Dolman, 1841); Figure 7.1, Fold-out wooden stereoscope with glass stereograph, *c.*1870; Figure 7.2, Phiz, 'Pantomime Night', *Illustrated London News* (8 January 1848); Figure 7.3, 'A. W. Hamilton's Voyage Around the World', Large Mechanics' Hall, Nottingham (1881); Figure 7.4, Alhambra Theatre programme, Leicester Square, London, 3 August 1896; Figure 8.1, '"The Times" Office. New Printing Machine', *The Ladies' Treasury* 4 (1860); Figure 10.1, Gideon Mantell, 'Fossil Teeth of Mammalia', *A Pictorial Atlas of Fossil Remains* (London: H. G. Bohn, 1850); Figure 10.2, 'The Two Giants of the Time (steam and electricity)', *Punch* 33 (1857).

Andrew King for Figure 8.2, 'Ellen De Vere and the Ayah in the Picture Gallery', *The London Journal: A Weekly Record of Literature, Science and Art* 16 (15 January 1853).

Every effort has been made to trace rights holders, but if any have been inadvertently overlooked the publishers would be pleased to make the necessary arrangements at the first opportunity.

This is a book born out of the shared intellectual endeavour of the members of the Centre for Victorian Studies at the University of Exeter. It was finished in collaboration with Birkbeck, University of London, following Ana Parejo Vadillo's move there in the course of its completion. It is, above all, a collegial effort, shaped by many informal discussions as well as by individuals being responsible for particular sections. Ana Parejo Vadillo and John Plunkett acted as lead editors, and were responsible for five of the sections as well as the introduction; the other sections were composed, either individually or jointly, by Regenia Gagnier, Angelique Richardson, Rick Rylance and Paul Young. Ana and John would like to thank their colleagues for their efforts in bringing their sections together.

We are very grateful to the research assistants who have greatly aided the preparation of this volume: Sunie Fletcher, Kate Hext and Andrew Griffiths (and to the Department of English at Exeter who granted us the funds to employ them). We are particularly thankful for Andrew's assistance with the final stages of the manuscript.

As this book was nearing completion, the international Victorian Studies community mourned the untimely death of Professor Sally Ledger. All of the editors of this volume benefited enormously from her energy, enthusiasm and scholarship; it is to her that we dedicate this book.

Series Editor's Preface

For at least 25 years, questions about the relation between literature and the historical period in which it was created have formed the central focus and methodology of critics. From the early 1980s, crucially, a range of literary scholars have sought to explore and define the parallels and differences between the representational language deployed in creative texts, and uses of similar rhetorical strategies in other contemporary cultural sources, such as journals, court documents, diaries and religious tracts. This kind of historicist reconsideration of literature has had far-reaching consequences in the academy and beyond, and the drive better to understand the dialogue established between texts and their originating period has brought new dynamism to ideas of context and contextualization.

The *Sourcebooks* series aims to provide a comprehensive and suggestive selection of original cultural sources for each of the major artistic moments from the medieval period onward. Edited by internationally renowned British and American experts in their chosen area, each volume presents within suitable subsections a panoply of materials relating to everything, from historical background to gender, philosophy, science and religion, which will be of use both to students and to scholars seeking to contextualize creative work in any given period. It has been a particular ambition of the series to put back into circulation ephemeral original texts from magazines, newspapers, and even private sources, in order to offer a more representative sense of any one period's cultural debates and processes. Literature remains the primary focus of the volumes, but each contains documents relating to the broader artistic and cultural context which will be of interest and use to everyone working in the humanities area.

Each volume contains an informative general Introduction giving an overview of pertinent historical and cultural movements and pressures of its time. Each document is edited to a high scholarly standard through the use of headnotes and other supportive apparatus, in order to make the document accessible for further study. This apparatus is not prescriptive in determining the relation between any one literary text and these background resources, although each volume contains instances where documents directly alluded to by major writers are specifically excerpted. Generally, however, the series seeks to further historicist study and research by making available important or intriguing materials which might act to instigate further thought and reflection, so aiding to determine a more substantial picture of any literary work's moment of coming into being.

Steven Matthews

Timeline of Historical Events

1801 Union of Great Britain and Ireland

1807 Abolition of the Slave Trade Act outlaws trading in (though not owning) slaves

1828 Repeal of Test and Corporation Act allowed Protestant dissenting groups (Unitarians, Methodists, Quakers, Wesleyans) to hold official public office

1829 Catholic Relief Act; Roman Catholics allowed to sit as MPs in Parliament

1830 Accession of William IV

1832 Reform Act, properly the Representation of the People Act 1832, increases the franchise from 217,000 to 435,000

1833 Slavery Abolition Act; slavery abolished throughout the British Empire

1834 Poor Law Amendment Act abolishes 'outdoor' relief and makes workhouses central to support for the poor. Tolpuddle Martyrs: a group of Dorset agricultural workers transported to Australia for forming a proto-trade union, the Friendly Society of Agricultural Labourers. Houses of Parliament burn down; reconstruction according to designs by Augustus Pugin and Charles Barry continues to c.1867

1836 Reduction of newspaper tax from 4d to 1d

1837 Accession of Queen Victoria, niece of William IV

1838 Publication of Charter calling for parliamentary reform. National Gallery opens in London

1840 Marriage of Queen Victoria to Prince Albert of Saxe-Coburg-Gotha

1841 *Punch*, a humorous and satirical journal, commences

1842 Mines Act; it bans women and children under 10 from working underground

1845 John Henry Newman converts to Roman Catholicism

1845–9 Potato blight in Ireland leads to famine and widespread starvation

1846 Repeal of the Corn Laws, which placed import tariffs on cheaper foreign wheat, enables free trade in this staple food

1847 Factory Act, also known as the Ten Hours Act, limited the hours worked by children and women to ten hours a day

1848 Revolution in France causes abdication of King Louis-

Philippe; establishment of
Second Republic; revolution-
ary uprisings across Europe.
Chartist petition presented to
Parliament following mass
demonstration on
Kennington Common,
London.
Formation of the Pre-
Raphaelite Brotherhood

1850 Factory Act limits working
hours for women and chil-
dren and makes Saturday a
half-day.
Public Libraries Act introduces publicly funded lend-
ing libraries in boroughs with
populations of over 10,000

1851 The Great Exhibition, housed
in the Crystal Palace, opens
in Hyde Park

1852 Founding of South
Kensington Museum, later
the Victoria and Albert
Museum

1853–6 Crimean War

1855 Abolition of Stamp Duty on
newspapers, significantly
reducing their price

1857 Matrimonial Causes Act
transfers divorce proceedings
from ecclesiastical to civil
courts.
Obscene Publications Act
allows police to search book-
sellers' premises, and
Customs Officers and Post
Office officials to destroy
offending works and prosecute offenders

1857–8 Indian 'Mutiny'

1859 Charles Darwin, *On the Origin
of Species*; J. S. Mill, *On Liberty*

1861 Death of Prince Albert, the

Prince Consort.
William Morris and associates
form an interior design
company, Morris, Marshall,
Faulkner and Company,
which was important to the
development of the Arts and
Crafts Movement

1862 International Exhibition of
1862 held at South
Kensington, London

1864 Contagious Diseases Acts; the
Act allows police to arrest
suspected prostitutes in ports
and garrison towns, and to
hold them for mandatory
physical examination and
medical treatment.
International Workingmen's
Association (or First
International), an alliance of
left-wing groups, founded in
London

1865 William Booth founds the
Christian Mission, later
named the Salvation Army

1866 First successful transatlantic
telegraph cable laid

1867 Second Reform Act enfran-
chises most male urban
householders.
Karl Marx, *Das Kapital*

1870 Elementary Education Act
provided legislation for local
authorities to provide schools
for all children aged between
five and twelve.
Married Women's Property
Act; women's earnings, inher-
itances and investments were
no longer automatically the
property of their husbands

1871 Charles Darwin, *The Descent
of Man*

1873   Impressionist artists Monet, Renoir, Pissarro and Sisley (soon joined by Renoir, Morisot and Degas) form the *Société Anonyme Coopérative des Artistes Peintres, Sculpteurs, Graveurs*.
Walter Pater, *The Renaissance*

1877   Grosvenor Gallery opens, exhibiting art from outside the mainstream.
James Abbott McNeill Whistler sues the critic Ruskin for describing his painting of *Nocturne in Black and Gold: The Falling Rocket* as 'flinging a pot of paint in the public's face'

1884   Third Reform Bill, the Representation of the People Act 1884, extended the franchise to working-class men in rural areas

1885   Criminal Law Amendment Act raises the age of consent for girls from 13 to 16 years of age. Labouchère Amendment to the same act criminalizes 'acts of gross indecency' between men

1886   Repeal of Contagious Diseases Acts

1886   First Irish Home Rule Bill defeated in the House of Commons

1889   Great Dock Strike (London) won by workers; the dispute helped bring union organization to unskilled labour

1893   Second Irish Home Rule Bill passed by House of Commons, but defeated in House of Lords

1893   Independent Labour Party formed

1895   In Paris, brothers Auguste and Louis Lumière hold first public screening of moving pictures at which admission is charged.
Oscar Wilde tried for gross indecency, sentenced to two years' hard labour

1899–
1902   Boer War

1900   Sigmund Freud, *The Interpretation of Dreams*

1901   Death of Queen Victoria; succeeded by her son as Edward VII

Introduction

At the beginning of his waspish retrospective *Eminent Victorians* (1918), Lytton Strachey declares, 'The history of the Victorian Age will never be written: we know too much about it.'[1] A member of the modernist Bloomsbury Group, who had nonetheless been born in 1880, Strachey's comment was meant in two ways: that the Victorians were still too much part of his own life for measured comprehension; and that they had left too vast a documentary record for him to be able to interpret them. Strachey's difficulties remain with us: there is still a fascination with the period because of its formative role both upon his time and ours. Kelly Boyd and Rohan McWilliam have observed that we remain 'haunted by the ghosts of the Victorians. We live in the houses they built, or, if we do not, regularly stroll past buildings they erected. We work in the global marketplace they did so much to construct . . . We continue to read their novels'.[2] What has remained equally prominent, though, is the inability of the period to be pinned down by virtue of its scale and quantity of documentation; an assembly of popular characteristics of the Victorians could only ever produce a series of contradictions: an age of discovery, progress and industry but also of slum dwellings, the workhouse and exploited factory workers; a period where the dominant ideals of bourgeois sobriety and respectability were challenged by gin palaces and prostitution; a queen on the throne who gave her name to the age, yet at a time when women were not entitled to vote.

Our sourcebook brings together a range of key social, political and scientific documents in order to help students and researchers explore Victorian literature in all its complexity. As Strachey realized, any summary of the period risks generalization, so this introduction seeks instead to outline a series of pathways to help open up the study of Victorian literature. Its aim is threefold: to reflect on the label of 'the Victorian' and why debates over its meaning raise important questions about the way we approach it as a period; to suggest how this sourcebook might be used and to reflect on the interdisciplinary methodologies developed by Victorian Studies scholarship over the last two decades; and, finally, to provide a brief overview of Victorian literature and the movements and genres most likely to be encountered in studying it.

---

1 Lytton Strachey, *Eminent Victorians: Cardinal Manning, Florence Nightingale, Dr Arnold, General Gordon* (London: Chatto and Windus, 1918), vii.
2 Kelly Boyd and Rohan McWilliam, 'Introduction: Rethinking the Victorians', in *The Victorian Studies Reader*, ed. Kelly Boyd and Rohan McWilliam (London: Routledge, 2007), 5.

The Victorian era ostensibly covers the period of Queen Victoria's long reign, from 1837 to 1901. Yet this straightforward and convenient dating belies a number of issues over precisely when the period was, and what exactly the label stands for. Revealingly, the term 'Victorian' was initially a contemporary appellation. Miles Taylor has pithily noted that 'the Victorians invented many things – including themselves'.[3] As early as 1843, the satirical journal *Punch* published an article announcing 'The Victorian, In Contradistinction to the Elizabethan Style'; by the mid- to late 1850s, it had pieces such as a poem on the 'Wonders of the Victorian Age'.[4] The self-confident assertions of a distinct and exceptional Victorian era (albeit one that often harked back to Elizabethan splendour) were, in a large measure, engendered by Britain's position as the first industrial nation, and its corresponding economic and imperial dominance in global affairs.

Our sourcebook uses the term 'Victorian' because it sees it as the period's most useful and powerful trademark (typically the Victorians were the first to provide legal protection to trademarks). It is also recognized in academia as an important area within the curriculum. It is important, though, to question what exactly the label means, what it covers (in terms of both characteristics and chronology), and whether the historical and critical baggage it has accumulated means that it needs to be used with a degree of care. A recent revisionary movement has seen a number of challenges to the grand narrative that the Victorians – eagerly followed by some subsequent critics – told to celebrate their own achievements as a distinct 'age'. This impetus has come from various fronts. Historians such as Richard Price have convincingly argued that key moments and ideas associated with the period, for example the rise of the middle classes or even the Industrial Revolution itself, can be traced back to the eighteenth century, and have made a strong case for speaking instead of a 'long eighteenth-century' lasting until 1850s.[5]

At one level, attempting to lay down a marker for the beginning of a period is obviously reductive given the arbitrariness of using individual dates to mark transitions. Scholars have been right to challenge the presumed uniqueness of some of the characteristics associated with the period. Nonetheless, the sourcebook consists of pieces predominantly from the period 1830 to 1900. In the 1830s, a plethora of legislative, social and technological events, culminating with the accession of the young Princess Victoria in 1837, created the distinct perception of a new 'modern' period.[6] To give just a few examples: the Catholic Relief Act (1829) removed restrictions upon Catholics holding parliamentary

---

3 Miles Taylor, 'Introduction', in *The Victorians Since 1901: Histories, Representations and Revisions*, ed. Miles Taylor and Michael Wolff (Manchester: Manchester University Press, 2004), 5.

4 'The Victorian, In Contradistinction to the Elizabethan Style', *Punch* (1843), 249; 'Wonders of the Victorian Age', *Punch* 29 (1 September 1855), 83.

5 Richard Price, 'Historiography, Narrative and the Nineteenth Century', *Journal of British Studies* 35.2 (April 1996), 220–56.

6 On a robust defence of the 'Victorian', see Martin Hewitt, 'Why the Notion of Victorian Britain *Does* Make Sense', *Victorian Studies* 48.3 (Spring 2006), 395–438.

office; the Reform Bill (1832) expanded the electorate and created voting constituencies for the new industrial cities; the New Poor Law (1834) introduced a system of welfare relief based on the workhouse. Elsewhere, the Liverpool and Manchester Railway opened in 1830; in 1834 Charles Babbage envisaged his analytic engine, regarded as the forerunner of the modern computer; Charles Darwin set off on HMS *Beagle* in December 1831; and Tennyson and Dickens began their literary careers with *Poems, Chiefly Lyrical* (1830) and *Sketches By Boz* (1833–6) respectively.

The clustering of events in the 1830s, exciting yet disorientating, liberating yet threatening, was not lost on those living through it; as the novelist Edward Bulwer-Lytton remarked:

> We live in an age of visible transition – an age of disquietude and doubt – of the removal of time-worn landmarks, and the breaking up of hereditary elements of society – old opinions, feelings – ancestral customs and institutions are crumbling away, and both the spiritual and temporal worlds are darkened by the shadows of change. The commencement of one of these epochs – periodical in the history of mankind – hailed by the sanguine as the coming of a new Millennium – a great iconoclastic reformation, by which all false gods shall be overthrown. To me such epochs appear but as the dark passages in the appointed progress of mankind – the times of greatest unhappiness to our species – passages into which we have no reason to rejoice at our entrance, save from the hope of being sooner landed on the opposite side.[7]

Bulwer-Lytton perfectly captures the ambivalence of transition in the years around Victoria's accession: the hopes of those aspiring towards a more democratic future are qualified by his own darker anxieties over the uncertainties that progress would inevitably bring.

In a fashion similar to debates over the beginning of the period, many critics have noted that the break between the Victorian era and modernism is equally fuzzy, despite the finitude that was created by the *fin de siècle* coinciding with Queen Victoria's death in 1901. A clear example is T. S. Eliot's high modernist poem *The Waste Land* (1922), one of whose foundational texts is James Thomson's 1873 urban sequence *The City of Dreadful Night*. Just as eighteenth-century critics have argued for a 'long eighteenth century', nineteenth-century critics often use the term 'the long nineteenth century' to describe a period that does not end with the death of Victoria but continues well into the twentieth century, up until the beginning of the First World War. While modernist art and literature relished its rejection of its Victorian forebears, creating an equivocal relationship with the period that cast a long shadow for much of the twentieth

---

7 Edward Bulwer-Lytton, *England and the English* (1833), ed. Standish Meacham (Chicago: University of Chicago Press, 1970), 318–19.

century, anthologies and sourcebooks for studying modernism now begin with the revolutions of 1848, the rise of Marxist theory and urbanism, all of which are reconceptualized as pivotal moments and processes in its emergence.

At the same time as the external boundaries of 'the Victorian' have been questioned, it is equally worth considering the way that the label elides internal differences. While the term 'Victorian' has granted and grants visibility to an area of research, it has also had the adverse effect of homogenizing its vast history and diversity. In his important early reappraisal of Victorian literary studies, *The Victorian Temper* (1951), Jerome H. Buckley argued against the basic tenets of this homogenization by showing that Victorians themselves 'were quite unable to view their long era as a static entity, a unique whole to be described by a single sweeping formula'.[8] Since then, Victorian scholars have continued to provide major re-evaluations of the literatures of the period, including most recently Philip Davis, who in his insightful discussion of *Why Victorian Literature Still Matters* (2008) reminds us that though we might be speaking of one single epoch, '1830 is as different from 1880 as most so-called "ages" are from one another'.[9]

The difference between the early, mid- and late Victorian period is matched by the diversity of experiences within the society at any one moment in time. One obvious example of this is the impact of urbanization, which created dramatically expanding cities, predominantly in northern England, that were wholly alien in their physical and social make-up to those still working on the land or in provincial towns. The 1851 census revealed that, for the first time, just over half the population of England lived in cities. The speed of urbanization is evident in the fact that, in 1831, it was still the case that three-quarters of the nation had lived in rural areas.[10] The population of Manchester rose from 75,000 in 1801 to 303,000 in 1851, while that of London rose from 800,000 in the early 1800s to five million by 1900. While industrialization and urbanization accentuated a split between city and country, north and south (themes explored by Elizabeth Gaskell's eponymous novel *North and South*), they also created a socio-economic structure characterized by lack of interaction between those of different classes. As Disraeli famously declared in *Sybil* (1845), Britain was not one nation but two:

> 'Well, society may be in its infancy,' said Egremont, slightly smiling; 'but, say what you like, our Queen reigns over the greatest nation that ever existed.'
> 'Which nation?' asked the younger stranger, 'for she reigns over two.'
> The stranger paused; Egremont was silent, but looked inquiringly.
> 'Yes,' resumed the younger stranger after a moment's interval. 'Two nations;

8 Jerome H. Buckley, *The Victorian Temper: A Study in Literary Culture* (Cambridge, MA: Harvard University Press, 1951), 7.

9 Philip Davis, *Why Victorian Literature Still Matters* (Oxford: Wily-Blackwell, 2008), 1.

10 See Philip Davis, *The Oxford English Literary History 1830–1880: The Victorians* (Oxford: Oxford University Press, 2002), 13–54.

between whom there is no intercourse and no sympathy; who are as ignorant of each other's habits, thoughts, and feelings, as if they were dwellers in different zones, or inhabitants of different planets; who are formed by a different breeding, are fed by a different food, are ordered by different manners, and are not governed by the same laws.'
'You speak of —' said Egremont, hesitatingly
'THE RICH AND THE POOR.'[11]

In this sense, Karl Marx's statement that all history is the history of class struggle can be understood as definitively Victorian in its universalism.

Perhaps, above all else then, this sourcebook offers a compendium of voices that demonstrate the impossibility of any monolithic understanding of 'the Victorian'. The diverse voices (and languages, with several pieces reproduced in translation) that make up the sourcebook not only reflect the range of influences upon the period, but the different social groups and identities which, in keeping with the democratic impulses of the time, were increasingly making their voices heard. In the pages below, a Sikh soldier's account of the Indian Mutiny jostles with Karl Marx writing about class war in Europe; Florence Nightingale's impassioned frustration at her domestic constraints challenges those pieces that essentialize women's social role because of biology or theology.

There is one caveat, however, to the heterogeneity of voices found in the sourcebook. Disraeli's lament over the existence of the two nations of rich and poor was intended as a clarion call to create communities that would overcome division, fragmentation and alienation. He was far from alone in his anxieties; the sourcebook is punctuated with extracts that record technological and legislative achievements, and the cultural anxieties and aspirations they are inseparable from, which worked to accentuate the sense of the nation as an imagined, unified whole. Examples range from the hopes of Augustus Pugin, John Ruskin and William Morris that Gothic medievalism would aid social reformation to Mathew Arnold's argument that the function of culture was precisely to mitigate the division of society into three groups he labelled as Barbarians, Philistines and Populace, broadly corresponding to the aristocracy, bourgeoisie and working class.

Efforts to use art and culture to create social cohesion and community had a counterpart in the extraordinary advances in communication and transportation technologies, particularly the railway and telegraph networks. The railway network was one of the industrial creations that the Victorians were most proud of. Its impact was far-reaching in the mobility, freedom and connectivity it created. The railways linked disparate regions and ultimately fostered a more homogenous nationhood. As John Mason Neale unflatteringly put it in *Hierologus; or The Church Tourists* (1843), railways made 'England into one huge manufacturing town – amalgamating into one senseless heap the various usages of different localities – mixing, as opticians do, the clear and beautiful tints of

---

11 Benjamin Disraeli, *Sybil; or The Two Nations* (London: Henry Colburn, 1845), 79.

local habits, feelings, prejudices, affections, into one colourless and monotonous mass . . . thus turning us into cosmopolites, most odious name!'[12] Neale's
warning against the erosion of local difference belies the excitement and freedom of the railways. The railways, along with the international telegraph
network, exemplify the compression of time and space that is often regarded as
constitutive of modernity.

The global connectivity of the telegraph network (the first transatlantic cable
to be successfully laid was in 1866) hints at one other way that the notion of
'the Victorian' sometimes works to obscure an important aspect of nineteenth-
century society and culture, namely its international character. So as well as the
questions of *when* and *what* the Victorian period was, there is also the issue of
where it was. Victorianism tends to be associated primarily with Britain, yet this
risks downplaying its relations with Europe and the rest of the world. Marx and
Engels acutely observed that the restless dynamism of industrial capitalism
needed to constantly seek out new markets and materials. At street level, the
fervent belief in free trade in a global marketplace was evident in the burgeoning
number of foreign goods and luxuries that were available, as reflected in a
description of London shops in 1850:

> in the space of a single mile [the shopper] may travel from the North Pole to
> the Polynesian Isles – from Western Europe to Japan, and contemplate, and
> handle if he choose, the infinite productions of every latitude and every race.
> If he be an Englishman, he will probably feel some justifiable pride in the
> universal extent of that commerce, the evidence of whose success is in all
> directions so abundantly manifest.[13]

Many of the exotic goods appearing in Britain were products of its burgeoning
empire, and it is the increasingly imperial character of the nation that is probably the most potent example of the imaginative and ideological engagement
with overseas territories and peoples. Victorian literature was deeply inflected by
the spatial imagination of the empire; characters emigrating or arriving from
distant parts of the world are commonplace as plot devices in many novels not
ostensibly concerned with empire (the arrival of George Talboys from Australia
at the beginning of *Lady Audley's Secret* and the emigration of Mary and Jem to
Canada at the end of *Mary Barton* are typical); later in the century, the boys' own
adventure stories of Rider Haggard, G. A. Henty and Robert Louis Stevenson,
among many others, was one of the most successful publishing genres of the
period. The ideological contours of British imperialism are described in the
Empire and Race section of this book, while, elsewhere, the importance of
European thinkers to the intellectual currents of the period are particularly

12 John Mason Neale, *Hierologus or, The Church Tourists* (London: James Burns, 1843), 92.
13 'Shops, Shopkeepers, Shopmen and Shop Morality', *Chambers's Edinburgh Journal*, 14 September
    1850, 161. Qtd. in Catherine Waters, *Commodity Culture in Dickens's Household Words: The Social Life
    of Goods* (Aldershot: Ashgate, 2008), 102–3.

reflected in the Philosophy and Ideas section, which include George Eliot's and Harriet Martineau's translations of Feuerbach and Comte respectively.

This is a sourcebook to contextualize and enrich the study of Victorian literature. If there is one thing that unifies Victorian literature it is its intertextuality, its deep and active engagement with the social, political, religious and scientific writing of the period. Victorian literature often seems overdetermined by its contexts. Novelists' preoccupation with responding to the new industrial environment is typified by the advent of the 'Condition of England' novel during the 1840s and 1850s, a genre of fiction that includes such major works as Disraeli's *Coningsby* (1844), Dickens's *Bleak House* (1852–3), Gaskell's *Mary Barton* (1848) and Kingsley's *Alton Locke* (1850). The genres of Sensation and New Woman fiction were similarly tied to changes in the social and economic position of women. Both challenged the dominant boundaries of accepted feminine propriety; New Woman fiction such as Grant Allen's *The Woman Who Did* (1895), George Egerton's *Keynotes* (1893) and Sarah Grand's *The Heavenly Twins* (1893) focused on independent and unconventional women and the oppressive double standard operating in gender and sexual relations.

As an area of scholarship, Victorian Studies has always had a strongly interdisciplinary character, concerned with creating an enriched understanding of the literature of the period by drawing on research and subject matter from the fields of history, politics, history of science, art, sociology, geography and gender studies.[14] Dickens, for example, is often read alongside contemporary portrayals of Victorian London, while Charlotte Brontë is studied alongside debates over the Woman Question. This sourcebook will of course enable such readings. Our sourcebook, however, is intended to do more than simply provide pieces that act as an historical backdrop to whatever novel, drama or poem is being studied. Rather, our aim is to emphasize the fuzziness of the text/context distinction and to encourage what is often described as an interdisciplinary approach. There are two interrelated reasons for this: the first stems from the nature of Victorian culture and society; the second from the way contemporary scholars of Victorian literature and culture have attempted to better understand the period by analysing different types of non-literary text. Regenia Gagnier has defined interdisciplinarity as 'a way to combine the objects and methods of different disciplines to solve a particular problem or tell a particular story'.[15] Examining different types of text, which at first glance might belong more to the disciplinary provinces of sociology, history, medicine, politics or the history of art and architecture, is an initial step in helping to fill out the unavoidably partial answers that Victorian literature provides to the complex questions posed by the culture it was part of. One reason for making this literary sourcebook a collaborative venture of six authors is because

---

14 On the history of Victorian Studies see Boyd and McWilliam, 'Introduction: Rethinking the Victorians', in *The Victorian Studies Reader*, 1–47.

15 Regenia Gagnier, 'Why Interdisciplinarity?' *2009 Compass Interdisciplinary Virtual Conference 2009*; http://compassconference.wordpress.com/2009/10/19/gagnier/

the rich and multifaceted nature of Victorian culture requires a range of expertise to do it justice.

The sourcebook is made up of many types of text, including parliamentary speeches, diaries, newspaper reports, scientific treatises, sermons, reviews, poems, biography and autobiography; this heterogeneity is necessary to begin to think through the multiple factors affecting social and individual identity in the period – whether that be in terms of class, sexual relations, popular enjoyments and desires, the experience of beauty, or individuals' struggle for progress and self-fulfilment. Recent work has often emphasized the discursive formation of individual and group identities, the ideological power that different textual narratives and modes have in representing individuals and groups to one another and to themselves. Many of the pieces in this sourcebook exemplify discursive positions that had an important agency in constructing social identities. To take just one example: the dominance of industrialization went hand in hand with the emergence of a new class structure that did much to shape the character of Victorian society, yet class has been demonstrated to be more than a simple reflection of an individual's relative position in the economic structure; rather it is fashioned by the different discourses used by inhabitants of the period to describe the social structure and their position within it. The Society, Politics and Class section deals most fully with the formation of class identity, but pieces in other sections both fill out the picture and, crucially, suggest that class was not the only way that people thought about themselves.

A good example of the way literary scholars have enthusiastically adopted an interdisciplinary approach is recent scholarship on the relationship between literature and science. As Stephen G. Brush has posited, the relationship between nineteenth-century science and literature is multidirectional:

> An idea from culture may enter science, where it can stimulate certain lines of theorizing, and (perhaps) suggest new experiments and lead to new discoveries. . . Conversely, scientific facts and theories may have a direct influence on those who construct philosophical systems, write novels, or criticize society. Thus, the mechanistic materialism of mid-nineteenth-century physics and biology was reflected by 'realism' in philosophy and literature, and by 'positivism' in the social sciences. A third possibility is that the same notion may appear at about the same time in both science and culture without any apparent causal influence one way or the other. Such was the case with the principle of dissipation of energy in physics, and the corresponding theory of degeneration in biology, both of which flourished in the pessimistic atmosphere of the latter part of the nineteenth century.[16]

Recent years have seen critics explore all the directions of influence between literature and science. The influence of the evolutionary ideas of Charles Darwin

---

16 Steven G. Brush, *The Temperature of History* (New York: Burt Franklin and Co., 1978), 1–2.

upon writers such as George Eliot, Alfred Tennyson and Thomas Hardy have been explored at length, as have the interactions between the newly emerging discipline of psychology and the novel, both of which were concerned, in their own unique way, with interiority, affect, and the life of the mind. As importantly though, scientific writing has been analysed for its discursive and imaginative properties. Writing of Darwin's *On the Origin of Species* (1859), Gillian Beer has argued that because 'of its preoccupation with time and with change evolutionary theory has inherent affinities with the problems and processes of narrative'.[17]

There are, however, risks in reading scientific or political works as if they were literary texts. The focus on the textual qualities of different discourses can flatten the material and intellectual contours of the way it was engaging in debates that had particular disciplinary histories and methods. Sensitivity to different forms of debate is to the fore in the third type of relationship that Brush posits between literature and science, one where there is no direct influence between texts but where works produced at the same time wrestle with similar issues in a way appropriate to their mode and method. This kind of relationship is strongly in evidence throughout the sourcebook in that many pieces provide standpoints on similar concerns. One of the ways in which this sourcebook can be used is by comparing pieces from different sections that engage with similar concerns; we have accordingly provided a number of cross-references. Issues about the relationship between the individual and their environment, for example, run across many nineteenth-century texts; it was key to Darwin's thinking about evolution and natural selection, Marx's and Engel's thinking about class, and formed a key element of many Victorian novels. *Middlemarch*, for example, is a working through of George Eliot's assertion in the novel that 'there is no creature whose inward being is so strong that it is not greatly determined by what lies outside it'.[18]

Victorian Fiction and Prose

One of the most striking things about a text like Darwin's *On the Origin of Species* is its accessibility to a general reader. It was a book written at a time when scientific debate was conducted in widely read periodicals and reviews, and prior to science evolving into an exclusive, professional and highly specialized community. The accessibility of *On the Origin of Species* reveals much about the character of the Victorian public sphere and the agency of literary and non-literary texts. Strachey's sense of being overwhelmed at the excess of information produced by the period was, in effect, a reaction against the unprecedented number of books,

---

17 Gillian Beer, *Darwin's Plots: Evolutionary Narrative in Darwin, George Eliot and Nineteenth-Century Fiction* (1983; Cambridge: Cambridge University Press, 2000), 5.
18 George Eliot, *Middlemarch*, ed. Rosemary Ashton (Harmondsworth: Penguin, 1994), 838.

journals and pamphlets being published. A defining characteristic of the period is the expansion of discursive prose in its different forms, whether essay, tract, novel, autobiography, conduct manual, travelogue, literary criticism or biography. The role of publishing in making a more open public sphere is reflected in Carlyle's assertion that the man of letters was the modern-day hero:

> Printing, which comes necessarily out of Writing, I say often, is equivalent to Democracy: invent Writing, Democracy is inevitable. Writing brings Printing; brings universal everyday extempore Printing, as we see at present. Whoever can speak, speaking now to the whole nation, becomes a power, a branch of government, with inalienable weight in law-making, in all acts of authority. It matters not what rank he has, what revenues or garnitures. The requisite thing is, that he have a tongue which others will listen to; this and nothing more is requisite.[19]

Carlyle's pronouncement was made at the very beginning of Victoria's reign, when the expansion of the publishing industry was having a particularly marked impact on the growth of the periodical press. This was a form that was crucial to nineteenth-century literature, intellectual life, and society in general. Its impact is evident in the number of extracts in this sourcebook that are periodical articles.

Periodicals and journals were obviously not invented by the period; nonetheless, they played a unique role in its culture. Their nineteenth-century growth began with the quarterly reviews: the Whig *Edinburgh Review*, founded in 1802, was followed by the Tory *Quarterly Review* in 1809. The quarterlies consisted of articles on a wide range of subjects – science, history, politics, and literature – a practice continued by subsequent reviews and many other popular journals such as the *Fortnightly Review* (1865–1954) and *Contemporary Review* (1866–ongoing). Writing of the quarterlies, Joanne Shattock has noted, 'The crucial assumption of each number was that all areas of knowledge were not only accessible, but potentially of interest and part of one's general cultivation.'[20] Contributors included most of the key intellectuals, writers and politicians of the period. That debates in different areas were open and understandable to many is one of the foundation stones for the intertextuality of Victorian literature.

The deep engagement of discursive prose with a wide general readership feeds into two other important reasons why the pieces in this sourcebook are of interest to those studying Victorian literature. The first is that the many influential texts and writers elude simple definition, calling into question any easy distinction between the literary and non-literary, text and context. Writers such as Thomas Carlyle, George Eliot, John Stuart Mill, Harriet Martineau, John

---

19 Thomas Carlyle, *On Heroes, Hero Worship and the Heroic in History* (London: James Fraser, 1841), 273.
20 Joanne Shattock, *Politics and Reviewers: The 'Edinburgh' and the 'Quarterly' in the Early Victorian Age* (Leicester: Leicester University Press, 1989), 10.

Ruskin, Walter Pater and Matthew Arnold were intellectual polymaths, writing at a time before specialization became the norm; their work contributed to debates in the fields of literature, art, economics, and politics, and have remained of interest to scholars in these different disciplines. They are important 'sources' that aid the study of Victorian literature, but deserve equal consideration as works of literature. Arnold, for example, was a school inspector for many years, but also served as Professor of Poetry at the University of Oxford; he was the author of distinguished works of literary and cultural criticism that addressed the overall state of the nation, as well as such poems as 'Dover Beach' and 'The Scholar Gypsy', which are standard inclusions in anthologies of Victorian poetry. John Stuart Mill worked for the East India Company. As their lives, so their work: Ruskin's *The Stones of Venice* (1851–3) is a treatise on medieval Gothic architecture that famously frames a profound argument about the importance of creative labour in an industrial age; similarly, Henry Mayhew's *London Labour and the London Poor* (1861) is a work of investigative journalism, a quasi-sociological study of the urban poor, and contains the most vividly realized autobiographical narratives of the urban underclass recorded during the nineteenth century.

The success of the novel as a form was a fundamental part of the dominance of prose. Writing in 1870, Anthony Trollope declared, 'We have become a novel-reading people [. . .] Poetry also we read and history, biography and the social and political news of the day. But all our other reading put together hardly amounts to what we read in novels.'[21] As with the period itself, to generalize the character of the Victorian novel invariably traduces its different genres and forms. Several recurring features are worth mentioning, though. The first, which is itself part of the explanation for the number of novelistic genres, is the way the novel evolved through addressing itself to the new social and economic realities of the period, including the transformation in the conditions of its own production. Gothic fiction, for example, was refigured so that instead of being set in the medieval past, the portrayal of modern urban spaces often took on a dark, mysterious and unknowable character. Dickens's London is sometimes full of energy but in *Bleak House* (1852–3), *Our Mutual Friend* (1864–5) and *Little Dorrit* (1855–7) it was just as often seen in gothic terms. Similarly, in *Dracula* (1897), the vampiric Count travels from Transylvania to haunts the streets of late Victorian London: contemporary fears of degeneration are expressed through a 400-year-old supernatural figure who threatens to bring chaos to the world's most powerful metropolis.

The way that the novel was shaped by commercial pressures is exemplified by the economic and creative influence that new groups of readers were able to exert. Probably the most important of these was women, who were prominent as both writers and readers of novels; in 1855, Margaret Oliphant, herself a

---

21 Anthony Trollope, 'On English Prose Fiction as a Rational Amusement', *Four Lectures*, ed. Morris L. Parrish (London: Constable, 1938), 108.

prolific author, famously declared that the period 'which is the age of so many things – of enlightenment, of science, of progress – is quite as distinctly the age of female novelists'.[22] Since the 1980s, the strong influence of gender studies on the period has brought to the fore not just what the Victorian called 'the Woman Question' but also the need to remap the literary landscape. Feminist critics have highlighted the importance of a large body of work by women writers that, for much of the twentieth century, was left outside the so-called Victorian canon. It is perhaps the imaginative voice that the novel provided women writers with that accounts, in part, for the prominence of the female *Bildungsroman* through such well-known works such as *Jane Eyre* (1847), *Villette* (1853) and *The Mill on the Floss* (1860), which narrate the development of a self and the internal and external pressures that each heroine faces. Centrally concerned with change, growth and socialization, certainly not all *Bildungsromans* were concerned with women, though; *Great Expectations* (1861), *David Copperfield* (1851) and *The Picture of Dorian Gray* (1890) follow the development of their male protagonists.

As to genres, the novel was the biggest beneficiary of the growth of the literary marketplace, whose readership now included children and the working class. Authors were equally beneficiaries of this commercial success though, the celebrity status of Dickens and his numerous reading tours being the most obvious example. The popularity of crime fiction among working-class readers soon spilled over into novels aimed at more genteel readers, from the criminal brio of the Artful Dodger in *Oliver Twist* (1838) and Count Fosco in *The Woman in White* (1860) to the sleuthing of Mr Bucket in *Bleak House* and the enormously successful stories of the arch-reasoner Sherlock Holmes. In the latter decades of the century, educational reform and increasing literacy levels similarly led to the burgeoning number of books and annuals aimed at juvenile readers, including works such as Robert Louis Stevenson's *Treasure Island* (1883), Lewis Carroll's *Alice's Adventures in Wonderland* (1865) and Rudyard Kipling's *The Jungle Book* (1894).

A second concern that weaves through the Victorian novel is the issue of realism. Fiction conceived itself as representing the external world, a question often articulated in the way in which the novel figured the relationship between the individual self and broader social relations. Henry James claimed that 'the air of reality (solidity of specification) seems to me to be the supreme virtue of a novel – merit on which all its other merits . . . helplessly and submissively depend'.[23] Not all would have agreed with James's stress on creating realism through the materiality of detail, but his comments are indicative of the importance attached to the form through which novels chose to represent the world. Citing Michael McKeon's claim that 'the instability of generic categories

---

22 [Margaret Oliphant], 'Modern Novelists – Great and Small', *Blackwood's Edinburgh Magazine* 77 (May 1855), 555.

23 Henry James, 'The Art of Fiction', *The House of Fiction*, ed. Leon Edel (London: Mercury Books, 1962), 33.

registers an epistemological crisis, a major cultural transition in attitudes towards how to tell the truth', George Levine has argued that the Victorian novel's preoccupation with conventions of realism is keyed into the broader epistemological questioning of the nature of truth and moral and spiritual authority that absorbed the period.[24] Realism, at least in the way James formulated it, is probably most fully associated with the mid-Victorian novel; during the final third of the century, the movements of Aestheticism and Naturalism pulled the conventions of realism in contrary directions. Aestheticism encouraged a turn away from the exploration of social experience to the inner consciousness, evident in works like Pater's *Marius the Epicurean* (1885), while naturalism went out of its way to stress the harsh determining effects of material forces such as hereditary influence and poverty, evident in works like Gissing's *The Nether World* (1889). By the *fin de siècle*, the commercialism that had so facilitated the growth of the novel was increasingly felt to restrict experimentation with its form and themes, particularly in the portrayal of sexual relations, creating a split between popular and avant-garde writing that would be fully taken up by modernism.

Victorian Poetry

Whereas the high-Victorian novel often has a capaciousness that attempts to encompass and explore the dynamic relations that made up society as a whole, poetry tended to have a more reflexive and complex engagement with the utilitarian and materialistic spirit of the age. In spite of the challenges it faced from the rising power of fiction and science, Victorian poetry was widely read. The figures speak for themselves. As Linda K. Hughes writes: 'Tennyson's *In Memoriam* [1849] sold 60,000 copies in three to four years and *Enoch Arden* [1864] 40,000 in mere weeks. Nearly 400,000 copies of John Keble's *The Christian Year* (1827) had been purchased when its copyright expired in 1873.'[25] Poetry, like prose, fiction and other genres, benefited from the new world of print culture and was just as eagerly consumed in book form as it was in journals and magazines.

Early Victorian poetry found itself in the shadow of Romantic poets such as Lord Bryon, Percy Bysshe Shelly and William Wordsworth, who would be Poet Laureate until 1850. Although Wordsworth is generally considered the link between Romantic and Victorian poetics, early Victorian poets and critics rejected Wordsworth's poetics on account of its philosophical reflexivity. As Joseph Bristow has pointed out, these early critics began to articulate the branching off of Romanticist and Victorian poetics into two different poetics –

---

24 George Levine, *How to Read the Victorian Novel* (Oxford: Blackwell, 2008), 16.
25 Linda K. Hughes, *The Cambridge Introduction to Victorian Poetry* (Cambridge: Cambridge University Press, 2010), 1.

what Arthur Henry Hallam called the poetry of the intellect (represented by Wordsworth) and the poetry of emotion and sensation (present in the work of Keats and Shelley but rearticulated by Tennyson in his 1830 collection *Poems, Chiefly Lyrical*).[26] Critics generally agree that the publication of Tennyson's *Poems, Chiefly Lyrical* (1830) and *Poems* (1832) marked the beginnings of Victorian poetics. In poems such as 'The Lady of Shalott' Tennyson articulated many of the challenges lying ahead for Victorian poets, most notably whether modern poets should engage with the world or retreat into the realm of the purely aesthetic. These dates are, in addition, particularly significant because they coincide with the 1832 Reform Bill, which was opposed by William Wordsworth. As Isobel Armstrong has argued, Victorian poetry emerged out of this moment as 'two systems of concentric circles', 'one exploring various strategies for democratic, radical writing, the other developing in different forms, a conservative poetry'.[27] Poets such as Ebenezer Elliott and Robert Browning belonged to the first group, while Tennyson belonged to the second.

While this poetry of feeling and emotion expressed in lyric form continued to dominate Victorian poetics and would be picked up and transformed later in the century by the Pre-Raphaelites, at the same time poetry itself became self-consciously aware of the position of the lyric and the lyric self in the world. Poets such as Felicia Hemans and Robert Browning presented this experiential self through a new poetic form, the dramatic monologue, perhaps the most important poetic experiment developed in the nineteenth century. A complex form, it is defined by Alan Sinfield as a first-person poem 'where the speaker is indicated not to be the poet'.[28] It represented dramatized speech (often in the form of soliloquies, monologues, dramatis personae) where an auditor might not be present. In the dramatic monologue, not only is the self deeply historical (belonging to a time, place, social and political structure), but the form allows the speaker to express unconsciously his or her innermost thoughts. The self of the poem is both the subject of his or her utterance and, unconsciously, the object of enquiry. In the dramatic lyrics of Tennyson, Browning, Dora Greenwell, Augusta Webster and Dante Gabriel Rossetti, to name but a few, form, experience and cultural critique are united in the speaker's expressive utterance. The flexibility of this form explains its extraordinary success with both male and female poets, as it enabled poets to intervene in key political and social issues of the period. Questions of gender, politics, social reformation, religion, empire, psychology and class are at the core of works such as Tennyson's *Maud* (1855), Browning's *Men and Women* (1855), Webster's *Medea in Athens* (1870) and Amy Levy's *Xantippe and Other Verse* (1881). Indeed, through positioning the 'I' in the poem in the midst of history and culture, readers were conscious of the social and cultural constraints the speakers in these poems, and

---

26 See Joseph Bristow, 'Reforming Victorian Poetry: Poetics After 1832', in *The Cambridge Companion to Victorian Poetry*, ed. Joseph Bristow (Cambridge: Cambridge University Press, 2000), 1–24.

27 Isobel Armstrong, *Victorian Poetry: Poetry, Poetics, Politics* (London: Routledge, 1993), 7.

28 Alan Sinfield, *Dramatic Monologue* (London: Methuen, 1977), 42.

by implication the readers themselves, were subjected to. It must be added, however, that though the dramatic monologue could be seen as a departure from one of those quintessential nineteenth-century forms, the lyric or verse drama, it did not supplant it.

Up to the mid-nineteenth century, the concept of poetry had been intrinsically linked to prophecy. As Thomas Carlyle famously put it, the poet was a 'prophet', a seer, who with 'his' poetry could illuminate 'the sacred mystery of the Universe'.[29] Poetry had the power to illuminate an individual and an individual's life because it spoke the truth about the self and the world. Such a unique identification of poetry with truth and knowledge had placed the genre at the centre of religious experience and at the core of a metaphysical, more philosophical (even secular) understanding of the world. Thus on the one hand, while the fervid religious debates of the nineteenth century animated Victorian poetry in many ways (see for example Adelaide Anne Proctor's and Christina Rossetti's Tractarian poetry, or the Catholic poetics of Gerald Manley Hopkins), poetry saw its position nonetheless undermined by science. This threat had been foreseen by John Stuart Mill, who in his essays on the nature of poetry spoke of two distinct types of knowledge: objective knowledge (the object of science) and subjective, experiential knowledge offered by poetry. As science became the paradigmatic form of knowledge in the nineteenth century, poetry lost its position as the beholder of truth and meaning. But, like the novel, Victorian poetry's deeply interdisciplinary nature meant that it could engage with objective, scientific knowledge and it used such interdisciplinarity to reclaim for itself a place as the metaphysical discourse of the self and the universe, sometimes by using scientific discourses (for example Tennyson's *In Memoriam*, 1850), sometimes through irony and critique (Constance Naden's 'Scientific Wooing', 1887).

Even more powerful was the competition brought about by fiction and the novel in the mid-nineteenth century. As the century progressed, Victorian poetry tried to offset the power of fiction in a number of ways, one of which was poetic experimentation. The dramatic monologue created a series of fictions of the self that would become extremely popular, not just because of the versatility of its subjects but also because the form, as we have seen, enabled the reader to understand the psychology of character. One might argue that the most original experiment in this context was Elizabeth Barrett Browning's 'verse-novel' *Aurora Leigh* (1856). Thematically speaking, the poem engages with the so-called 'Woman Question'. As an epic following in the tradition of Milton's *Paradise Lost*, Barrett Browning's novel in verse challenged gendered stereotypes about the poetess, claiming for both the eponymous heroine and for herself the position of 'Poet'.

But just as the long poem was establishing itself in the mid-Victorian period, the changing cultural and political landscape of the 1850s brought about another impetus in poetic experimentation. Elizabeth Barrett Browning, George

---

29 Carlyle, *On Heroes, Hero Worship and the Heroic in History*, 92.

Meredith, Dante Gabriel Rossetti, Christina Rossetti and others began to work in the 1850s with shorter poetic forms, most notably the sonnet. In their hands, the sonnet and the sonnet sequence became forms with which to discuss issues such as marriage, religion, love and desire. Barrett Browning's *Sonnets from the Portuguese* (1850), Meredith's *Modern Love* (1862), Dante Gabriel Rossetti's 'The House of Life' (1870) and Christina Rossetti's 'Monna Innominata' (1881) all explored the complexity of human sexuality and desire in the context of gender, religion and patriarchy.

The publication of Rossetti's *Poems* (1870), which included the unfinished sonnet sequence 'The House of Life', occasioned the most heated debate over poetics during the period, and pointed towards an important new shift in the cultural landscape. Influenced by the writings of Walter Pater, poets like A. C. Swinburne, D. G. Rossetti and William Morris rejected Arnold's imperative that 'art possessed a moral function'. In his infamous article 'The Fleshly School of Poetry' (1871), a review of Rossetti's *Poems*, Robert Buchanan accused this new poetic school of fleshiness, of focusing on sensuality and sexual desire. Dante Gabriel Rossetti's poetry belonged to what came to be called the Aesthetic Movement, which comprised not just poetry and prose but also the arts (painting, book illustrations, ceramics, furniture, etc.). Indeed, many of the poets of this generation excelled in other arts too (Dante Gabriel Rossetti was both a painter and a poet; the polymathic Morris was also a poet, decorator and book illustrator). Influenced by French aesthetic models, most notably Gautier's philosophy of 'art for art's sake', late Victorian poets, aesthetes and decadents rejected the materialism that had dominated the nineteenth century and would argue for a return to aesthetic values using as models not just French literature but the past. Poets such as Arthur Symons, Oscar Wilde, Amy Levy, Michael Field and others turned to Hellenism, the Italian and French Renaissance, Arthurian legends and Celtic themes in search of new poetic models. The publication of Arthur Symons's important essay 'The Decadent Movement in Literature' (1893) closes Victorian poetics by signalling the beginnings of a new poetic movement, symbolism, which would mark the poetics of, among others, W. B. Yeats and Symons himself.

Victorian Drama

Most students of Victorian literature encounter the drama of the period through a narrow canon of works from the 1890s, constituted by plays such as Oscar Wilde's *The Importance of Being Earnest* (1895), *Salomé* (1891) and *A Woman of No Importance* (1893); Henrik Ibsen's *Ghosts* (1881; first British performance, 1891) and *Hedda Gabler* (1891); Arthur Wing Pinero's *The Second Mrs Tanqueray* (1893); and George Bernard Shaw's *Mrs Warren's Profession* (1893). These plays are often studied as much for their links to movements such as Naturalism and Decadence as for their dramaturgy; Wilde's *Salomé*, for example is at least as well known for the accompanying erotic illustrations by Aubrey Beardsley as for any individual scene: it resonates more on the page as a literary text than in performance. Equally, Victorian lyric drama (reinvented in the late nineteenth century by Alfred Tennyson, A. C. Swinburne and Michael Field) lies forgotten on library selves. The limited canon of Victorian plays owes much to theatre's reinvention of its aesthetic and social respectability at the end of the century; as Nina Auerbach has noted, 'It was in the 1890s that the theatre, like the novel, grew ashamed of mere popularity and aspired to high art.'[30] The legacy of this attitude still survives; the rest of Victorian drama continues to remain something of a hinterland, leavened only by references to Dickens's interest in popular theatre either through his acting or through well-known journalistic pieces such as 'Amusements of the People' (1850), wherein he condescendingly describes an East End theatre audience.

The focus on drama-as-art during the 1890s is a back-handed testimony to the thriving commonality and popular appeal of drama during the period. Simon Shepherd and Peter Womack are not overstating their case when they claim that 'there were probably more performances in more theatres seen by more people than at any other period, including the present'.[31] Victorian drama was central to popular culture, and the form primarily responsible for this was melodrama, which created a structure of feeling through which audiences could understand the fast-changing world around them, not only inside the theatre but beyond in their everyday lives. As David Mayer has emphasized, the appeal of melodrama lay partly in its emotional or sentimental explanation of the world:

> Melodrama tries to respond with emotional, rather than intellectual answers to a world where explanations of why there is pain and chaos and discord are flawed or deeply and logically inconsistent, where there are all-too-visible discrepancies between readily observed calamities and palliative answers. Melodrama provides an emotionally intelligible picture of the world to deracinated western cultures, severed by science and technology from former religious and spiritual 'truths'.[32]

Kate Newey has similarly noted the 'black and white' character of melodrama, arguing that it can be 'defined as a dramatic form which offers a truncated dialectic of moral choice between good and evil, dramatized simply, directly and effectively'.[33] Plays such as Douglas Jerrold's *Black Ey'd Susan* (1829) and *The Rent Day* (1832) dealt with naval authoritarianism, rural privation and negligent

---

30 Nina Auerbach, 'Introduction', in *The Cambridge Companion to Victorian and Edwardian Theatre*, ed. Kerry Powell (Cambridge: Cambridge University Press, 2004), 6.

31 Cited in Katherine Newey, 'Theatre', in *The Cambridge Companion to Victorian Culture*, ed. Francis O'Gorman (Cambridge: Cambridge University Press, 2009), 124.

32 David Mayer, 'Encountering Melodrama', in *The Cambridge Companion to Victorian and Edwardian Theatre*, ed. Kerry Powell (Cambridge: Cambridge University Press, 2004), 148.

33 Newey, 'Theatre', 127.

landlords, while the 'sensation dramas' of Dion Boucicault such as *The Colleen Bawn* (1860) incorporated new technologies for their audience.

The preponderance of melodrama on the Victorian stage exerted a creative influence upon the fiction and politics of the period. For example, the opening of chapter 17 in *Oliver Twist* explains to its readers why the setting and emotional pace of the novel is now changing from Fagin's den back to Mr Bumble and the town from which Oliver first fled by declaring: 'It is the custom on the stage: in all good, murderous melodramas: to present the tragic and the comic scenes, in as regular alternation, as the layers of red and white in a side of streaky, well-cured bacon.'[34] Dickens's novel deliberately flaunts its indebtedness to melodrama as part of its popular credentials. Later in the century, a play such as Wilde's *The Importance of Being Earnest* owed much to melodramatic conventions, even as it delightfully parodied them: hidden ancestry, secret kinship, sensational action and crucial items that could resolve the plot – for example Miss Prism's handbag and Jack's cigarette case – were all melodramatic devices reused by Wilde. For students of Victorian literature, the crossover between theatre and fiction is demonstrable by considering just how many works of fiction reproduce the melodramatic structures described by Mayer and Newey.

Conclusion

Scholarly debates about the shifting identity of the Victorian period are connected to its ongoing re-envisioning in popular Anglophone culture. Nowhere is this more evident than in the success of the neo-Victorian novel, exemplified by works such as John Fowles's *The French Lieutenant's Woman* (1969), A. S. Byatt's *Possession* (1990), Sarah Waters's *Tipping the Velvet* (1999) and Michael Faber's *The Crimson Petal and the White* (2002). While some contemporary reworkings, such as cinematic versions of classic works of Victorian literature, might ossify the period into an airbrushed heritage costume drama, most neo-Victorian novels knowingly rewrite the Victorian past, their historicism attempting to expand, fill in for, or expose those elements that history itself somehow left incomplete or hidden. Neo-Victorian novels create what Walter Benjamin called a constellation; for Benjamin, the practice of writing history should not be sequential or linear but should work towards the establishing of constellations, whereby 'what has been comes together in a flash with the now to form a constellation'.[35] In the best neo-Victorian novels, the relationship between past and present is always dialectical, whereby each thinks through the other. Our sourcebook attempts something analogous: in exploring nineteenth-century ideas about globalization, bio-ethics, environmental change, citizen-

---

34 Charles Dickens, *Oliver Twist* (London: Richard Bentley, 1838), 271.
35 Walter Benjamin, *The Arcades Project*, trans. Howard Eiland and Kevin McLaughlin (Cambridge, MA: Belknapp Press, 1999), 462.

ship, technology and the self, consumerism and free trade we hope to provide a fresh perspective not only on the Victorian period but also on contemporary debates upon the self-same issues.

Note on the Selected Texts

Where possible the earliest or first published edition of each of the works excerpted here has been used. Similarly we have always sought to reproduce original or first translations of foreign works in order to allow readers to read them as the Victorians would have done.

Where the following symbol appears '[. . .]', it signifies that the editors have omitted some material from the original text. Square brackets around an author's name signify the piece was first published anonymously.

1

Key Historical Events

Introduction

The defining events of the Victorian period are typically disparate; the extracts in this section describe military conflicts, parliamentary legislation, royal celebrations, mass starvation, technological innovation and working-class revolution. Nonetheless, certain shared concerns run through them that exemplify the social and political character of the period.

To begin with, the very diversity of voices, ranging from Prince Albert celebrating the Great Exhibition to a native Indian soldier describing his experiences of the Indian Mutiny signals, the proliferation of the number and type of narratives in the public sphere, all jostling to fashion the way that the Victorian period understood itself. Nonetheless, the events documented by this section still testify to the continued centrality of power in particular places (London) and particular institutions (the Houses of Parliament and the British armed forces), as well as its exercise by particular social classes long accustomed to seeing it as their right (principally male members of the aristocracy). Revealingly, though, such extracts are often anxiously concerned with the way that the traditional order of things was being challenged by the interlinked impact of industrialization, urbanization, and the changing class structure of Britain. An extract by the Whig politician Thomas Babington Macaulay, from a parliamentary speech given in 1831, is one such example. He is advocating a Reform Bill that would grant the vote to the burgeoning middle class and give parliamentary representation to those cities that had grown rapidly due to industrialization. For Macaulay, this social change to the established political structure was necessary to defuse the threat of revolution. A similar process of social assimilation could be seen at work in the development of a national education system, which, as the extract below on the Elementary Education Act of 1870 suggests, was a means of training individuals to be responsible workers and citizens.

A concern over who or what best represented the nation – in a way that took account of its modern industrial character – defines many of the extracts in this section. This concern fed into the decision to host the world's first international industrial display, the Great Exhibition of the Works of Industry of all Nations, which was housed in the Crystal Palace in Hyde Park, London, and which ran for six months in 1851. Featuring British products alongside those from

America, Asia and Europe, the Exhibition was a tremendous success, and was seen by many Victorians to generate a positive picture concerning the state of the nation in a world increasingly bound together by science, technology and trade.

Extracts offering a progressive, even triumphant, definition of British nationhood, and indeed what it meant to be 'Victorian', need to be set against pieces from those groups, particularly women and the working class, who had to fight for legislative and political recognition. Working-class radicalism centred upon Chartism, a mass political movement that campaigned for universal male suffrage and which was at its strongest in the late 1830s and 1840s. While working-class men were enfranchised by the end of the period, women would not receive the vote until 1918. Nonetheless, as the nineteenth century wore on women became increasingly vocal in challenging traditional structures of power and patriarchal conceptions of their role (for more on this see the section on Gender and Sexuality). A notable step in the improvement of women's legal, educational and economic rights was the Matrimonial Causes Act of 1857, which began the process of giving a woman a legal, physical and economic identity that was not subsumed under that of her husband. The legislation was shaped by the pioneering campaign of Caroline Norton – from one of whose pamphlets we include an extract.

While political, legal and social reform was important to the way that individual identity was refigured and different groups were made to feel part of the nation, other developments similarly encouraged a sense of citizenship and belonging. Advances in transport and communications technology, epitomized by the development of the railway and telegraph networks, more closely linked disparate regions and cities. They helped to reinforce a sense of belonging to the *imagined* community of the nation, circulating ideas, commodities and people. Appropriately, the first extract in the section documents the opening of the Liverpool and Manchester railway in September 1830 (see also the extracts 10.4 and 10.6 on the railways and communication in Section 10).

The self-confidence engendered by Britain's economic strength, backed up by its seeming ability to democratize its political structures without serious class unrest, led to proclamations of national uniqueness and superiority. This attitude is epitomized by characters like Mr Podsnap from Dickens's *Our Mutual Friend*:

> Mr Podsnap's world was not a very large world, morally; no, nor even geographically: seeing that although his business was sustained upon commerce with other countries, he considered other countries, with that important reservation, a mistake, and of their manners and customs would conclusively observe, 'Not English!' when, PRESTO! with a flourish of the arm, and a flush of the face, they were swept away.[1]

---

1 Charles Dickens, *Our Mutual Friend*, ed. Adrian Poole (Penguin: Harmondsworth, 1994), 119.

Podsnap's refusal to recognize the world of 'Not English' dramatizes the way that Victorian Britain – for all its proclaimed coming together as an inclusive community – remained an unequal amalgamation of parts: the dominant values of Englishness often stood in for the nation as a whole.

Ireland provided a particularly glaring example of this type of internal geopolitical inequality. The United Kingdom of Great Britain and Ireland had been created in 1801, with Ireland subsequently being ruled directly from the Houses of Parliament in London. Yet when potato blight struck Ireland, the resultant famine of 1845–51 was exacerbated by the British government's ineffectual response to the crisis, which was itself a product of longstanding disregard for the welfare of Ireland's Catholic peasantry.

That Podsnap felt able to dismiss anything 'Not English' ignored the extent to which Britain was influenced by and engaged in various overseas activities, including events in Europe and, increasingly, its burgeoning empire. The European revolutions of 1848; the Crimean War in the Balkans; the Indian Mutiny; the imperial celebration of Queen Victoria's Golden Jubilee of 1887: the below extracts narrating these episodes demonstrate how deeply the identity of Victorian Britain was shaped by events outside its borders (see also Section 5 for the influence of Continental philosophy and Section 9 on Empire and Race).

1.1 Samuel Smiles, 'The Opening of the Liverpool and Manchester Railway', *The Life of George Stephenson: Railway Engineer* (London: John Murray, 1857)

Railways were the quintessential symbol of Victorian industrial progress and modernity. Compressing time and space, they were instrumental in fostering a social world founded upon speed, mobility and the continuous circulation of goods and people. Towns and cities were brought closer together, often mitigating regional differences in favour of a more homogenous national culture. The successful running of the railway network necessitated all stations and passengers keeping to a standard national time – a potent symbol of the uniformity and discipline imposed by industrialization. The spread of railways was phenomenal: in 1840 there were 1,497 miles of track; by 1870 there were 13,388 miles criss-crossing Britain. While the early nineteenth century saw steam locomotives used by collieries, the onset of the railway era can be dated to the event described below – the opening of the Liverpool and Manchester railway line in September 1830. The line was built under the aegis of the engineer George Stephenson (1781–1848), whose engine, the 'Rocket', had also won the competition to be the locomotive responsible for running the line. Stephenson's efforts were widely celebrated as a model of industry and innovation, as in the biography by Samuel Smiles from which the below extract is taken. See p. 59–60 for a biographical note on Smiles.

About the middle of 1829 the tunnel at Liverpool was finished; and being lit up with gas, it was publicly exhibited one day in each week. Many thousand persons visited the tunnel, at a charge of a shilling a head, – the fund thus raised being appropriated partly to the support of the families of labourers who had been injured on the line, and partly in contributions to the Manchester and Liverpool infirmaries. [. . .]

Thus, in June, 1830, a trial trip was made between Liverpool and Manchester and back, on the occasion of the board meeting being held at the latter town. A great concourse of people assembled at both termini, and along the line to witness the spectacle. The train consisted of two carriages filled with about forty persons, and seven wagons laden with stores – in all about thirty-nine tons. The 'Rocket', light though it was compared with modern engines, drew the train from Liverpool to Manchester in two hours and one minute, and performed the return journey in an hour and a half. The speed of the train over Chat Moss was at the rate of about twenty-seven miles an hour.

The public opening of the railway took place on the 15th of September, 1830. Eight locomotive engines had now been constructed by the Messrs. Stephenson, and placed upon the line. The whole of them had been repeatedly tried, and with success, weeks before. A high paling had been erected for miles along the deep cuttings near Liverpool, to keep off the pressure of the multitude, and prevent them from falling over in their constant eagerness to witness the opening ceremony. Constables and soldiers were there in numbers, to assist in keeping the railway clear. The completion of the work was justly regarded as a great national event, and was celebrated accordingly. The Duke of Wellington, then prime minister, Sir Robert Peel, secretary of state, Mr. Huskisson, one of the members for Liverpool and an earnest supporter of the project from its commencement, were present, together with a large number of distinguished personages. The 'Northumbrian' engine took the lead of the procession, and was followed by the other locomotives and their trains, which accommodated about 600 persons.[2] Many thousands of spectators cheered them on their way, – through the deep ravine of Olive Mount; up the Sutton incline, over the Sankey viaduct, beneath which a multitude of persons had assembled, – carriages filling the narrow lanes and barges crowding the river. The people gazed with wonder and admiration at the trains which sped along the line, far above their heads, at the rate of twenty-four miles an hour.

At Parkside, seventeen miles from Liverpool, the engines stopped to take in water. Here a deplorable accident occurred to one of the most distinguished of the illustrious visitors present, which threw a deep shadow over the subsequent proceedings of the day. The 'Northumbrian' engine, with the carriage containing the Duke of Wellington, was drawn up on one line, in order that the whole of the trains might pass in review before him and his party on the other. Mr Huskisson had, unhappily, alighted from the carriage, and was landing on the

---

2 *Original Note*: The engines with which the line was opened on the 15th of September were the following:—1. The 'Northumbrian', driven by George Stephenson; 2. The 'Phoenix', by Robert Stephenson; 3. The 'North Star', by Robert Stephenson, senior (brother of George); 4. The 'Rocket', by Joseph Locke; 5. The 'Dart', by Thomas I. Gooch; 6. The 'Comet', by William Allcard; 7. The 'Arrow', by Frederick Swanwick; 8. The 'Meteor', by Anthony Harding.

opposite road, along which the 'Rocket' engine was observed rapidly coming up. At this moment the Duke of Wellington, between whom and Mr Huskisson some coolness had existed, made a sign of recognition, and held out his hand. A hurried but friendly grasp was given; and before it was loosened there was a general cry from the bystanders of 'Get in, get in!' Flurried and confused, Mr. Huskisson endeavoured to get round the open door of the carriage, which projected over the opposite rail; but in so doing he was struck down by the 'Rocket', and falling with his leg doubled over the rail, the limb was instantly crushed. His first words, on being raised, were, 'I have met my death,' which unhappily proved too true, for he expired that same evening in the neighbouring parsonage of Eccles. It was cited at the time as a remarkable fact, that the 'Northumbrian' engine conveyed the wounded body of the unfortunate gentleman a distance of about fifteen miles in twenty-five minutes, or at a rate of thirty-six miles an hour. This incredible speed burst upon the world with the effect of a new and unlooked-for phenomenon.

The lamentable accident threw a gloom over the rest of the day's proceedings. The Duke of Wellington and Sir Robert Peel expressed a wish that the procession should return to Liverpool. It was, however, represented to them that a vast concourse of people had assembled at Manchester to witness the arrival of the trains; that report would exaggerate the mischief, if they did not complete the journey; and that a false panic on that day might seriously affect future railway travelling and the value of the Company's property. [. . .]

It is scarcely necessary that we should speak here of the commercial results of the Liverpool and Manchester Railway. Suffice it to say that success was complete and decisive. The anticipations of its projectors were, however, in many respects at fault. They had based their calculations almost entirely on heavy merchandise traffic – such as coal, cotton, and timber – relying little upon passengers; whereas the receipts derived from the conveyance of passengers far exceeded those derived from merchandise of all kinds, which, for a time, continued a subordinate branch of the traffic. In the evidence given before the House of Commons, the promoters stated their expectation of obtaining about one-half of the whole number of passengers that the coaches then running could take, which was from 400 to 500 a day. But the railway was scarcely opened before it carried on average about 1200 passengers a day; and five years after opening it carried nearly half a million of persons yearly.

1.2 Lord Macaulay, 'A Speech: Delivered in the House of Commons on the 2nd of March, 1831', *The Complete Works of Lord Macaulay*, vol. XI (London: Longmans, Green and Co., 1898)

The Reform Act of 7 June 1832 significantly changed the political make-up of Britain. It introduced liberal reform to a parliamentary system that was at best antiquated and at worst corrupt. The Reform Act enfranchised newly industrialized cities whose population had expanded rapidly yet had no parliamentary representation: Birmingham, Manchester, Leeds and Sheffield had MPs for the first time. The act also removed the worst of the 'rotten boroughs', so called because their small number of eligible voters meant that the MP was effectively appointed by the local landowner. The electorate rose from 217,000 to 435,000, making around one in five adult men eligible to vote. As Macaulay's speech makes clear, the Act marked the political assimilation of the new middle class; it also sought to defuse widespread agitation for reform (the 1832 Act was only passed after several attempts had been blocked, and Macaulay's speech stems from the Whigs' first attempt to introduce a bill in 1831). Macaulay (1800–59) was a Whig politician who would subsequently become renowned as an essayist and historian, most notably for his five-volume The History of England from the Accession of James the Second *(1848–61).*

I have seen with delight the perfect concord which prevails among all who deserve the name of reformers in this House; and I trust that I may consider it as an omen of the concord which will prevail among reformers throughout the country. I will not, Sir, at present express any opinion as to the details of the bill; but having given the most diligent consideration to its general principles, I have no hesitation in pronouncing it a wise, noble and comprehensive measure, skilfully framed for the healing of great distempers, for the securing at once of public liberties and of the public repose, and for the reconciling and knitting together of all the orders of the State. [...]

Their principle is plain, rational and consistent. It is this, to admit the middle class to a large and direct share in the representation, without any violent shock to the institutions of our country. [...]

I consider this, Sir, as a practical question. I rest my opinion on no general theory of government. I will not positively say, that there is any form of polity which may not, in some conceivable circumstances, be the best possible. I believe that there are societies in which every man may safely be admitted to vote. Gentlemen may cheer, but such is my opinion. I say, Sir, that there are countries in which the condition of the labouring classes is such that they may safely be entrusted with the right of electing Members of the Legislature. If the labourers of England were in that state in which I, from my soul, wish to see them, if employment were always plentiful, wages always high, food always cheap, if a large family were considered not as an encumbrance but as a blessing, the principal objections to Universal Suffrage would, I think, be removed. Universal Suffrage exists in the United States without producing any very frightful consequences; and I do not believe, that the people of those States, or of any part of the world, are in any good quality naturally superior to our own countrymen. But, unhappily, the labouring classes in England, and in all the old countries, are occasionally in a state of great distress. Some of the causes of this distress are, I fear, beyond the control of the Government. We know what effect distress produces, even on people more intelligent than the great body of labouring classes can possibly be. We know that it makes even wise men irritable,

unreasonable, credulous, eager for immediate relief, heedless of remote consequences. There is no quackery in medicine, religion, or politics, which may not
impose even on a powerful mind, when that mind has been disordered by pain
or fear. It is therefore no reflection on the poorer class of Englishmen, who are
not, and who cannot in the nature of things be, highly educated, to say that
distress produces on them its natural effects, those effects which it would
produce on the Americans, or on any other people, that it blinds their judgement, that it inflames their passions, that it makes them prone to believe those
who flatter them, and to distrust those who would serve them. For the sake,
therefore, of the whole society, for the sake of the labouring classes themselves,
I hold it to be clearly expedient that, in a country like this, the right of suffrage
should depend on a pecuniary qualification.

But, Sir, every argument which would induce me to oppose Universal
Suffrage, induces me to support the plan which is now before us. I am opposed
to Universal Suffrage, because I think that it would produce a destructive revolution. [...]

All history is full of revolutions, produced by causes similar to those which
are now operating in England. A portion of the community which had been of
no account expands and becomes strong. It demands a place in the system,
suited, not to its former weakness, but to its present power. If this is granted, all
is well. If this is refused, then comes the struggle between the young energy of
one class and the ancient privileges of another. [...] Such, finally, is the struggle
which the middle classes in England are maintaining against an aristocracy of
mere locality, against an aristocracy the principle of which is to invest a hundred
drunken potwallopers in one place, or the owner of a ruined hovel in another,
with powers which are withheld from cities renowned to the furthest ends of the
earth, for the marvels of their wealth and of their industry.

But these cities, says my honourable friend, the member for the University of
Oxford, are virtually, though not directly, represented. Are not the wishes of
Manchester, he asks, as much consulted as those of any town which sends
members to parliament? Now, Sir, I do not understand how a power which is
salutary when exercised virtually can be noxious when exercised directly. If the
wishes of Manchester have as much weight with us as they would have under a
system which should give Representatives to Manchester, how can there be any
danger in giving Representatives to Manchester? [...]

Renew the youth of the State. Save property, divided against itself. Save the
multitude, endangered by its own ungovernable passions. Save the aristocracy,
endangered by its own unpopular power. Save the greatest, and fairest, and most
highly civilised community that ever existed, from calamities that may in a few
days sweep away all the rich heritage of so many ages of wisdom and glory. The
danger is terrible. The time is short. If this bill should be rejected, I pray to God
that none of those who concur in rejecting it may ever remember their votes
with unavailing remorse, amidst the wreck of laws, the confusion of ranks, the
spoliation of property, and the dissolution of social order.

· 1.3   THE PEOPLE'S CHARTER; Being the Outline of an Act to Provide for the Just Representation of the People of Great Britain and Ireland In the Commons' House of Parliament, Embracing the Principles of Universal Suffrage, No Property Qualification, Annual Parliaments, Equal Representation, Payment of Members, and Vote By Ballot (London: Working Men's Association, 1838)

The 'People's Charter', published in May 1838, became the keystone of the Chartist movement, launching a political campaign that was as momentous for its creation of the first large-scale working-class movement as for its specific demands. Following radicals' disappointment over the limited electoral changes introduced by the 1832 Reform Act (see previous extract), the six points of the Charter demanded suffrage for all men over 21; voting by secret ballot; equal electoral districts; abolition of property qualifications for MPs; payment of MPs; and annual parliamentary elections. The origins of Chartism lie in the burgeoning number of radical groups formed during the 1820s and 1830s, which were themselves a product of the increasingly class-based structure of British society. Three great petitions were presented to Parliament in support of the Charter in 1839, 1842 and 1848 (their size is typified by the 3,315,752 signatures on the second petition). Chartism faded as a movement following the failure of the 1848 petition and the dissipation of that year's revolutionary fervour (see extract 1.5); nonetheless, all but one of their original demands eventually became law.

    Prepared by a Committee of Twelve Persons, Six Members of Parliament and Six Members of the London Working Men's Association, and addressed to the People of the United Kingdom.

    Whereas, to insure, as far as it is possible by human forethought and wisdom, the just government of the people, it is necessary to subject those who have the power of making laws to a wholesome and strict responsibility to those whose duty it is to obey them when made.

    And whereas, this responsibility is best enforced through the instrumentality of a body which emanates directly from and is itself immediately subject to, the whole people, and which completely represents their feelings and their interests;

    And, whereas, as the Commons' House of Parliament now exercises, in the name, and on the supposed behalf of he people, the power of making the laws, it ought, in order to fulfil with wisdom and with honesty the great duties imposed on it, to be made the most faithful and accurate representation of the people's wishes, feelings and interests;

    Be it therefore enacted, That from and after the passing of this Act, every male inhabitant of these realms be entitled to vote for the election of a Member of Parliament; subject, however, to the following conditions: –

1. That he be a native of these realms, or a foreigner who has lived in this country upwards of two years, and been naturalized.
2. That he be twenty-one years of age.
3. That he be not proved insane when the lists of voters are revised.
4. That he be not *undergoing the sentence of the law at the time when called upon to exercise the electoral right.*
5. That his electoral rights be not suspended for bribery at elections, or for personation, or for forgery of election certificates, according to the penalties of this Act.

ELECTORAL DISTRICTS.

Be it enacted, I. That for the purpose of obtaining an equal representation of the people in the Commons' House of Parliament, the united kingdom be divided into three hundred electoral districts.[3]

II. That each such district contain, as nearly as may be, an equal number of inhabitants.

III. That the number of inhabitants be taken from the last census, and as soon as possible after the next ensuing decennial census shall have been taken, the electoral districts be made to conform thereto.

IV. That each electoral district be named after the principal city of borough within its limits.

V. That each electoral district return one representative to sit in the Commons' House of Parliament. [...]

ARRANGEMENTS FOR ELECTIONS.

Be it enacted, I. That a general election of Members of Parliament for all the electoral districts of the United Kingdom take place on the first Monday in June each year; and that all vacancies by death or otherwise, shall be filled up as nearly as possible within eighteen days after they occur. [...]

DURATION OF PARLIAMENT.

Be it enacted, I. That the members of the House of Commons chosen as aforesaid, shall meet on the first Monday in June in each year, and continue their sittings from time to time as they may deem it convenient, till the first Monday in June following, when the next new Parliament *shall* be chosen; they shall be eligible to be re-elected.

II. That during an adjournment they be liable to be called together by the Executive in case of emergency.

III. That a register be kept of the daily attendance of each member, which, at the close of the session shall be printed as a sessional paper, showing how the Members have attended.

---

3 *Original Note:* There are, say 6,000,000 of men eligible to vote; this number, divided by 300, gives 20,000 to each member.

PAYMENT OF MEMBERS.

Be it enacted, I. That every Member of the House of Commons be entitled at the close of the session, to a writ of expenses on the Treasury, for his legislative duties in the public service; and shall be paid per annum.[4] [...]

1.4 'Distress in Cork', *The Times*, 24 December 1846

Between 1845 and 1851, Ireland was afflicted by a disastrous famine that had a profound impact on its demographic and social structure. The initial cause was potato blight, which caused successive failure of the potato crop at a time when potatoes were the principal foodstuff of the poor (in 1846, around 75 per cent of the crop was lost). The privation of the rural poor was accentuated by the British government's misdirected and ineffective response to the crisis. An attachment to free-market ideology, widespread belief in the inefficiency of Irish agriculture, and a longstanding disregard for the Catholic peasantry led to political reluctance to devote enough energy and resources to large-scale welfare support. Figures vary, but it is estimated that around one million people died from starvation and disease, and at least one million emigrated to England, Canada and the United States. The famine killed around one-eighth of the population.

The reports from Cork continue extremely unfavourable. The following is an extract of a letter dated 'Bantry, Saturday', supplied by the special reporter of the *Cork Examiner*: –

As regards the influence exercised by the sudden and extraordinary deaths which are daily occurring, it is not confined to the families or individuals immediately affected, – it extends to all the labourers employed for miles around, and excites in their imaginations the most dreadful anticipations regarding their ultimate condition. It is, I have heard from numbers of those labourers themselves, and as I have been credibly informed by the Catholic clergy, their firm and undoubted belief that they are all reserved for the same fate as is daily occurring to their neighbours, – that they are doomed, without either expectation of relief or release, to expire before the termination of a few months, – that they will be found either in fields or on mountains, without either the consolations of clergy or the comfort of friends.

And what reason have the people for anticipating any other change in their present protracted sufferings? With hundreds unemployed – still further retrenchment of expenditure appears to be the Government policy, still greater strictness characterizes their present proceedings. In the remote and extreme

---

4 *Original Note:* The Committee understand that the DAILY payment of Members of Parliament has operated beneficially in Canada: but they fear that such mode of payment holds out a motive for lengthening the sessions unnecessarily: and if the time of sitting is limited by law, it may lead to too hasty legislation, both of which evils are obviated by an annual payment.

districts of the parish that I at present refer to, the individuals composing the families of employed labourers are obliged to travel a distance of 20 miles to the nearest available market for the purchase of perhaps one stone of flour or meal, and they are compelled to return the same distance before their hungry families can receive one morsel of food. [. . .]

That these statements are not over-coloured may be gathered from a letter addressed to the Duke of Wellington by Mr. N. Cumming, a magistrate of the county of Cork; it is as follows: –

'My Lord Duke, – Without apology or preface, I presume so far as to trespass on your Grace as to state to you, and by the use of your illustrious name, to present to the British public the following statement of what I have myself seen within the last three days.

Having for many years been intimately connected with the western portion of the county of Cork, and possessing some small property there, I thought it right personally to investigate the truth of the several lamentable accounts which had reached me, of the appalling state of misery to which that part of the country was reduced.

I accordingly went on the 15th inst. to Skibbereen, and to give the instance of one townland which I visited, as an example of the state of the entire coast district, I shall state simply what I there saw. It is situated on the eastern side of Castlehaven harbour, and is named South Reen, in the parish of Nyross. Being aware that I should have to witness scenes of frightful hunger, I provided myself with as much bread as five men could carry, and on reaching the spot I was surprised to find the wretched hamlet apparently deserted. I entered some of the hovels to ascertain the cause, and the scenes that presented themselves were such as no tongue or pen can convey the slightest idea of. In the first, six famished and ghastly skeletons, to all appearance dead, were huddled in a corner on some filthy straw, their sole covering what seemed a ragged horse-cloth, their wretched legs hanging about, naked above the knees. I approached with horror, and found by a low moaning they were alive – they were in fever, four children, a woman, and what had once been a man. It is impossible to go through the detail. Suffice it to say, that in a few minutes I was surrounded by at least 200 of these phantoms, such frightful spectres as no words can describe. By far the greater number were delirious, either from famine or from fever. Their demoniac yells are still ringing in my ears, and their horrible images are fixed upon my brain. My heart sickens at the recital, but I must go on.

In another case, decency would forbid what follows, but it must be told. My clothes were nearly torn off in my endeavour to escape from the throng of pestilence around, when my neckcloth was seized from behind by a gripe which compelled me to turn. I found myself grasped by a woman with an infant just born in her arms, and the remains of a filthy sack across her loins – the sole covering of herself and babe. The same morning the police opened a house on the adjoining lands, which was observed shut for many days, and two frozen corpses were found, lying upon the mud floor, half devoured by the rats.

A mother, herself in a fever, was seen the same day to drag out the corpse of her child, a girl about 12, perfectly naked, and leave it half covered with stones. In another house, within 500 yards of the cavalry station at Skibbereen, the dispensary doctor found several wretches lying, unable to move, under the same cloak. One had been dead many hours, but the others were unable to move either themselves or the corpse.

To what purpose should I multiply such cases? If these be not sufficient, neither would they hear who have the power to send relief and do not, even 'though one came from the dead.' Let them, however, believe and tremble, that they shall one day hear the Judge of all the earth pronounce their tremendous doom, with the addition, 'I was an hungered and ye gave me no meat, thirsty and ye gave me no drink, naked and ye clothed me not.'

But I forget to whom this is addressed. My Lord, you are an old and justly honoured man. It is yet in your power to add another honour to your age, to fix another star, and that the brightest in your galaxy of glory. You have access to our young and gracious Queen. Lay these things before her. She is a woman. She will not allow decency to be outraged. She has at her command the means of at least mitigating the sufferings of the wretched survivors in this tragedy. They will soon be few indeed in the district I speak of, if help be longer withheld. [. . .]

1.5 'The King of Prussia to Queen Victoria' and 'Prince Albert to Lord John Russell', *The Letters of Queen Victoria: A Selection from Her Majesty's Correspondence Between the Years 1837 and 1861*, ed. Arthur Christopher Benson and Viscount Esher, vol. 2 (London: John Murray, 1908)

The year 1848 was a momentous year in which a spirit of revolution spread across mainland Europe. The political upheaval began in France in February 1848, when King Louis-Philippe, whose reign had been increasingly conservative and divisive, abdicated following popular unrest in Paris. Revolution against monarchical rule soon extended to the German states (including Austria, Prussia, Saxony, Baden and Bavaria). Protests demanding liberal reform and/or the removal of conservative regimes took place in the Italian states, the Austrian Habsburg Empire, Hungary and Greater Poland. Unsurprisingly, these revolutions provoked shock and fear on the part of the ruling monarchs, who, as the letter from the King of Prussia below indicates, were in frequent contact with Queen Victoria. The British royal family also watched nervously as the radical fervour wafted across the English Channel. A large Chartist rally planned for Kennington Common, London, on 10 April 1848, provoked much anxiety, and is the subject of the letter below from Prince Albert. However, despite fears of impending insurrection, the presence of 8,000 soldiers and large numbers of police ensured that the Chartist protest passed off peacefully.

The King of Prussia to Queen Victoria
27th February 1848.

MOST GRACIOUS QUEEN AND SISTER, – Even at this midnight hour of the day, on the evening of which the awful news from Paris has arrived, I venture to address these lines to your Majesty. God has permitted events which decisively threaten the peace of Europe.

It is an attempt to 'spread the principles of the Revolution by *every* means throughout the whole of Europe'. This programme binds together both these individuals and their parties. The consequences for the peace of the world are *clear* and *certain*. If the revolutionary party carries out its programme, 'The sovereignty of the people', my minor crown will be broken, no less certainly than the mighty crowns of you Majesty, and a fearful scourge will be laid upon the nations; a century [will follow] of rebellion, of lawlessness, and of godlessness. The late king [Louis-Philippe] did not dare to write 'by the Grace of God'. *We*, however, call ourselves King 'by the Grace of God', because it is true. Well, then, most gracious Queen, let us now show to men, to the peoples now threatened with disruption and nameless misery, both *that* we understand our sacred office and *how* we understand it. God has placed in your Majesty's hands, in the hands of the two Emperors, in those of the German Federation, and in mine, a power, which, if it now acts in union and harmony, with reliance on Heaven, is able humanly speaking, to enforce, with certainty, the maintenance of the peace of the world. This power is *not that of arms*, for these, more than ever, must only afford the *ultima ratio*. [. . .]

With these words I fall at your Majesty's feet, most gracious Queen, and remain you Majesty's most faithfully devoted, most attached Servant and good Brother, FREDERIC WILLIAM.

P.S. – The Prince I embrace. He surely feels with me, and justly appraises my endeavours.

Post scriptum, 28th, in the evening.

I venture to open my letter again, for this day has brought us news from France, which one can only call *horrible*. According to what we hear, there is no longer left a King in France. A regency, a government, and the most complete anarchy has ensued, under the name of the Republic – a condition of things in which, at first, there will be no possibility of communicating with the people, infuriated with crime. In case a Government should evolve itself out of this chaos, I conscientiously hold that the 'united word' of the great Powers, such as I have indicated in the preceding pages, should be made known, *without any modification, to the new holders of power*. Your Majesty's gracious friendship will certainly not take amiss this addition to my letter, though it be not comfortable to strict etiquette.

The fate of the poor old King, of the Duchess of Orleans, of the whole honourable and amiable family, cuts me to the heart, for up to this time we do not know what has become of any one of them. We owe Louis Philippe eighteen

Figure 1.1 'Specimens from Mr. Punch's Industrial Exhibition of 1850', *Punch* 18 (1850), 145

happy years of peace. No noble heart must forget that. And yet – who would not recognise the avenging hand of the King of kings in all this?

I kiss your Majesty's hands.

The Prince Albert to Lord John Russell.[5]
OSBORNE, 10th April 1848.

MY DEAR LORD JOHN, – To-day the strength of the Chartists and all evil-disposed people in the country will be brought to the test against the force of the law, the Government, and the good sense of the country. I don't feel doubtful for a moment who will be found the stronger, but should be exceedingly mortified if anything like a commotion was to take place, as it would shake *that* confidence which the whole of Europe reposes in our stability at this moment, and upon which will depend the prosperity of the country. I have enquired a good deal into the state of employment about London, and I find, to my great regret, that the number of workmen of all trades out of employment is *very* large, and that it has been increased by the reduction of all the works under Government, owing to the clamour for economy in the House of Commons. Several hundred workmen have been discharged at Westminster Palace; at Buckingham Palace much fewer hands

5 Lord John Russell (1792–1878), Liberal politician and Prime Minister 1846–52.

Figure 1.2 'The Exterior', *Dickinson's Comprehensive Pictures of the Great Exhibition of 1851: From the originals painted for H.R.H. Prince Albert by Messrs. Nash, Haghe and Roberts*

are employed than are really wanted; the formation of Battersea Park has been suspended, etc., etc. Surely this is not the moment for the tax-payers to economise upon the working classes! And though I don't wish our Government to follow Louis Blanc in his system of *organisation du travail*,[6] I think the Government is bound to do what it can to help the working classes over the present moment of distress. It may do this consistently with real economy in its own works, whilst the reductions on the part of the Government are followed by all individuals as a sign of the times. I have before this spoken to Lord Morpeth[7] upon this subject, but I wish to bring it specially under your consideration at the present moment.

Ever yours truly,
ALBERT.

1.6 Henry Cole, *Official Descriptive and Illustrated Catalogue of the Great Exhibition 1851*, vol. 1 (London: Spicer Brothers, 1851)

Opened by Queen Victoria on 1 May 1851, 'The Great Exhibition of the Works of Industry of All Nations' was a momentous display of the most innovative products of industrialization, all housed within the iconic Crystal Palace in Hyde Park. The excerpt

---

6 Louis Blanc, French politician who became a member of the government after the fall of Louis-Philippe. Blanc pioneered government-funded cooperative workshops to ensure that workers had jobs.

7 Lord Morpeth (1802–64), Chief Commissioner of Woods and Forests.

*below is from the introduction to the official catalogue and expounds the vision of
Henry Cole (1808–82) and Prince Albert (1819–61), two leading figures in the conception and organization of the Great Exhibition. In part the event celebrated a new world
order based on the spread of industrial capitalism which, it was idealistically hoped,
would consequently bring freedom and progress to all. Truly international in conception, with exhibits from colonies such as Canada and India as well as numerous
European countries and the United States of America, the first 'World's Fair' was seen
by many to confirm Britain's status as the leading industrial, global power. By the time
it was officially closed on 15 October 1851 over six million visitors had attended the
exhibition.*

The activity of the present day chiefly develops [*sic*] itself in commercial industry, and it is in accordance with the spirit of the age that the nations of the world
have now collected together their choicest productions. It may be said without
presumption, that an event like this Exhibition could not have taken place at
any earlier period, and perhaps not among any other people than ourselves. The
friendly confidence reposed by other nations in our institutions; the perfect
security for property; the commercial freedom, and the facility of transport,
which England pre-eminently possesses, may all be brought forward as causes
which have operated in establishing the Exhibition in London. Great Britain
offers a hospitable invitation to all the nations of the world, to collect and
display the choicest fruits of their industry in her Capital; and the invitation is
freely accepted by every civilized people, because the interest both of the guest
and host is felt to be reciprocal. [...]

HIS ROYAL HIGHNESS THE PRINCE ALBERT, as President of the Society, had
of course been fully informed, from time to time, of all these proceedings, which
had received His Royal Highness's sanction and approval; but immediately after
the termination of the session of 1849, the Prince took the subject under his
own personal superintendence. He proceeded to settle the general principles on
which the proposed exhibition for 1851 should be conducted, and to consider
the mode in which it should be carried out.

His Royal Highness has himself fully expressed the views which prompted
him to take the lead in carrying out the Exhibition, and on the occasion of the
banquet to promote the Exhibition, given by Mr. FARNCOMB, the Lord Mayor
of London, to the municipal authorities of the United Kingdom, His Royal
Highness declared these views in the following terms: –

It must, indeed, be most gratifying to me, to find that a suggestion which I
had thrown out, as appearing to me of importance at this time, should have met
with such universal concurrence and approbation; for this has proved to me that
the view I took of the peculiar character and requirements of our age was in
accordance with the feelings and opinions of the country. Gentlemen, I
conceive it to be the duty of every educated person closely to watch and study
the time in which he lives; and, as far as in him lies, to add his humble mite of
individual exertion to further the accomplishment of what he believes

Providence to have ordained. Nobody, however, who has paid any attention to the particular features of our present era, will doubt for a moment that we are living at a period of most wonderful transition, which tends rapidly to the accomplishment of that great end to which, indeed, all history points – the realization of the unity of mankind. Not a unity which breaks down the limits, and levels the peculiar characteristics of the different nations of the earth, but rather a unity the result and product of those very national varieties and antagonistic qualities. The distances which separated the different nations and parts of the globe are gradually vanishing before the achievements of modern invention, and we can traverse them with incredible ease; the languages of all nations are known, and their acquirements placed within the reach of everybody; thought is communicated with the rapidity and even by the power of lightning. On the other hand, the great principle of division of labour, which may be called the moving power of civilization, is being extended to all branches of science, industry, and art. Whilst formerly the greatest mental energies strove at universal knowledge, and that knowledge was confined to the few, now they are directed to specialties, and in these again even to the minutest points; but the knowledge acquired becomes at once the property of the community at large. Whilst formerly discovery was wrapt in secresy [sic], the publicity of the present day causes that no sooner is a discovery or an invention made, than it is already improved upon and surpassed by competing efforts; the products of all quarters of the globe are placed at our disposal, and we have only to choose which is the best and cheapest for our purposes, and the powers of production are intrusted to the stimulus of competition and capital. So man is approaching a more complete fulfilment of that great and sacred mission which he has to perform in this world. His reason being created after the image of God, he has to use it to discover the laws by which the Almighty governs his creation, and, by making these laws his standard of action, to conquer Nature to his use – himself a divine instrument. Science discovers these laws of power, motion, and transformation: industry applies them to the raw matter, which the earth yields us in abundance, but which becomes valuable only by knowledge: art teaches us the immutable laws of beauty and symmetry, and gives to our productions forms in accordance with them. Gentlemen, – THE EXHIBITION of 1851 is to give us a true test and a living picture of the point of development at which the whole of mankind has arrived in this great task, and a new starting point from which all nations will be able to direct their further exertions.

1.7 Caroline Norton, *A Letter to the Queen on Lord Chancellor Cranworth's Marriage and Divorce Bill* (London: Longman, Brown, Green and Longmans, 1855)

The Matrimonial Causes Act of 1857 marked the first small step in improving the legal rights of women in marriage and divorce. Previously an option only for the most wealthy, the Act made divorce more accessible by transferring legal proceedings from the ecclesiastical to the civil courts. A husband who had deserted his wife was no longer entitled to her earnings. Crucially, a woman who was legally separated or divorced from her husband was also granted the property rights of a single woman. Nonetheless, the divorce laws retained a sexual double standard: a husband was able to divorce his wife on the grounds of her adultery, but a wife could only do so if – in addition to adultery – her husband had also committed bestiality, bigamy, cruelty, rape or incest. The passing of the Act owed much to the campaigning of Caroline Norton (1808–77), writer, society beauty and advocate of women's rights, following a disastrous marriage and separation. As Caroline Sheridan, she had married George Norton in 1826; they subsequently separated due to his violent and abusive behaviour, yet he retained custody of their children and she found she was legally unable to divorce him. In addition to the above pamphlet, which was produced following the initial introduction of a Matrimonial Causes bill in 1854, Norton published numerous other leaflets urging reform of laws concerning marriage and divorce. (For other extracts on the roles and rights of women, see Section 3.)

I connect your Majesty's name with these pages from a different motive; for two reasons: of which one, indeed, is a sequence to the other. First, because I desire to point out the grotesque anomaly which ordains that married women shall be 'non-existent' in a country governed by a female Sovereign; and secondly, because, whatever measure for the reform of these statutes may be proposed, it cannot become 'the law of the land' without your Majesty's assent [. . .]

A married woman in England has *no legal existence*: her being is absorbed in that of her husband. Years of separation or desertion cannot alter this position. Unless divorced by special enactment in the House of Lords, the legal fiction holds her to be '*one*' with her husband, even though she may never see or hear of him.

She has no possessions, unless by special settlement; her property is *his* property. [. . .] An English wife has no legal right even to her clothes or ornaments; her husband may take them and sell them if he pleases, even though they be the gifts of relatives or friends, or bought before marriage.

An English wife cannot make a will. She may have children or kindred whom she may earnestly desire to benefit; – she may be separated from her husband, who may be living with a mistress; no matter: the law gives what she has to him, and no will she could make would be valid.

An English wife cannot legally claim her own earnings. Whether wages for manual labour, or payment for intellectual exertion, whether she weed potatoes, or keep a school, her salary is *the husband's*; and he could compel a second payment, and treat the first as void, if paid to the wife without his sanction.

An English wife may not leave her husband's house. Not only can he sue her for 'restitution of conjugal rights', but he has a right to enter the house of any friend or relation with whom she may take refuge, and who may 'harbour her', – as it is termed, – and carry her away by force, with or without the aid of the police.

If the wife sue for separation for cruelty, it must be 'cruelty that endangers life or limb', and if she has once forgiven, or, in legal phrase, '*condoned*' his offences, she cannot plead them; though her past forgiveness only proves that she endured as long as endurance was possible.

If her husband take proceedings for a divorce, she is not, in the first instance, allowed to defend herself. She has no means of providing the falsehood of his allegations. She is not represented by attorney, nor permitted to be considered a party to the suit between him and her supposed lover, for 'damages'. [...]

If an English wife be guilty of infidelity, her husband can divorce *her* so as to marry again; but she cannot divorce the husband *a vinculo*,[8] however profligate he may be. No law court can divorce in England. A special Act of Parliament annulling the marriage, is passed for each case. The House of Lords grants this almost as a matter of course to the husband, but not to the wife. In only four instances (two of which were cases of incest), has the wife obtained a divorce to marry again. [. . .]

Her being [. . .] of spotless character, and without reproach, gives her no advantage in law. She may have withdrawn from his roof knowing that he lives with 'his faithful housekeeper': having suffered personal violence at his hands; having 'condoned' much, and being able to prove it by unimpeachable testimony: or he may have shut the doors of her house against her: all this is quite immaterial: the law takes no cognisance of which is to blame. As *her husband*, he has a right to all that is hers: as *his wife*, she has no right to anything that is his. As her husband he may divorce her (if truth or false swearing can do it): as his wife, the utmost 'divorce' she could obtain, is permission to reside alone, – married to his name. The marriage ceremony is a civil bond for him, – and an indissoluble sacrament for her; and the rights of mutual property which that ceremony is ignorantly supposed to confer, are made absolute for him, and null for her.

1.8 [Sītā Rām], *From Sepoy to Subadar: Being the Life and Adventures of a Native Officer of the Bengal Army, Written and Related By Himself,* trans. Lieut-Colonel Norgate and ed. Lieut-Colonel C. C. Phillott (1873; Calcutta: Baptist Mission Press, 1911)

In May 1857 a rebellion against British rule in India broke out, led by soldiers of the Bengal army. The uprising spread through large parts of northern and central India. Shocked at the challenge to British rule, and horrified by tales of the massacre of women and children at Cawnpore, British retribution against the leaders of the rebellion was fierce, brutal and bloody. The revolt was only finally quelled in the summer of 1858. In its aftermath the British Crown took over the responsibility for ruling India from the East India Company. These memoirs were originally written in Hindi by a native officer of

---

8 Divorce *a vinculo matrimonii* constitutes an absolute dissolution and severance of the marriage; the alternative, divorce *a mensa et thoro*, simply separates the two parties.

the Bengal army, and the blame the piece ascribes to Muslim soldiers for the Mutiny needs to be set in the context of religious tension existing within India and the author's loyalty to the British. The memoirs were translated by a member of the Bengal Staff Corps and first published in an Indian periodical in 1861; they were subsequently published in book form in 1873 (this extract is from the third edition of 1911).

Preface by Translator

I have attempted to render into English the Life and Adventures of this Native Officer, and in so doing, have often been obliged to give the general meaning, rather than adhere to a literal translation of many sentences and ideas, the true idiom of which it is almost impossible to transpose into English [. . .]

For the opinions contained in the work, I am not responsible: they are those of a Hindoo, not a Christian [. . .]

It is believed that this is one of the first attempts of any native soldier, to give his thoughts and ideas to the world, and it occasioned great trouble, and a great amount of assurances had to be given, before the Soobadar would part with his memoirs [. . .]

From Sepoy to Soobadar, Being the Autobiography of a Sepoy

It chanced that about this time the Sirkar[9] sent chosen parties of men from each regiment to different stations to be instructed in the use of the new rifle; the men went on with their drill for some time, when by some means or other a report got about that the cartridges used for these new arms were greased with the fat of cows and pigs. The men from our regiment wrote to the others telling them of this, and great excitement began to be felt in every regiment. Some of the men said they had served the Sirkar for forty years, during which time nothing had ever been done to insult their religion; still, as I have mentioned, the minds of men had been made unsteady by the seizure of Oude; interested parties always pointed out, that the great aim of the English was to make the natives all Christians, and by the cartridge it was to be bought about, as both Mahomedans and Hindoos would be alike defiled. [. . .]

When I returned to my own village, the whole place was talking about the news. In a short time the entire country was in a ferment, and every regiment in it was said to be ready to mutiny; every day reports came in, that the regiments at the different stations had all risen and killed their officers. I went again to see the Deputy Commissioner, and offered to collect the furlough men of my own regiment, and also any pensioners who could use arms; he thanked me, and promised to let me know if it would be required.

Shortly after this, the regiments at Lucknow, Setapore, and other stations in Oude broke out into open mutiny, and the country was overrun with sepoys of those regiments. [. . .]

---

9 A term used in India to designate the government or ruling authority; from the Persian *sarkar*, meaning 'head of affairs'.

I now discovered that I was watched, and was suspected of giving the civil officers information. One day a large body of sepoys of one of the mutinied regiments came through my village, and I tried to persuade them to go quietly to their houses, and pointed out to them the folly of going against the English Government; but these men were so intoxicated with the plunder they had taken, and the prospects of rewards from the Emperor of Delhi, that they turned on me, and were about to shoot me on the spot for having dared to speak about the Sirkar *Ungreese*; they called me a traitor, and at last made me a prisoner, and put heavy irons on me and a chain round my neck, declaring they would take me to Lucknow, where they would secure a large reward for having seized me, and where my punishment would be to have melted lead poured down my throat for daring to uphold the English rule under which I had served and eaten my salt, so many years. I was treated with every indignity; the men boasted of the deeds they had done, and how the Sahebs had been so easily killed, or frightened into the jungles like hares; they were fully persuaded that the English rule had come to an end throughout India [. . .]

I had never known the Sirkar interfere with our religion or our caste ever since I had been a soldier in its service certainly, but my mind was filled with some doubts. I remembered the treatment of many regiments as to the *batta*[10] – how it had been in the first place promised and then withheld; then that the Sirkar had seized Oude without any just cause. I had also observed the increase in late years of Padree Sahebs,[11] who stood up in the streets and cities and told the people their cherished religion was all false, entreating them to become Christians; they always said they were not employed by the Sirkar, and that they received no money from it, but how could they say what they did, without their permission? Everybody believed they were secretly employed by it: why should they take such trouble if they were not ordered? Then I remembered how the Sirkar had been a protector to me, and that I had eaten its salt for forty years, and I determined never to go against it as long as it remained, but to do all I could for it.

My Lord, you must not forget that at this time I was bound with chains, and to all appearances being taken to a terrible death. Day after day when I heard city after city, station after station, were in the hands of the people, I cannot but say the thought sometimes came into my mind that the mighty Companee Raj was passing away, as all its guns had been taken, and its arsenals also; how could I help thinking otherwise? [. . .]

The Mussulmans were the first instigators of the mutiny; and the Hindoos followed, like a flock of sheep over the bank of a river.[12] The chief thing that bred the rebellion was the knowledge of the power the sepoys had, and the little

---

10 *Original Note*: *Bhattā*, derived from *bhāt*, cooked rice. – *Ed.*
11 An Indian term for chaplains.
12 *Original Note*: When crossing a stream one sheep is forcibly pushed into the water first, when the remainder followed. – *Ed.*

control the Sahebs were allowed to exert over them. They naturally from this fancied the Sirkar must be afraid of them; whereas it only trusted them too well. But as a son is not discarded by his parent for once rebelling against his authority, I will hope that the chastisement of the rebellious son received for this, will have a lasting effect, and that wickedness will never be allowed to attack the hearts of the sepoys again [. . .]

Let the English Sirkar look well to its Hindoo servants; remove as much as possible all causes of complaint, and they will not resist it; besides which they will seldom commence a rebellion, but will follow in its track when once begun. Let it remember the words of an old man who knows them: never trust the Mussulmans; they are the instigators and principal movers in all disturbances, always having an ill-feeling against the Sirkar. The Mussulman is the snake that the man put in his bed to keep warm, and in return it stung him; the snake's nature is to sting, therefore, obeying its nature, it stung. The religion of the Mussulman enforces on him the necessity of slaying what he calls an infidel, and promises him seven heavens seven times over for every one he slays.[13]

1.9 William Forster on the 'Elementary Education Bill', Hansard's Parliamentary Debates. Third Series. Comprising the period from the eighth day of February 1870, to the fifteenth day of March 1870 (London: Cornelius Buck, 1870)

On 12 February 1870, William Forster (1818–86) introduced the Elementary Education Act into Parliament. It was a pioneering piece of legislation that created a national framework for the educational provision of children between the ages of five and twelve inclusive. Where provision was lacking, schools could be set up by education boards, publicly funded by local rates. As his House of Commons speech suggests, Forster's bill aimed to remedy the existing patchwork system of public and voluntary schools, which meant many working-class children received limited or no schooling. The Act laid the foundations for a national education system: there were 3,692 board schools by 1883. It remained the case, however, that parents had to pay for their children and attendance was not made compulsory until 1880. Forster was a Liberal-radical politician and industrialist; his leading role in framing the legislation is reflected in the fact that it is often referred to as Forster's Education Act.

[William Forster] I believe I can give pretty correctly the figures with regard, at all events, to Liverpool, and they are figures which may well alarm us. It is calculated that in Liverpool the number of children between five and thirteen who ought to receive an elementary education is 80,000; but as far as

---

13 *Original Note:* This is, of course, only Sita Rama's idea. – *Ed.*

we can ascertain, 20,000 of them attend no school whatever, while at least another 20,000 attend schools where they get an education not worth having. [. . .]

I have stated to the House what now exists, and I have endeavoured to form an estimate of what does not exist in regard to the education of the people. Now, what are the results? They are what we might have expected; much imperfect education and much absolute ignorance; good schools become bad schools for children who attend them for only two or three days in the week, or for only a few weeks in the year; and though we have done well in assisting the benevolent gentlemen who have established schools, yet the result of the State leaving the initiative to volunteers, is, that where State help has been most wanted, State help has been least given, and that where it was desirable that State power should be most felt it was not felt at all. In helping those only who help themselves, or who can get others to help them, we have left unhelped those who most need help. Therefore, notwithstanding the large sums of money we have voted, we find a vast number of children badly taught, or utterly untaught, because there are too few schools and too many bad schools, and because there are large numbers of parents in this country who cannot, or will not, send their children to school. Hence comes a demand from all parts of the country for a complete system of national education, and I think it would be as well for us at once to consider the extent of that demand. I believe that the country demands from us that we should at least try to do two things, and that it shall be no fault of ours if we do not succeed in doing them – namely, cover the country with good schools, and get the parents to send their children to those schools. I am aware, indeed, that to hope to arrive at these two results may be thought Utopian; but our only hope of getting over the difficulties before us, is to keep a high ideal before our minds, and to realize to ourselves what it is we are expected to try to do. [. . .]

We must not delay. Upon the speedy provision of elementary education depends our industrial prosperity. It is of no use trying to give technical teaching to our artisans without elementary education; uneducated labourers – and many of our labourers are utterly uneducated – are, for the most part, unskilled labourers, and if we leave our work-folk any longer unskilled, notwithstanding their strong sinews and determined energy, they will become overmatched in the competition of the world. Upon this speedy provision depends also, I fully believe, the good, the safe working of our constitutional system. To its honour, Parliament has lately decided that England shall in future be governed by popular government. I am one of those who would not wait until the people were educated before I would trust them with political power. If we had thus waited we might have waited long for education; but now that we have given them political power we must not wait any longer to give them education.

Figure 1.3 'For Queen and Empire!!' *Punch* 112 (1897), 296–7

1.10 Lewis Morris, 'A Song of Empire', from *Songs for Britain* (London: Kegan Paul, Trench & Co., 1887)

On 20 June 1887, Queen Victoria celebrated 50 years on the throne. The centrepiece of her Golden Jubilee was an enormous military procession through London, ending with an open-air thanksgiving service at St Paul's. There was also a large naval display at Portsmouth and many thousands of local processions in towns and cities across Britain and her empire. The scale and organization of Queen Victoria's Golden Jubilee (and that of her Diamond Jubilee in 1897) reflect the imperial reinvention of the monarchy following Prime Minister Benjamin Disraeli's bestowal upon her of the title Empress of India in 1877. As this extract from Morris's long poem demonstrates, Victoria became the overarching, unifying figure who bound together the disparate colonies of the empire. From Calcutta to Cape Town, her feminine virtues, her motherly concern for her subjects, were used to emphasize the existence of an imperial family and to soften the imposition of British rule. Morris (1833–1907) was a popular late Victorian poet, who narrowly missed becoming laureate following the death of Tennyson in 1892; his work included several odes commemorating royal and imperial events.

> First Lady of our English race,
> In Royal dignity and grace
> Higher than all in old ancestral blood,
> But higher still in love of good,
> And care for ordered Freedom, grown
> To a great tree where'er
> In either hemisphere,

Its vital seeds are blown;
Where'er with every day begun
Thy English bugles greet the coming sun!

Thy life is England's. All these fifty years
Thou from thy lonely Queenly place
Hast watched the clouds and sunshine on her face;
Hast marked her changing hopes and fears;
Her joys and sorrows have been always thine;
Always thy quick and Royal sympathy
Has gone out swiftly to the humblest home,
Wherever grief and pain and suffering come.

Therefore is it that we
Take thee for head and symbol of our name.
For fifty years of reign thou wert the same,
Therefore today we make our jubilee.
Firm set on ancient right, as on thy people's love,
Unchecked thy wheels of empire onward move.
Not as theirs is thy throne
Who, though their hapless subjects groan,
Sit selfish, caring not at all,
Until the fierce mob surges and they fall,
Or the assassin sets the down-trod free.
Not such thy fate on this thy jubilee,
But love and reverence in the hearts of all.

Oh England! Empire wide and great
As ever from the shaping hand of fate
Did issue on the earth, august, large grown!
What were the Empires of the past to thine,
The old, old Empires ruled by kings divine –
Egypt, Assyria, Rome? What rule was like thine own,
Who over all the round world bearest sway?
Not those alone who thy commands obey
Thy subjects are; but in the boundless West
Our grandsires lost, still is thy reign confest.
'The Queen' they call thee, the young People strong,
Who, being Britons, might not suffer wrong,
But are reknit with us in reverence for thee;
Therefore it is we make our jubilee.

See what a glorious throng they come,
Turned to their ancient home,

The children of England! See
What vigorous company
Thou sendest, Greater England of the Southern Sea!
Thy stately cities, thick with domes and spires,
Chase the illumined night with festal fires
In honour of their Queen, whose happy reign
Began when, 'mid their central roar,
The naked savage trod the pathless plain.
Thousands of miles, North, South, East, West, to-day,
Their countless herds and flocks unnumbered stray.
Theirs are the vast primeval forest depths profound;
Yet everywhere are found
The English laws, the English accents fair,
'Mid burning North or cooler Southern air.
A world within themselves, and with them blent
Island with continent. [. . .]
Flash, festal fires, high on the joyous air!
Clash, joy-bells! joy-guns, roar! and, jubilant trumpets, blare!
Let the great noise of our rejoicing rise!
Gleam, long-illumined cities, to the skies
Round all the earth, in every clime,
So far your distance half confuses time!
As in the old Judæan history,
Fling wide the doors and set the prisoners free!
Wherever England is o'er all the world,
Fly, banner of Royal England, stream unfurled!
The proudest Empire that has been, to-day
Rejoices and makes solemn jubilee.
For England! England! we our voices raise!
Our England! England! England! in our Queen we praise!
We love not war, but only peace,
Yet never shall our England's power decrease!
Whoever guides our helm of State,
Let all men know it, England shall be great!
We hold a vaster Empire than has been!
Nigh half the race of man is subject to our Queen!
Nigh half the wide, wide earth is ours in fee!
And where her rule comes, all are free.
And therefore 'tis, oh Queen, that we,
Knit fast in bonds of temperate liberty,
Rejoice to-day, and make our solemn jubilee!

2
Society, Politics and Class

Introduction

In 1800 about 80 per cent of the population of Great Britain lived in the countryside; in 1900 about 80 per cent in the towns and cities. When considering this massive demographic shift, the result of property enclosures and the Industrial Revolution, students of the Victorian period must be careful to guard against idealized conceptions of pre-Victorian Britain as a natural or 'organic' society, an unchanging, localized rural order distinguished by stable, prosperous communities. Equally, it is worth remembering that although after the middle of the nineteenth century agriculture was no longer the hub around which the entire British economy turned, it was only in 1901 that transport and the metal industries surpassed it as the main employers of the British population. Notwithstanding, it remains the case that Victorian society was dramatically marked by the twofold processes of industrialization and urbanization, and it is important to recognize the extent to which Britain was transformed by new living conditions, working environments, modes of social interaction and organization – and the possibilities and pressures associated with such changes. As Marx and Engels famously noted, it was a period when it seemed that 'All that is solid melts into air'. Victorian society, politics and culture were energized at once by excitement and anxiety.

Particularly after an upturn in economic prosperity around the midpoint of the nineteenth century, many commentators were optimistic about the state of the nation. Theories of social advancement derived from the discipline of political economy maintained that increasingly complex divisions of labour would, as a result of rationalized production techniques and expanding market competition, connect peoples in mutually beneficial and dynamic ways, generating wealth, health and happiness. According to this model of progress, British society was very definitely changing for the better. Allied with its strong financial base and maritime supremacy, the capacity of growing or newly emerging towns and cities to turn out mass-produced manufactured products created tremendous wealth. Britain dominated international commerce, supplying cheap goods and financial services to foreign nations. Drawing upon a strong spirit of evangelical religiosity, commentators were keen to stress that Britain's status as the 'Workshop of the World' was the result of dominant political and cultural values

– an emphasis upon individual liberty, a good work ethic, a strong character and a developed sense of duty – as well as environmental factors (exemplified below by the extract from Samuel Smiles's *Self-Help*).

Faith in Britain's world-leading institutions and ideals, as well as its industrial and economic strength, added to Victorian optimism. Three Reform Acts of 1832, 1867 and 1884 provided substance to a belief that, unlike on the Continent, Britain's long-established traditions, laws and customs allowed its political system to develop without the need for revolution. Under pressure of popular campaigning, the 1832 Reform Bill began the process of giving parliamentary recognition to the new (middle-class) towns alongside the old (aristocratic) counties (see extract 1.2); it increased the electorate from under 400,000 in England and Wales in 1831 to 652,777 in 1833, around 17.2 per cent of all adult males.[1] However, although the 1867 and 1884 Acts increased enfranchisement, in 1891 it remained the case that only 60 per cent of the male population in England had the vote. Women would have to wait for suffrage until well after the death of Queen Victoria. As for the monarchy as an institution, Queen Victoria was often celebrated, not always justifiably, for being a modern monarch who adopted a constitutional role above party politics (the perceived weakness of women in high politics encouraging an impression of the monarchy's declining power). The extract below from Walter Bagehot's *The English Constitution* demonstrates the attachment to, and reinvention of, the function of the House of Lords. Other significant legislation and developments included the 1870 Education Act (see p. 41), an impressive programme of public and private building, and a burgeoning commodity culture. All these factors heightened middle-class optimism in particular. However, notwithstanding the changing fabric of Victorian society, and the importance attached to the 'self-made man', the rise of industrial entrepreneurs should not hide the fact that much economic and political power remained concentrated with older landed and banking interests.

For a variety of socio-economic, political and cultural reasons, 'class', over and above older societal designations such as 'ranks' or 'orders', became increasingly significant in the Victorian period as a category with which to understand both the material and the mental lives of a British populace undergoing rapid growth and experiencing fluctuating fortunes. In *The Communist Manifesto*, Marx and Engels declared that the history of 'all hitherto existing society is the history of class struggle'. Set against positive nineteenth-century accounts of cohesion and mobility between classes were radical analyses of society that emphasized the structural inevitability of class conflict, alienation and exploitation. So, despite increases in wealth, scientific and technological advances, and ongoing political emancipation, there was the feeling throughout the nineteenth century that the blessings the Chartist William Lovett labelled 'Bread, Knowledge and Freedom' were distributed unevenly. This feel-

---

1 K. Theodore Hoppen, *The Mid-Victorian Generation* (Oxford: Oxford University Press, 2000), 238.

ing was especially pronounced in the 1830s and 1840s when economic depression exacerbated ongoing political agitation. Chartism was at its strongest during the 'Hungry Forties', and the extracts by Benjamin Disraeli and Thomas Carlyle typify anxieties caused by a society increasingly defined and divided by class identity (see also p. 27 for the six points of the Charter). While the Chartists' demands were rejected, they provoked fear of possible revolution. More broadly, the Chartists were only one voice among many questioning the supposedly beneficent connection between labour, technological progress and the market. During the 1840s and 1850s, the 'Condition of England', 'Industrial' or 'Social Problem' novel dramatized the gap opening up between 'masters' or industrialist financiers and 'men' or working people. Powerful social journalism, represented below by William Cobbett, Henry Mayhew and William Booth, also sought to document the lives of those living in poverty, those who paid the price of, or were left behind by, the onward march of progress.

While industrialization brought material benefits to some members of society, many thought that the doctrinal positions associated with political economy and utilitarianism supported a pernicious system that denied the sympathetic fellow-feeling and imaginative freedom central to a moral, pious and full life. Maintaining that industrialization allied with laissez-faire economics had an alienating, 'atomistic' and instrumentalist impact upon individuals and communities, conservative and radical commentators alike were drawn to theorize strategies of resistance and to propose alternative modes of life.

The end of the nineteenth century saw the rise of new political movements – including labour unions, socialism, women's rights, ecology and conservation – which mounted a challenge to interests and values that might be loosely defined as bourgeois and patriarchal. Ongoing innovation in manufacturing allied with rising living standards also saw sections of society define their class identity more in relation to consumption than production, the gratification of desires as opposed to need, or aesthetics as opposed to utility. Politics also became increasingly 'jingoistic' as it was inflected by an aggressive phase of 'new imperialism', when Britain's colonial possessions grew tremendously (see extracts 1.10, 9.6 and 9.8). But colonial expansion and conflicts sapped resources and confidence, while there was an ever-growing threat to Britain's dominant global position posed by the rise of America and Germany. This threat from abroad was intensified by post-Darwinian fears that British society, led by the working-class inhabitants of crowded cities, was degenerating. Questions concerning the health of the 'Great' British nation converged around interrelated issues involving class, race, gender and sexuality. Such anxieties were bound up with a millenarian dimension of pessimism at the *Fin de siècle*. Although degeneration operated as a dominant late Victorian structure of feeling, it is also true that its dialectical opposite was regeneration, and the turn of the century encouraged many commentators to look forward optimistically.

2.1   William Cobbett, 'Down the Valley of the Avon in Wiltshire', *Rural Rides* (London: William Cobbett, 1830)

William Cobbett (1763–1835) was a publican's son, self-educated and committed to educating the people. A prolific journalist, he became a radical advocate of parliamentary reform in the first decade of the century (a retreat from his conservative stance of the 1790s, when he wrote under the name of Peter Porcupine from self-imposed exile in America). Cobbett was sentenced to two years' imprisonment in Newgate prison for libel in 1810, during which time he published attacks on the banking system and the insubstantiality of paper money. Hazlitt said his style was 'plain, broad, downright English'. In 1830, he collected from his journal, the weekly Political Register, *his* Rural Rides, *a travel diary recording how, between 1822 and 1826, he had ridden through the countryside of southern England, observing its natural wealth and beauty, its human depopulation due to impoverishment, and the hypocrisy and indifference of the landed gentry. Following the Reform Act of 1832, he was elected to Parliament for the new borough of Oldham. His writing is typically descriptive or realistic, empirical and elegiac of times past or fading. Modern critics often use him as an example of a transitional figure, before the rationalization of knowledge into factual and fictitious disciplines.*

In taking my leave of this beautiful vale I have to express my deep shame, as an Englishman, at beholding the general *extreme poverty* of those who cause this vale to produce such quantities of food and raiment. This is, I verily believe it, the *worst used labouring people upon the face of the earth.* Dogs and hogs and horses are treated with *more civility*; and as to food and lodging, how gladly would the labourers change with them! This state of things never can continue many years! *By some means or other* there must be an end to it; and my firm belief is, that that end will be dreadful. In the mean while I see, and I see it with pleasure, that the common people *know they are ill used*; and that they cordially, most cordially, hate those who ill-treat them.

During the day I crossed the river about fifteen or sixteen times; and in such hot weather it was very pleasant to be so much amongst meadows and water. I had been at NETHERAVON about eighteen years ago, where I had seen a great quantity of hares.[2] It is a place belonging to Mr Hicks BEACH, or BEECH, who was once a member of parliament. I had found the place *altered* a good deal; out of repair; the gates rather rotten; and (a very bad sign!) the *roof of the dog-kennel falling in!* There is a church, at this village of NETHERAVON, large enough to hold *a thousand or two* of people, and the whole parish contains only 350 souls, men, women and children. This Netheravon was formerly a great lordship, and in the parish there were three considerable manor-houses, besides the one near the church. These mansions are all down now; and it is curious enough to see the former *walled gardens* become *orchards*, together with other changes, all tend-

---

2 Netheravon is a village in the county of Avon in southern England.

ing to prove the gradual decay in all except what appertains merely to *the land* as a thing of production for the distant market. But, indeed, the people and the means of enjoyment *must go away*. They are *drawn* away by the taxes and the paper money. How are *twenty thousand new houses* to be, all at once, building in the WEN, without people and food and raiment going from this valley towards the WEN? It must be so; and this unnatural, this dilapidating, this ruining and debasing work must go on, until that which produces it be destroyed.

2.2 Thomas Carlyle, *Chartism* (London: James Fraser, 1840)

As the son of a Scottish Calvanist stonemason, Thomas Carlyle's (1795–1881) upbringing fed strongly into his puritanical valuation of the work ethic. It took an engagement with German philosophy – most prominently Kant and Goethe – in order for Carlyle to develop a transcendental spiritualism with which to combat what he believed to be the limiting, soul-destroying over-emphasis of his own age upon rationalist philosophies, material interests and mechanistic organization. Railing in particular against Benthamite utilitarianism (see extract 5.2) and labelling political economy as the 'dismal science', Carlyle developed a singular brand of socio-economic critique against the efficacy of the 'cash nexus' and the emancipatory beneficence of democratic reforms. Inspired by the Chartist movement, the extract below typifies Carlyle's radical willingness to attack the failure of a church and landowning elite to protect the working classes from the ravages of industrial capitalism. Far less radical, however, is his proposal that the solution to such societal ills and revolutionary threat lay in the hands of strong, heroic leaders, which Carlyle associated with pre-bourgeois forms of society (see extract 9.1 for his deeply conservative views on race). While not always agreeing with him, prominent figures, including Dickens, Marx and John Stuart Mill, were inspired by Carlyle's capacity to bring to the fore the questions they too considered urgent.

One inference, but one inclusive of all, shall content us here; this namely: That *Laissez-faire* has as good as done its part in a great many provinces; that in the provinces of the Working Classes, *Laissez-faire* having passed its New Poor-Law,[3] has reached the suicidal point, and now, as *felo-de-se*, lies dying there, in torch-light meetings and suchlike; that, in brief, a government of the under classes by the upper on the principle of *Let-alone* is no longer possible in England in these days. This is the one inference inclusive of all. For there can be no acting or doing of any kind, till it be recognised that there is a thing to be done; the thing once recognised, doing in a thousand shapes becomes possible. The Working Classes cannot any longer go on without government; without being *actually* guided and governed; England cannot subsist in peace till, by some means or other, some guidance or governance is found.

3 The New Poor Law, or Poor Law Amendment Act of 1834, established workhouses to provide for the destitute.

For, alas, on us too the rude truth has come home. Wrappages and speciosities all warned off, the haggard naked fact speaks to us: Are these millions taught? Are these millions guided? We have a Church, the venerable embodiment of an idea which may well call itself divine; which our fathers for long ages, feeling it to be divine, have been embodying as we see: it is a Church well furnished with equipments and appurtenances; educated in universities; rich in money; set on high places that it may be conspicuous to all, honoured of all. We have an Aristocracy of landed wealth and commercial wealth, in whose hands lies the law-making and the law-administering: an Aristocracy rich, powerful, long secure in its place; an Aristocracy with more faculty put free into its hands than was ever before, in any country or time, put into the hands of any class of men. This Church answers: Yes, the people are taught. This Aristocracy, astonishment in every feature, answers: Yes, surely the people are guided! Do we not pass what Acts of Parliament are needful; as many as thirty-nine for the shooting of the partridges alone? Are there not treadmills, gibbets; even hospitals, poor-rates, New Poor-Law? So answers Church; so answers Aristocracy, astonishment in every feature. – Fact, in the mean while, takes his lucifer-box, sets fire to wheat-stacks; sheds an all-too dismal light on several things. Fact searches for his third-rate potato, not in the meekest humour, six-and-thirty weeks each year; and does not find it. Fact passionately joins Messiah Thom of Canterbury, and has himself shot for a new fifth-monarchy brought in by Bedlam. Fact holds his fustian-jacket *Femgericht* in Glasgow City. Fact carts his Petition over the London streets, begging that you would simply have the goodness to grant him a universal suffrage and 'the five points', by the way of remedy.[4] These are not the symptoms of teaching and guiding. [. . .]

What is the meaning of the 'five points', if we will understand them? What are all popular commotions and maddest bellowings, from Peterloo[5] to the Place-de-Grève[6] itself? Bellowings, *in*articulate cries of a dumb creature in rage and pain; to the ear of wisdom they are inarticulate prayers: 'Guide me, govern me! I am mad and miserable, and cannot guide myself!' Surely of all 'rights of man', this right of the ignorant man to be guided by the wiser, to be, gently or forcibly, held in the true course by him, is the indisputablest. Nature herself ordains it from the first; Society struggles towards perfection by enforcing and accomplishing it more and more. If Freedom have any meaning, it means enjoyment of this right, wherein all other rights are enjoyed. It is a sacred right and duty, on both sides; and the summary of all social duties whatsoever between the two. [. . .]

Democracy, we are well aware, what is called 'self-government' of the multitude by the multitude, is in words the thing everywhere passionately

---

4 'Five points' refers to the demands of the Charter; see p. 27.

5 A pro-reform demonstration at St Peter's Field, Manchester in 1819 was violently dispersed by soldiers. Several protestors were killed and hundreds injured. The name 'Peterloo' is an ironic comparison to Waterloo.

6 The Place-de-Grève: the main place of execution in Paris until 1830.

clamoured for at present. [. . .] And yet all men may see, whose sight is good for much, that in democracy can lie no finality; that with the completest winning of democracy there is nothing yet won – except emptiness, and the free chance to win! [. . .] In Rome and Athens, as elsewhere, if we look practically, we shall find that it was not by loud voting and debating of many, but by wise insight and ordering of a few that the work was done. So is it ever, so will it ever be.

2.3 Benjamin Disraeli, *Sybil; or The Two Nations* (London: Henry Colburn, 1845)

Benjamin Disraeli (1804–81) was elected as a Tory MP in 1837; he had, however, published his first novel, Vivien Grey, *as early as 1826. He rose to political prominence in the early 1840s as the leading figure in the Young England movement. Created by a group of aristocratic Tory MPs, the Young England movement opposed the utilitarian and industrial temper of the times. In response to the social and political unrest of the late 1830s and early 1840s, they advocated a romantic programme of reform based upon a return to Christian chivalry and feudal paternalism, complete with a revivified monarchy, aristocracy, Church, and harmonious social relations. It was a Pre-Raphaelitism of politics. Sybil; or The Two Nations was the second of a trilogy of novels –* Coningsby *(1844),* Sybil *(1845) and* Tancred *(1847) – which analysed the condition of England and promoted Disraeli's political views. Often the victim of anti-Semitism (despite having been baptised at 13), Disraeli was twice Prime Minister, briefly in 1868, and again from 1874 to 1880.*

'In great cities men are brought together by the desire of gain. They are not in a state of co-operation, but of isolation, as to the making of fortunes; and for all the rest they are careless of neighbours. Christianity teaches us to love our neighbour as ourself; modern society acknowledges no neighbour.'

'Well, we live in strange times,' said Egremont, struck by the observation of his companion, and relieving a perplexed spirit by an ordinary exclamation, which often denotes that the mind is more stirred than it cares to acknowledge, or at the moment is able to express.

'When the infant begins to walk, it also thinks that it lives in strange times,' said his companion.

'Your inference?' asked Egremont.

'That society, still in its infancy, is beginning to feel its way.'

'This is a new reign,' said Egremont, 'perhaps it is a new era.'

'I think so,' said the younger stranger.

'I hope so,' said the elder one.

'Well, society may be in its infancy,' said Egremont, slightly smiling; 'but, say what you like, our Queen reigns over the greatest nation that ever existed.'

'Which nation?' asked the younger stranger, 'for she reigns over two.'

Figure 2.1 [John Tenniel], 'Cartoon No. V. Capital and Labour', Punch 5 (July–December 1843), 49

The stranger paused; Egremont was silent, but looked inquiringly.

'Yes,' resumed the younger stranger after a moment's interval. 'Two nations; between whom there is no intercourse and no sympathy; who are as ignorant of each other's habits, thoughts, and feelings, as if they were dwellers in different zones, or inhabitants of different planets; who are formed by a different breeding, are fed by a different food, are ordered by different manners, and are not governed by the same laws.'

'You speak of —' said Egremont, hesitatingly

'THE RICH AND THE POOR.'

2.4 Karl Marx and Friedrich Engels, *The Communist Manifesto*, trans. Samuel Moore in cooperation with Friedrich Engels (1848; London: William Reeves, 1888)

'A spectre is haunting Europe – the spectre of Communism.' When The Communist Manifesto *first appeared in February 1848, the opening words of Karl Marx (1818–83) and Friedrich Engels (1820–95) resonated powerfully with a series of revolutions that had broken out across the Continent. While these revolutions were prompted by wide-ranging socio-economic concerns, and while Victorian society did not experience*

revolt, there were genuine fears within Britain and beyond that the Manifesto's plea for the workers of the world to unite might indeed be heeded.

The extract below, the first of the Manifesto's four sections, dramatically under-scores capitalism's irresistible capacity to alter conditions of life in the nineteenth century. It provides an account of the way in which the bourgeoisie, driven by the need to extend markets and exploit fully the potential for economic growth afforded by devel-oping manufacturing and communication technologies, were transforming all social relations. The imperial character of nineteenth-century globalization is also manifest, alongside a pronounced attention to industrial capitalism's dehumanizing impact upon the proletariat. But as is also clear, Marx and Engels's materialist conception of histor-ical progress meant that they considered the world-changing power of capitalism neces-sary to the revolutionary realization of a socialist destiny.

The bourgeoisie cannot exist without constantly revolutionizing the instru-ments of production, and thereby the relations of production, and with them the whole relations of society. Conservation of the old modes of production in unaltered form, was, on the contrary, the first condition of existence for all earlier industrial classes. Constant revolutionising of production, uninterrupted disturbance of all social conditions, everlasting uncertainty and agitation distin-guish the bourgeois epoch from all earlier ones. All fixed, fast-frozen relations, with their train of ancient and venerable prejudices and opinions, are swept away, all new-formed ones become antiquated before they can ossify. All that is solid melts into air, all that is holy is profaned, and man is at last compelled to face with sober senses his real conditions of life, and his relations with his kind.

The need of a constantly expanding market for its products chases the bour-geoisie over the entire surface of the globe. It must nestle everywhere, settle everywhere, establish connexions everywhere.

The bourgeoisie has through its exploitation of the world market given a cosmopolitan character to production and consumption in every country. [. . .] In place of the old wants, satisfied by the productions of the country, we find new wants, requiring for their satisfaction the products of distant lands and climes. In place of the old local and national seclusion and self-sufficiency, we have intercourse in every direction, universal inter-dependence of nations. [. . .]

The bourgeoisie, by the rapid improvement of all instruments of production, by the immensely facilitated means of communication, draws all, even the most barbarian, nations into civilisation. The cheap prices of its commodities are the heavy artillery with which it batters down all Chinese walls, with which it forces the barbarians' intensely obstinate hatred of foreigners to capitulate. It compels all nations, on pain of extinction, to adopt the bourgeois mode of production; it compels them to introduce what it calls civilization into their midst, i.e., to become bourgeois themselves. In one word, it creates a world after its own image. [. . .]

Modern bourgeois society with its relations of production, of exchange and of property, a society that has conjured up such gigantic means of production and of exchange, is like the sorcerer who is no longer able to control the powers of the nether world whom he has called up by his spells. [. . .]

But not only has the bourgeoisie forged the weapons that bring death to itself; it has also called into existence the men who are to wield those weapons – the modern workers – the proletarians.

In proportion as the bourgeoisie, i.e., capital, is developed, in the same proportion is the proletariat, the modern working class, developed – a class of labourers, who live only so long as they find work, and who find work only so long as their labour increases capital. These labourers, who must sell themselves piecemeal, are a commodity, like every other article of commerce, and are consequently exposed to all the vicissitudes of competition, to all the fluctuations of the market. [. . .]

Modern Industry has converted the little workshop of the patriarchal master into the great factory of the industrial capitalist. Masses of labourers, crowded into the factory, are organised like soldiers. As privates of the industrial army they are placed under the command of a perfect hierarchy of officers and sergeants. Not only are they slaves of the bourgeois class, and of the bourgeois State; they are daily and hourly enslaved by the machine, by the overlooker, and, above all, by the individual bourgeois manufacturer himself. The more openly this despotism proclaims gain to be its end and aim, the more petty, the more hateful and the more embittering it is.

The less the skill and exertion of strength implied in manual labour, in other words, the more modern industry becomes developed, the more is the labour of men superseded by that of women. Differences of age and sex have no longer any distinctive social validity for the working class. All are instruments of labour, more or less expensive to use, according to their age and sex.

No sooner is the exploitation of the labourer by the manufacturer, so far, at an end, that he receives his wages in cash, than he is set upon by the other portions of the bourgeoisie, the landlord, the shopkeeper, the pawnbroker, etc. [. . .]

In depicting the most general phases of the development of the proletariat, we traced the more or less veiled civil war, raging within existing society, up to the point where that war breaks out into open revolution, and where the violent overthrow of the bourgeoisie lays the foundation for the sway of the proletariat. [. . .]

[H]ere it becomes evident, that the bourgeoisie is unfit any longer to be the ruling class in society, and to impose its conditions of existence upon society as an over-riding law. It is unfit to rule because it is incompetent to assure an existence to its slave within his slavery, because it cannot help letting him sink into such a state, that it has to feed him, instead of being fed by him. Society can no longer live under this bourgeoisie, in other words, its existence is no longer compatible with society. [. . .]

What the bourgeoisie therefore produces, above all, are its own grave-diggers. Its fall and the victory of the proletariat are equally inevitable.

2.5 [Henry Mayhew], 'Letter II', *Morning Chronicle*, 23 October 1849; 'Letter VII', *Morning Chronicle*, 13 November 1849

Satirical, anti-establishment, irreverent, bohemian, Henry Mayhew (1812–87) was the greatest of the Victorian 'social explorers', the middle-class ethnographers of the condition of the people, who included Royal Commission Reporters from the 1830s through journalists such as James Greenwood and Andrew Mearns to Margaret Harkness, Eleanor Marx and Beatrice Webb in the 1890s. Co-founder of the satirical journal Punch *and commonly acknowledged as the founder of the technique of oral history, Mayhew produced richly reflexive empirical investigations of the poor and working classes while exhibiting a rage for the taxonomies, tables and charts that characterized early social science. In the prestigious* Morning Chronicle, *he published a series of letters between 19 October 1849 and 12 December 1850, which provide the closest look we have of the London urban poor and their trades 'according as they* will work, they can't *work, and they* won't *work'. Commenced as an effort in social reconciliation – after the revolutionary events of 1848 in Europe; the cholera epidemic of 1848, which provoked waves of social conscience; and the last flickers of Chartism in England – they evoked a seminal public correspondence on the causes and cures of poverty.*

Mayhew directed his interviews around wages and working conditions. In the end he blamed unregulated competition for poverty, demonstrated the astonishing productivity and resourcefulness of the poor, and recorded the taxonomic subversion of the status quo. Although Mayhew's work was expanded into a four-volume edition, London Labour and the London Poor *(1861), he produced little of note after his Letters, and died in obscurity. The extract here consists of two interviews: the first, with a Spitalfields silk weaver, describes the brutalization of living conditions in light of the beauty of their products; the second reveals the shame of prostitution among needlewomen.*

'Letter II'

'Yes, I was comfortable in '24. I kept a good little house, and I thought as my young ones growed up – why I thought as I should be comfortable in my old age, and 'stead of that, I've got no wages. I could live by my labour then, but now, why it's wretched in the extreme. Then, I'd a nice little garden and some nice tulips for my hobby when my work was done. There they lay, up in my old hat now. As for animal food, why it's a stranger to us. Once a week, may be, we gets a taste of it, but that's a hard struggle, and many a family don't have it once a month – a joint we never sees. Oh, it's too bad! There's seven of us here in this room – but it's a very large room to some weavers' – their's [*sic*] a'n't about half the size of this here. The weavers is in general five or six all living and working in the same room. There's four on us here in this bed. One head to foot – one at our back on the bolster; and me and my wife side by side. An' there's four on 'em over there. My brother Tom makes up the other one. There's a nice state in a Christian land! How many do you think lives in this house? Why 23 souls. Oh! a'n't' too bad! But the

Figure 2.2 After a daguerreotype by Beard, 'The Wallflower Girl', from Henry Mayhew, London Labour and the London Poor, vol. 1 (London: Griffin, Bohn and Co, 1861), 127

people is frightened to say how bad they're off, for fear of their masters and losing their work, so they keeps it to themselves – poor creatures. But oh, there's many worse then me. Many's gone to the docks, and some turned coster-mongers. But none goes a stealing nor sojering, that I hears on. They goes out to get a loaf of bread – oh, it's a shocking scene! I can't say what I thinks about the young 'uns. Why you loses your nat'ral affection for 'em. The people in general is ashamed to say how they thinks on their children. It's wretched in the extreme to see one's children, and not be able to do to 'em as a parent ought; and I'll say this here after all you've heerd me state – that the Government of my native land ought to inter-pose their powerful arm to put a stop to such things. Unless they do, civil society with us all is at an end. Everybody is becoming brutal – unnatural. Billy, just turn up that shell now, and let the gentleman see what beautiful fabrics we're in the habit of producing – and then he shall say whether we ought to be in the filthy state we are. Just show the light, Tilly! That's for ladies to wear and adorn them, and make them handsome.' (It was an exquisite piece of maroon coloured velvet, that, amidst all the squalor of the place, seemed marvellously beautiful, and it was a wonder to see it unsoiled amid all the filth that surrounded it). 'I say, just turn it up Billy, and show the gentleman the back. That's cotton, partly, you see, sir, just for the manufacturers to cheat the public, and get a cheap article, and have all the gold out of the poor working creatures they can, and don't care nothing about them. [. . .]

'Letter VII'

During the course of my investigation into the condition of those who are dependent upon the needle for their support, I had been so repeatedly assured that the young girls were mostly compelled to resort to prostitution to eke out their subsistence, that I was anxious to test the truth of the statement. I had seen much want, but I had no idea of the intensity of the privations suffered by the needlewomen of London until I came to inquire into this part of the subject. But the poor creatures shall speak for themselves. I should inform the reader, however, that I have made enquiries into the truth of the almost incredible statements here given, and I can in most of the particulars at least vouch for the truth of the statement. Indeed, in one instance – that of the last case here recorded – I travelled nearly twenty miles in order to obtain the character of the young woman. The first case is that of a good-looking girl. Her story is as follows: – [. . .]

'My father died when I was five years of age. My mother is a widow, upwards of 66 years of age, and seldom has a day's work. Generally once in the week she is employed pot-scouring – that is, cleaning publicans' pots. She is paid 4d. a dozen for that, and does about four dozen and a half, so that she gets about 1s. 6d. in the day by it. For the rest she is dependent upon me. I am 20 years of age the 25th of this month. We earn together, to keep the two of us, from 4s. 6d. to 5s. each week. Out of this we have to pay 1s. rent, and there remains 3s. 6d. to 4s. to find us both in food and clothing. It is of course impossible for us to live upon it, and the consequence is I am obliged to go a bad way. I have been three years working at slop-work.

'I was virtuous when I first went to work, and I remained so till this last twelvemonth. I struggled very hard to keep myself chaste, but I found I couldn't get food and clothing for myself and mother, so I took to live with a young man. He is turned 20. He is a tinman. He did promise to marry me, but his sister made mischief between me and him, so that parted us. I have not seen him now for about six months, and I can't say whether he will keep his promise or not. I am now pregnant by him, and expect to be confined in two months' time. He knows of my situation, and so does my mother. My mother believed me to be married to him. She knows otherwise now. I was very fond of him, and had known him for two years before he seduced me. He could make 14s. a week. He told me if I came to live with him he'd take care I shouldn't want, and both my mother and me had been very bad off before. He said, too, he'd make me his lawful wife, but I hardly cared so long as I could get food for myself and mother.

'Many young girls at the shop advised me to go wrong. They told me how comfortable they was off; they said they could get plenty to eat and drink, and good clothes. There isn't one young girl as can get her living by slop work. The masters all know this, but they wouldn't own to it of course. It stands to reason that no one can live and pay rent, and find clothes, upon 3s. a week, which is the most they make clear, even the best hands, at the moleskin and cord trowsers work. The shirt work is worse and worse still. There's poor people moved out of our house that was making ¾d. shirts. I am satisfied there is not one young girl that works at slop work that is virtuous, and there are some thousands in the trade. They may do very well if they have got mothers and fathers to find them a home and food, and to let them have what they earn for clothes. Then they may be virtuous, but not without. I've heard of numbers who have gone from slop work to the streets altogether for a living, and I shall be obliged to do the same thing myself unless something better turns up for me.

'If I was never allowed to speak no more, it was the little money I got by my labour that led me to go wrong. Could I have honestly earnt enough to have subsisted upon, to find me in proper food and clothing, such as is necessary, I should not have gone astray; no, never.

'As it was I fought against it as long as I could – that I did – to the last. I hope to be able to get a ticket for a midwife; a party has promised me as much, and, he says, if possible, he'll get me an order for a box of linen. My child will only increase my burdens, and if my young man won't support the child I must go on the streets altogether. I know how horrible all this is. It would have been much better for me to have subsisted upon a dry crust and water rather than be as I am now. But no one knows the temptations of us poor girls in want. Gentlefolks can never understand it. If I had been born a lady it wouldn't have been very hard to have acted like one. To be poor and to be honest, especially with young girls, is the hardest struggle of all. There isn't one in a thousand that can get the better of it. I am ready to say again, that it was want and nothing more that made me transgress. If I had been better paid I should have done better. Young as I am, my life is a curse to me. If the Almighty would please to take me before my child is born, I should die happy.'

2.6 Samuel Smiles, *Self-Help: With Illustrations of Conduct and Perseverance* (London: John Murray, 1859)

Samuel Smiles (1812–1904), Scottish didact and biographer, studied medicine at Edinburgh and became active in the campaign for parliamentary reform, serving in the 1840s as the first secretary of the Leeds Parliamentary Reform Association; he also campaigned against the Corn Laws. He became disillusioned with Chartism and began to stress the importance of individual reform, abandoning, by the 1850s, the idea of parliamentary reform. Self-Help *originated as a series of lectures given to the Leeds Mutual Improvement Society in 1845. Eventually published in 1859, it sold 20,000 copies within the first year; by 1905 it had sold over a quarter of a million. It was also widely translated.* Self-Help *elaborates Smiles's belief that social advance and national progress would be achieved through individuals developing their work ethic, character, thrift and duty, rather than via state support (see extract 3.3 for the way this influenced his views on gentlemanliness). The work combines his political radicalism with aspects of the dutiful morality of his early Calvinist education and the educational emphasis of the Unitarians. He developed his ideas in* Character *(1871),* Thrift *(1875),* Duty – with Illustrations of Courage, Duty and Endurance *(1880) and* Life and Labour, or Characteristics of Men of Industry, Culture and Genius *(1887). In 1898 his publisher, Murray, turned down his last manuscript,* Conduct; *the late nineteenth century was no longer so receptive to his ideas.*

'The worth of a State, in the long run, is the worth of the individuals composing it.' – *J. S. Mill*
'We put too much faith in systems, and look too little to men.' – *B. Disraeli*

'Heaven helps those who help themselves' is a well-tried maxim, embodying in a small compass the results of vast human experience. The spirit of self-help is the root of all genuine growth in the individual; and, exhibited in the lives of many, it constitutes the true source of national vigour and strength. Help from without is often enfeebling in its effects, but help from within invariably invigorates. Whatever is done *for* men or classes, to a certain extent takes away the stimulus and necessity of doing for themselves; and where men are subjected to over-guidance and over-government, the inevitable tendency is to render them comparatively helpless.

Even the best institutions can give a man no active help. Perhaps the most they can do is, to leave him free to develop himself and improve his individual condition. But in all times men have been prone to believe that their happiness and well-being were to be secured by means of institutions rather than by their own conduct. Hence the value of legislation as an agent of human advancement has usually been much over-estimated. To constitute the millionth part of a Legislature, by voting for one or two men once in three or five years, however conscientiously this duty may be performed, can exercise but little active influence upon any man's life and character. Moreover, it is every day becoming more clearly understood, that the function of Government is negative and restrictive, rather than positive and active; being resolvable principally into protection – protection of life, liberty, and property. Laws, wisely administered, will secure men in the enjoyment of the fruits of their labour, whether of mind or body, at a comparatively small personal sacrifice; but no laws, however stringent, can make the idle industrious, the thriftless provident, or the drunken sober. Such reforms can only be effected by means of individual action, economy, and self-denial; by better habits, rather than by greater rights. [. . .]

The spirit of self-help, as exhibited in the energetic action of individuals, has in all times been a marked feature in the English character, and furnishes the true measure of our power as a nation. Rising above the heads of the mass, there were always to be found a series of individuals distinguished beyond others, who commanded the public homage. But our progress has also been owing to multitudes of smaller and less known men. Though only the generals' names may be remembered in the history of any great campaign, it has been in a great measure through the individual valour and heroism of the privates that victories have been won. And life, too, is 'a soldier's battle' – men in the ranks having in all times been amongst the greatest of workers.

2.7 [Harriet Martineau], 'Female Industry', *Edinburgh Review* 109 (April 1859), 293–336.

Harriet Martineau (1802–76) came to prominence at the start of the 1830s, when her Illustrations of Political Economy *appeared to general acclaim, establishing her as an influential social and political commentator. She enjoyed a 40-year career, becoming widely regarded as a liberal and, at times, radical figure, in which she was able to articulate accessibly – through fiction and non-fiction writing alike – historical and philosophical issues, trends and controversies. The daughter of a Norwich manufacturer, Martineau was a firm believer in the progressive character of industrial capitalist civilization, and a particular proponent of the free market. But her faith in laissez-faire economics did not blind her to social prejudices and injustices, especially as regards the position of women. Informed by statistics garnered from the 1851 census, the extract below sees Martineau demanding that women's substantive and wide-ranging contribution to the 'public' world of work be at once recognized and further promoted. The piece registers her liberal advocacy of the 'natural laws' of the market alongside her feminist recognition that the politics and mores of patriarchal society worked to distort or prohibit the proper functioning of those laws. (On women's work and the lack thereof, see also extracts 3.2 and 7.6.)*

There was a time when continental visitors called England 'the hell of horses, the purgatory of servants, and the paradise of women', from the two former having everything to do, and the latter nothing. The lapse of centuries has materially altered this aspect of affairs. The railways have annihilated the hardest-worked class of horses; improvements in the arts of life have relieved our servants of a great amount of toil, while on the whole elevating their condition; whereas the women of the United Kingdom have been led forth from their paradise into a life of labour and care, more strongly resembling that of men than either the men or women of old times could have anticipated.

Wearied as some of us are with the incessant repetition of the dreary story of spirit-broken governesses and starving needlewomen, we rarely obtain a glimpse of the full breadth of the area of female labour in Great Britain; and it requires publication of the 'Results of the Census', or some such exhibition of hard facts, to make us understand and feel that the conditions of female life have sustained as much alteration as the fortunes of other classes by the progress of civilisation. Sooner or later it must become known, in a more practical way than by the figures of the census returns, that a very large proportion of the women of England earn their own bread; and there is no saying how much good may be done, and how much misery may be saved, by a timely recognition of this simple truth. [. . .]

In those days, therefore, the supposition was true which has now become false, and ought to be practically admitted to be false; – that every woman is supported (as the law supposes her to be represented) by her father, her brother, or her husband. In those days, unmarried women were rare; and convents were the refuge of celibacy. It was not only in royal families that children were betrothed in their cradles. In all ranks, parents made matches for their children at any age that suited the family convenience; and the hubbub that ensued, when a daughter refused to marry at her parents' bidding, shows what a disaster it was considered to have a woman in the house who would neither marry nor become a nun. There was in such a society, no call for female industry, except within the establishment; – whether it were the mansion, the farm, the merchant's dwelling, or the cottage. From that time (the uprising of a middle class) to this, the need and the supply of female industry have gone on increasing, and latterly at an unparalleled rate, while our ideas, our language, and our arrangements have not altered in any corresponding degree. We go on talking as if it were still true that every woman is, or ought to be, supported by father, brother, or husband: we are only beginning to think of the claim of all workers; – that their work should be paid for by its quality, and its place in the market, irrespective of the status of the worker: – we are only beginning to see that the time must come when such artificial depreciation must cease, under the great natural laws of society. We are (probably to a man) unaware of the amount of the business of life in England done by women; and if we do not attend to the fact in time, the knowledge will be forced upon us in some disadvantageous or disagreeable way. A social organisation framed for a community of which half stayed at home, while the other half went out to work, cannot answer the purposes of a society, of which a quarter remains at home while three-quarters go out to work. This seems to be clear enough. It does not follow that changes in the law are needed; or that anybody is called upon to revolutionise his thoughts or his proceedings. The natural laws of society will do whatever has to be done, when once recognised and allowed to act. They will settle all considerable social points, – and all the controversies of the labour-market, and the strifes about consideration and honour. All that we contend for at this moment is, that the case should be examined and admitted. Under a system like ours, in which the middle class of society constitutes the main strength of the whole organisation, women have become industrial in the sense of being supporters of themselves and of a large proportion of households: and their industrial production is rapidly on the increase. The census of 1851 affords some idea of how the matter stands. 'While the female population has increased' (between 1841 and 1851) in the ratio of 7 to 8, the number of 'women returned as engaged in independent industry has increased in the far greater ratio of 3 to 4.' (*Industrial and Social Position of Women*, p. 219.) [. . .]

So far from our countrywomen being all maintained, as a matter of course, by us 'the breadwinners,' three millions out of six of adult Englishwomen work for subsistence; and two out of three in independence. With this new condition of affairs, new duties and new views must be accepted. Old obstructions must be removed; and the aim must be set before us, as a nation as well as in private life, to provide for the free development and full use of the powers of every member of the community. In other words, we must improve and extend education to the utmost; and then open a fair field to the powers and energies we have educed. This will secure our welfare, nationally and in our homes, to which few elements can contribute more vitally and more richly than the independent industry of our countrywomen.

2.8 Walter Bagehot, *The English Constitution* (London: Chapman and Hall, 1867)

Walter Bagehot (1828–77) is often considered the anthropologist of British politics, observing not what politics says it is doing but what it actually does in practice, the daily exercise of power. An experienced banker by family trade, he was politically influential as editor of the Economist *from 1861 to 1877. Like Mill, he was a Liberal who welcomed the transfer of political power to the middle classes after 1832; his* English Constitution *(1867) was published the same year as Marx's* Das Kapital, *and while they differed in perspective, their descriptions of bourgeois power often converged.*

Bagehot discovered the Cabinet as 'the efficient secret' of the constitution. Government are merely the managers of the state, and they manage in their own interests; but tradition and habit are as significant as self-interest. Bagehot called the Lords and Monarch the 'dignified' parts of the Constitution, while the Commons and Cabinet were the 'efficient' parts; the first were for impressing, the other for ruling, the people. In the doctrine of Cabinet responsibility, the Cabinet efficiently fuses the executive and legislative powers through a combination of party loyalty, collective responsibility and secrecy. Bagehot described the period of parliamentary government from 1832 to 1867, before the extension of the suffrage in 1867 and the creation of party machines, and before the emergence of an independent Civil Service administering a vast welfare state. This extract describes the function of the House of Lords, illustrating Bagehot's attraction to an even then disempowered aristocracy, but also the constraints on its potential to regulate the House of Commons.

The fancy of the mass of men is incredibly weak; it can see nothing without a visible symbol, and there is much that it can scarcely make out with a symbol. Nobility is the symbol of mind. It has the marks from which the mass of men always used to infer mind, and often still infer it. A common clever man who goes into a country place will get no reverence; but the 'old squire' will get reverence. Even after he is insolvent, when everyone knows that his ruin is but a question of time, he will get five times as much respect from the common peasantry as the newly rich man who sits beside him. The common peasantry will listen to his nonsense more submissively than to the new man's sense. An old lord will get infinite respect. His very existence is so far useful that it awakens the sensation of obedience to a *sort* of mind in the coarse, dull, contracted multitude, who could neither appreciate nor perceive any other.

The order of nobility is of great use, too, not only in what it creates, but in what it prevents. It prevents the rule of wealth – the religion of gold. [. . .]

But it is not true that the reverence for rank – at least, for hereditary rank – is as base as the reverence for money. As the world has gone, manner has been half-hereditary in certain castes, and manner is one of the fine arts. It is the *style* of society; it is in the daily-spoken intercourse of human-beings what the art of literary expression is in their occasional written intercourse. In reverencing wealth we reverence not a man, but an appendix to a man; in reverencing inherited nobility, we reverence the probable possession of a great faculty – the faculty of bringing out what is in one. The unconscious grace of life *may* be in the middle-classes; finely mannered persons are born everywhere; but it *ought* to be in the aristocracy: and a man must be born with a hitch in his nerves if he has not some of it. It is a physiological possession of the race, though it is sometimes wanting in the individual. [. . .]

This is the mode in which the House of Lords came to be what it now is, a chamber with (in most cases) a veto of delay, with (in most cases) a power of revision, but with no other rights or powers. The question we have to answer is, 'the House of Lords being such, what is the use of the Lords?'

The common notion evidently fails, that it is a bulwark again immanent revolution. As the Duke's letter in every line evinces, the wisest members, the guiding members of the House, know that the House must yield to the people if the people is determined. The two cases – that of the Reform Act and the corn laws – were decisive cases. The great majority of the Lords thought the Reform revolution, Free-trade confiscation, and the two together ruin. If they could ever have been trusted to resist the people, they would have resisted it. But in truth it is idle to expect a second chamber – a chamber of nobles – ever to resist a popular chamber; a nation's chamber, when the chamber is vehement and the nation vehement too. There is no strength in it for that purpose. [. . .]

The very nature, too, as has been seen of the Lords in the English Constitution, shows that it cannot stop revolution. The constitution contains an exceptional provision to prevent it stopping it. The executive, the appointee of the popular chamber and the nation, can make new peers, and so create a majority in the peers; it can say to the Lords, 'Use the powers of your House as we like, or you shall not use them at all. We will find others to use them; your virtue shall go out of you if it is not used as we like, and stopped when we please.' An assembly under such a threat cannot arrest, and could not be intended to arrest, a determined and insisting executive.

In fact, the House of Lords, as a House, is not a bulwark that will keep out revolution, but an index that revolution is unlikely. Resting as it does upon old deference, and inveterate homage, it shows that the spasm of new forces, the outbreak of new agencies, which we call revolution, is for the first time simply impossible. So long as many old leaves linger on the November trees, you know that there has been little frost and no wind; just so while the House of Lords retains much power, you may know that no desperate in the country, no wild agency likely to cause a great demolition. [. . .]

The best test of a machine is the work it turns out. Let anyone who knows what legal documents ought to be, read first a will he has just been making and then an Act of Parliament; he will certainly say, 'I would have dismissed my attorney if he had done my business as the legislature has done the nation's business.' While the House of Commons is what it is, a good revising, regulating and retarding House would be a benefit to a great magnitude. [. . .]

But is the House of Lords such a chamber? Does it do this work? [. . .]

The House of Lords, being an hereditary chamber, cannot be of more than common ability. It may contain – it almost always has contained, it almost always will contain – extraordinary men. But its average born law-makers cannot be extraordinary. Being a set of eldest sons picked out by chance and history, it cannot be very wise. It would be a standing miracle if such a chamber possessed a knowledge of its age superior to the other men of the age; if it descried what they did not discern, and saw truly that which they saw, indeed, but saw untruly.

2.9 Matthew Arnold, *Culture and Anarchy: An Essay in Political and Social Criticism* (London: Smith, Elder and Co., 1869)

Matthew Arnold (1822–88) was a noted poet and cultural critic, who, between 1851 and 1886, also worked as a school inspector. He gave up writing poetry in favour of cultural criticism because he felt the latter would have greater social impact; and Culture and Anarchy *propounds his belief in the capacity of culture to act 'as the great help out of our present difficulties'. The difficulties to which he was referring concerned the tendency of Victorian society (and particularly middle-class 'Philistines') to promote a form of life lacking the capacity to develop those inward, spiritual qualities and virtues Arnold believed should distinguish human existence. The 'anarchy' Arnold associated with industrial capitalist modernity could mean public disorder, but more generally it signalled an unimaginative and debilitating emphasis upon material progress and individual liberty. 'Freedom, like Industry,' Arnold would note in*

Friendship's Garland, *'is a very good horse to ride; – but to ride somewhere.'*[7] *Culture was to provide the necessary corrective to modernity's lack of an adequate* telos, *and Arnold maintained it was the crucial role of the 'disinterested' critic to identify those cultural forms capable of promoting social cohesion, moral sentiment and spiritual improvement (see extract 8.7 for Arnold on the function of criticism).*

If culture, then, is a study of perfection, and of harmonious perfection, general perfection, and perfection which consists in becoming something rather than having something, in an inward condition of the mind and spirit, not in an outward set of circumstances, – it is clear that culture, instead of being the friv-olous and useless thing which Mr Bright, and Mr Frederic Harrison, and many other Liberals are apt to call it, has a very important function to fulfil for mankind.[8] And this function is particularly important in our modern world, of which the whole civilisation is, to a much greater degree than the civilisation of Greece and Rome, mechanical and external, and tends constantly to become more so. But above all in our own country has culture a weighty part to perform, because here that mechanical character, which civilisation tends to take every-where, is shown in the most eminent degree. Indeed, nearly all the characters of perfection, as culture teaches us to fix them, meet in this country with some powerful tendency which thwarts them and sets them at defiance. The idea of perfection as an *inward* condition of the mind and spirit is at variance with the mechanical and material civilisation in esteem with us, and nowhere, as I have said, so much in esteem with as with us. The idea of perfection as a *general* expansion of the human family is at variance with our strong individualism, our hatred of all limits to the unrestrained swing of the individual's personality, our maxim of 'every man for himself'. Above all, the idea of perfection as a *harmonious* expansion of human nature is at variance with our want of flexibility, with our inaptitude for seeing more than one side of a thing, with our intense ener-getic absorption in the particular pursuit we happen to be following. So culture has a rough task to achieve in this country. Its preachers have, and are likely long to have, a hard time of it, and they will much oftener be regarded, for a great while to come, as elegant or spurious Jeremiahs than as friends and bene-factors. That, however, will not prevent their doing in the end good service if they persevere. [. . .]

Plenty of people will try to indoctrinate the masses with the set of ideas and judgements constituting the creed of their own profession or party. Our religious and political organisations give an example of this way of working on the masses. I condemn neither way; but culture works differently. It does not try to

---

7 Mathew Arnold, *Friendship's Garland: Being the Conversations, Letters, and Opinions of the Late Arminius, Baron von Thunder-Ten-Tronckh* (1871; London: Smith, Elder and Co., 1897), 147.

8 John Bright (1811–89), radical Liberal MP who was a leading proponent of parliamentary reform. Frederic Harrison (1831–1923), positivist and academic. Harrison campaigned on a number of polit-ical issues, publishing several articles in favour of electoral reform, an issue on which he clashed with Arnold.

teach down to the level of inferior classes; it does not try to win them for this or that sect of its own, with ready-made judgements and watchwords. It seeks to do away with classes; to make the best that has been thought and known in the world current everywhere; to make all men live in an atmosphere of sweetness and light, where they may use ideas, as it uses them itself, freely, – to be nourished, and not bound by them.

This is the *social idea*; and the men of culture are the true apostles of equality. The great men of culture are those who have had a passion for diffusing, for making prevail, for carrying from one end of society to the other, the best knowledge, the best ideas of their time; who have laboured to divest knowledge of all that was harsh, uncouth, difficult, abstract, professional, exclusive; to humanise it, to make it efficient outside the clique of the cultivated and the learned, yet still remaining the *best* knowledge and thought of the time, and a true source, therefore, of sweetness and light. [. . .]

For a long time, as I have said, the strong feudal habits of subordination and deference continued to tell upon the working class. The modern spirit has now almost entirely dissolved those habits, and the anarchical tendency of our worship of freedom in and for itself, of our superstitious faith, as I say, in machinery, is becoming very manifest. More and more, because of this our blind faith in machinery, because of our want of light to enable us to look beyond machinery to the end for which machinery is valuable, this and that man, and this and that body of men, all over the country, are beginning to assert and put in practice an Englishman's right to do what he likes; his right to march where he likes, meet where he likes, enter where he likes, hoot as he likes, threaten as he likes, smash as he likes.

2.10 William Morris, 'The Society of the Future' (1887), from *William Morris: Artist, Writer, Socialist*, ed. May Morris, vol. 2 (Oxford: Blackwell, 1936)

On 13 November 1887, on the eve of military repression of the rising called Bloody Sunday, William Morris (1843–96) delivered a lecture to the Hammersmith Branch of the Socialist League. 'The Society of the Future' described his ideal future state. Personally one of the wealthiest men in England, Morris was nonetheless committed to a revolution that would bring about the redistribution of wealth. He used his admiration of medievalism and his travels in Iceland to critique modern inequality and ugliness; wrote epic literature with distinctly cosmopolitan tolerance that recalled simpler, heroic times; founded the Arts and Crafts movement not so much for its art objects as for 'the pleasurable exertion of our faculties'; and ultimately, although he retained a distaste for party politics, became a revolutionary in the Social Democratic Federation and Socialist League, editing its journal The Commonweal. *Morris upheld the development of individual capacities without believing in liberal individualism. For him the social unit that enabled or disabled individual growth was always society or the collec-*

tive. In this excerpt, we see his egalitarianism, cosmopolitanism, environmentalism and anti-asceticism.

It is a society which does not know the meaning of rich and poor, or the rights of property, or law or legality, or nationality: a society which has no conscious-ness of being governed; in which equality of condition is a matter of course, and in which no man is rewarded for having served the community by having the power given him to injure it.

It is a society conscious of a wish to keep life simple, to forgo some of the power over nature won by past ages in order to be more human and less mechanical, and willing to sacrifice something to this end. It would be divided into small communities varying much within the limits allowed by due social ethics, but without rivalry between each other, looking with abhorrence at the idea of a holy race.

Being determined to be free, and therefore contented with a life not only simpler but even rougher than the life of slave-owners, division of labour would be habitually limited: men (and women too, of course) would do their work and take their pleasure in their own persons, and not vicariously: the social bond would be habitually and instinctively felt, so that there would be no need to be always asserting it by set forms: the family of blood relationship would melt into that of the community and of humanity. The pleasures of such a society would be founded on the free exercise of the senses and passions of a healthy human animal, so far as this did not injure the other individuals of the community and so offend against a social unity: no one would be ashamed of humanity or ask for anything better than its due development.

But from this healthy freedom would spring up the pleasures of intellectual development, which the men of civilisation so foolishly try to separate from sensuous life, and to glorify at its expense. Men would follow knowledge and the creation of beauty for their own sake, and not for the enslavement of their fellows, and they would be rewarded by finding their most necessary work grow interest-ing and beautiful under their hands without their being conscious of it. [. . .]

And amidst this pleasing labour, and the rest that went with it, would disap-pear from the earth's face all the traces of the past slavery. Being no longer driven to death by anxiety and fear, we should have time to avoid disgracing the earth with filth and squalor, and accidental ugliness would disappear along with that which was the mere birth of fantastic perversity.

2.11 General William Booth, *In Darkest England and the Way Out* (London: International Headquarters of the Salvation Army, 1890)

If there was no more powerful register of Victorian Britain's economic and industrial power than the growth of its towns and cities, it is perhaps also true that nothing gener-

ated more unrest and unease than the extremities of class division and poverty that accompanied industrialization and urbanization. Owing a debt to Henry Mayhew's earlier social exploration, William Booth (1829–1912), a Methodist preacher and founder of the Salvation Army, was concerned to expose the social ills and spiritual destitution endured by the inhabitants of those built-up but unknown spaces he characterized as 'a great lost land' (see extract 4.9 for another description of Booth's work). In this bestselling work, Booth attacked the complacent faith in Britain's civilized progress, arguing that market fluctuations and dreadful urban conditions worked against cherished principles of self-help and demanded, instead, a far more active degree of state and church intervention. Without such support, Booth was one of many commentators who feared widespread and increasing social degeneration. As the extract below shows, such fears drew upon Social Darwinism, tapping into anxieties about race as well as class.

This summer the attention of the civilised world has been arrested by the story which Mr Stanley has told of 'Darkest Africa' and his journeyings across the heart of the Lost Continent.[9] In all that spirited narrative of heroic endeavour, nothing has so much impressed the imagination, as his description of the immense forest, which offered an almost impenetrable barrier to his advance. [. . .] The mind of man with difficulty endeavours to realise this immensity of wooded wilderness, covering a territory half as large again as the whole of France, where the rays of sun never penetrate, where in the dark, dank air, filled with the steam of the heated morass, human beings dwarfed into pygmies and brutalised into cannibals lurk and live and die. [. . .]

It is a terrible picture, and one that has engraved itself deep on the heart of civilisation. But while brooding over the awful presentation of life as it exists in the vast African forest, it seemed to me only too vivid a picture of many parts of our own land. As there is a darkest Africa is there not also a darkest England? Civilisation, which can breed its own barbarians, does it not also breed its own pygmies? May we not find a parallel at our own doors, and discover within a stone's throw of our cathedrals and palaces similar horrors to those which Stanley has found existing in the great Equatorial forest? [. . .]

A population sodden with drink, steeped in vice, eaten up with every social and physical malady, these are the denizens of Darkest England amidst whom my life has been spent, and to whose rescue I would now summon all that is best in the manhood and womanhood of our land. [. . .]

Darkest England may be described as consisting broadly of three circles, one within the other. The outer and widest circle is inhabited by the starving and the homeless, but honest Poor. The second by those who live by Vice; and the third and innermost region at the centre is peopled by those who exist by Crime. The

9 Henry Morton Stanley (1841–1904) was an explorer renowned for 'finding' David Livingstone in 1871. In 1890 he published *In Darkest Africa*, the story of the controversial Emin Pasha Relief Expedition.

whole of the three circles is sodden with Drink. Darkest England has many more public-houses than the Forest of the Aruwimi has rivers, of which Mr Stanley sometimes had to cross three in half-an-hour.

The borders of this great lost land are not sharply defined. They are continually expanding or contracting. Whenever there is a period of depression in trade, they stretch; when prosperity returns, they contract. So far as individuals are concerned, there are none among the hundreds of thousands who live upon the outskirts of the dark forest who can truly say that they or their children are secure from being hopelessly entangled in its labyrinth. The death of the bread-winner, a long illness, a failure in the City, or any one of a thousand other causes which might be named, will bring within the first circle those who at present imagine themselves free from all danger of actual want. [. . .]

I am labouring under no delusions as to the possibility of inaugurating the Millennium by any social specific. In the struggle of life the weakest will go to the wall, and there are so many weak. The fittest in tooth and claw, will survive. All that we can do is to soften the lot of the unfit and make their suffering less horrible than it is at present. No amount of assistance will give a jelly-fish a back-bone. No outside propping will make some men stand erect. All material help from without is useful only in so far as it develops moral strength within. And some men seem to have lost even the faculty of self-help. There is an immense lack of common sense and of vital energy on the part of the multitudes. [. . .]

How can we marvel if, after leaving generation after generation to grow up uneducated and underfed, there should be developed a heredity of incapacity, and that thousands of dull-witted people should be born into the world, disinherited before their birth of their share in the average intelligence of mankind? [. . .]

All this is true, and it is one of the things that makes the problem almost insoluble. And insoluble it is, I am absolutely convinced, unless it is possible to bring new moral life into the soul of these people. This should be the first object of every social reformer, whose work will only last if it is built on the solid foundation of a new birth, to cry 'You must be born again.'

To get a man soundly saved it is not enough to put on him a pair of new breeches, to give him regular work, or even to give him a University education. These things are all outside a man, and if the inside remains unchanged you have wasted your labour. You must in some way or other graft upon the man's nature a new nature, which has in it the element of the Divine. All that I propose in this book is governed by that principle.

3
Gender and Sexuality

Introduction

When the young Princess Victoria ascended the throne in 1837, women were defined legally, by the doctrine of coverture, as objects rather than subjects with rights: a husband owned his wife's property and was responsible for her actions. The decades that followed saw unprecedented change in the political, social and economic position of women, and attitudes towards femininity and masculinity underwent transformation in dialogue with developments in medical and scientific thought.

Was gender an expression of nature or culture? This, in various guises, was arguably the abiding – and unresolved – question of the nineteenth century and can be seen at work in several of the extracts. The Woman Question really was a question, a debate rather than a series of pronouncements, conducted by the middle class primarily in print, and richly explored in fiction. It was both a cause and a symptom of the rethinking of the nature of the sexes.

With the demise of eighteenth-century coffee-house culture, middle-class masculine life had become more centred in the family home and improvements in standards of sanitation and medical knowledge, combined with a lack of knowledge about contraception, were leading to larger families. The 1830s saw the emergence of a domestic ideal of feminine virtue, exemplified in the conduct books of Sarah Stickney Ellis (see extract 3.1), which gave rise to the powerful ideology of separate spheres. The sanctity of marriage and the home, and the role of women as moral guardians, maintaining the sanctity of the hearth amid the anxious turmoil of modern public life, was a defining feature of the period. In Charles Dickens's *Bleak House* (1852–3), the morally virtuous and self-effacing Esther Summerson, with her jangling house keys, is an embodiment of mid-Victorian domestic ideology and a striking contrast with another of the novel's women, Mrs Jellyby, who neglects her family in favour of philanthropy on behalf of African missionaries. But philanthropy was another expression of the emphasis on duty which characterized nineteenth-century conceptions of the role of women.

Victorian feminism had pragmatic beginnings. The census of 1851 had revealed 400,000 surplus women; 42 per cent of women between the ages of 20 and 40 were unmarried. In light of this, how attainable was the domestic ideal expressed in the title of Coventry Patmore's poem about marriage, *The Angel in the House*? Not all middle-class women could be guaranteed the possibility of such a role. The early women's movement focused on improving the employment prospects of single women, running classes to train them as bookkeepers, shop assistants and clerks. Education was also seen to have a positive effect on the social good, as the extracts from John Ruskin and Florence Nightingale illustrate in their different ways. The 1850s saw the beginning of the establishment of girls' secondary schools in Britain; other measures, notably the 1870 Elementary Education Act (see extract 1.9) and the introduction of compulsory attendance at elementary schools in 1880 opened up opportunities for women as elementary schoolteachers and members of the school boards. They were also beginning to enter traditionally male professions such as medicine. Elizabeth Blackwell was placed on the first British Medical Register in 1858, Elizabeth Garrett Anderson in 1866. With Sophia Jex Blake, Thomas Huxley and others they established the London School of Medicine for Women in 1874.

Middle-class women also began to be admitted into higher education. Queen's and Bedford Colleges at London University accepted women at the end of the 1840s and Oxford and Cambridge established women's colleges in the 1860s and 1870s but did not grant women fully accredited degrees until 1922 and 1947 respectively. In the 1870s the Girls' Public Day School Trust sought with Cheltenham Ladies College and other new institutions to improve the provision of education for teenage girls. There was a growing insistence in the later part of the century that middle-class women were physically as well as morally fit, and not the frail or mentally vulnerable subjects the medical men (and some of the novelists) sometimes seemed to suggest (see extract 7.10).

The legal status of women was gradually improved though the reform of marital law. Prior to the creation of a new Court of Divorce and Matrimonial Causes by the Divorce and Matrimonial Causes Act of 1857 divorce had only been possible for the very wealthy (see extract 1.7). Nonetheless, it remained only within reach of the moderately wealthy and the grounds for divorce were not made the same until 1923. It was also not until 1891 that a High Court ruling denied the husband the right to imprison his wife in pursuit of his conjugal rights.

The 1870 Married Women's Property Act allowed a woman to retain earnings or property acquired after her marriage but all that she owned on marriage passed into her husband's ownership. The Married Women's Property Act of 1882 marked a more significant change in the legal status of women, giving them rights to the property they acquired before and during marriage. A woman now no longer surrendered her legal existence on marriage and prospects for the success of the campaign for women's suffrage were thus improved.

In 1867 John Stuart Mill had proposed an amendment to the Representation of the People bill (which became the 1867 Second Reform Act), suggesting that the clause containing the term 'man' be amended to read 'person'. The bill was defeated by 196 votes to 73. In the following decade women's suffrage societies, which were forming in most of the major cities of Britain, submitted petitions to Parliament demanding female suffrage. In 1897, the societies united to form the National Union of Women's Suffrage Societies (NUWSS), but it was not until 1918 that the Representation of the People Act finally gave the vote to women of Great Britain aged 30 and over who were householders, wives of householders, university graduates or occupiers of property with an annual rent of £5.

Opposition to the idea of women's social and political equality came from men and women who argued for the complementary nature of the sexes; as the extracts demonstrate, it came especially from science and medicine. The work of men of science, notably Herbert Spencer, Charles Darwin, Henry Maudsley and George Romanes, describing secondary sexual characteristics – differences which had developed through sexual and natural selection but which were not directly connected to reproduction – lent credence to the idea that men were more capable of abstract thought, and naturally aggressive, while women were intuitive, nurturing and non-competitive. The moral function of women was given an increasingly biological basis and a one-sex model of humanity, which held that the sexes were on a continuum, and that woman was merely an inferior version of man, was gradually replaced by a two-sex model, which held that the sexes were fundamentally different.

Female sexuality came increasingly under the spotlight in these years of social transformation. The conservative social and political essayist W. R. Greg, writing in the *Westminster Review* in 1850, argued for the passivity of women's sexuality, a view which received medical support from the surgeon William Acton who argued in the *Functions and Disorders of the Reproductive Organs* (1857) that women seldom desired sexual pleasure. By contrast George Drysdale, free-thinker and advocate of contraception, equated male and female sexuality and argued in *Elements of Social Science* (1857) that it was repression rather than indulgence that led to sexual problems. Attempts to police sexuality increased during the century and can be seen in the Contagious Diseases Acts of 1864, 1866 and 1869. These mandated the compulsory inspection of women suspected of being prostitutes and their detention in lock hospitals, and appeared to give state backing to the sexual double standard; they were repealed in 1886 as a result of organized resistance under the leadership of Josephine Butler. The close of the century saw the development of sexology, a term coined by the Berlin dermatologist Iwan Bloch in 1906 as the German *Sexualwissenschaft*. Bringing both male and female sexuality under medical scrutiny it was potentially liberating (as extract 3.11 from *Sexual Inversion* shows), arguing for the tolerance rather than penalization of unconventional or homosexual desires.

The final decade saw the entry onto the scene of the New Woman. In her most radical form, threatening to rewrite sex roles and overthrow the institution of marriage, the New Woman was to a large extent a media cipher; even one of the most far-seeing of the New Woman writers, Mona Caird, included here, advocated the reform rather than the abolition of marriage. The debates of the last decade were complex, with some women advocating a break from the past but others seeking continuity and a reworking of traditional values and roles. A new moral, gendered, citizenship of duty rather than entitlement, informed by emergent eugenic discourse, developed in a context of urban poverty and degeneration, and the role of women was reshaped as one with the potential to regenerate a flailing imperial race, working outwards from the home and turned more actively to the social good.

3.1 Mrs [Sarah Stickney] Ellis, *The Women of England, Their Social Duties, and Domestic Habits* (London: Fisher, Son & Co., 1839)

Sarah Stickney Ellis (1812–72) was the second wife of a missionary, William Ellis, with whom she had four children. Brought up as a Quaker, she joined the Congregational Church and became an active temperance campaigner. The Women of England, first published in 1839, and dedicated by permission to Queen Victoria, was a popular conduct manual which set out the mid-Victorian ideal of femininity. Going through 13 editions in its first year, and widely reprinted in the United States, it made a considerable contribution to the early years of the Woman Question. Its essentialist appeal was underpinned, as the title suggests, by a sense of women's national duty. Ellis advocated a life of self-sacrifice and service towards men but she also argued for a notable degree of autonomy for women in their own sphere, emphasizing their moral authority. Her intended readers were middle-class women, those 'who are restricted to the services of from one to four domestics, – who on the one hand, enjoy the advantages of a liberal education, and, on the other, have no pretension to family rank'. Ellis stressed the responsibility of women to recreate English society through their influence in the domestic sphere, emphasizing the importance of practical intelligence and women's role in maintaining the home as a place of moral virtue; education was of value for social and moral, rather than intellectual, reasons. In 1844 Ellis co-founded a non-denominational school for girls, Rawdon House School, which, unusually, included practical instruction in cookery and household management, putting her theories into practice. She went on to write more specific manuals for women at different stages of their lives: The Daughters of England *(1842),* The Mothers of England *(1843) and* The Wives of England *(1843). (See extract 8.3 for Ellis's views on women's reading habits.)*

When the cultivation of the mental faculties had so far advanced as to take precedence of the moral, by leaving no time for domestic usefulness, and the practice of personal exertion in the way of promoting general happiness, the character of the women of England assumed a different aspect, which is now beginning to tell upon society in the sickly sensibilities, the feeble frames, and the useless habits of the rising generation. [. . .] This state of listless indifference, my sisters, must not be. You have deep responsibilities, you have urgent claims;

a nation's moral wealth is in your keeping. Let us inquire then in what way it may be best preserved. Let us consider what you are, and have been, and by what peculiarities of feeling and habit you have been able to throw so much additional weight into the scale of your country's worth. [. . .]

Time was when the women of England were accustomed, almost from their childhood, to the constant employment of their hands. It might be sometimes in elaborate works of fancy, now ridiculed for their want of taste, and still more frequently in household avocations, now fallen into disuse from their incompatibility with modern refinement. [. . .]

In short, the customs of English society have so constituted women the guardians of the comfort of their homes, that, like the Vestals of old, they cannot allow the lamp they cherish to be extinguished, or to fail for want of oil, without an equal share of degradation attaching to their names.

In other countries, where the domestic lamp is voluntarily put out, in order to allow the women to resort to the opera, or the public festival, they are not only careless about their home-comforts, but necessarily ignorant of the high degree of excellence to which they might be raised. In England there is a kind of science of good household management, which, if it consisted merely in keeping the house respectable in its physical character, might be left to the effectual working out of hired hands; but, happily for the women of England, there is a philosophy in this science, by which all their highest and best feelings are called into exercise. [. . .]

From Chapter 2: Influence of the Women of England

How often has man returned to his home with a mind confused by the many voices, which in the mart, the exchange, or the public assembly, have addressed themselves to his inborn selfishness, or his worldly pride; and while his integrity was shaken, and his resolution gave way beneath the pressure of apparent necessity, or the insidious pretences of expediency, he has stood corrected before the clear eye of woman, as it looked directly to the naked truth, and detected the lurking evil of the specious act he was about to commit. Nay, so potent may have become this secret influence, that he may have borne it about with him like a kind of second conscience, for mental reference, and spiritual counsel, in moments of trial; and when the snares of the world were around him, and temptations from within and without have bribed over the witness in his own bosom, he has thought of the humble monitress who sat alone, guarding the fireside comforts of his distant home; and the remembrance of her character, clothed in moral beauty, has scattered the clouds before his mental vision, and sent him back to that beloved home, a wiser and a better man.

[. . .] It is a fact well worthy of our most serious attention, and one which bears immediately upon the subject under consideration, that the present state of our national affairs is such as to indicate that the influence of woman in counteracting the growing evils of society is about to be more needed than ever.

From Chapter 8: Domestic Habits – Consideration and Kindness

[. . .] In her intercourse with man, it is impossible but that woman should feel her own inferiority; and it is right that it should be so. Yet, feeling this, it is also impossible but that the weight of social and moral duties she is called upon to perform, must, to an unsanctified spirit, at times appear oppressive. She has innumerable sources of disquietude, too, in which no man can partake; and from the very weakness and susceptibility of her own nature, she has need of sympathies which it would be impossible for him to render. She does not meet him upon equal terms. Her part is to make sacrifices, in order that his enjoyment may be enhanced. She does this with a willing spirit; but, from error of judgment, or from want of consideration, she does it so often without producing any adequate result, and so often without grateful acknowledgment, that her spirit sometimes sinks within her, and she shrinks back from the cares and anxieties of every day, with a feeling that the burden of life is too heavy to be borne.

Nor is man to be blamed for this. He knows not half the foolish fears that agitate her breast. He could not be made to know, still less to understand, the intensity of her capability of suffering, from slight, and what to him would appear inadequate causes. But women *do* know what their sex is formed to suffer; and for this very reason, there is sometimes a bond existing between sisters, the most endearing, the most pure and disinterested, of any description of affection which this world affords.

3.2 Florence Nightingale, 'Cassandra', in Ray Strachey, *The Cause: A Short History of the Women's Movement in Britain* (1852; London, G. Bell and Sons Ltd., 1928)

Florence Nightingale (1820–1910), reformer of the Army Medical Services and of the organization of nursing, wrote the fragment 'Cassandra' in 1852. It was conceived initially as a novel and then revised to form the concluding essay of the second volume (subheaded 'Practical Deductions') of her three-volume Suggestions for Thought to Searchers after Religious Truth. *This she had written in a state of despair in response to opposition from her family to her desire for active public work. In 1853 she took up a post as superintendent of the Institution for the Care of Sick Gentlewomen in Distressed Circumstances, known also as the Harley Street Nursing Home, where the changes she introduced were greatly appreciated by the patients. The following year she left for the Crimea. She returned in 1856, by now internationally renowned, and revised 'Suggestions' (which was never made publicly available); 'Cassandra' was first published in Ray Strachey's* The Cause: A Short History of the Women's Movement in Great Britain *(1928). In this emphatic denouncement of the constraints of the lives of middle-class women, her only piece on the Woman Question, Nightingale noted the suffering, including physical suffering, that women underwent from a lack of worth-*

while occupation. Virginia Woolf referred to it in A Room of One's Own *(1929) as 'shrieking aloud in agony'. Nightingale asked for economic reform before the franchise; she advocated the right of women to property and to undertake worthwhile and paid work but she did not campaign on behalf of their right to become physicians. While she did not campaign actively for the suffrage she joined the National Society for Women's Suffrage and opposed the Contagious Diseases Acts.*

Passion, intellect, moral activity – these three have never been satisfied in a woman. In this cold and oppressive conventional atmosphere, they cannot be satisfied. To say more on this subject would be to enter into the whole history of society, of the present state of civilisation.

Look at that lizard – 'It is not hot,' he says, 'I like it. The atmosphere which enervates you is life to me.' The state of society which some complain of makes others happy. Why should these complain to those? *They* do not suffer. *They* would not understand it, any more than that lizard would comprehend the sufferings of a Shetland sheep. [. . .]

Poetry and imagination begin life. A child will fall on its knees on the gravel walk at the sight of a pink hawthorn in full flower, when it is by itself, to praise God for it.

Then comes intellect. It wishes to satisfy the wants which intellect creates for it. But there is a physical, not moral, impossibility of supplying the wants of the intellect in the state of civilisation at which we have arrived. The stimulus, the training, the time, are all three wanting to us; or, in other words, the means and inducements are not there. [. . .]

Now, why is it more ridiculous for a man than for a woman to do worsted work and drive out every day in the carriage? Why should we laugh if we were to see a parcel of men sitting round a drawing-room table in the morning, and think it all right if they were women?

Is man's time more valuable than woman's? or is the difference between man and woman this, that woman has confessedly nothing to do? [. . .]

The family uses people, *not* for what they are, nor for what they are intended to be, but for what it wants them for – its own uses. It thinks of them not as what God has made them, but as the something which it has arranged that they shall be. If it wants someone to sit in the drawing-room, *that* someone is supplied by the family, though that member may be destined for science, or for education, or for active superintendence by God, *i.e.* by the gifts within.

This system dooms some minds to incurable infancy, others to silent misery.

And family boasts that it has performed its mission well, in as far as it has enabled the individual to say, 'I have *no* peculiar work, nothing but what the moment brings me, nothing that I cannot throw up at once at anybody's claim'; in as far, that is, as it has *destroyed* the individual life. And the individual thinks that a great victory has been accomplished, when, at last, she is able to say that she has 'no personal desires or plans'. What is this but throwing the gifts of God aside as worthless, and substituting for them those of the world?

Marriage is the only chance (and it is but a chance) offered to women for escape from this death; and how eagerly and how ignorantly it is embraced!

At present we live to impede each other's satisfactions; competition, domestic life, society, what is it all but this? We go somewhere where we are not wanted and where we don't want to go. What else is conventional life? *Passivity* when we want to be active. So many hours spent every day in passively doing what conventional life tells us, when we would so gladly be at work.

And is it a wonder that all individual life is extinguished?

Women dream of a great sphere of steady, not sketchy benevolence, of moral activity, for which they would fain be trained and fitted, instead of working in the dark, neither knowing nor registering whither their steps lead, whether farther from or nearer to the aim. [. . .]

Women long for an education to teach them *to teach*, to teach them the laws of the human mind and how to apply them – and knowing how imperfect, in the present state of the world, such an education must be, they long for experience, not patch-work experience, but experience followed up and systematised, to enable them to know what they are about and *where* they are 'casting their bread', and whether it is *'bread'* or a stone. [. . .]

Nothing can well be imagined more painful than the present position of woman, unless, on the one hand, she renounces all outward activity and keeps herself within the magic sphere, the bubble of her dreams; or, on the other, surrendering all aspiration, she gives herself to her real life, soul and body. For those to whom it is possible, the latter is best; for out of activity may come thought, out of mere aspiration can come nothing.

3.3 Samuel Smiles, 'Character – The True Gentleman', *Self-Help: With Illustrations of Conduct and Perseverance* (London: John Murray, 1859)

In Self-Help, *his influential work on moral character and individual reform, Smiles argued that 'the highest patriotism and philanthropy consist, not so much in altering laws and modifying institutions, as in helping and stimulating men to elevate and improve themselves by their own free and independent action'. As a consequence, male virtue for Smiles was based on action and work, self-reliance and self-control. The true gentleman was not someone of inherited privilege but someone who was polite, civil, tolerant and forbearing, regardless of their social rank. Real gentlemen might be of any rank or class, and the parvenu became a gentleman not by aping his 'betters' but by remaining true to himself.* Self-Help *is aimed at the working and lower middle classes. The heroes of* Self-Help *are self-made men, inventors, producers and captains of industry, and manliness becomes the attribute of the self-made man. (For a biographical note on Smiles see p. 59–60, and also extracts 1.1 and 2.6).*

The inbred politeness which springs from right-heartedness and kindly feelings, is of no exclusive rank or station. The mechanic who works at the bench may possess it, as well as the clergyman or the peer. It is by no means a necessary condition of labour that it should in any respect be either rough or coarse. The politeness and refinement which distinguish all classes of the people in many continental countries show that those qualities might become ours too – as doubtless they will become with increased culture and more general social intercourse – without sacrificing any of our more genuine qualities as men. From the highest to the lowest, the richest to the poorest, to no rank or condition in life has nature denied her highest boon, – the great heart. There never yet existed a gentleman but was lord of a great heart. [. . .]

Riches and rank have no necessary connexion with genuine gentlemanly qualities. The poor man may be a true gentleman, – in spirit and in daily life. He may be honest, truthful, upright, polite, temperate, courageous, self-respecting, and self-helping, – that is, be a true gentleman. The poor man with a rich spirit is in all ways superior to the rich man with a poor spirit. To borrow St. Paul's words, the former is as 'having nothing, yet possessing all things', while the other, though possessing all things, has nothing. The first hopes everything, and fears nothing; the last hopes nothing, and fears everything. Only the poor in spirit are really poor. He who has lost all, but retains his courage, cheerfulness, hope, virtue, and self-respect, is still rich. For such a man, the world is, as it were, held in trust; his spirit dominating over its grosser cares, he can still walk erect, a true gentleman. [. . .]

There are many tests by which a gentleman may be known; but there is one that never fails – How does he *exercise power* over those subordinate to him? How does he conduct himself towards women and children? How does the officer treat his men, the employer his servants, the master his pupils, and man in every station those who are weaker than himself? The discretion, forbearance, and kindliness, with which power in such cases is used, may indeed be regarded as the crucial test of gentlemanly character.

3.4 Eliza Lynn Linton, 'The Girl of The Period', *Saturday Review*, 14 March 1868, 339–40

Eliza Lynn Linton (1822–98) was a successful journalist and novelist. This sensational, anti-feminist piece is one of her more extreme essays. First published anonymously in the Saturday Review *and then as a hugely popular pamphlet, it first appeared under her name in 1883 in* The Girl of the Period and Other Social Essays. *Linton herself was a contradictory figure. She was the first woman journalist in England to earn a fixed salary, and her second novel,* Amymone: A Romance in the Days of Pericles *(1848), was an impassioned defence of women's rights. From 1864 she lived apart from her husband William James Linton whom she had married six years earlier. She became increasingly conservative, writing as a critic of women in the*

Saturday Review *and other Victorian periodicals, and became more outspoken in her opposition as women gained more rights. Linton continued writing into the 1890s when she contributed a number of essays on the New Woman to the periodical debates and attacked the New Woman in two of her late – and less successful – novels,* The One Too Many *(1894) and* In Haste and at Leisure *(1895). 'The Girl of the Period' expresses a strong sense of nationalist pride and a belief in nature as determining; its vision of femininity is underpinned by the commonplace binary opposition of virgin and whore. The piece makes no reference to the suffrage and questions of education or employment, central issues of the decade, advocating instead an ideal of domestic virtue which the surplus of women and the growing number of women in the workplace was already making unsustainable.*

Time was when the stereotyped phrase, 'a fair young English girl', meant the ideal of womanhood; to us, at least, of home birth and breeding. It meant a creature generous, capable, and modest; something franker than a Frenchwoman, more to be trusted than an Italian, as brave as an American but more refined, as domestic as a German and more graceful. It meant a girl who could be trusted alone if need be, because of the innate purity and dignity of her nature, but who was neither bold in bearing nor masculine in mind; a girl who, when she married, would be her husband's friend and companion, but never his rival; one who would consider their interests identical, and not hold him as just so much fair game for spoil; who would make his house his true home and place of rest, not a mere passage-place for vanity and ostentation to go through; a tender mother, an industrious house-keeper, a judicious mistress. We prided ourselves as a nation on our women. We thought we had the pick of creation in this fair young English girl of ours, and envied no other men their own. We admired the languid grace and subtle fire of the South; the docility and childlike affectionateness of the East seemed to us sweet and simple and restful; the vivacious sparkle of the trim and sprightly Parisienne was a pleasant little excitement when we met with it in its own domain; but our allegiance never wandered from our brown-haired girls at home, and our hearts were less vagrant than our fancies. This was in the old time, and when English girls were content to be what God and nature had made them. Of late years we have changed the pattern, and have given to the world a race of women as utterly unlike the old insular ideal as if we had created another nation altogether. The girl of the period, and the fair young English girl of the past, have nothing in common save ancestry and their mother-tongue; and even of this last the modern version makes almost a new language, through the copious additions it has received from the current slang of the day.

    The girl of the period is a creature who dyes her hair and paints her face, as the first articles of her personal religion; whose sole idea of life is plenty of fun and luxury; and whose dress is the chief object of such thought and intellect as she possesses. Her main endeavour is to outvie her neighbours in the extravagance of fashion [. . .] With purity of taste she has lost also that far more precious purity and delicacy of perception which sometimes mean more than appears on the surface. [. . .]

The Girl of the Period envies the queens of the *demi-monde*[1] far more than she abhors them. She sees them gorgeously attired and sumptuously appointed, and she knows them to be flattered, fêted, and courted with a certain disdainful admiration of which she catches only the admiration while she ignores the disdain. [. . .] But she [The Girl of the Period] does not marry easily. Men are afraid of her; and with reason. They may amuse themselves with her for an evening, but they do not take her readily for life. Besides, after all her efforts, she is only a poor copy of the real thing; and the real thing is far more amusing than the copy, because it is real. [. . .]

[W]hen they become again what they were once they will gather round them the love and homage and chivalrous devotion which were then an Englishwoman's natural inheritance. The marvel, in the present fashion of life among women, is how it holds its ground in spite of the disapprobation of men. It used to be an old-time notion that the sexes were made for each other, and that it was only natural for them to please each other, and to set themselves out for that end. But the girl of the period does not please men. She pleases them as little as she elevates them; and how little she does that, the class of women she has taken as her model of itself testifies. All men whose opinion is worth having prefer the simple and genuine girl of the past, with her tender little ways and pretty bashful modesties, to this loud and rampant modernization, with her false red hair and painted skin, talking slang as glibly as a man, and by preference leading the conversation to doubtful subjects. She thinks she is piquante and exciting when she thus makes herself the bad copy of a worse original; and she will not see that though men laugh with her they do not respect her, though they flirt with her they do not marry her; she will not believe that she is not the kind of thing they want, and that she is acting against nature and her own interests when she disregards their advice and offends their taste. We do not see how she makes out her account, viewing her life from any side; but all we can do is to wait patiently until the national madness has passed, and our women have come back again to the old English ideal, once the most beautiful, the most modest, the most essentially womanly in the world.

3.5 John Stuart Mill, *The Subjection of Women* (London: Longmans, Green, Reader and Dyer, 1869)

For a biographical note on Mill (1806–73) see p. 139; the breadth and influence of his thinking is also evident in extracts 5.7, 6.1, and 9.2. The Subjection of Women, the last and most rhetorical of his political tracts, was drafted in 1861 and published in 1869. The work is a sustained, polemical appeal for the recognition of women's

---

1 High class of women kept by wealthy men.

personal, legal and political rights, including the right to higher education, to work outside the home, and to equal rights in marriage. It draws on Harriet Taylor's Westminster Review *essay 'The Enfranchisement of Women' (1851) and shares her critique of the practice of affording women superior moral status in lieu of actual political and legal power. Mill in his* Autobiography *spoke of his indebtedness to Taylor; he also noted that the work had been suggested by his stepdaughter Helen Taylor and enriched with her ideas. The four chapters argue that the legal subordination of one sex to the other, the principle that regulated social relations between the sexes, ought to be replaced by a principle of perfect equality. Mill is concerned both with justice and utility: the subjection of women is not only intrinsically wrong but it is also the cause of much social ill: 'all the selfish propensities, the self-worship, the unjust self-preference, which exist among mankind, have their source and root in, and derive their principal nourishment from, the present constitution of the relation between men and women'. Mill argues that what appears to be natural is simply customary, and that this is no more true than in relation to the Woman Question. He insists that no useful evidence yet exists as to the question of women's essential nature and that men and women are further from a state of nature in England than in any other country. The Subjection* of Women *was a crucial text for the campaigners for women's suffrage.*

From Chapter One

The object of this Essay is to explain as clearly as I am able, the grounds of an opinion which I have held from the very earliest period when I had formed any opinions at all on social or political matters, and which, instead of being weakened or modified, has been constantly growing stronger by the progress of reflection and the experience of life: That the principle which regulates the existing social relations between the two sexes – the legal subordination of one sex to the other – is wrong in itself, and now one of the chief hindrances to human improvement; and that it ought to be replaced by a principle of perfect equality, admitting no power or privilege on the one side, nor disability on the other. [. . .]

So true is it that unnatural generally means only uncustomary, and that everything which is usual appears natural. The subjection of women to men being a universal custom, any departure from it quite naturally appears unnatural. But how entirely, even in this case, the feeling is dependent on custom, appears by ample experience. Nothing so much astonishes the people of distant parts of the world, when they first learn anything about England, as to be told that it is under a queen: the thing seems to them so unnatural as to be almost incredible. To Englishmen this does not seem in the least degree unnatural, because they are used to it; but they do feel it unnatural that women should be soldiers or members of Parliament. In the feudal ages, on the contrary, war and politics were not thought unnatural to women, because not unusual; it seemed natural that women of the privileged classes should be of manly character, inferior in nothing but bodily strength to their husbands and fathers. [. . .]

But, it will be said, the rule of men over women differs from all these others in not being a rule of force: it is accepted voluntarily; women make no complaint, and are consenting parties to it. In the first place, a great number of women do not accept it. Ever since there have been women able to make their sentiments known by their writings (the only mode of publicity which society permits to them), an increasing number of them have recorded protests against their present social condition: and recently many thousands of them, headed by the most eminent women known to the public, have petitioned Parliament for their admission to the Parliamentary Suffrage. The claim of women to be educated as solidly, and in the same branches of knowledge, as men, is urged with growing intensity, and with a great prospect of success; while the demand for their admission into professions and occupations hitherto closed against them, becomes every year more urgent. Though there are not in this country, as there are in the United States, periodical Conventions and an organised party to agitate for the Rights of Women, there is a numerous and active Society organised and managed by women, for the more limited object of obtaining the political franchise. [. . .]

All causes, social and natural, combine to make it unlikely that women should be collectively rebellious to the power of men. [. . .] The masters of all other slaves rely, for maintaining obedience, on fear; either fear of themselves or religious fears. The masters of women wanted more than simple obedience, and they turned the whole force of education to effect their purpose. All women are brought up from the very earliest years in the belief that their ideal of character is the very opposite to that of men; not self-will, and government by self-control, but submission, and yielding to the control of others. All the moralities tell them that it is the duty of women, and all the current sentimentalities that it is their nature, to live for others; to make complete abnegation of themselves, and to have no life but in their affections. And by their affections are meant the only ones they are allowed to have – those to the men with whom they are connected, or to the children who constitute an additional and indefeasible tie between them and a man. When we put together three things – first, the natural attraction between opposite sexes; secondly, the wife's entire dependence on the husband, every privilege or pleasure she has being either his gift, or depending entirely on his will; and lastly, that the principal object of human pursuit, consideration, and all objects of social ambition, can in general be sought or obtained by her only through him, it would be a miracle if the object of being attractive to men had not become the polar star of feminine education and formation of character. And, this great means of influence over the minds of women having been acquired, an instinct of selfishness made men avail themselves of it to the utmost as a means of holding women in subjection, by representing to them meekness, submissiveness, and resignation of all individual will into the hands of a man, as an essential part of sexual attractiveness. [. . .]

What is now called the nature of women is an eminently artificial thing – the result of forced repression in some directions, unnatural stimulation in others. It may be asserted without scruple, that no other class of dependents have had their character so entirely distorted from its natural proportions by their relation with their masters; for, if conquered and slave races have been, in some respects, more forcibly repressed, whatever in them has not been crushed down by an iron heel has generally been let alone, and if left with any liberty of development, it has developed itself according to its own laws; but in the case of women, a hot-house and stove cultivation has always been carried on of some of the capabilities of their nature, for the benefit and pleasure of their masters. [. . .]

Even the preliminary knowledge, what the differences between the sexes now are, apart from all question as to how they are made what they are, is still in the crudest and most incomplete state. Medical practitioners and physiologists have ascertained, to some extent, the differences in bodily constitution; and this is an important element to the psychologist: but hardly any medical practitioner is a psychologist. Respecting the mental characteristics of women; their observations are of no more worth than those of common men. It is a subject on which nothing final can be known, so long as those who alone can really know it, women themselves, have given but little testimony, and that little, mostly suborned. [. . .]

When we further consider that to understand one woman is not necessarily to understand any other woman; that even if he could study many women of one rank, or of one country, he would not thereby understand women of other ranks or countries; and even if he did, they are still only the women of a single period of history; we may safely assert that the knowledge which men can acquire of women, even as they have been and are, without reference to what they might be, is wretchedly imperfect and superficial, and always will be so, until women themselves have told all that they have to tell.

And this time has not come; nor will it come otherwise than gradually. It is but of yesterday that women have either been qualified by literary accomplishments or permitted by society, to tell anything to the general public. As yet very few of them dare tell anything, which men, on whom their literary success depends, are unwilling to hear. [. . .]

From Chapter Three

It will be said, perhaps, that the greater nervous susceptibility of women is a disqualification for practice, in anything but domestic life, by rendering them mobile, changeable, too vehemently under the influence of the moment, incapable of dogged perseverance, unequal and uncertain in the power of using their faculties. [. . .] But women brought up to work for their livelihood show none of these morbid characteristics, unless indeed they are chained to an excess of sedentary work in confined and unhealthy rooms. Women who in their early years have shared in the healthful physical education and bodily freedom of their brothers, and who obtain a sufficiency of pure air and exercise in after-life, very rarely have any excessive susceptibility of nerves which can disqualify them for active pursuits. [. . .]

3.6 John Ruskin, 'Of Queen's Gardens', *Sesame and Lilies. Revised and enlarged edition* (1865; London: Smith Elder and Co., 1871)

Ruskin (1819–1900) made his name as a critic of painting – especially in his defence of the work of J. M. W. Turner – and then of architecture (see Section 6: Art and Aesthetics). In his later writings he turned increasingly to social, political and economic questions. Ruskin actively supported girls' schools and colleges through the 1860s and was involved with Margaret Bell's innovative school for girls, Winnington Hall School in Cheshire, where he taught in person and by letter. 'Of Kings' Treasuries' was the first of two lectures he delivered in Rusholme near Manchester in 1864, 'Of Queens' Gardens' the second; the first was to raise money for a library of the Rusholme Institute, the second to establish schools in an impoverished area of the city. The images of kingship and queenship stand respectively for masculine leadership and feminine nurture. The lectures were first published together as Sesame and Lilies *the following year; they were revised and republished with an additional essay in 1871. In 'Of Queens' Gardens' Ruskin advocates free access to books and emphasizes that the education of girls must be serious, underlining the importance of the social good as an end of education. Recently scholars have explored the complexity of Ruskin's gender politics and instead of positioning him against Mill, as previous critics had tended to do, his views have begun to be seen as complementary, focusing on education reform as Mill focused on the legal and political rights of women. Ruskin saw the duties of women as praise, moral and social responsibility, and reverence; while he emphasized the importance of the home the concept seems for Ruskin to have been more a spiritual state than a physical entity, which complicates and broadens his vision of feminine virtue and influence.*

We are foolish, and without excuse foolish, in speaking of the 'superiority' of one sex to the other, as if they could be compared in similar things. Each has what the other has not: each completes the other, and is completed by the other: they are in nothing alike, and the happiness and perfection of both depends on each asking and receiving from the other what the other only can give.

68. Now their separate characters are briefly these. The man's power is active, progressive, defensive. He is eminently the doer, the creator, the discoverer, the defender. His intellect is for speculation and invention; his energy for adventure, for war, and for conquest, wherever war is just, wherever conquest necessary. But the woman's power is for rule, not for battle, – and her intellect is not for invention or creation, but for sweet ordering, arrangement, and decision. She sees the qualities of things, their claims, and their places. Her great function is Praise: she enters into no contest, but infallibly adjudges the crown of contest. By her office, and place, she is protected from all danger and temptation. The man, in his rough work in open world, must encounter all peril and trial; – to him, therefore, must be the failure, the offence, the inevitable error: often he must be wounded, or subdued; often misled; and *always* hardened. But he guards the

woman from all this; within his house, as ruled by her, unless she herself has sought it, need enter no danger, no temptation, no cause of error or offence. This is the true nature of home – it is the place of Peace; the shelter, not only from all injury, but from all terror, doubt, and division. In so far as it is not this, it is not home; so far as the anxieties of the outer life penetrate into it, and the inconsistently-minded, unknown, unloved, or hostile society of the outer world is allowed by either husband or wife to cross the threshold, it ceases to be home; it is then only a part of that outer world which you have roofed over, and lighted fire in. [. . .]

And wherever a true wife comes, this home is always round her. The stars only may be over her head; the glowworm in the night-cold grass may be the only fire at her foot: but home is yet wherever she is; and for a noble woman it stretches far round her, better than ceiled with cedar, or painted with vermilion, shedding its quiet light far, for those who else were homeless. [. . .]

74. I believe, then, with this exception [theology], that a girl's education should be nearly, in its course and material of study, the same as a boy's; but quite differently directed. A woman, in any rank of life, ought to know whatever her husband is likely to know, but to know it in a different way. His command of it should be foundational and progressive; hers, general and accomplished for daily and helpful use. Not but that it would often be wiser in men to learn things in a womanly sort of way, for present use, and to seek for the discipline and training of their mental powers in such branches of study as will be afterwards fittest for social service; but, speaking broadly, a man ought to know any language or science he learns, thoroughly – while a woman ought to know the same language, or science, only so far as may enable her to sympathise in her husband's pleasures, and in those of his best friends.

75. Yet, observe, with exquisite accuracy as far as she reaches. There is a wide difference between elementary knowledge and superficial knowledge – between a firm beginning, and an infirm attempt at compassing. A woman may always help her husband by what she knows, however little; by what she half-knows, or mis-knows, she will only tease him.

And indeed, if there were to be any difference between a girl's education and a boy's, I should say that of the two the girl should be earlier led, as her intellect ripens faster, into deep and serious subjects: and that her range of literature should be, not more, but less frivolous; calculated to add the qualities of patience and seriousness to her natural poignancy of thought and quickness of wit; and also to keep her in a lofty and pure element of thought.

3.7 Charles Darwin, *The Descent of Man, and Selection in Relation to Sex*, vol. 2 (London: John Murray, 1871)

In On the Origin of Species *(1859), Darwin (1809–88) advanced the theory of natural selection; 12 years later he published* The Descent of Man, and Selection in

Relation to Sex, *which applied the theory to humans (for a biographical note on Darwin, see p. 275, and extracts 9.7 and 10.7). By the time of* The Descent, *Darwin saw sexual selection as playing a greater and more distinct part in the process of evolution. Over two-thirds of the work was devoted to a description of sexual selection in the animal kingdom. Among humans, Darwin argued, each aboriginal society had its own ideal of beauty which, through sexual selection, had led to the divergence of the human races. Noting that in almost all species females were the choice makers, he observed that the dominance of men in the selection of sexual partners, in keeping with Victorian courting convention, made the human love-plot exceptional in the animal kingdom: 'the males, instead of having been selected, are the selectors'. He noted a further difference: 'with civilized people the arbitrament of battle for the possession of the women has long ceased'. In human reproduction men were the choosers, leaving women as the passive embodiments of Victorian femininity. Among the 'civilized', aesthetic principles overruled physical strength. Sexual selection highlighted physical and mental differences between the sexes, explaining them as advantageous in finding mates, and thus potentially lent new authority and evolutionary purpose to Victorian ideas of gender. Darwin argued in* The Descent *for fundamental differences between men and women. In spite of his earlier emphasis in the* Origin *on change and mutability, his study of humans offered no challenge to sexual stereotyping. Nonetheless, he did not rule out possibilities for social change.*

WITH mankind the differences between the sexes are greater than in most species of Quadrumana, but not so great as in some, for instance, the mandrill. Man on an average is considerably taller, heavier, and stronger than woman, with squarer shoulders and more plainly-pronounced muscles. Owing to the relation which exists between muscular development and the projection of the brows,[2] the superciliary ridge is generally more strongly marked in man than in woman. His body, and especially his face, is more hairy, and his voice has a different and more powerful tone. In certain tribes the women are said, whether truly I know not, to differ slightly in tint from the men; and with Europeans, the women are perhaps the more brightly coloured of the two, as may be seen when both sexes have been equally exposed to the weather.

Man is more courageous, pugnacious, and energetic than woman, and has a more inventive genius. His brain is absolutely larger, but whether relatively to the larger size of his body, in comparison with that of woman, has not, I believe been fully ascertained. In woman the face is rounder; the jaws and the base of the skull smaller; the outlines of her body rounder, in parts more prominent; and her pelvis is broader than in man;[3] but this latter character may perhaps be considered rather as a primary than a secondary sexual character. She comes to maturity at an earlier age than man. [. . .]

---

2 *Original Note*: Schaaffhausen, translation in *Anthropological Review*, Oct. 1868, p. 419, 420, 427.

3 *Original Note*: Ecker, translation in *Anthropological Review*, Oct. 1868, pp. 351–6. The comparison of the form of the skull in men and women has been followed out with much care by Welcker.

There can be little doubt that the greater size and strength of man, in comparison with woman, together with his broader shoulders, more developed muscles, rugged outline of body, his greater courage and pugnacity, are all due in chief part to inheritance from some early male progenitor, who, like the existing anthropoid apes, was thus characterised. These characters will, however, have been preserved or even augmented during the long ages whilst man was still in a barbarous condition, by the strongest and boldest men having succeeded best in the general struggle for life, as well as in securing wives, and thus having left a large number of offspring. It is not probable that the greater strength of man was primarily acquired through the inherited effects of his having worked harder than woman for his own subsistence and that of his family; for the women in all barbarous nations are compelled to work at least as hard as the men. With civilised people the arbitrament of battle for the possession of the women has long ceased; on the other hand, the men, as a general rule, have to work harder than the women for their mutual subsistence; and thus their greater strength will have been kept up.

Difference in the Mental Powers of the two Sexes.—With respect to differences of this nature between man and woman, it is probable that sexual selection has played a very important part. I am aware that some writers doubt whether there is any inherent difference; but this is at least probable from the analogy of the lower animals which present other secondary sexual characters. No one will dispute that the bull differs in disposition from the cow, the wild-boar from the sow, the stallion from the mare, and, as is well known to the keepers of menageries, the males of the larger apes from the females. Woman seems to differ from man in mental disposition, chiefly in her greater tenderness and less selfishness; and this holds good even with savages, as shewn by a well-known passage in Mungo Park's Travels, and by statements made by many other travellers. Woman, owing to her maternal instincts, displays these qualities towards her infants in an eminent degree; therefore it is likely that she should often extend them towards her fellow-creatures. Man is the rival of other men; he delights in competition, and this leads to ambition which passes too easily into selfishness. These latter qualities seem to be his natural and unfortunate birthright. It is generally admitted that with woman the powers of intuition, of rapid perception, and perhaps of imitation, are more strongly marked than in man; but some, at least, of these faculties are characteristic of the lower races, and therefore of a past and lower state of civilisation.

The chief distinction in the intellectual powers of the two sexes is shewn by man attaining to a higher eminence, in whatever he takes up, than woman can attain – whether requiring deep thought, reason, or imagination, or merely the use of the senses and hands. If two lists were made of the most eminent men and women in poetry, painting, sculpture, music, – comprising composition and performance, history, science, and philosophy, with half-a-dozen names under each subject, the two lists would not bear comparison. We may also infer, from the law of the deviation of averages, so well illustrated by Mr. Galton, in his work on 'Hereditary Genius', that if men are capable of decided eminence over women in many subjects, the average standard of mental power in man must be above that of woman.

The half-human male progenitors of man, and men in a savage state, have struggled together during many generations for the possession of the females. But mere bodily strength and size would do little for victory, unless associated with courage, perseverance, and determined energy. With social animals, the young males have to pass through many a contest before they win a female, and the older males have to retain their females by renewed battles. They have, also, in the case of man, to defend their females, as well as their young, from enemies of all kinds, and to hunt for their joint subsistence. But to avoid enemies, or to attack them with success, to capture wild animals, and to invent and fashion weapons, requires the aid of the higher mental faculties, namely, observation, reason, invention, or imagination. These various faculties will thus have been continually put to the test, and selected during manhood; they will, moreover, have been strengthened by use during this same period of life. Consequently, in accordance with the principle often alluded to, we might expect that they would at least tend to be transmitted chiefly to the male offspring at the corresponding period of manhood. [. . .]

With animals in a state of nature, many characters proper to the males, such as size, strength, special weapons, courage and pugnacity, have been acquired through the law of battle. The semi-human progenitors of man, like their allies the Quadrumana, will almost certainly have been thus modified; and, as savages still fight for the possession of their women, a similar process of selection has probably gone on in a greater or less degree to the present day. Other characters proper to the males of the lower animals, such as bright colours and various ornaments, have been acquired by the more attractive males having been preferred by the females. There are, however, exceptional cases in which the males, instead of having been the selected, have been the selectors. We recognise such cases by the females having been rendered more highly ornamented than the males, – their ornamental characters having been transmitted exclusively or chiefly to their female offspring. One such case has been described in the order to which man belongs, namely, with the Rhesus monkey.

Man is more powerful in body and mind than woman, and in the savage state he keeps her in a far more abject state of bondage than does the male of any other animal; therefore it is not surprising that he should have gained the power of selection. Women are everywhere conscious of the value of their beauty; and when they have the means, they take more delight in decorating themselves with all sorts of ornaments than do men. They borrow the plumes of male birds, with which nature decked this sex in order to charm the females. As women have long been selected for beauty, it is not surprising that some of the successive variations should have been transmitted in a limited manner; and consequently that women should have transmitted their beauty in a somewhat higher degree to their female than to their male offspring. Hence women have become more beautiful, as most persons will admit, than men. Women, however, certainly transmit most of their characters, including beauty, to their offspring of both sexes; so that the continued preference by the men of each race of the more attractive women, according to their standard of taste, would tend to modify in the same manner all the individuals of both sexes belonging to the race.

3.8 Henry Maudsley, 'Sex in Mind and Education', *Fortnightly Review* 15 (April 1874), 466–83

In this notorious and controversial essay the English psychiatrist Dr Henry Maudsley (1835–1918) argued that social organization was an expression of evolutionary differentiation, and that mental differences between the sexes were the product of the evolutionary process and not to be challenged. Maudsley draws on Herbert Spencer who in Education: Intellectual, Moral and Physical *(1861) argued that women had been arrested intellectually to conserve their energy for reproduction; Maudsley argues that if women attempted to achieve the educational standards of men they would lack the resources necessary for childbearing and rearing. The essay refers to* Sex in Education *by the Harvard physician Edward H. Clarke, published earlier that year, which offered an emphatic warning that girls were reaching breaking point on account of intellectual work. Arguing that there was 'sex in mind as distinctly as there is sex in body', Maudsley declared, 'sex is fundamental, lies deeper than culture, cannot be ignored or defied with impunity'. Maudsley's views provoked a cogent response from the physician Elizabeth Garrett Anderson (the first female member of the British Medical Association) in the following issue of the* Fortnightly Review. *She explored Maudsley's objections to an equal education for women, resisting the idea that the male body was the norm and emphasizing, instead, that women needed to be considered on their own terms.*

When we thus look the matter honestly in the face, it would seem plain that women are marked out by nature for very different offices in life from those of men, and that the healthy performance of her special functions renders it improbable she will succeed, and unwise for her to persevere, in running over the same course at the same pace with him. For such a race she is certainly weighted unfairly. Nor is it a sufficient reply to this argument to allege, as is sometimes done, that there are many women who have not the opportunity of getting married, or who do not aspire to bear children; for whether they care to be mothers or not, they cannot dispense with those physiological functions of their nature that have reference to that aim, however much they might wish it, and they cannot disregard them in the labour of life without injury to their health. They cannot choose but to be women; cannot rebel successfully against the tyranny of their organization, the complete development and function whereof must take place after its kind. This is not the expression of prejudice nor of false sentiment; it is the plain statement of a physiological fact. Surely, then, it is unwise to pass it by; first or last it must have its due weight in the determination of the problem of women's education and mission; it is best to recognize it plainly, however we may conclude finally to deal with it.

It is sometimes said, however, that sexual difference ought not to have any place in the culture of mind, and one hears it affirmed with an air of triumphant satisfaction that there is no sex in mental culture. This is a rash statement, which argues want of thought or insincerity of thought in those who make it. There is sex in mind as distinctly as there is sex in body; and if the mind is to receive the best culture of which its nature is capable, regard must be had to the mental qualities which correlate differences of sex. To aim, by means of education and pursuits in life, to assimilate the female to the male mind, might well be pronounced as unwise and fruitless a labour as it would be to strive to assimilate the female to the male body by means of the same kind of physical training and by the adoption of the same pursuits. Without doubt there have been some striking instances of extraordinary women who have shown great mental power, and these may fairly be quoted as evidence in support of the right of women to the best mental culture; but it is another matter when they are adduced in support of the assertion that there is no sex in mind, and that a system of female education should be laid down on the same lines, follow the same method, and have the same ends in view, as a system of education for men.

3.9 Edward Aveling and Eleanor Marx Aveling, 'The Woman Question: From a Socialist Point of View', *Westminster Review* 125 (January 1886), 207–22

Eleanor Marx (1855–98) and Edward Aveling (1851–98) present in this essay a Marxist reading of the Woman Question, ostensibly a review of an English translation of the German socialist August Bebel's Woman under Socialism *which had been banned in Germany. Drawing on Engels's* Origins of the Family, Private Property and the State *(first published in 1879) they emphasize the economic basis of women's oppression in capitalism, drawing an analogy between women and the working class, and denounce mercenary marriage, prostitution, inadequate sex education and 'unnatural' chastity, arguing that class relations, through the unequal distribution of property, lie at the root of women's oppression (see also extract 2.7). They write that in a socialist society, which they, like many Marxists, saw as inevitable, economic independence would allow women to reach their full potential and to achieve genuine equality with men, having the same educational and social opportunities. They urge the need for women to organize themselves in the struggle for emancipation, something which both the oppressed classes – women and the immediate producers – must understand, and extend Karl Marx's dictum that the emancipation of the working class must be the act of the working class itself: 'their emancipation will come from themselves'; they could not be freed by men.*

[T]hose who attack the present treatment of women without seeking for the cause of this in the economics of our latter-day society are like doctors who treat a local affection without inquiring into the general bodily health.

This criticism applies not alone to the commonplace person who makes a jest of any discussion into which the element of sex enters. It applies to those higher natures, in many cases earnest and thoughtful, who see that women are in a parlous state, and are anxious that something should be done to better their condition. These are the excellent and hard-working folk who agitate for that perfectly just aim, woman suffrage; for the repeal of the Contagious Diseases Act, a monstrosity begotten of male cowardice and brutality; for the higher education of women; for the opening to them of universities, the learned professions, and all callings, from that of teacher to that of bagman. In all this work – good as far as it goes – three things are especially notable. First, those concerned in it are of the well-to-do classes, as a rule. With the single and only partial exception of the Contagious Diseases agitation, scarcely any of the women taking a prominent part in these various movements belong to the working class. We are prepared for the comment that something very like this may be said, as far as concerns England, of the larger movement that claims our special efforts. Certainly, Socialism is at present in this country little more than a literary movement. It has but a fringe of working men on its border. But we can answer to this criticism that in Germany this is not the case, and that even here Socialism is now beginning to extend among the workers.

The second point is that all these ideas of our *advanced* women are based either on property, or on sentimental or professional questions. Not one of them gets down through these to the bedrock of the economic basis, not only of each of these three, but of society itself. [. . .]

The truth, not fully recognised even by those anxious to do good to woman, is that she, like the labour-classes, is in an oppressed condition; that her position, like theirs, is one of merciless degradation. Women are the creatures of an organised tyranny of men, as the workers are the creatures of an organised tyranny of idlers. Even where this much is grasped, we must never be weary of insisting on the non-understanding that for women, as for the labouring classes, no solution of the difficulties and problems that present themselves is really possible in the present condition of society. All that is done, heralded with no matter what flourish of trumpets, is palliative, not remedial. Both the oppressed classes, women and the immediate producers, must understand that their emancipation will come from themselves. Women will find allies in the better sort of men, as the labourers are finding allies among the philosophers, artists, and poets. But the one has nothing to hope from man as a whole, and the other has nothing to hope from the middle class as a whole. [. . .]

Some wonder that John Stuart Mill wrote, *Marriage is at the present day the only actual form of serfdom recognised by law.* The wonder to us is that he never saw this serfdom as a question, not of sentiment, but of economics, the result of our capitalistic system. [. . .]

3.10 Mona Caird, 'Marriage', *Westminster Review* 130 (August 1888), 186–229

Mona Caird (1853–1932) was one of the most radical and outspoken of the New Women and this essay inspired the most famous newspaper debate of the nineteenth century, with the Daily Telegraph *responding with the question 'Is Marriage a Failure?'. The paper could claim the largest circulation in the world (average sales were in excess of 500,000), and it received 27,000 responses, with a striking number in agreement, before closing the correspondence in September 1888. Caird's essay draws on earlier ideas of feminist thinkers such as Wollstonecraft, who argued for the importance of education for women, urging their capacity for reason. Caird's article argues that contemporary marriage was derived from rule of force, and urges an alternative model underpinned by affection and sympathy. Exposing a twin system of marriage and prostitution, she stresses the importance of economic independence of women for healthy relationships.*

It is not difficult to find people mild and easy-going about religion, and even politics may be regarded with wide-minded tolerance; but broach social subjects, and English men and women at once become alarmed and talk about the foundations of society and the sacredness of the home! Yet the particular form of social life, or of marriage, to which they are so deeply attached, has by no means existed from time immemorial; in fact, modern marriage, with its satellite ideas, only dates as far back as the age of Luther. Of course the institution existed long before, but our particular mode of regarding it can be traced to the era of the Reformation, when commerce, competition, the great *bourgeois* class, and that remarkable thing called 'Respectability', also began to arise.

Before entering upon the history of marriage, it is necessary to clear the ground for thought upon this subject by a protest against the careless use of the words 'human nature' and especially 'woman's nature'. History will show us, if anything will, that human nature has an apparently limitless adaptability, and that therefore no conclusion can be built upon special manifestations which may at any time be developed. Such development must be referred to certain conditions, and not be mistaken for the eternal law of being. With regard to 'woman's nature', concerning which innumerable contradictory dogmas are held, there is so little really known about it, and its power of development, that all social philosophies are more or less falsified by this universal though sublimely unconscious ignorance.

The difficulties of friendly intercourse between men and women are so great, and the false sentiments induced by our present system so many and so subtle, that it is the hardest thing in the world for either sex to learn the truth concerning the real thoughts and feelings of the other. If they find out what they mutually think about the weather it is as much as can be expected – consistently, that is, with genuine submission to present ordinances. Thinkers, therefore, perforce take no count of the many half-known and less understood ideas and emotions

Figure 3.1 [John Tenniel], 'An "Ugly Rush!" Mr. Bull. "Not if I know it!"', *Punch* 58 (January–June 1870), 212

of women, even as these actually exist at the moment, and they make still smaller allowance for potential developments which at the present crisis are almost incalculable. Current phrases of the most shallow kind are taken as if they expressed the whole that is knowable on the subject.

There is in fact no social philosophy, however logical and far-seeing on other points, which does not lapse into incoherence as soon as it touches the subject of women. The thinker abandons the thought-laws which he has obeyed until that fatal moment; he forgets every principle of science previously present to his mind, and he suddenly goes back centuries in knowledge and in the conscious-ness of possibilities, making schoolboy statements, and 'babbling of green fields' in a manner that takes away the breath of those who have listened to his former reasoning and admired his previous delicacies of thought-distinction. Has he been overtaken by some afflicting mental disease? Or does he merely allow himself to hold one subject apart from the circulating currents of his brain judg-ing it on different principles from those on which he judges every other subject?

3.11 Havelock Ellis and John Addington Symonds, *Sexual Inversion* (London: Wilson and Macmillan, 1897)

Written by Ellis (1859–1939), in collaboration with the critic and poet John Addington Symonds (1840–93), Sexual Inversion, first published in Germany in 1896 and in England in 1897, posits an interpretation of homosexuality as an innate congenital condition over which the individual had little control. It appeared three years after the sentencing of Oscar Wilde for committing acts of 'gross indecency' with other men. In his general preface Ellis declared, 'I regard sex as the central problem of life.' Sexual Inversion, part of the emerging field of sexology, contains 27 original case histories on men and four on women. It concludes with the idea that pathology is only physiology working under new conditions and thus ultimately normalizes perceived abnormality. It was updated in 1915 to take account of psychoanalysis, and Ellis resisted the revival by Freudians of the idea that homosexuality was acquired rather than innate.

One of the political aims of Sexual Inversion is legal reform, which it seeks through recourse to the language of medicine. The first English editions were suppressed following the arrest and conviction of a London bookseller who sold a copy to an undercover policeman in 1898. The Lancet refused to review it, observing that the editors were unconvinced that 'homosexuality is anything else than an acquired and depraved manifestation of the sexual passion', and concluding 'it is especially important that such matters should not be discussed by the man in the street, not to mention the boy and girl in the street'. Ellis did not think homosexuality or 'gross indecency' should be penal offences, arguing that any attempt to repress 'abnormal sexuality' would foster blackmailing, and concluding that if two persons of either or both sexes, having reached years of discretion, 'privately consent to practise some perverted mode of sexual relationship, the law cannot be called upon to interfere'.

From 'Preface'

I had not at first proposed to devote a whole volume to sexual inversion. It may even be that I was inclined to slur it over as an unpleasant subject, and one that it was not wise to enlarge on. But I found in time that several persons for whom I felt respect and admiration were the congenital subjects of this abnormality. At the same time I realized that in England, more than in any other country, the law and public opinion combine to place a heavy penal burden and a severe social stigma on the manifestations of an instinct which to those persons who possess it frequently appears natural and normal. It was clear that the matter was in special need of elucidation and discussion. [. . .]

There can be no doubt that a peculiar amount of ignorance exists regarding the subject of sexual inversion. I know medical men of many years' general experience who have never, to their knowledge, come across a single case. We may remember, indeed, that some fifteen years ago the total number of cases recorded in scientific literature scarcely equalled those of British race which I have obtained, and that before my first cases were published not a single British case, unconnected with the asylum or the prison, had ever been recorded. Probably not a very large number of people are even aware that the turning in of the sexual instinct toward persons of the same sex can ever be regarded as in-born, so far as any sexual instinct is in-born. [. . .] [I]n most [sexually inverted men and women] the inverted tendency seems to be instinctive, and appears at a somewhat early age. In any case, however, it must be realized that in this volume we are not dealing with subjects belonging to the lunatic asylum or the prison. We are concerned with individuals who live in freedom, some of them suffering intensely from their abnormal organization, but otherwise ordinary members of society. In a few cases, we are concerned with individuals whose moral or artistic ideals have widely influenced their fellows who know nothing of the peculiar organization which has largely moulded those ideals. [. . .]

From 'Introduction'

It must be remembered that, in dealing with a northern country like England – and in the present volume I am chiefly dealing with England – homosexual phenomena do not present themselves in the same way as they do in southern Italy today, or in ancient Greece. In Greece the homosexual impulse was recognized and idealized; a man could be an open homosexual lover, and yet, like Epaminondas, be a great and honoured citizen of his country. There was no reason whatever why a man who in mental and physical constitution was perfectly normal should not adopt a custom that was regarded as respectable, and sometimes as even specially honourable. But it is quite otherwise in a country like England or the United States.[4] Here all our traditions and all our moral ideals, as well as the law, are energetically opposed to every manifestation of homosexual passion. It requires a very strong impetus to go against this compact social force which on every side constrains the individual into the paths of heterosexual love. That impetus, in a well-bred individual who leads the normal life of his fellow-men and who feels the ordinary degree of respect for the social feeling surrounding him, can only be supplied by a fundamental – usually, it is probable, inborn – perversion of the sexual instinct, rendering the individual organically abnormal. [. . .]

From 'Chapter IV: Sexual Inversion In Women'

It has been stated by many observers who are able to speak with some authority – in America, in France, in Germany, in England – that homosexuality is increasing among women.[5] It seems probable that this is true. There are many influences in our civilization today which encourage such manifestations. The modern movement of emancipation – the movement to obtain the same rights and duties, the same freedom and responsibility, the same education and the same work – must be regarded as, on the whole, a wholesome and inevitable movement. But it carries with it certain disadvantages. It has involved an increase in feminine criminality and in feminine insanity, which are being elevated towards the masculine standard. In connection with these – we can scarcely be surprised to find an increase in homosexuality which has always been regarded as belonging to an allied, if not the same, group of phenomena. Women are, very justly, coming to look upon knowledge and experience gener-

---

4 *Original Note:* It is true that in the solitude of great modern cities it is possible for small homosexual coteries to form, in a certain sense, an environment of their own favourable to their abnormality; yet, this fact hardly modifies the general statement made in the text.

5 *Original Note*: There are few traces of feminine homosexuality in English social history. In Charles II's court, the *Mémoires de Grammont* tell us (as Dr. Kiernan has reminded me), that Miss Hobart was credited with Lesbian tendencies [. . .].

ally as their right as much as their brothers' right. But when this doctrine is applied to the sexual sphere it finds certain limitations. Intimacies of any kind between young men and young women are as much discouraged socially now as ever they were; as regards higher education, the mere association of the sexes in the lecture-room or the laboratory or the hospital is discouraged in England and in America. Marriage is decaying, and while men are allowed freedom, the sexual field of women is becoming restricted to trivial flirtation with the opposite sex, and to intimacy with their own sex; having been taught independence of men and disdain for the old theory which placed women in the moated grange of the home to sigh for a man who never comes, a tendency develops for women to carry this independence still further and to find love where they find work. I do not say that these unquestionable influences of modern movements can directly cause sexual inversion, though they may indirectly, in so far as they promote hereditary neurosis; but they develop the germs of it, and they probably cause a spurious imitation. This spurious imitation is due to the fact that the congenital anomaly occurs with special frequency in women of high intelligence who, voluntarily or involuntarily, influence others. [. . .]

From Chapter VII: Conclusions

We can seldom, therefore, safely congratulate ourselves on the success of any 'cure' of inversion. [. . .] When I review the cases I have brought forward and the mental history of inverts I have known, I am inclined to say that if we can enable an invert to be healthy, self-restrained, and self-respecting, we have often done better than to convert him into the mere feeble simulacrum of a normal man. [. . .]

It should be the function of the law in this matter to prevent violence, to protect the young, and to preserve public order and decency. Whatever laws are laid down beyond this must be left to the individuals themselves, to the moralists and to social opinion.

4

Religion and Belief

Introduction

In Britain, the nineteenth century was a period of feverish religious debates marked by three distinct but interrelated forces: the decline of the established Anglican Church (Church of England), the growth of doubt and secularization, and the emergence of other groups and religious denominations within and outside the Church of England.

At the beginning of the nineteenth century, and as a result of the increase in population in urban areas, the Anglican Church pressed the government to take action over the lack of church accommodation in cities. The result was the 1818 Church Building Act, which secured funds of one million pounds for the building of new churches. An additional half a million was added in 1824, and by 1833, thanks to the involvement of private enterprises, a further six million pounds had been raised. 'There followed,' Andrew Saint has showed, 'a rash of fashionable, competitive church-building with little regard for demand, reaching a perilous climax in the 1860s and 1870s.'[1] Part of the reason for this growth in church building was that the results of the religious census of 1851, the first and last of its kind, showed that 'less than half the population of England had attended any church or chapel at all, and of them, less than half had attended an Anglican Church'.[2] The aim of the census was to assess the religious practices of Victorian Britain by quantifying the Sunday attendances at a place of worship and to determine whether the number of churches and seats were enough for the population. But as its author, Horace Man, suggested, what the census showed was that 'a sadly formidable portion of the English people' were 'habitual neglecters of the public ordinances of religion'.[3] In addition, the census showed the success of Evangelicalism and dramatically demonstrated the challenge to the status of the Anglican Church as the official ecclesiastical body of the state.

One might argue that the publication in 1833 of John Keble's sermon *National Apostasy* (an excerpt from which is included below) marked the begin-

---

1 Andrew Saint, 'Anglican Church-Building in London, 1890–1890: From State Subsidy to the Free Market', in *The Victorian Church: Architecture and Society*, ed. Chris Brooks and Andrew Saint (Manchester: Manchester University Press, 1995), 30.

2 Liza Picard, *Victorian London: The Tale of a City, 1840–1870* (London: St Martin's Press, 2006), 283.

3 Picard, *Victorian London*, 282.

ning of the demise of the Anglican Church, even though it also energized it. John Henry Newman regarded this sermon as the catalyst for the Oxford Movement, so called because its origins lie within Oxford University. The movement's central figures were John Keble, John Henry Newman and Edward Bouverie Pusey, and their aim was to save the Anglican Church 'from both Dissent and secularization'.[4] They issued a series of *Tracts for the Times* with the aim of reviving Anglicanism through a return to the primitive, Early Church. Its doctrines included Baptismal Regeneration, Apostolic Succession and the Real Presence. The movement generated a revival of the Anglican Church, attracting poets such as William Wordsworth and Christina Rossetti and politicians such as William Gladstone. But many accused the Tractarians (as they were also called) of being 'Romish', especially as the movement's liturgical elements reminded them of the Catholic Church. Queen Victoria (head of state and of the Church of England), for example, wrote that she was 'shocked and grieved' to see 'the higher classes and so many of the young clergy tainted with this leaning towards Rome'.[5] The conversion to the Roman Catholic faith of Newman and later of another leading Tractarian, Henry Manning, in 1845 and 1851 respectively, shook the foundations of the Oxford Movement and of the Anglican Church, and as a result reinvigorated the position of Catholicism in Britain.

The publication of Darwin's *On the Origin of Species* in 1859 has often been taken to signify the beginning of doubt and secularization in the nineteenth century (see extracts 10.7 and 10.8). As John Hedley Brooke has put it, Darwin's representation of evolution through 'the image of a branching tree or branching coral, made it difficult to believe in the unfolding of a divine plan'.[6] How to respond to scientific discoveries, and the rationalist, secular mode of post-Enlightenment thinking in general, became an unresolved, focal problem for religion in the nineteenth century. While some believed that science and religion could walk hand in hand (Unitarians), for many others they belonged to different spheres of knowledge. However, the crisis of faith that lay at the heart of Victorian England had its roots not only in science (exemplified by texts such as Darwin's *On the Origins of the Species* and *The Descent of Man*) but also in the emerging tradition of biblical scholarship of Higher Criticism. Christine Krueger argues that 'people with a sense of spiritual vocation, ordained or lay, regardless of denomination, shared one common ground: the Bible'.[7] Yet Higher Criticism, through the pioneering work of D. F. Strauss, Ludwig Feuerbach and Ernest Renan, discredited the infallibility of the Bible (see extract 4.4). Scholars questioned both its divine origin and the historicity of the events in the Old

---

4 Mark Knight and Emma Mason, *Nineteenth-Century Religion and Literature: An Introduction* (Oxford: Oxford University Press, 2006), 90.

5 Quoted in Picard, *Victorian London*, 287.

6 John Hedley Brooke, 'Darwin and Victorian Christianity', in *The Cambridge Companion to Darwin*, ed. Jonathan Hodge and Gregory Radick (Cambridge: Cambridge University Press, 2003), 195.

7 Christine Krueger, 'Clerical', in *A Companion to Victorian Literature and Culture*, ed. Herbert Tucker (Oxford: Blackwell, 1999), 142.

Testament. Their conclusions shook the foundations of Victorian Christianity by challenging its most sacred text, of which the inevitable consequence was a 'crisis of faith'.

The result of such crisis was the increasing visibility and influence in the later part of the nineteenth century of two different but related movements, atheism and agnosticism. Atheism came to the fore through the work of secularist figures like Charles Bradlaugh, who became the first publicly declared atheist to become a Member of Parliament. Agnosticism, however, was not synonymous with atheism. As Herbert Schlossberg explains, 'the agnostic project did not entail the abolition of religion, but the substitute of secular dogmas for the traditional religion'.[8] Agnostics such as T. H. Huxley (who coined the term), W. K. Clifford and Leslie Stephen refused the Theist claim that God was knowable. They asserted instead 'the broadest range of items that [they did] know, including Darwinism as the key to the mysteries of life, the unreliability of the Bible, the untruth of both atheism and a purely mechanistic explanation for life' among others.[9]

Though Victorian England was predominantly a Christian culture, other important religious denominations made their mark in nineteenth-century England. The most important of these was Judaism. At the beginning of the nineteenth century the Jewish population was extremely small. Jews could not enter the university, the army or Parliament. But as the century progressed, new waves of immigration increased the Anglo-Jewish population, culminating with the mass immigration from the pogroms of Eastern Europe in the 1880s and 1890s. Throughout the nineteenth century, the Jewish population eventually increased both in number and in power. Cynthia Scheinberg has argued that in Victorian England the persistence of a 'Jewish identity and belief in the Diaspora' posed 'a problem for Christianity, calling into question the assumed universality of Christian truth'.[10] This was more so the case considering the religious turbulence of these years: the loss of power of the Anglican Church and the rise of Evangelicalism, Catholicism, Darwinism and historical biblical criticism. 'Against this backdrop,' she claims, 'the increased economic and political success of the Jewish community and the very public debates about Jewish political enfranchisement were necessarily causes for Christian scrutiny.'[11] Fighting anti-Semitism, Anglo-Jewish theologians had to keep a difficult balance: to bring to the forefront political and social advancements whilst maintaining and fostering their faith in a predominantly Christian culture.

Just as immigration ensured cross-cultural encounters between the different religious denominations, emigration and, more particularly, British imperialism

---

8 Herbert Schlossberg, *Conflict and Crisis in the Religious Life of Victorian England* (New Brunswick and London: Transaction Publishers, 2009), 262.

9 Ibid., 262.

10 Cynthia Scheinberg, *Women's Poetry and Religion in Victorian England: Jewish Identity and Christian Culture* (Cambridge: Cambridge University Press, 2002), 37.

11 Ibid., 37.

transformed the world-wide religious picture. From one point of view, imperialism opened Victorian Britain to other religions: Buddhism, Hinduism and Islam perhaps being the most significant. But, from another point of view, while in Britain the Anglican Church was experiencing a loss of power, through foreign mission activity, the Anglican Church was transforming itself into a global organization in the name of both Church and state. Missionaries sought to Christianize and civilize; their role in propagating British cultural imperialism is exemplified by the extract from Edward Steere, Bishop of Zanzibar, while the text from William Booth, founder of the Salvation Army, records similar work in the East End of London.

4.1 John Keble, *National Apostasy Considered in a Sermon, Preached in St Mary's Oxford, Before His Majesty's Judges of Assize, on Sunday July 14, 1833* (Oxford: J. H. Parker, 1833)

John Keble (1792–1866) was a leading Church of England clergyman whose importance stems from his position as one of the founders of the Oxford Movement. He was equally well known as a poet, though; his volume of devotional verse, The Christian Year *(1827) is often considered to be the best-selling poetry collection of the nineteenth century (he served as Professor of Poetry at Oxford from 1831 to 1841). Keble wrote his influential 'National Apostasy' sermon (which John Henry Newman regarded as the catalyst for beginning of the Oxford Movement) as a response to the government's act of reducing by ten the number of bishops in Ireland. The sermon uses Jewish history, in particular the Israelites' rejection of theocracy in preference for the establishment of a monarchy, to set up a parallel with the situation in England. Keble fears that Christianity is losing ground and suggests that the current indifference to religion was influenced by the state's intervention in matters of the Church. His attack on the undermining of the Church by the state was founded on his belief in Apostolic Succession, that is, the transference of authority that Christ gave to his Apostles to the current generation of bishops, negating therefore the power of the state in matters of the Church.*

One of the most alarming, as a symptom, is the growing indifference, in which men indulge themselves, to other men's religious sentiments. Under the guise of charity and toleration we are come almost to this pass; *that no difference, in matters of faith, is to disqualify for our approbation and confidence, whether in public or domestic life.* Can we conceal it from ourselves, that every year the practice is becoming more common, of trusting men unreservedly in the most delicate and important matters, without one serious inquiry, whether they do not hold principles which make it impossible for them to be loyal to their CREATOR, REDEEMER, and SANCTIFIER? Are not offices conferred, partnerships formed, intimacies courted, – nay, (what is almost too painful to think of,) do not parents commit their children to be educated, do they not encourage them to intermarry, in houses, on which Apostolical Authority would rather teach them to set a mark, as unfit to be entered by a faithful servant of CHRIST? [. . .]

The point really to be considered is, whether, according to the coolest estimate, the fashionable liberality of this generation be not ascribable, in a great measure, to the same temper which led the Jews voluntarily to set about degrading themselves to a level with the idolatrous Gentiles?[12] And, if it be true any where, that such enactments are forced on the Legislature by public opinion, is APOSTASY too hard a word to describe the temper of that nation? [. . .]

They will have the more reason to suspect themselves, in proportion as they see and feel more of that *impatience under pastoral authority*, which our SAVIOUR Himself has taught us to consider as a never-failing symptom of an unchristian temper. 'He that heareth you, heareth Me; and he that despiseth you, despiseth Me.'[13] Those words of divine truth put beyond all sophistical exception, what common sense would lead us to infer, and what daily experience teaches; – that disrespect to the Successors of the Apostles, *as such*, is an unquestionable symptom of enmity to Him, who gave them their commission at first, and has pledged Himself to be with them for ever. Suppose such disrespect general and national, suppose it also avowedly grounded not on any fancied tenet of religion, but on mere human reasons of popularity and expediency, either there is no meaning at all in these emphatic declarations of our LORD, or that nation, how highly soever she may think of her own religion and morality, stands convicted in His sight of a direct disavowal of His Sovereignty.

To this purpose it may be worth noticing, that the ill-fated chief, whom GOD gave to the Jews,[14] as the prophet tells us, in His anger,[15] and whose disobedience and misery were referred by himself to his 'fearing the people, and obeying their voice',[16] whose conduct, therefore, may be fairly taken as a sample of what public opinion was at that time supposed to require, – his first step in apostasy was an intrusion on the sacrificial office,[17] as the last and greatest of his crimes was persecuting David, whom he well knew to bear GOD's special commission.[18] GOD forbid, that any Christian land should ever, by her prevailing temper and policy, revive the memory and likeness of Saul, or incur a sentence of reprobation like his. But if such a thing should be, the crimes of that nation will probably begin in infringement on Apostolical Rights; she will end in persecuting the true Church; and in the several stages of her melancholy career, she will contin-

---

12 A non-Jew, Keble draws here a parallel between the Jews' rejection of God's prophets to lead the country and their insistence on wanting a king, with disastrous consequences, and the situation of Britain, where the state rules over matters of the Church.

13 *Original Note:* Luke x. 16.

14 Israel was governed by judges, but the Israelites, disobeying God, demanded a king to defend themselves from their enemies. Saul was crowned as King of the Israelites but he failed to carry out God's instructions as spoken by the prophet Samuel.

15 *Original Note:* Hos. xiii. 11.

16 *Original Note:* 1 Sam. xv. 24.

17 *Original Note:* 1 Sam. xiii. 8–14.

18 King Saul mistrusted David (of David and Goliath fame) and attempted to kill him.

ually be led on from bad to worse by vain endeavours at accommodation and compromise with evil. Sometimes *toleration* may be the word, as with Saul when he spared the Amalekites;[19] sometimes *state security*, as when he sought the life of David; sometimes *sympathy with popular feeling*, as appears to have been the case, when violating solemn treaties, he attempted to exterminate the remnant of the Gibeonites,[20] in his zeal for the children of Israel and Judah.[21] Such are the sad but obvious results of separating religious resignation altogether from men's notions of civil duty.

4.2 Thomas Arnold, 'Sermon III', *Christian Life, Its Course, Its Hindrances, and Its Helps: Sermons, Preached Mostly in the Chapel of Rugby School* (London: B. Fellowes, 1841)

Thomas Arnold (1795–1842) became headmaster of Rugby School in 1828. A member of the liberal 'Broad Church' and a champion of learning, Arnold's educational reforms transformed Rugby into 'a by-word for "serious" education, in which moral tone and a sense of demanding vocation in life were the pre-eminent goals'.[22] His aim was to instil a sense of discipline and Christian duty into his pupils. The text reproduced here, from Sermon III, presents the basis of what came to be known as 'Christian manliness', which was popularized by Thomas Hughes, a former pupil, in his influential novel Tom Brown's Schooldays *(1857). In Victorian Britain, the male body was often perceived as a site of struggle for the control of bodily desires. Arnold, Charles Kingsley and Hughes, by contrast, emphasized the importance of the body to Christian life. Boys developed into Christian moral men through muscular and physical activities.*

It is seen, that some young men of great ambition, or remarkable love of knowledge, do really injure their health, and exhaust their minds, by an excess of early study. I always grieve over such cases exceedingly; not only for the individual's sake who is the sufferer, but also for the mischievous effect of his example. It affords a pretence to others to justify their own want of exertion; and those to whom it is in reality the least dangerous, are always the very persons who seem to dread it the most. But we should clearly understand, that this excess of intellectual exertion at an early age, is by no means the same thing with hastening the change from childishness to manliness. We are all enough aware, in common life, that a very clever and forward boy may be, in his conduct, exceeding childish, that those whose talents and book-knowledge are by no means remarkable, may be, in their conduct, exceedingly manly. Examples of both

---

19 Enemies of the Jews. Saul disobeyed God and allowed their King Agag to live.

20 Saul broke a covenant by which the Gibeonites were condemned to perpetual protection and instead massacred them.

21 *Original Note*: 2 Sam. xxi. 2.

22 John Tosh, *Manliness and Masculinities in Nineteenth-Century Britain* (New York: Pearson Education, 2005), 84.

these truths instantly present themselves to my memory, and perhaps may do so to some of yours. I may say farther, that some whose change from childhood to manhood had been, in St Paul's sense of the terms, the most remarkably advanced, were so far from being distinguished for their cleverness or proficiency in their school-work, that it would almost seem as if their only remaining childishness had been displayed there. What I mean, therefore, by the change from childhood to manhood, is altogether distinct from a premature advance in book-knowledge, and involves in it nothing of that over-study which is dreaded as so injurious. [. . .]

Or, if we turn to the third point of change from childhood to a Christian manhood, the change from selfishness to unselfishness, neither can we find any possible danger in hastening this. This cannot hurt our health or strain our faculties; it can but make life at every age more peaceful and more happy. Nor indeed do I suppose that any one could fancy that such a change was otherwise than wholesome at the earliest possible period.

There may remain, however, a vague notion, that, generally, if what we mean by an early change from childishness to manliness be that we should become religious, then, although it may not exhaust the powers, or injure the health, yet it would destroy the natural liveliness and gaiety of youth, and by bringing on a premature seriousness of manner and language, would be unbecoming and ridiculous. Now, in the first place, there is a great deal of confusion and a great deal of folly in the common notions of the gaiety of youth. If gaiety mean real happiness of mind, I do not believe that there is more of it in youth than in manhood; if for this reason only, that the temper in youth being commonly not yet brought into good order, irritation and passion are felt, probably, oftener than in after life, and these are sad drawbacks, as we all know, to a real cheerfulness of mind. And of the outward gaiety of youth, there is a part also which is like the gaiety of a drunken man; which is riotous, insolent, and annoying to others; which, in short, is a folly and a sin. There remains that which strictly belongs to youth, partly physically – the lighter step and the livelier movement of the growing and vigorous body; partly from circumstances, because a young person's parents or friends stand between him and many of the cares of life, and protect him from feeling them altogether; partly from the abundance of hope which belongs to the beginning of every thing, and which continually hinders the mind from dwelling on past pain. And I know not which of these causes of gaiety would be taken away or lessened by the earlier change from childhood to manhood. True it is, that the question, 'What must I do to be saved?' is a grave one, and must be considered seriously; but I do not suppose that any one proposes that a young person should never be serious at all. True it is, again, that if we are living in folly and sin, this question may be a painful one; we might be gayer for a time without it. But, then, the matter is, what is to become of us if we do not think of being saved? – shall we be saved without thinking of it? And what is it to be not saved but lost? I cannot pretend to say that the thought of God would not very much disturb the peace and gaiety of an ungodly and sinful mind; that it would not interfere with the mirth of the bully, or the drunkard, or the reveller, or the glutton, or the idler, or the fool. It would, no doubt; just as the hand that was seen to write on the wall threw a gloom over the guests at Belshazzar's festival. I never meant or mean to say, that the thought of God, or that God himself, can be other than a plague to those who do not love Him. The thought of Him is their plague here; the sight of Him will be their judgment for ever. But I suppose the point is, whether the thought of Him would cloud the gaiety of those who were striving to please Him. It would cloud it as much, and be just as unwelcome and no more, as will be the very actual presence of our Lord to the righteous, when they shall see Him as He is. Can that which we know to be able to make old age, and sickness, and poverty, many times full of comfort, – can that make youth and health gloomy? When to natural cheerfulness and sanguineness, are added a consciousness of God's ever present care, and a knowledge of his rich promises, are we likely to be the more sad or the more unhappy?

What reason, then, is there for any one's not anticipating the common progress of Christian manliness, and hastening to exchange, as I said before, ignorance for wisdom, selfishness for unselfishness, carelessness for thoughtfulness?

4.3 Grace Aguilar, *The Spirit of Judaism*, ed. Isaac Leeser (Philadelphia: 1842)

Grace Aguilar (1816–47) is the most important Anglo-Jewish writer of the early to mid-nineteenth century. In a prolific but short career as a poet, novelist, theologian and religious reformer, her writings brought to the fore her unique position as a Jewish woman in Victorian Britain. She argued for both Jews' emancipation in Victorian England and women's emancipation in the Jewish world. The Spirit of Judaism was first published in America in 1842, edited by Isaac Leeser, who, without her consent, introduced footnotes when his views were in conflict with Aguilar's (as the long footnote at the end of this excerpt demonstrates). The book was extremely well received by Jews and Christians in England and across the Atlantic. It advocates English tolerance towards the Jewish community and religion while also emphasizing the need for Jewish religious reform. The text reproduced below reveals how Aguilar felt about and dealt with what was perhaps the key issue for the Jewish community in nineteenth-century Britain: assimilation.

To the mothers of every faith and every class these hints may be equally applicable; but to Jewish mothers more particularly. We have but to study the Book of Life, and every history of our nation: and we shall not fail to perceive that the religion Moses taught was intended to unite the thought of God with our every action. If a Christian writer finds sufficient foundation for the assertion that 'there can be no half measures in devotion, religion must be *all* or nothing:' how much more powerfully should *we* feel it, we – who are a peculiar people, the first-born of the Lord, thus called by the Eternal Himself, and therefore absolutely *set apart*, to exalt by our conduct His glory amidst the nations. It is urged perhaps, our situation is not now what it was, that it does not depend on us alone, 'to magnify the Lord', that we are but as a handful amidst the nations that now worship Him; yet this fact in no way decreases our responsibility. It is rather increased; for it was easy to divide the worship of the one true God from idolatry, – many civil as well as religious customs did this; but now mingling intimately with the nations that worship God, though not as we do, living under the same civil jurisdiction, acknowledging the same sovereign: unless the adherence to the laws of Moses be even more exact, it is more than likely our nationality would be entirely lost, as well as all pride, all glory in the Hebrew faith.

To prevent this great evil should be the Hebrew mother's aim. The youngest child may be taught that he is a member of a distinct and peculiar nation. The great mercies and unchanging love of the Lord will, if well related, find very early an answering chord in the youthful heart. The wonderful providence, the stupendous miracles, the innumerable instances of our Father's long suffering and loving kindness, which our eventful history records, might be related as interesting tales in those many leisure hours that the child looks up so clingingly and fondly to his mother for amusement. Vividly and interestingly might these narratives be opened to the young and eager mind, till almost insensibly he feels it a privilege, even at this long lapse of years, to belong to a nation so peculiarly blessed, so singularly the object of God's gracious providence; and that false shame, now alas, but too familiar to the Hebrew, would never flush the cheek, or lead the tongue to falsehood. [. . .]

There is yet another most important reason for impressing carefully and deeply the awful sins of Israel on the youthful Hebrew. He sees the present degraded and wandering state of his nation; he perceives our condition is widely different from that of other kingdoms; he is ready to feel and acknowledge we are cast off from the favour of the Lord, that His countenance is for ever darkened towards us; and if he have not been instructed in the cause of this, if he have not studied long and deeply the history of his nation and read there, – in our continued rebellions, apostasy, transgressions as varied as they are innumerable, disobedience to every given law, – the *real* and *only* origin of our dispersions and fearful sufferings: he is quite prepared to embrace the creed of the Christian, and believe with him, that all our miseries originate in our rejection of their messiah, that the Eternal has cast us off because, according to the creed and charge of the Christian, we crucified His son.*

* [Isaac Leeser] *Original note:* Without the least intention of weakening the force of the evil depicted as arising from the want of a Jewish education, exhibited in the text, I cannot help remarking that the non-adoption of our system by no means opens the way for the embracing of Christianity. It is possible that there are some, for argument's sake I will say many, who are so struck by the pretended fulfilment of the gospel prediction with regard to our dispersion, as to admit the truth of the dogmas embraced in the new testament. But for a philosophical mind, or one well versed in Scripture, such a result must seem very singular. [. . .]

[T]his much we may assert without fear of offending our Christian friends, or of asserting an untruth, that *legitimate* convictions or where the converts can give a reasonable account of the reasons which sway them for the abandonment of Judaism, are very rare indeed; or else we should not hear so frequently of recantations, or returnings to the fold of Israel. – I say again we need not fear conversions as much as hypocrisy or indifference. Many may pretend to a change of religion for the sake of a tangible advantage, such as office, high-standing, or an advantageous matrimonial connexion; but we have yet to learn that persons acquainted with Scripture, who have enjoyed the benefits of a Jewish education in ever so moderate a degree, could by any possibility be induced to adopt the doctrine of a trinity with the accessory belief in a mediator. We do not deny nor gainsay that Christians of late have had a plentiful harvest of apostates; but they were apostates in very deed, apostates – deniers of their God for worldly gain. Solitary exceptions may perhaps be adduced; but they will be found to proceed from the individual's having been always under Christian tuition or exposed through ignorance to some unfortunate influence of friends who took advantage of moments of weakness to urge their views with a success which they themselves could hardly have expected at another time. – So well are European governments, anxious as they are from political purposes to consolidate their empire over the minds of all their subjects no less than their bodies, convinced of the uselessness of mere preaching, that they attach political advantages in some shape or other as bribes or bounties for conversions; no doubt under the persuasion, that though the parents will make bad Christians, the children will be like those of other Christians, that is believers in the popular system from the ignorance of the principles and hopes of the Jewish faith. Hence it is that, though we hear much of conversions to Christianity in Prussia, Poland, and England, such events are extremely rare in France, Holland, and America, and unheard of in the Ottoman countries. In the catholic countries of Spain and her former colonies, the Jew hides his religion; under governments where he is free to act as he pleases he cares for no belief if he values not his own. Let the experiment be made of treating Jews and converts alike, and but few of the latter will ever be obtained. Interest is a powerful stimulus, but conscientious conviction a thing of slow growth, too slow indeed to convert a Jew into any thing else. The same is also the case with the reverse; Christians by education are not apt to see error in their creed; our views to the contrary notwithstanding. Hence Miss A. says truly in urging mutual charity and forbearance whilst enforcing steadfastness in the path we have been pursuing from the time of Moses to our own days. – I. L.

4.4 Ernest Renan, *The Life of Jesus* (1863; London: Trübner and Co., 1864)

Ernest Renan (1823–92) began training for a life serving the Church but was led to question the orthodoxies of the Catholic Church by his interest in the sciences. He gained a doctorate in philosophy and subsequently studied philology and religion, trav-

elling to the Holy Land. He achieved high scholarly distinction in the study of Semitic languages. These studies led him to a view of religion as fundamentally material and historical: this perspective is evident in the extract below. Renan published numerous works before his death after a brief illness in 1892, including The Life of Jesus *(the first volume of* The History of the Origins of Christianity*),* History of the People of Israel *and* Recollections of My Youth. *Highly respected in France, Renan was elected to the Académie Française in 1878.*

La Vie de Jesus *(1863) was a hugely influential publication; it continued with the tradition of Higher Criticism of German biblical scholars such as Frederick Strauss, but Renan's emphasis on a naturalistic, non-miraculous life of Jesus marked a departure from these works. Renan's biography accepted Jesus's historical existence but denied his divinity; he rejected the dogma that Jesus was the son of God and argued that 'miracles are things which never happen, and, therefore, things which Jesus never did'. The Life of Jesus was an instant sensation; it sold more than 60,000 copies within six months and was soon translated into more than 10 languages (the first English translation by Charles Wilbour was published in 1864). But it also received fierce criticism from the Church; Pope Pius XI described him as 'the European blasphemer'. A second controversial element in Renan's work was his negative characterization of Jewishness in terms of both religion and race. Judaism was criticized as stultifying and inferior to Christianity, while Renan's corresponding portrayal of Jesus's development from Jew to Christian was highly charged, considering Europe was debating Jewish emancipation.*

From Chapter XXVIII. Essential Character of the Work of Jesus

Jesus, it will be seen, limited his action entirely to the Jews. Although his sympathy for those despised by orthodoxy led him to admit pagans into the kingdom of God, – although he had resided more than once in a pagan country, and once or twice we surprise him in kindly relations with unbelievers,[23] – it may be said that his life was passed entirely in the very restricted world in which he was born. He was never heard of in Greek or Roman countries; his name appears only in profane authors of a hundred years later, and then in an indirect manner, in connection with seditious movements provoked by his doctrine, or persecutions of which his disciples were the object.[24] Even on Judaism, Jesus made no very durable impression. Philo,[25] who died about the year 50, had not the slightest knowledge of him. Josephus,[26] born in the year 37, and writing in the last years of the century, mentions his execution in a few lines,[27] as an event of secondary importance, and in the enumeration of the sects of his time, he omits the Christians altogether.[28] In the *Mishnah*,[29] also, there is no trace of the

---

23 *Original Note*: Matt. viii. 5, and following; Luke vii. 1, and following; John xii. 20, and following. Comp. Jos., *Ant.*, XVIII. iii. 3.

24 *Original Note*: Tacitus, *Ann.*, XV. 45; Suetonius, *Claudius*, 25.

25 Philo of Alexandria, a Hellenistic Jewish philosopher.

26 First-century Jewish philosopher.

27 *Original Note*: *Ant.* XVIII. iii. 3. This passage has been altered by a Christian hand.

28 *Original Note*: *Ant.* XVIII. i.; *B.J.*, II. viii.; *Vita*, 2.

29 The first major written transcription of the 'Oral Torah' (or the 'Oral Law').

new school; the passages in the two Gemaras[30] in which the founder of Christianity is named, do not go further back than the fourth or fifth century.[31] The essential work of Jesus was to create around him a circle of disciples, whom he inspired with boundless affection, and amongst whom he deposited the germ of his doctrine. To have made himself beloved, 'to the degree that after his death they ceased not to love him', was the great work of Jesus, and that which most struck his contemporaries.[32] His doctrine was so little dogmatic, that he never thought of writing it or of causing it to be written. Men did not become his disciples by believing this thing or that thing, but in being attached to his person and in loving him. A few sentences collected from memory, and especially the type of character he set forth, and the impression it had left, were what remained of him. Jesus was not a founder of dogmas, or a maker of creeds; he infused into the world a new spirit. The least Christian men were, on the one hand, the doctors of the Greek Church, who, beginning from the fourth century, entangled Christianity in a path of puerile metaphysical discussions, and, on the other, the scholastics of the Latin Middle Ages, who wished to draw from the Gospel the thousands of articles of a colossal system. To follow Jesus in expectation of the kingdom of God, was all that at first was implied by being Christian.

It will thus be understood how, by an exceptional destiny, pure Christianity still preserves, after eighteen centuries, the character of a universal and eternal religion. It is, in fact, because the religion of Jesus is in some respects the final religion. [. . .]

'Christianity' has thus become almost a synonym of 'religion'. All that is done outside of this great and good Christian tradition is barren. Jesus gave religion to humanity, as Socrates gave it philosophy, and Aristotle science. There was philosophy before Socrates and science before Aristotle. Since Socrates and since Aristotle, philosophy and science have made immense progress; but all has been built upon the foundation which they laid. In the same way, before Jesus, religious thought had passed through many revolutions; since Jesus, it has made great conquests: but no one has improved, and no one will improve upon the essential principle Jesus has created; he has fixed for ever the idea of pure worship. The religion of Jesus in this sense is not limited. The Church has had its epochs and its phases; it has shut itself up in creeds which are, or will be but temporary: but Jesus has founded the absolute religion, excluding nothing, and determining nothing unless it be the spirit. His creeds are not fixed dogmas, but images susceptible of indefinite interpretations. We should seek in vain for a theological proposition in the Gospel. All

---

30 Critical commentaries and analysis of the *Mishnah*.

31 *Original Note*: Talm. of Jerusalem, *Sanhedrim*, xiv. 16; *Aboda zara*, ii, 2; *Shabbath*, xiv, 4; Talm. of Babylon, *Sanhedrim*, 43*a*, 67*a*; *Shabbath*, 104*b*. 116*b*. Comp. *Chagiga*, 4*b*; *Gittin*, 57*a*, 90*a*. The two Gemarans derive the greater part of their data concerning Jesus from a burlesque and obscene legend, invented by the adversaries of Christianity, and of no historical value.

32 *Original Note*: Jos., *Ant.*, XVIII. iii. 3.

confessions of faith are travesties of the idea of Jesus, just as the scholasticism of the middle ages, in proclaiming Aristotle the sole master of a completed science, perverted the thought of Aristotle. Aristotle, if he had been present in the debates of the schools, would have repudiated this narrow doctrine; he would have been of the party of progressive science against the routine which shielded itself under his authority; he would have applauded his opponents. In the same way, if Jesus were to return among us, he would recognize as disciples, not those who pretend to enclose him entirely in a few catechismal phrases, but those who labour to carry on his work. The eternal glory, in all great things, is to have laid the first stone. It may be that in the 'Physics', and in the 'Meteorology' of modern times, we may not discover a word of the treatises of Aristotle which bear these titles; but Aristotle remains no less the founder of natural science. Whatever may be the transformations of dogma, Jesus will ever be the creator of the pure spirit of religion; the Sermon on the Mount will never be surpassed. Whatever revolution takes place will not prevent us attaching ourselves in religion to the grand intellectual and moral line at the head of which shines the name of Jesus. In this sense we are Christians, even when we separate ourselves on almost all points from the Christian tradition which has preceded us. [. . .]

Is it more just to say that Jesus owes all to Judaism, and that his greatness is only that of the Jewish people? No one is more disposed than myself to place high this unique people, whose particular gift seems to have been to contain in its midst the extremes of good and evil. No doubt, Jesus proceeded from Judaism; but he proceeded from it as Socrates proceeded from the schools of the Sophists, as Luther proceeded from the Middle Ages, as Lamennais from Catholicism, as Rousseau from the eighteenth century. A man is of his age and his race even when he reacts against his age and his race. Far from Jesus having continued Judaism, he represents the rupture with the Jewish spirit. The general direction of Christianity after him does not permit the supposition that his idea in this respect could lead to any misunderstanding. The general march of Christianity has been to remove itself more and more from Judaism. It will become perfect in returning to Jesus, but certainly not in returning to Judaism. The great originality of the founder remains then undiminished; his glory admits no legitimate sharer.

Doubtless, circumstances much aided the success of this marvelous revolution; but circumstances only second that which is just and true. Each branch of the development of humanity has its privileged epoch, in which it attains perfection by a sort of spontaneous instinct, and without effort. No labour of reflection would succeed in producing afterwards the masterpieces which nature creates at those moments by inspired geniuses. That which the golden age of Greece was for arts and literature, the age of Jesus was for religion.

4.5 Iconoclast [Charles Bradlaugh], 'A Plea for Atheism', *Two Nights' Discussion, Between Thomas Cooper and Charles Bradlaugh, On the Being of a God as the Maker and Moral Governor of the Universe, to which is added, A Plea For Atheism* (London: Austin and Co., 1864)

A member of a number of radical groups, amongst them the Reform League, Land Law Reformers and Secularists, Charles Bradlaugh (1833–91) was an outspoken atheist and a prominent republican. In 1860 he became the editor of the National Reformer, *a periodical considered so radical that in 1868 it was prosecuted by the government on charges of blasphemy and sedition. Bradlaugh was undeterred and continued to publish works such as James Thomson's* The City of Dreadful Night, *first published in 1874 in its pages. With Annie Besant in 1876, he reissued a pamphlet by Charles Knowlton that advocated birth control,* The Fruits of Philosophy, or the Private Companion of Young Married Couples. *They were both prosecuted for obscenity (Charles Darwin refused to give evidence in their defence). In 1866, he also founded, and became the first president of, the National Secular Society. Bradlaugh was elected as a Member of Parliament in 1880; however, although he offered to take the Oath of Allegiance as a formality (he was an atheist), this was against the law and he was forced to forfeit his seat. It was not until 1886, following a series of challenges by Bradlaugh and his supporters, that the law was changed; he was finally permitted to take his seat in Parliament. A new Oaths Act of 1888 allowed MPs to solemnly affirm their allegiance to the Crown rather than swearing it to God.*

If you speak to the Atheist of God as creator, he answers that the conception of creation is impossible. We are utterly unable to construe it in thought as possible that the complement of existence has been either increased or diminished, much less can we conceive an absolute origination of substance. We cannot conceive either, on the one hand, nothing becoming something, or on the other, something becoming nothing. The Theist who speaks of God creating the universe must either suppose that Deity evolved it out of himself, or that he produced it from nothing. But the Theist cannot regard the universe as evolution of Deity, because this would identify Universe and Deity, and be Pantheism rather than Theism. There would be no distinction of substance – in fact no creation. Nor can the Theist regard the universe as created out of nothing, because Deity is, according to him, necessarily eternal and infinite. His existence being eternal and infinite, precludes the possibility of the conception of vacuum to be filled by the universe if created. No one can even think of any point in extent or duration and say, here is the point of separation between the creator and the created. Indeed, it is not possible for the Theist to imagine a beginning to the universe. It is not possible to conceive either an absolute commencement, or an absolute termination of existence; that is, it is impossible to conceive beginning before which you have a period when the universe has yet to be; or to conceive an end, after which the universe, having been, no longer exists. It is impossible in thought to originate or annihilate the universe. The Atheist affirms that he cognises to-day effects; that these are at the same time, causes and effects – causes to the effects they precede, effects to the causes they follow. Cause is simply everything without which the effect would not result, and with which it must result. Cause is the means to an end, consummating itself in that end. The Theist who argues for creation must assert a point of time that is, of duration, when the created did not yet exist. At this point of time either something existed or nothing; but something must have existed, for out of nothing nothing can come. Something must have existed, because the point fixed upon is that of the duration of something. This something must have been either finite or infinite; if finite it could not have been God, and if the something were infinite, then creation was impossible: it is impossible to add to infinite existence. [. . .]

While Theism, asserting God as the creator and governor of the universe, hinders and checks man's efforts by declaring God's will to be the sole directing and controlling power, Atheism, by declaring all events to be in accordance with natural laws – that is, happening in certain ascertainable sequences – stimulates man to discover the best conditions of life, and offers him the most powerful inducements to morality. While the Theist provides future happiness for a scoundrel repentant on his death-bed, Atheism affirms present and certain happiness for the man who does his best to live here so well as to have little cause for repenting hereafter.

Theism declares that God dispenses health and inflicts disease, and sickness and illness are regarded by the Theist as visitations from an angered Deity, to be borne with meekness and content. Atheism declares that physiological knowledge may preserve us from disease by preventing our infringing the law of health, and that sickness results not as the ordinance of offended Deity, but from ill-ventilated dwellings and workshops, bad and insufficient food, excessive toil, mental suffering, exposure to inclement weather, and the like – all these finding root in poverty, the chief source of crime and disease; that prayers and piety afford no protection against fever, and that if the human being be kept without food he will starve as quickly whether he be Theist or Atheist, theology being no substitute for bread.

4.6 John Henry Newman, *Apologia Pro Vita Sua: Being a Reply to a Pamphlet Entitled 'What, Then, Does Dr. Newman Mean?'* (London: Longman, Green, Longman, Roberts and Green, 1864)

A Fellow of Oriel College, Oxford, and a minister at the University's Church, St Mary, John Henry Newman (1801–90) found that his fascination with the ancient Catholic Church led him to question why many of its doctrines, such as the sacramental system and the Apostolic succession, had been abandoned by Anglicans. In 1833, with the support of fellow Oxford scholars John Keble and Edward Bouverie Pusey, he set out to restore ancient doctrines that had been gradually abandoned by the Anglican Church.

The group became known as the Oxford Movement and, alternatively, as the Tractarians following their publication of Tracts for the Times *(1833–41). But many regarded these tracts as 'Romish corruptions' of the Gospel. As the Anglican Church began to disapprove of their teaching, many began to convert to Catholicism. In 1841, Newman published Tract Ninety, in which he explained that the Thirty-Nine Articles, the foundation of the Anglican Church, should be read in the most Catholic sense. Dramatically, in 1845, he converted to Roman Catholicism.* Apologia Pro Vita Sua *(A Defence of One's Life) is one of the most significant religious texts of the nineteenth century. Its publication stems from a famous public controversy between Charles Kingsley and Newman. In an article in* Macmillan's Magazine *in 1864, Kingsley, whose anti-Catholic views were evident from his novels, accused Newman and Catholic clergy in general of disregarding the truth. In response, Newman decided to write an autobiographical account that rationally justified his conversion into Roman Catholicism.*

In 1843, I took two very important and significant steps: – 1. In February, I made a formal Retractation of all the hard things which I had said against the Church of Rome. 2. In September, I resigned the Living of St. Mary's, Littlemore inclusive: – I will speak of these two acts separately.

1. The words, in which I made my Retractation, have given rise to much criticism. After quoting a number of passages from my writings against the Church of Rome, which I withdrew, I ended thus: – 'If you ask me how an individual could venture, not simply to hold, but to publish such views of a communion so ancient, so wide-spreading, so fruitful in Saints, I answer that I said to myself, "I am not speaking my own words, I am but following almost a *consensus* of the divines of my own Church. They have ever used the strongest language against Rome, even the most able and learned of them. I wish to throw myself into their system. While I say what they say, I am safe. Such views, too, are necessary for our position." Yet I have reason to fear still, that such language is to be ascribed, in no small measure, to an impetuous temper, a hope of approving myself to persons I respect, and a wish to repel the charge of Romanism.'

These words have been, and are, cited again and again against me, as if a confession that, when in the Anglican Church, I said things against Rome which I did not really believe.

For myself, I cannot understand how any impartial man can so take them; and I have explained them in print several times. I trust that by this time they have been sufficiently explained by what I have said in former portions of this narrative; still I have a word or two to say about them, which I have not said before. I apologized in the lines in question for saying out charges against the Church of Rome which I fully believed to be true. What is wonderful in such an apology?

There are many things a man may hold, which at the same time he may feel that he has no right to say publicly. The law recognizes this principle. In our own time, men have been imprisoned and fined for saying true things of a bad king. The maxim has been held, that, 'The greater the truth, the greater is the libel.' And so as to the judgment of society, a just indignation would be felt against a writer who brought forward wantonly the weaknesses of a great man, though the whole world knew that they existed. No one is at liberty to speak ill of another without a justifiable reason, even though he knows he is speaking truth, and the public knows it too. Therefore, I could not speak ill against the Church of Rome, though I believed what I said, without a good reason. I did believe what I said; but had I a good reason for saying it? I thought I had; viz. I said what I believed was simply necessary in the controversy, in order to defend ourselves; I considered that the Anglican position could not be defended, without bringing charges against the Church of Rome. Is not this almost a truism? is it not what every one says, who speaks on the subject at all? does any serious man abuse the Church of Rome, for the sake of abusing her, or because it justifies his own religious position? What is the meaning of the very word 'Protestantism', but that there is a call to speak out? This then is what I said; 'I know I spoke strongly against the Church of Rome; but it was no mere abuse, for I had a serious reason for doing so.' [. . .]

But there was a far deeper reason for my saying what I said in this matter, on which I have not hitherto touched; and it was this: – The most oppressive thought, in the whole process of my change of opinion, was the clear anticipation, verified by the event, that it would issue in the triumph of Liberalism. Against the Anti-dogmatic principle I had thrown my whole mind; yet now I was doing more than any one else could do, to promote it. I was one of those who had kept it at bay in Oxford for so many years; and thus my very retirement was its triumph. The men who had driven me from Oxford were distinctly the Liberals; it was they who had opened the attack upon Tract 90, and it was they who would gain a second benefit, if I went on to retire from the Anglican Church. But this was not all. As I have already said, there are but two alternatives, the way to Rome, and the way to Atheism: Anglicanism is the halfway house on the one side, and Liberalism is the halfway house on the other. How many men were there, as I knew full well, who would not follow me now in my advance from Anglicanism to Rome, but would at once leave Anglicanism and me for the Liberal camp.

4.7 Rev. R. M. Heanley, *A Memoir of Edward Steere, D.D., LL.D.: Third Missionary Bishop in Central Africa* (London: George Bell and Sons, 1888)

In 1857, the explorer David Livingstone, in a series of lectures at the universities of Oxford and Cambridge, appealed to graduates and undergraduates to go to Africa as missionaries. He declared he was going back to Africa 'to make an open path for commerce and Christianity' and encouraged his audience to follow his example. The universities' direct response was the creation of 'The Universities' Mission to Central

Africa'. As Rev. Henry Rowley put it in one of the first histories of the movement (The Story of the Universities' Mission to Central Africa, *1866), the object was to estab-lish outposts in central Africa 'which would serve as centres of Christianity and civili-sation, for the promotion of true religion, the encouragement of agriculture and lawful commerce, and the ultimate extinction of the slave trade'. The first mission was led by Bishop Charles Mackenzie, who died of malaria only one year after his placement (1862), and later by William George Tozer. Edward Steere (1828–82) succeeded Tozer as Bishop of Zanzibar in 1874. Steere had arrived in Zanzibar in 1864 and immedi-ately began to learn the local language, Swahili. He set up a printing press and published a number of works including his celebrated* Handbook of the Swahili Language as Spoken in Zanzibar *and* Swahili Tales *(in the original language with English translations). His ultimate aim was to publish the first Bible in Swahili. The extract below is from a memoir of Steere's life and work, which drew copiously on his letters home. It provides an insightful account of the Anglican Church's encounter with Islam in Africa and gives an important account of the religious debates taking place in Africa itself. (See also Section 9 for further accounts of the range of British imperial activity.)*

We are bound to add, that our gratitude for the past cannot blind us to the truth that our Church and nation have not yet risen up to the true recognition of the value of the Universities' Mission as the best agent of civilizing and Christianizing the peoples and nations with which it comes in contact in the dark continent.

What though, when Bishop Steere sank to his last rest, he left behind him thirty-four European helpers, as well as a large force of native Christians to carry on the work to which, with one fellow helper and five starving slave boys, he had eighteen years before set his hand? What though, at the present time, Bishop Smythies has a staff of sixty-two Europeans, and some twenty-five native catechists and school-teachers? It is but a poor instalment of the debt that England owes to Africa, and a very inadequate occupation of the opportunities still open to her of repaying it.

England may have forgotten, but the African only too well remembers, the English pirates, who came to prey upon the Portuguese commerce, and left behind them no honourable memory of Englishmen and Christians. After them came slave-dealers of every nation, but the most eager of them our own coun-trymen, all professing the utmost benevolence, seeking only to get the people, and most of all their children, into their power, and then they fastened them below hatches and sailed away. Here is an evil name that has been most justly earned, a long series of evil doings which have to be atoned for. Surely an Englishman and a Christian cannot rest under such a burden as this. Many thousand Africans have died in miserable slavery in order that Englishmen might make fortunes and build up families; and if we could but realize the debt that we owe them and give but one tithe of English lives for the lives that Africa has given us, we should send out missionaries, not by twos or threes, but by hundreds and thousands. So might we hope to wipe out the reproaches of the past, and show these nations that Christianity is something better than a hollow name.

Again, in Central Africa *we are fighting against time*. On all sides we are met by signs that the stagnation of Africa is past. The various trading, exploring, and missionary expeditions that have penetrated into all parts of Central Africa, have opened the eyes of the natives to their ignorance, backwardness, and weakness. Even the very antagonism of the Mohammedans to Christianity has done good in its way, by arousing the natives out of their lethargic state with regard to religion, and making them enquire into the differences between Christianity and Islam. The whole future of Central Africa is trembling in the balance. The Africans will not remain as they are; they are seeking for a religion, and they will have one. They are calling to England for teachers, even begging for men to teach them the faith of Christ. The false faith of Islam is at their door, they have not yet accepted it, but if through lack of men with the apostolic spirit, the English Church is unable to answer their appeal for missionaries, they have no alterative, they must accept Islam, and in all probability be lost to Christianity, civilization and freedom for ever. For, as so unbiased a witness as Mr Palgrave wrote in the 'Cornhill Magazine' for August, 1878, 'Sooner or later the nation that casts in its lot with Islam is stricken as by a blight; its freshness, its plasticity, disappear first, then its reparative and reproductive power, and it petrifies or perishes.'[33] [. . .]

It remains to speak of the Bishop's evidence as to the true nature of the spread of Mohammedism among the natives of East Africa.

Writing to the Home Committee of the Mission in 1876, he said of the 'Shambala' tribes:

> The more thoughtful have unavoidably looked hitherto to the coast Mohammedans as the only people who had a religion to give them. The coast people baptize them by dipping in a river, give them Arab names, charge them not to drink palm wine, not to eat pork or the meat of any animal not slaughtered with the invocation of God's name, teach them an Arabic formula or two, fix them in the professed belief of one only God, and leave them all their old charms and superstitions. The best taught learn very little, and seldom understand what they learn.
>
> It is especially acceptable to the natives as giving them a recognized civilization. One can see in a moment what an immense social advantage it is to be admitted into such a community. A Mohammedan feels himself at once a man; the rest, as the Zanzibar men say of the negroes, are merely like sheep and oxen. The grand kind of Freemasonry of Mohammedanism, especially valuable to merchants and travellers, helps to win it acceptance with Africans and the Malays.

---

33 *Original Note*: Archdeacon Farler, 'Christ in Central Africa', p. 8.

But with many, their nearer acquaintance with Mohammedans has bred no liking for them. The greediness and treachery of the coastmen and the open violence they use when they dare, give great point to the objection to their religion generally, that it tries to prove itself by mere brute force. Those who go in terror of their lives and liberties from the Mohammedans can understand that a prophet of God should come with some other message than a sword.

I heard myself a Mohammedan who was vapouring about their achievements in war silenced by the answer that there was war enough in the world before without God sending a prophet to teach men to kill one another. A series of ready answers to Mohammedan cavils and self-recommendations is a necessity wherever traders go, and most of all among natives who are conscious of their old inferiority and want to get civilized connections by the easiest road. Some, as for instance, that the enjoyments promised to the blessed in Paradise are exactly what are condemned on earth as sins, are obvious enough. Others need more elaboration, and we hope to get out a series of tractlets in Swahili, in Arabic characters, which will be valuable along the coast, as well as for our own and other missions in the interior.

4.8 Madame Blavatsky, *The Secret Doctrine: The Synthesis of Science, Religion and Philosophy* (1888; London: Theosophical Publishing House, 1893)

Though Spiritualism had been in vogue in England since the 1850s (Elizabeth Barrett Browning, for example, attended the séances of the medium David Home, much to Robert Browning's regret), the end of the nineteenth century saw a new wave of interest in spiritual mysticism led by the charismatic Russian Helena Petrovna Blavatsky (1831–91). Blavatsky was one of the founders of the Theosophical Society (formed in 1875), one of whose aims was to combine Spiritualism with Buddhism. After periods in the United States of America and India (where she met Rudyard Kipling), Blavatsky arrived in London in the early 1880s, where she would remain until her death in 1891. Members of the Theosophical Society included the poet W. B. Yeats and the socialist thinker Annie Besant, who succeeded Blavatsky as the movement's leader. One of the movement's key texts was The Secret Doctrine, *first published in 1888. In the extract below from the revised third edition of 1893, Blavatsky explains the importance of the Eastern concept of karma in the context of new scientific discoveries. One further note about the text: it is less important to know the specific associations of the Hindu and Buddhist deities Blavatsky invokes here than to see her method of drawing upon Eastern religion.*

From 'Cyclic Evolution and Karma'
    It is the Spiritual evolution of the *inner*, immortal Man that forms the fundamental tenet in the Occult Sciences. To realize even distantly such a process, the

student has to believe (*a*) in the One Universal Life, independent of Matter (or what Science regards as Matter); and (*b*) in the individual Intelligences that animate the various manifestations of this Principle. Mr Huxley[34] does not believe in Vital Force; others [*sic*] Scientists do. Dr J. H. Hutchinson Stirling's work *As Regards Protoplasm*[35] has made no small havoc of this dogmatic negation. Professor Beale's decision is also in favour of a Vital Principle; and Dr B. W. Richardson's lectures on Nervous Ether have been sufficiently quoted. Thus, opinions are divided.

The One Life is closely related to the One Law which governs the World of Being – KARMA. Exoterically, this is simply and literally 'action', or rather an 'effect-producing cause'. Esoterically it is quite a different thing in its far-reaching moral effects. It is the unerring LAW OF RETRIBUTION. To say to those ignorant of the real significance, characteristics and awful importance of this eternal immutable Law, that no theological definition of a Personal Deity can give an idea of this impersonal, yet ever present and active Principle, is to speak in vain. Nor can it be called Providence. For Providence, with the Theists – the Protestant Christians, at any rate – rejoices in a personal male gender, while with the Roman Catholics it is a female potency. 'Divine Providence tempers His blessings to secure their better effects', Wogan tells us. Indeed 'He' tempers them, which Karma – a sexless principle – does not.

Throughout the first two Parts, it has been shown that, at the first flutter of renascent life, Svabhâvat, '*the Mutable Radiance of the Immutable Darkness unconscious in Eternity*', passes, at every new rebirth of Kosmos, from an inactive state into one of intense activity; that it differentiates, and then begins its work through that differentiation. This work is KARMA.

The Cycles are also subservient to the effects produced by this activity.

The one Cosmic Atom becomes seven Atoms on the plane of Matter, and each is transformed into a centre of energy; that same Atom becomes seven Rays on the plane of Spirit, and the seven creative Forces of Nature, radiating from the Root-Essence ... follow, one the right, the other the left path, separate till the end of the Kalpa, and yet in close embrace. What unites them? Karma.

The Atoms emanated from the Central Point emanate in their turn new centres of energy, which, under the potential breath of *Fohat*, begin their work from within without, and multiply other minor centres. These, in the course of evolution and involution, form in their turn the roots or developing causes of new effects, from worlds and 'man-bearing' globes, down to the genera, species, and classes of all the *seven* kingdoms, of which we know only *four*. For as says the *Book of the Aphorisms of Tson-Ka-Pa*:

'The blessed workers have received the Thyan-kam, in the eternity'

34 Thomas Henry Huxley (1825–95): a biologist whose defence of evolutionary theory earned him the nickname 'Darwin's Bulldog'. (See extract 10.8.)

35 James Hutchinson Stirling (1820–1909) published *As Regards Protoplasm* in 1872. The text was a direct critique of Huxley's work.

Thyan-kam is the power or knowledge of guiding the impulses of Cosmic Energy in the right direction.

The true Buddhist, recognising no 'personal God', nor any 'Father' and 'Creator of Heaven and Earth', still believes in an *Absolute Consciousness*, Adi-Buddhi; and the Buddhist Philosopher *knows* that there are Planetary Spirits, the Dhyân Chohans. But though he admits of 'Spiritual Lives', yet, as they are temporary in eternity, even they, according to his Philosophy, are 'the Mâyâ of the Day', the Illusion of a 'Day of Brahmâ', a short Manvantara of 4,320,000,000 years. The Yin-Sin is not for the speculations of men, for the Lord Buddha has strongly prohibited all such inquiry. If the Dhyân Chohans and all the Invisible Beings – the Seven Centres and their direct Emanations, the minor centres of Energy – are the direct reflex of the One Light, yet men are far removed from these, since the whole of the visible Kosmos consists of '*self-produced* beings, the creatures of Karma'. Thus regarding a personal God 'as only a gigantic shadow thrown upon the void of space by the imagination of ignorant men',[36] they teach that only 'two things are [objectively] eternal, namely Âkâsha and Nirvâna'; and that these are *one* in reality, and but a Mâyâ when divided.

Everything has come out of Âkâsha (or Svabhâvat on our earth) in obedience to a law of motion inherent in it, and after a certain existence passes away. Nothing ever came out of nothing. We do not believe in miracles; hence we deny creation and cannot conceive of a creator.[37]

If a Vedântic Brâhman of the Advaita Sect, were asked whether he believed in the existence of God, he would probably answer, as Jacolliot was answered – 'I am myself "God";' while a Buddhist (a Sinhalese especially) would simply laugh, and say in reply, 'There is no God; no Creation.' Yet the root Philosophy of both Advaita and Buddhist scholars is *identical*, and both have the same respect for animal life, for both believe that every creature on Earth, however small and humble, 'is an immortal portion of the immortal Matter' – Matter having with them quite another significance from that which it has with either Christian or Materialist – and that every creature is subject to Karma.

4.9 General William Booth, *In Darkest England and the Way Out* (London: International Headquarters of The Salvation Army, 1890)

In Darkest England and the Way Out *compared the situation of the urban poor in London to the situation of people in Africa. By referring in its title to the explorer Henry Stanley's dubbing of Africa as the Dark Continent, William Booth's aim was to bring attention to the plight of the urban poor in 'Darkest London' (see also extract 2.11). Booth (1829–1912) was a Methodist preacher who founded the Christian Revival Society in 1865 in the East End of London, which was renamed the Salvation Army in*

---

36 *Original Note: Buddhist Catechism*, by H. S. Olcott, President of the Theosophical Society, 51.
37 *Original Note*: Ibid., 51, 52.

1878. The Salvation Army became an international Christian organization with a quasi-military structure (it was led by a 'General'), which undertook evangelic, social and rescue work. In Darkest England *was ghostwritten by the polemical journalist W. T. Stead, author of* The Maiden Tribute of Modern Babylon *(1885), an exposé of child prostitution in London. Using the sensationalist language of the New Journalism of the 1880s and 1890s, Booth's aim was to energize the middle classes into charity work. The extract below, from the Preface, demonstrates how, for Booth, charity work was a necessary step in the evangelization of the urban poor.*

The progress of The Salvation Army in its work amongst the poor and lost of many lands has compelled me to face the problems which are more or less hopefully considered in the following pages. The grim necessities of a huge Campaign carried on for many years against the evils which lie at the root of all the miseries of modern life, attacked in a thousand and one forms by a thousand and one lieutenants, have led me step by step to contemplate as a possible solution of at least some of those problems the Scheme of Social Selection and Salvation which I have here set forth.

When but a mere child the degradation and helpless misery of the poor Stockingers of my native town, wandering gaunt and hunger-stricken through the streets droning out their melancholy ditties, crowding the Union or toiling like galley slaves on relief works for a bare subsistence, kindled in my heart yearnings to help the poor which have continued to this day and which have had a powerful influence on my whole life. At last I may be going to see my longings to help the workless realised. I think I am.

The commiseration then awakened by the misery of this class has been an impelling force which has never ceased to make itself felt during forty years of active service in the salvation of men. During this time I am thankful that I have been able, by the good hand of God upon me, to do something in mitigation of the miseries of this class, and to bring not only heavenly hopes and earthly gladness to the hearts of multitudes of these wretched crowds, but also many material blessings, including such commonplace things as food, raiment, home, and work, the parent of so many other temporal benefits. And thus many poor creatures have proved Godliness to be 'profitable unto all things, having the promise of the life that now is as well as of that which is to come'.

These results have been mainly attained by spiritual means. I have boldly asserted that whatever his peculiar character or circumstances might be, if the prodigal would come home to his Heavenly Father, he would find enough and to spare in the Father's house to supply all his need both for this world and the next; and I have known thousands nay, I can say tens of thousands, who have literally proved this to be true, having, with little or no temporal assistance, come out of the darkest depths of destitution, vice and crime, to be happy and honest citizens and true sons and servants of God.

And yet all the way through my career I have keenly felt the remedial measures usually enunciated in Christian programmes and ordinarily employed by

Christian philanthropy to be lamentably inadequate for any effectual dealing with the despairing miseries of these outcast classes. The rescued are appallingly few – a ghastly minority compared with the multitudes who struggle and sink in the open-mouthed abyss. Alike, therefore, my humanity and my Christianity, if I may speak of them in any way as separate one from the other, have cried out for some more comprehensive method of reaching and saving the perishing crowds.

No doubt it is good for men to climb unaided out of the whirlpool on to rock of deliverance in the very presence of the temptations which have hitherto mastered them, and to maintain a footing there with the same billows of temptation washing over them. But, alas! with many this seems to be literally impossible. That decisiveness or character, that moral nerve which takes hold of the rope thrown for the rescue and keeps its hold amidst all the resistances that have to be encountered, is wanting. It is gone. The general wreck has shattered and disorganised the whole man.

Alas, what multitudes there are around us everywhere, many known to my readers personally, and any number who may be known to them by a very short walk from their own dwellings, who are in this very plight! Their vicious habits and destitute circumstances make it certain that without some kind of extraordinary help, they must hunger and sin, and sin and hunger, until, having multiplied their kind, and filled up the measure of their miseries, the gaunt fingers of death will close upon them and terminate their wretchedness. And all this will happen this very winter in the midst of the unparalleled wealth, and civilisation, and philanthropy of this professedly most Christian land.

Now, I propose to go straight for these sinking classes, and in doing so shall continue to aim at the heart. I still prophesy the uttermost disappointment unless that citadel is reached. In proposing to add one more to the methods I have already put into operation to this end, do not let it be supposed that I am the less dependent upon the old plans or that I seek anything short of the old conquest. If we help the man it is in order that we may change him. The builder who should elaborate his design and erect his house and risk his reputation without burning his bricks would be pronounced a failure and a fool. Perfection of architectural beauty, unlimited expenditure of capital, unfailing watchfulness of his labourers, would avail him nothing if the bricks were merely unkilned clay. Let him kindle a fire. And so here I see the folly of hoping to accomplish anything abiding, either in the circumstances or the morals of these hopeless classes, except there be a change effected in the whole man as well as in his surroundings. To this everything I hope to attempt will tend. In many cases I shall succeed, in some I shall fail; but even in failing of this my ultimate design, I shall at least benefit the bodies, if not the souls, of men; and if I do not save the fathers, I shall make a better chance for the children.

It will be seen, therefore, that in this or in any other development that may follow, I have no intention to depart in the smallest degree from the main principles on which I have acted in the past. My only hope for the permanent deliv-

erance of mankind from misery, either in this world or the next, is the regeneration or remaking of the individual by the power of the Holy Ghost through
Jesus Christ. But in providing for the relief of temporal misery I reckon that I am
only making it easy where it is now difficult, and possible where it is now all but
impossible, for men and women to find their way to the Cross of our Lord Jesus
Christ.

5

Philosophy and Ideas

Introduction

There were two great philosophical or ideological problems of the nineteenth century: the problem of idealism and materialism, and that of freedom and determinism. The first, deriving from advances in the social and natural sciences, especially psychology, logic, geology and biology, was concerned with how to reconcile materialism with idealism and spiritualism. What was the relation of human thought to matter? How did biblical time relate to historical evolution? Could scripture be married with natural science? Victorian notions of reason and progress were informed by Immanuel Kant's idealism in the domains of the Good (ethics), the True (science) and the Beautiful (aesthetics) – that we could not perceive the truth of nature unmediated by our own perceptual and cognitive apparatuses, that the world was rational and progressive, and that the human mind was capable of discerning the Good and acting on it.

Utilitarianism was one of the most influential schools of nineteenth-century philosophical and social thinking. Its founder, Jeremy Bentham, was resisting idealism when he insisted that Nature had placed humankind under the governance of two sovereign masters, pain and pleasure, which governed us in all we do, and that every effort to throw off our subjection would but serve to confirm it. His principle of utility aimed to increase the pleasure and decrease the pain of the greatest number, and he did not distinguish between higher and lower pleasures: push-pin was as good as poetry. Bentham's main intellectual and personal ally was James Mill, whose son, John Stuart Mill, went on in *Utilitarianism* (1863) to refine and elevate human pleasures to include the intellectual and emotional pleasures (especially sympathy) and to emphasize the intersubjective or collective nature of pleasure, lest it be interpreted as merely individual sensual gratification.

The divergent approaches of materialism and idealism were keenly expressed through the way Victorian philosophers grappled with the limits of knowledge and, in particular, the limits of the knower. Romantic subjectivity (the 'mirror' of self-consciousness) and scientific objectivity (the 'lamp' held up to reveal nature) were the dialectical opposites that most fruitfully generated knowledge. In the extract below, Walter Pater writes of the individual's state of subjectivity, isolated 'by that thick wall of personality through which no real voice has ever pierced' from external reality, or 'that which we can only conjecture to be without'.

Social science was heavily informed by Auguste Comte's Positivism as it amassed empirical data that sought to make sense of social change and social relations. Philosophical anthropologists like Johann Gottfried Herder and Higher Critics of the Bible like Ludwig Feuerbach (see Section 4, p. 98ff) humanized scripture by demonstrating how religious ideas were the objectified projections of human need and desire, thereby showing a uniquely self-conscious humankind reflecting on its own constraints and limitations. Marx and Engels similarly thought that all human history could be seen through the historical development and practical uses of the prehensile thumb, recognizing that all human senses and capacities developed through concrete and specific material conditions.

The oppositions of mind and matter, nature and culture, individual and collective, were resolved in Hegelian dialectics. In dialectical logic, we start from a given position, find that this position contains within itself the seeds of its own destruction in the form of an internal contradiction, and then move to a third position that combines the positive aspects of its two predecessors: thesis, antithesis, synthesis.

This leads us to the second main philosophical problem of the century, the problem of freedom. After the French Revolution, the great promise of freedom pervaded the age, not only in Romantic philosophy but also in politics (liberal reform, the abolition of the slave trade and emancipation of slaves, the franchise for working-class men and women), economics (the free market) and religion (Protestant free conscience and self-reliance). The extracts below from Hegel, Mill, Bradley and Nietzsche are all concerned with the scope and limits of freedom, and, by extension, the determining influences upon individuals and their agency. Hegel, for example, saw the progress of the consciousness of freedom as the purpose and meaning in history.

One example of the intellectual stimulus provided by Continental philosophy is the influence of German idealist conceptions of Freedom as human destiny or Spirit unfolding through time to its ultimate self-consciousness; these were matched by British empirical traditions, going back to the seventeenth-century work of John Locke, which focused on the individual's freedom from interference as an individual right. The exemplar of nineteenth-century British liberalism, John Stuart Mill, took Reason to the extreme in supposing absolutely autonomous individuals (the classic liberal subject), in *On Liberty* calling for maximum toleration and respect for diversity, except in preventing harm to others.

The empirical tradition of Mill and Hume was challenged in the latter decades of the century by a group of British idealist philosophers, the most original of whom was the Oxford academic F. H. Bradley. Claiming that Benthamite utilitarianism, Kantian rationality and Hegelian idealism respectively did not provide genuine freedom, or self-realization, Bradley tried to reconcile empiricism and idealism in concrete universals. At the very end of the century, the ideology of freedom dialectically gave way to Nietzsche's idea of resentment, when freedom becomes a burden. Knowing that we are free, we feel resentment when we, for whatever biological, psychological or sociological reasons, fail to achieve it. And resentment was incendiary unless it could be contained by the mystifications of power.

The configuration of this section demonstrates that philosophy among the Victorians was predominantly a European, male and elite provenance. There was much communication between professional philosophers at the universities and through elite publishing houses but little scope for others in the conversation. From Bentham through Mill and Spencer, to Comte and Hegel, they created philosophical *systems* that did not invite casual engagement by those without formidable education and talent. Perhaps more importantly, they were not accessible to those outside the relevant social networks. Marx and Engels were the exception in consciously popularizing their work, claiming that the point was not only to interpret the world but to change it. While crediting Marx and Engels with world-historical influence in the twentieth century, we can safely say that nineteenth-century philosophy was primarily influential through universities and elite publication networks, with some dissemination through popular movements like Chartism and feminism.

John Stuart Mill was the exception who proved the rule in terms of the masculine bias of nineteenth-century philosophy. Mill did credit his wife Harriet Taylor Mill with the ideas in *The Subjection of Women* (see Section 3, p. 81); however, her own *Enfranchisement of Women* did not enjoy a contemporary circulation, or canonical status, comparable to the essay published under John Stuart's name. Similarly, Harriet Martineau and George Eliot, probably the most visible intellectual women of the age, translated very difficult philosophical texts of Comte, Strauss and Feuerbach, mediating the great philosophical systems. Yet they never received the status of philosophers among their male interlocutors. One of the most interesting generic and disciplinary questions of the age, given the talent of the female novelist-philosophers, is the nature of the difference between – and different statuses of – novelistic versus philosophical knowledge.

While Schopenhauer had been strongly influenced by Buddhism in his *The World as Will and Idea* (1819), it was not until the end of the century, through the new social movements of theosophy, socialism, feminism, back-to-nature-back-to-the-land and so forth, that the great works of Eastern philosophy began to appear regularly in academic and popular discourse. By then, American Transcendentalists like Emerson and Thoreau had also contributed to the extension of philosophical thought in Britain.

5.1 Immanuel Kant, *Critique of Judgment* (1790) [trans. J. H. Bernard, 1892] (London: Macmillan, 1914)

Probably the most famous statement in Western aesthetic philosophy is the referral by Kant (1724–1804) of the Beautiful to the morally Good. It is a statement of absolute value in an interrelated system of the Good, the True and the Beautiful, whose conception predates the nineteenth-century rationalization of knowledge. Yet it has haunted all later, more relativistic, conceptions of art. It refers to a freedom from desire or self-interest that harmonizes the self, and the self in relation to society. It is not about the object or its producer but about a process that occurs between the perceiving subject and the object; it is not about pleasure ('mere liking') but a system of equilibrium between ethics, truth and aesthetics.

A Kantian judgement of taste begins with the harmonious workings of the faculties when a perceiver is confronted with certain objects. At first this aesthetic feeling (the Beautiful) is subjective and phenomenal. But Kant insisted, in line with the logic of his entire system, that judgements of taste were also objective (the True), which introduced rational and objective elements. In the disinterested pleasure that comes to me without the element of desire or self-interest, I do not transcend the phenomenal sphere. But recognizing something in us that is common to the species, and something in each member of the species that is not owned but is universal property, we are freed from our former confinement and limitations.

In Kant, the moral good consists in acting autonomously, as one ought, rather than heteronomously, or from desire, emotion or self-interest. This freedom to act autonomously can only be achieved by Reason, but it can be prefigured by the feeling of freedom from desire or self-interest that we get when we perceive the beautiful object. When we perceive the beautiful object – which in Kant is typically a natural object theoretically accessible to all, rather than a work of art, which, Kant says, may give rise to an element of ego or possessiveness – the disjunction between our perception and our concept creates an excess, a free play of imagination, that prefigures moral freedom, or freedom from desire and self-interest. (I have no desire to possess the sunset, for there is enough of it for all; but I share with all the wonder of beholding it.) The free play prefigures the reconciliation between individual and social life that the moral good entails – that is, to act according to duty rather than desire or self-interest, to act in such a way that one's actions embody a universal principle for action. This taste for freedom is thus, notoriously, a form of discipline, a freedom from selfish desires. In Kant's Anthropology *(1798) the Man of Taste simultaneously perfects both aesthetic and ethical skills. Many people who are persuaded by Kant's phenomenology of aesthetic feeling – the free play of imagination synthesizing perception and concept – are not persuaded by his rationalizing or universalizing of it to make it a symbol of the moral good, or freedom.*

Now I say the Beautiful is the symbol of the morally Good, and that it is only in this respect (a reference which is natural to every man and which every man postulates in others as a duty) that it gives pleasure with a claim for the agreement of everyone else. By this the mind is made conscious of a certain ennoble-ment and elevation above the mere sensibility to pleasure received through sense, and the worth of others is estimated in accordance with a like maxim of their Judgment. [. . .]

We shall indicate some points of this analogy, while at the same time we shall note the differences.

(1) The beautiful pleases *immediately* (but only in reflective intuition, not, like morality, in its concept). (2) It pleases *apart from any interest* (the morally good is indeed necessarily bound up with an interest, though not with one which precedes the judgment upon the satisfaction, but with one which is first of all produced by it). (3) The *freedom* of the imagination (and therefore of the sensi-bility of our faculty) is represented in judging the beautiful as harmonious with the conformity to law of the Understanding (in the moral judgment the free-dom of the will is thought as the harmony of the latter with itself, according to universal laws of Reason). (4) The subjective principle in judging the beautiful is represented as *universal*, i.e. as valid for every man, though not cognizable through any universal concept. (The objective principle of morality is also expounded as universal, i.e. for every subject and for every action of the same subject, and thus as cognizable by means of a universal concept). Hence the moral judgment is not only susceptible of definite constitutive principles, but is possible *only* by grounding its maxims on these in their universality.

A reference to this analogy is usual even with the common understanding [of men], and we often describe beautiful objects of nature or art by names that seem to put a moral appreciation at their basis. We call buildings or trees majes-tic and magnificent, landscapes laughing and gay; even colours are called inno-cent, modest, tender, because they excite sensations which have something analogous to the consciousness of the state of mind brought about by moral judgments. Taste makes possible the transition, without any violent leap, from the charm of Sense to habitual moral interest; for it represents the Imagination in its freedom as capable of purposive determination for the Understanding, and so teaches us to find even in objects of sense a free satisfaction apart from any charm of sense.

5.2 Jeremy Bentham, *An Introduction to the Principles of Morals and Legislation* (1789; London: Wilson, 1823)

Bentham (1748–1832), moral philosopher and jurist, entered Queen's College, Oxford, at 12, and after graduation entered Lincoln's Inn and was admitted to the bar. He never practised but spent his life advocating in print utilitarian applications to British and international law. He was the leader in a radical group around the Westminster Review, *which he founded in 1823 as a journal for utilitarian philosophy, and was also influential in criminal law. Bentham's utilitarianism held that pleasure and pain were the only tests of good and evil and that they could be measured in intensity, dura-*

tion, proximity and after effects, and then summed up for all persons affected. The greatest pleasure for the greatest number was the good. It followed from this that evil was the causing of pain, and that causing pain was the only reason for punishment.

Recently Bentham has been best known for his panoptical prison system and characteristic mechanical calculation of happiness ('Quantity of pleasure being equal, push-pin is as good as poetry'), but these are crude reductions of Bentham's wide sympathies, thoughtful social planning, progressive tolerance and consistent justice. His friend J. S. Mill criticized him for not agreeing to a hierarchy of pleasures and wrote eloquently of a utilitarianism based less in individual hedonics than the Golden Rule: 'In the golden rule of Jesus of Nazareth, we read the complete spirit of the ethics of utility.' Although Mill most patiently delineated the altruism of utilitarianism, it was always present in Bentham, and today his reluctance to claim some pleasures as higher than others suits modern relativism rather more than Mill's refinements.

From Chapter I: Of the Principle of Utility

I. Nature has placed mankind under the governance of two sovereign masters, *pain* and *pleasure*. It is for them alone to point out what we ought to do, as well as to determine what we shall do. On the one hand the standard of right and wrong, on the other the chain of causes and effects, are fastened to their throne. They govern us in all we do, in all we say, in all we think: every effort we can make to throw off our subjection, will serve but to demonstrate and confirm it. In words a man may pretend to abjure their empire: but in reality he will remain subject to it all the while. The *principle of utility* recognizes this subjection, and assumes it for the foundation of that system, the object of which is to rear the fabric of felicity by the hands of reason and of law. Systems which attempt to question it, deal in sounds instead of sense, in caprice instead of reason, in darkness instead of light.

But enough of metaphor and declamation: it is not by such means that moral science is to be improved.

II. The principle of utility is the foundation of the present work: it will be proper therefore at the outset to give an explicit and determinate account of what is meant by it. By the principle of utility is meant that principle which approves or disapproves of every action whatsoever, according to the tendency it appears to have to augment or diminish the happiness of the party whose interest is in question: or, what is the same thing in other words to promote or to oppose that happiness. I say of every action whatsoever, and therefore not only of every action of a private individual, but of every measure of government.

III. By utility is meant that property in any object, whereby it tends to produce benefit, advantage, pleasure, good, or happiness, (all this in the present case comes to the same thing) or (what comes again to the same thing) to prevent the happening of mischief, pain, evil, or unhappiness to the party whose interest is considered: if that party be the community in general, then the happiness of the community: if a particular individual, then the happiness of that individual.

IV. The interest of the community is one of the most general expressions that can occur in the phraseology of morals: no wonder that the meaning of it is often lost. When it has a meaning, it is this. The community is a fictitious *body*, composed of the individual persons who are considered as constituting as it were its *members*. The interest of the community then is, what is it? – the sum of the interests of the several members who compose it.

V. It is in vain to talk of the interest of the community, without understanding what is the interest of the individual. A thing is said to promote the interest, or to be *for* the interest, of an individual, when it tends to add to the sum total of his pleasures: or, what comes to the same thing, to diminish the sum total of his pains.

VI. An action then may be said to be conformable to the principle of utility, or, for shortness sake, to utility, (meaning with respect to the community at large) when the tendency it has to augment the happiness of the community is greater than any it has to diminish it.

VII. A measure of government (which is but a particular kind of action, performed by a particular person or persons) may be said to be conformable to or dictated by the principle of utility, when in like manner the tendency which it has to augment the happiness of the community is greater than any which it has to diminish it.

VIII. When an action, or in particular a measure of government, is supposed by a man to be conformable to the principle of utility, it may be convenient, for the purposes of discourse, to imagine a kind of law or dictate, called a law or dictate of utility: and to speak of the action in question, as being conformable to such law or dictate.

IX. A man may be said to be a partisan of the principle of utility, when the approbation or disapprobation he annexes to any action, or to any measure, is determined by and proportioned to the tendency which he conceives it to have to augment or to diminish the happiness of the community: or in other words, to its conformity or unconformity to the laws or dictates of utility.

X. Of an action that is conformable to the principle of utility one may always say either that it is one that ought to be done, or at least that it is not one that ought not to be done. One may say also, that it is right it should be done; at least that it is not wrong it should be done: that it is a right action; at least that it is not a wrong action. When thus interpreted, the words *ought*, and *right* and *wrong* and others of that stamp, have a meaning: when otherwise, they have none.

5.3 Johann Gottfried Herder, *Treatise upon the Origin of Language* [trans. unknown] (1772; London: Longman, 1827)

Born in 1744 in East Prussia, Johann Herder formulated an account of human freedom that influenced Kant's anthropology, Marx and Engels's sense of species being, and British notions of the people and nation (this extract is from the first English transla-

tion of his Treatise). *In Herder's terms, 'man' is by far inferior to other animals in the intensity and reliability of his instincts and does not have what in many species we regard as innate artefactive skills and drives. Yet if humankind's senses are inferior in acuity to the senses of other species, then it is this that gives human senses the advantage of freedom. Because they are not senses for one spot, they become generalized senses for the universe. Unlike the precisely directed and perfectly achieved work of the spider and the bee, there is no single work of humanity in which its actions are not improvable, but it enjoys the freedom of exercise in many things and hence the freedom of improving itself forever. By means of humankind's receptivity, and underdetermined response, to its environment, it evolves into the diverse social groupings of 'race' and ethnicity. Herder provided a philosophical anthropology of human diversity that would haunt the more scientistic expositors of empire. Understanding the human being as sensuous, cognitive and wilful – as a human animal capable of sweet reason but liable to wilful perversity – he was a bulwark against both Romantic and scientific reductionism.*

Every animal has its peculiar sphere, to which it belongs from its birth, which it immediately enters, in which it remains during life, and in which it dies. It is however remarkable, that, 'the keener the animal's senses, and the more wonderful the products of its skill, the more contracted is its sphere, and the less varied its work of art'. I have investigated this relative condition, and universally observed, the astonishing reversed proportion between the extent of locomotion, nutrition, self-preservation, propagation, education, and association of animals, and their instinct and skill. The bee in its hive constructs with a wisdom which Egeria could not teach her Numa,[1] but out of these cells, and independently of its occupation within them, it is a mere nothing. The spider weaves with the art of Minerva, but all its skill is confined to the narrow space in which it spins. This is its world! How wonderful is the insect, yet how contracted is its sphere of action! On the other hand, the more manifold the operations, and appointments of animals, and the more diverted their attention towards different objects, the more unsettled their manner of life, in short the more extensive and varied their sphere; the more do we observe their senses subdivided and weakened. [. . .]

When infinitely delicate senses are confined within a small circle, and applied always to the same thing, to the exclusion of every thing else in the world, how penetrating must they become! When faculty of representation is confined within a contracted sphere, and endowed with an analogous sensitive power; how forcibly must it operate! And lastly when the senses, and their representations are all directed to one point, what but instinct could be the result? This will explain the sensibility, faculties, and impulses of animals, according to their rank and species.

---

1 In Roman legend Numa Pompilius, the second king of Rome, was advised by his consort, the wise nymph Egeria.

I may, therefore, lay down the following proposition: 'The sensibility, faculties, and instincts of animals, increase in strength, and intensity, in an inverse ratio, to the extent and manifoldness of their sphere of action.' Man, however, has no such uniform and contracted sphere, in which only one task awaits him; a world of occupations and appointments lie around him. His senses and organization are not so acute on one point, he has senses for all things, therefore taken individually, they are weaker and more obtuse. The faculties of his soul are diffused over the whole world; his ideas cannot be concentrated upon one point: consequently, he has neither instinctive dexterity, nor instinctive art; nor, what still more belongs to our subject, animal language. [. . .]

It follows then, that if man have senses, which, when referring to a confined plot of ground, to the cultivation and enjoyment of a span of the universe, are inferior in acuteness to the senses of those animals who live within such a space, he obtains in lieu, the privilege of freedom. His senses are intended to operate throughout the universe and therefore are not concentrated upon any one point. [. . .] Man is not confined to one particular task, in which of course he would be more perfect, but has free space, wherein to exercise himself in various ways, and thus to improve himself.

[. . .] [S]ince he does not blindly fall upon one point, and blindly there remain, but stands free, can select his sphere, and contemplate in himself the nature of his own being. No longer an infallible machine in the hand of nature, he is the object and aim for the application of his own powers.

However this disposition of his powers may be termed, whether understanding, reason, or reflection &c. [. . .] It is the total arrangement of all the human powers, the total œconomy of man's sentient and intellectual, of his intellectual and volitive nature, or rather, it is the positive power of reflection, which, connected with a certain organization of the body, is called reason in man, and the instinctive faculty in animals, which in the former, gives birth to freedom, and in the latter, to instinct. The difference consists not in degree, or accession of faculties, but in the entirely different tendency and development of all the powers.

5.4 Georg Wilhelm Friedrich Hegel, *Aesthetics. Lectures on Fine Art* (1835–8), translated by Bernard Bosanquet and published as *The Introduction to Hegel's Philosophy of Fine Art* (London: Kegan, Paul, Trench and Co., 1886)

Hegel's lectures on aesthetics were first delivered in Berlin in several series during the 1820s. Profoundly influenced by the French Revolution and Rights of Man, Hegel (1770–1831) saw history as the progress of consciousness of freedom to self-determination through reason. History was Mind or Spirit becoming conscious of itself, and material culture was its expression. Thus the impulse to historicize art, to read in art the history of social relations, goes back to Hegel, a student of political economy. Kant's examples in the third Critique *of the Sublime and the Beautiful are drawn from nature, for example, sublime mountains and cataracts or the beautiful song of a bird. Hegel, on the other hand, made representation central to his aesthetics, deriving the aesthetic impulse from the fact that it was human nature to represent ourselves to ourselves, to make us conscious of ourselves. Thus art is an index of its time, its producers, and their conditions of production. Marx and Engels derived their dialectical materialism from Hegel's historical idealism.*

Contra Kant, Hegel ranked natural beauty low in relation to art. Plants and animals were more beautiful, because closer to the Idea, than inanimate natural objects, but what we see of them is their outward coverings, not the soul within, for that is concealed by the visible feathers, scales, fur and the like that cover them. In the Philosophy of History, *Hegel opposed human creativity to natural beauty, which was the 'prose of the world': 'in nature there happens "nothing new under the sun", and the multiform play of its phenomena so far induces a feeling of* ennui'.

The universal and absolute need out of which art, on its formal side, arises has its source in the fact that man is a *thinking* consciousness, *i.e.* that he draws out of himself, and makes explicit *for himself*, that which he is, and, generally, whatever is. The things of nature are only *immediate and single*, but man as mind *reduplicates* himself, inasmuch as *prima facie* he *is* like the things of nature, but in the second place just as really is *for* himself, perceives himself, has ideas of himself, thinks himself, and only thus is active self-realizedness. This consciousness of himself man obtains in a twofold way: *in the first place theoretically*, in as far as he has inwardly to bring himself into his own consciousness, with all that moves in the human breast, all that stirs and works therein, and, generally, to observe and form an idea of himself, to fix before himself what thought ascertains to be his real being, and, in what is summoned out of his inner self as in what is received from without, to recognize only himself. Secondly, man is realized for himself by *practical* activity, inasmuch as he has the impulse, in the medium which is directly given to him, and externally presented before him, to produce himself, and therein at the same time to recognize himself. This purpose he achieves by the modification of external things upon which he impresses the seal of his inner being, and then finds repeated in them his own characteristics. Man does this in order as a free subject to strip the outer world of its stubborn foreignness, and to enjoy in the shape and fashion of things a mere external reality of himself. Even the child's first impulse involves this practical modification of external things. A boy throws stones into the river, and then stands admiring the circles that trace themselves on the water, as an effect in which he attains the sight of something that is his own doing. This need traverses the most manifold phenomena, up to the mode of self-production in the medium of external things as it is known to us in the work of art. And it is not only external things that man treats in this way, but himself no less, *i.e.* his own natural form, which he does not leave as he finds it, but alters of set purpose. This is the cause of all ornament and decoration [. . .]

The universal need for expression in art lies, therefore, in man's rational impulse to exalt the inner and outer world into a spiritual consciousness for himself, as an object in which he recognizes his own self. He satisfies the need of this spiritual freedom when he makes all that exists explicit for himself *within*, and in a corresponding way realizes this his explicit self *without*, evoking thereby, in this reduplication of himself, what is in him into vision and into knowledge for his own mind and for that of others. This is the free rationality of man, in which, as all action and knowledge, so also art has its ground and necessary origin.

5.5 Herbert Spencer, *Social Statics: or, The Conditions essential to Happiness specified, and the First of them Developed* (London: John Chapman, 1851)

Spencer (1820–1903), like J. S. Mill, was a genuine polymath. After studying natural science at a school near Bath, he became an assistant schoolmaster at Derby, a civil engineer on the Birmingham and Gloucester Railway, a sub-editor of The Economist, *and also served on the Jamaica Committee for the prosecution of Governor Eyre[2]. In 1858 he planned a system of synthetic philosophy covering biology, ethics, metaphysics, psychology and sociology, one contemporary equivalent of which might be systems analysis.*

In the course of the nineteenth century, the account of progress put forward by political economy – as deriving from the division of labour and advances in technology – was transformed by the influence of evolutionary biology. Drawing explicitly on models from political economy, Spencer biologized the division of labour, calling it the law of organic progress. This law hypothecated a change from the homogeneous or simple to the heterogeneous, complex, unique or individuated. All progress was progress towards individuation, and humankind would necessarily become, through inevitable individuation, perfectly fit for purpose. It is the classic statement of Victorian optimism, in which a perfectly functioning division of labour evolves with social consciousness and harmony. His progress through social evolution would be a guiding light of the New Liberalism at the end of the century.

Progress, therefore, is not an accident, but a necessity. Instead of civilization being artificial, it is a part of nature; all of a piece with the development of the embryo or the unfolding of a flower. The modifications mankind have undergone, and are still undergoing, result from a law underlying the whole organic creation; and provided the human race continues, and the constitution of things remains the same, those modifications must end in completeness. As surely as the tree becomes bulky when it stands alone, and slender if one of a group; as

---

2 The Jamaica Committee campaigned to prosecute Edward Eyre, Governor General of Jamaica , for his brutal suppression of the Morant Bay rebellion of 1865; many innocent Jamaicans were killed by the indiscriminate violence of British troops.

surely as the same creature assumes the different forms of cart-horse and race-horse, according as its habits demand strength or speed; as surely as a black-smith's arm grows large, and the skin of a labourer's hand thick; as surely as the eye tends to become long-sighted in the sailor, and short-sighted in the student; as surely as the blind attain a more delicate sense of touch; as surely as a clerk acquires rapidity in writing and calculation; as surely as the musician learns to detect an error of a semitone amidst what seems to others a very babel of sounds; as surely as a passion grows by indulgence and diminishes when restrained; as surely as a disregarded conscience becomes inert, and one that is obeyed active; as surely as there is any efficacy in educational culture, or any meaning in such terms as habit, custom, practice; – so surely must the human faculties be moulded into complete fitness for the social state; so surely must the things we call evil and immorality disappear; so surely must man become perfect.

5.6 Auguste Comte, *The Positive Philosophy*, vol. 2, freely translated and condensed by Harriet Martineau (1830–42; London: John Chapman, 1853)

Auguste Comte (1798–1857), who is generally thought to have coined the term 'soci-ology', believed that Bacon, Hobbes, Descartes, Galileo, and any who had made real contributions to modern science were the founders of the Positive philosophy. The key tenets of Positivism, which Comte outlined in his Cours de Philosophie Positive *(1830–42), were that we have no knowledge of anything but phenomena, and our knowledge of phenomena is not absolute but relative. The laws of phenomena in their ordering and consistency are all that we know respecting them; their essential nature and efficient or final causes are unknown and inscrutable to us. It was Comte's stress upon the description and observation of experienced phenomena, and his concomitant rejection of metaphysical speculation, which made him so influential in the develop-ment of social research.*

The modernity of Comte derives from the way Positivism was figured as an advance upon theological and metaphysical philosophies, which attributed the various agencies of Nature to real or imaginary Beings, or to powers and forces respectively. He was orig-inal in claiming that every distinct class of human conceptions passes sequentially through these three stages: theological, metaphysical and positive. There are two excerpts below; the first is on the social implications of Positivism, the second on the aesthetic – or expressive – contributions of Positivism in the European commonwealth.

The positive philosophy is the first that has ascertained the true point of view of social morality. The metaphysical philosophy sanctioned egotism; and the theo-logical subordinated real life to an imaginary one; while the new philosophy takes social morality for the basis of its whole system. The two former systems were so little favourable to the rise of the purely disinterested affections, that they often led to a dogmatic denial of their existence; the one being addicted to scholastic subtleties, and the other to considerations of personal safety. No set of feelings can be fully developed otherwise than by special and permanent exercise; and especially if they are not naturally very prominent; and the moral sense, – the social degree of which is its completest manifestation, – could be only imperfectly instituted by the indirect and factitious culture of a preparatory stage. We have yet to witness the moral superiority of a philosophy which connects each of us with the whole of human existence, in all times and places. The restriction of our expectations to actual life must furnish new means of connecting our individual development with the universal progression, the growing regard to which will afford the only possible, and the utmost possible, satisfaction to our natural aspiration after eternity. For instance, the scrupulous respect for human life, which has always increased with our social progression, must strengthen more and more as the chimerical hope dies out which disparages the present life as merely accessory to the one in prospect. The philosophical spirit being only an extension of good sense, it is certain that it alone, in its spontaneous form, has for three centuries maintained any general agreement against the dogmatic disturbances occasioned or tolerated by the ancient philosophy, which would have overthrown the whole modern economy if popular wisdom had not restrained the social application of it. The effects are, at best, only too evident; the practical intervention of the old philosophy taking place only in cases of very marked disorder, such as must always be impending and ever renewed while the intellectual anarchy which generates it yet exists. By its various aptitudes, positive morality will tend more and more to exhibit the happiness of the individual as depending on the complete expansion of benevolent acts and sympathetic emotions towards the whole of our race; and even beyond our race, by a gradual extension to all sentient beings below us, in proportion to their animal rank and social utility. The relative nature of the new philosophy will render it applicable, with equivalent facility and accuracy, to the exigencies of each case, individual or social, whereas we see how the absolute character of religious morality has deprived it of almost all force in cases which, arising after its institution, could not have been duly provided for. Till the full rational establishment of positive morality has taken place, it is the business of true philosophers, ever the precursors of their race, to confirm it in the estimation of the world by the sustained superiority of their own conduct, personal domestic, and social; giving the strongest conceivable evidence of the possibility of developing, on human grounds alone, a sense of general morality complete enough to inspire an invincible repugnance to moral offence, and an irresistible impulse to steady practical devotedness. [. . .]

One of the least anticipated results of this working out of opinions, morals, and institutions under the guidance of positive philosophy, is the development which must take place in the modes of expressing them. For five centuries, society has been seeking an aesthetic constitution correspondent to its civilization. In the time to come, – apart from all consideration of the genius that will arise, which is wholly out of the reach of anticipation, – we may see how Art must eminently fulfil its chief service, of charming and improving the humblest and the loftiest minds, elevating the one and soothing the other. For this service it must gain much by being fitly incorporated with the social economy, from which it has hitherto been essentially excluded. Our philosophical speculation has shown us how favourable the human view and collective spirit must be to the rise and spread of aesthetic tastes; and our historical survey had before taught us, that a progressive social condition, marked and durable, is indispensable to the completeness of such a development. On both grounds, the future is full of promise. The public life and military existence of antiquity are exhausted; but the laborious and pacific activity proper to modern civilization is scarcely yet instituted, and has never yet been aesthetically regarded; so the modern art, like the modern science and industry, is so far from being worn out, that it is as yet only half formed. The most original and popular species of modern art which forms a preparation for that which is to ensue, has treated of private life, for want of material in public life. But the public life will be such as will admit of idealization: for the sense of the good and the true cannot be actively conspicuous without eliciting a sense of the beautiful; and the action of the positive philosophy is in the highest degree favourable to all three. The systematic regeneration of human conceptions must also furnish new philosophical means of aesthetic expansion, secure at once of a noble aim and a steady impulsion. There must certainly be an inexhaustible resource of poetic greatness of the positive conception of Man as the supreme head of the economy of Nature, which he modifies at will, in a spirit of boldness and freedom, within no other limits than those of natural law. This is yet an untouched wealth of idealization, as the action of Man upon Nature was hardly recognized as a subject of thought till art was declining from the exhaustion of the old philosophy. The marvellous wisdom of Nature has been sung, in imitation of the ancients, and with great occasional exaggeration; and the conquests of Man over nature, with science for his instrument, and sociality for his atmosphere, remains, promising much more interest and beauty than the representation of an economy in which he has no share, and in which magnitude was the original object of admiration, and the material grandeur continues to be most dwelt upon. There is no anticipating what the popular enthusiasm will be when the representations of Art shall be in harmony with the noble instinct of human superiority, and with the collective rational convictions of the human mind. To the philosophical eye it is plain that the universal reorganization will assign to modern Art at once inexhaustible material in the spectacle of human power and achievement, and a noble social destination in illustrating and endearing the final economy of human life. What philosophy elaborates, Art will propagate and adapt for propagation, and will thus fulfil a higher social office than in its most glorious days of old. – I have here spoken of the first of the arts only, – of Poetry, which by its superior amplitude and generality has always superintended and led to the development of them all: but the conditions which are favourable to one mode of expression are propitious to all, in their natural succession. While the positive spirit remained in its first phase, the mathematical, it was reproached for its anti-aesthetic tendency: but we now see how, when it is systematized from a sociological centre, it becomes the basis of an aesthetic organization no less indispensible than the intellectual and social renovation from which it is inseparable.

The five elements of this great process will each bring their own special contribution to the new system, which will inseparably combine them all. France will bring a philosophical and political superiority; England, an earnest predilection for reality and utility; Germany, a natural aptitude for systematic generalization; Italy, its genius for art; and Spain, its familiar combined sense of personal dignity and universal brotherhood. By their natural co-operation, the positive philosophy will lead us onto a social condition the most conformable to human nature, in which our characteristic qualities will find their most perfect respective confirmation, their completest mutual harmony, and the freest expansion for each and all.

5.7 Ludwig Feuerbach, *The Essence of Christianity* (1841) translated by George Eliot (London: John Chapman, 1854)

In 1854 George Eliot translated Feuerbach's The Essence of Christianity, *which distinguished Christianity from other religions in the imputation of moral perfection to its Deity. What Feuerbach did that so impressed Marx, Engels, Eliot and G. H. Lewes was to locate the identifiable aspects of the Deity – omniscience, justice and love – as externalized aspects of humankind itself in its capacities of thinking, willing and loving. Religion is 'man's' consciousness of his own nature but viewed as a nature apart from his own. Conceived in the interiority of his own insufficiency, 'Man' objectified outside himself his need for truth and justice. Whereas all religions externalized knowledge in their deities, the specificity of Christianity arose from its imputation of moral perfection as well. Moral perfection depends on will. As sensuous beings, humans are inclined towards weak wills: they tend to opt for sensual gratification over duty or the social good. This introduces the third externalization. As human will is not perfect, love is needed to compensate for its failures, and Jesus is created to mediate between perfect God and imperfect men, sinless and sinful beings, the universal and the individual. For Feuerbach, mercy was the justice of sensuous life. Our sins were forgiven because we are not abstract beings, but creatures of flesh and blood.*

What was crucial for Eliot and others in the nineteenth century was not Christianity's moral perfection but rather its recognition that we could never attain it and therefore that we ought to be tolerant. If Christianity's main contribution to modernity was the sacred value of every individual soul, no matter how erring or humble, its logical extension was toleration. Eliot's translation of The Essence of Christianity *provided an anthropology of humans as biological, rational, affective and expressive, as sensuous beings capable of, but just as often incapable of, sweet reason. It was an account of human freedom and its limitations that resonated with the Victorian intelligentsia from Browning and Eliot to Marx. (See also Section 4, Religion and Belief, p. 98ff.)*

In the perceptions of the senses consciousness of the object is distinguishable from consciousness of self; but in religion, consciousness of the object and self-consciousness coincide. The object of the senses is out of man, the religious object is within him, and therefore as little forsakes him as his self-consciousness or his conscience; it is the intimate, the closest object. 'God,' says Augustine,[3] for example, 'is nearer, more related to us, and therefore more easily known by us, than sensible, corporeal things.' The object of the senses is in itself indifferent – independent of the disposition or of the judgment; but the object of religion is a selected object; the most excellent, the first, the supreme being; it essentially presupposes a critical judgment, a discrimination between the divine and the non-divine, between that which is worthy of adoration and that which is not worthy. And here may be applied, without any limitation, the proposition: the object of any subject is nothing else than the subject's own nature taken objectively. Such as are a man's thoughts and dispositions, such is his God; so much worth as a man has, so much and no more has his God. Consciousness of God is self-consciousness, knowledge of God is self-knowledge. By his God thou knowest the man, and by the man his God; the two are identical. Whatever is God to a man, that is his heart and soul; and conversely, God is the manifested inward nature, the expressed self of a man, – religion the solemn unveiling of a man's hidden treasures, the revelation of his intimate thoughts, the open confession of his love-secrets.

But when religion – consciousness of God – is designated as the self-consciousness of man, this is not to be understood as affirming that the religious man is directly aware of this identity; for, on the contrary, ignorance of it is fundamental to the peculiar nature of religion. To preclude this misconception, it is better to say, religion is man's earliest and also indirect form of self-knowledge. Hence, religion everywhere precedes philosophy, as in the history of the race, so also in that of the individual. Man first of all sees his nature as if *out* of himself, before he finds it in himself. His own nature is in the first instance contemplated by him as that of another being. Religion is the childlike condition of humanity; but the child sees his nature – man – out of himself; in childhood a man is an object to himself, under the form of another man. Hence the historical progress of religion consists in this: that what by an earlier religion was regarded as objective, is now recognised as subjective; that is, what was formerly contemplated and worshipped as God is now perceived to be something *human*. [. . .]

The identity of the subject and predicate is clearly evidenced by the progressive development of religion, which is identical with the progressive development of human culture. So long as man is in a mere state of nature, so long is his god a mere nature-god – a personification of some natural force. Where man inhabits houses, he also encloses his gods in temples. The temple is only a manifestation of the value which man attaches to beautiful buildings. Temples in honour of reli-

---

3 Saint Augustine (AD 354–430), philosopher and theologian.

gion are in truth temples in honour of architecture. With the emerging of man from a state of savagery and wildness to one of culture, with the distinction between what is fitting for man and what is not fitting, arises simultaneously the distinction between that which is fitting and that which is not fitting for God. God is the idea of majesty, of the highest dignity: the religious sentiment is the sentiment of supreme fitness. The later more cultured artists of Greece were the first to embody in the statues of the gods the ideas of dignity, of spiritual grandeur, of imperturbable repose and serenity. But why were these qualities in their view attributes, predicates of God? Because they were in themselves regarded by the Greeks as divinities. Why did those artists exclude all disgusting and low passions? Because they perceived them to be unbecoming, unworthy, un-human, and consequently ungodlike. The Homeric gods eat and drink; – that implies: eating and drinking is a divine pleasure. Physical strength is an attribute of the Homeric gods: Zeus is the strongest of the gods. Why? Because physical strength, in and by itself, was regarded as something glorious, divine. To the ancient Germans the highest virtues were those of the warrior; therefore their supreme god was the god of war, Odin, – war, 'the original or oldest law'. Not the attribute of the divinity, but the divineness or deity of the attribute, is the first true Divine Being. Thus what theology and philosophy have held to be God, the Absolute, the Infinite, is not God; but that which they have held not to be God is God: namely, the attribute, the quality, whatever has reality. Hence he alone is the true atheist to whom the predicates of the Divine Being, – for example, love, wisdom, justice, – are nothing; not he to whom merely the subject of these predicates is nothing. And in no wise is the negation of the subject necessarily also a negation of the predicates considered in themselves. These have an intrinsic, independent reality; they force their recognition upon man by their very nature; they are self-evident truths to him; they prove, they attest themselves. It does not follow that goodness, justice, wisdom, are chimæras because the existence of God is a chimæra, nor truths because this is a truth. The idea of God is dependent on the idea of justice, of benevolence; a God who is not benevolent, not just, not wise, is no God; but the converse does not hold. The fact is not that a quality is divine because God has it, but that God has it because it is in itself divine: because without it God would be a defective being. [. . .]

Of all the attributes which the understanding assigns to God, that which in religion, and especially in the Christian religion, has the pre-eminence, is moral perfection.

5.8 John Stuart Mill, *On Liberty* (London: J. W. Parker and Son, 1859)

Mill (1806–73) was probably the most educated and liberal thinker of the period. He was schooled by his radical utilitarian father at home, learning Greek at three and Latin at eight. At twelve he commenced logic, government and jurisprudence, and corrected the proofs of his father's History of India. *By thirteen he had embarked on a complete course of political economy. He was also unique among his peers in that religious practice played no part in his life. He worked for the East India Company for 35 years, which he considered 'leisure' from his pursuits of writing and politics. He defended the French Revolution, birth control, the North in the American Civil War, Irish Land Reform, women's suffrage, political refugees, and he chaired the Jamaica Committee of 1866 (see note 2, p. 133).*

In the locus classicus *of Western individualism,* On Liberty, *Mill argued that although there had been a time when men of strong will had had to be subdued for the good of society as a whole, 'Society has now fairly got the better of individuality; and the danger which threatens human nature is not the excess but the deficiency of personal impulses.' Against the repressive desublimation of modern mass media and commodification, or what Mill called the threat of stagnation due to the suppression of diversity, he proposed social tolerance and absolute liberty of thought and discussion, limited solely by society's right to self-protection. His critique of dogmatism, authoritarianism and intolerance of any kind was as outraged and thoroughgoing as Nietzsche's, though more abstract. That is, it relied solely on reason or ideas to effect toleration. Mill sought liberty through Reason, or the mind's ability to pursue a course to achieve an end. For him, Reason was always in the service of an objectively, that is, socially, good end. Thus economic freedom and inheritance, for example, should be limited by taxation to benefit the state. While Mill's argument is a rhetorical tour de force, he formulated an abstract individual who appeared to be entirely rational, neither buffed about by passions and emotions nor dependent on others in making decisions. As Freud and many others have pointed out, Mill's political programme was somewhat compromised by this abstract rationality, or naive psychology. (See extracts 3.5 and 6.1 for his views on gender and aesthetics respectively.)*

From 'Chapter I: Introductory'

The object of this Essay is to assert one very simple principle, as entitled to govern absolutely the dealings of society with the individual in the way of compulsion and control, whether the means used be physical force in the form of legal penalties, or the moral coercion of public opinion. The principle is, that the sole end for which mankind are warranted, individually or collectively, in interfering with the liberty of action of any of their number, is self-protection. That the only purpose for which power can be rightfully exercised over any member of a civilized community, against his will, is to prevent harm to others. His own good, either physical or moral, is not a sufficient warrant. He cannot rightfully be compelled to do or forbear because it will be better for him to do so, because it will make him happier, because, in the opinions of others, to do so would be wise, or even right. These are good reasons for remonstrating with him, or reasoning with him, or persuading him, or entreating him, but not for compelling him, or visiting him with any evil in case he do otherwise. To justify that, the conduct from which it is desired to deter him, must be calculated to produce evil to someone else. The only part of the conduct of any one, for which he is amenable to society, is that which concerns others. In the part which merely concerns himself, his independence is, of right, absolute. Over himself, over his own body and mind, the individual is sovereign.

It is, perhaps, hardly necessary to say that this doctrine is meant to apply only to human beings in the maturity of their faculties. We are not speaking of children, or of young persons below the age which the law may fix as that of manhood or womanhood. [. . .]

This, then, is the appropriate region of human liberty. It comprises, first, the inward domain of consciousness; demanding liberty of conscience, in the most comprehensive sense; liberty of thought and feeling; absolute freedom of opinion and sentiment on all subjects, practical or speculative, scientific, moral or theological. The liberty of expressing and publishing opinions may seem to fall under a different principle, since it belongs to that part of the conduct of an individual which concerns other people; but, being almost of as much importance as the liberty of thought itself, and resting in great part on the same reasons, is practically inseparable from it. Secondly, the principle requires liberty of tastes and pursuits; of framing the plan of our life to suit our own character; of doing as we like, subject to such consequences as may follow; without impediment from our fellow creatures, so long as what we do does not harm them, even though they should think our conduct foolish, perverse, or wrong. Thirdly, from this liberty of each individual, follows the liberty, within the same limits, of combination among individuals; freedom to unite, for any purpose not involving harm to others: the persons combining being supposed to be of full age, and not forced or deceived.

No society in which these liberties are not, on the whole, respected, is free, whatever may be its form of government; and none is completely free in which they do not exist absolute and unqualified. [. . .]

From 'Chapter II: Of the Liberty of Thought and Discussion'

[T]he peculiar evil of silencing the expression of an opinion is, that it is robbing the human race; posterity as well as the existing generation; those who dissent from the opinion, still more than those who hold it. If the opinion is right, they are deprived of the opportunity of exchanging error for truth: if wrong, they lose, what is almost as great a benefit, the clearer perception and livelier impression of truth, produced by its collision with error. [. . .]

We have now recognised the necessity to the mental well-being of mankind (on which all other well-being depends) of freedom of opinion, and freedom of the expression of opinion, on four distinct grounds; which we will now briefly recapitulate.

First, if any opinion is compelled to silence, that opinion may, for aught we can certainly know, be true. To deny this is to assume our own infallibility.

Secondly, though the silenced opinion be an error, it may, and very commonly does, contain a portion of truth; and since the general or prevailing opinion on any subject is rarely or never the whole truth, it is only by the collision of adverse opinions that the remainder of the truth has any chance of being supplied.

Thirdly, even if the received opinion be not only true, but the whole truth; unless it is suffered to be, and actually is, vigorously and earnestly contested, it will, by most of those who receive it, be held in the manner of a prejudice, with little comprehension or feeling of its rational grounds. And not only this, but fourthly, the meaning of the doctrine itself will be in danger of being lost, or enfeebled, and deprived of its vital effect on the character and conduct: the dogma becoming a mere formal profession, inefficacious for good, but cumbering the ground, and preventing the growth of any real and heartfelt conviction, from reason or personal experience.

5.9 Walter Pater, *The Renaissance: Studies in Art and Poetry* (1873; London: Macmillan, 1888)

The most famous statement of art for art's sake in English is Pater's 'Conclusion' to
The Renaissance, *which he omitted in the second edition because he thought 'it might possibly mislead some of those young men into whose hands it might fall'. A quiet don at Oxford for three decades, Pater (1839–94) developed a subjectivist analysis of one's most intense impressions, not to see the object as in itself it really was (Matthew Arnold), but to see one's own impression as it really was, which Oscar Wilde would later refine as, to see the object as in itself it really was not (see extract 6.10). This subjective intensity was the goal of life, rather than the more dutiful or progressive visions of earlier Victorians. To analyse and make us perceptive to the intensity of experience was the goal of philosophy, religion and art. The highest intensity for Pater was not to be found in sensuality but in art and song (see also Section 6.7, p. 169). As he grew older he recast the hedonics of art for art's sake into a unique fusion of aesthetics and Christianity. In* Marius the Epicurean *(1885), he combined the epicurean or hedonic good to feel intensely with the Christian good of sympathy with others' suffering.* Marius *uses the refined senses of Epicureanism to feel others' pain, so that the good is an ethical Epicureanism. What the most refined species feels is sympathy with others, and that refined sympathy is the highest good. Compared to this intensity of feeling for others, romantic love and sex were crude. The extract here is from the slightly revised and reissued 'Conclusion' to the third edition of 1888 (for the second edition of 1877, Pater also changed the original title,* Studies in the History of the Renaissance, *to that listed above).*

From 'Conclusion'

To regard all things and principles of things as inconstant modes or fashions has more and more become the tendency of modern thought. Let us begin with that which is without – our physical life. Fix upon it in one of its more exquisite intervals, the moment, for instance, of delicious recoil from the flood of water in summer heat. What is the whole physical life in that moment but a combination of natural elements to which science gives their names? But these elements, phosphorus and lime and delicate fibres, are present not in the human body alone: we detect them in places most remote from it. Our physical life is a perpetual motion of them – the passage of the blood, the wasting and repairing of the lenses of the eye, the modification of the tissues of the brain by every ray of light and sound – processes which science reduces to simpler and more elementary forces. Like the elements of which we are composed, the action of these forces extends beyond us; it rusts iron and ripens corn. Far out on every side of us these elements are broadcast, driven by many forces; and birth and gesture and death and the springing of violets from the grave are but a few out of ten thousand resulting combinations. That clear perpetual outline of face and limb is but an image of ours under which we group them – a design in a web, the actual threads of which pass out beyond it. This at least of flame-like our life has, that it is but the concurrence, renewed from moment to moment, of forces parting sooner or later on their ways. [. . .]

Experience, already reduced to a swarm of impressions, is ringed round for each one of us by that thick wall of personality through which no real voice has ever pierced on its way to us, or from us to that which we can only conjecture to be without. Every one of those impressions is the impression of the individual in his isolation, each mind keeping as a solitary prisoner its own dream of a world. [. . .]

Philosophiren, says Novalis, *ist dephlegmatisiren, vivificiren.*[4] The service of philosophy, of speculative culture, towards the human spirit, is to rouse, to startle it into sharp and eager observation. Every moment some form grows perfect in hand or face; some tone on the hills or sea is choicer than the rest; some mood of passion or insight or intellectual excitement is irresistibly real and attractive for us, – for that moment only. Not the fruit of experience, but experience itself is the end. A counted number of pulses only is given to us of a variegated, dramatic life. How may we see in them all that is to be seen in them by the finest senses? How shall we pass most swiftly from point to point, and be present always at the focus where the greatest number of vital forces unite in their purest energy?

To burn always with this hard, gemlike flame, to maintain this ecstasy, is success in life. In a sense it might even be said that our failure is to form habits; for, after all, habit is relative to a stereotyped world, and meantime it is only the roughness of the eye that makes any two persons, things, situations, seem alike. While all melts under our feet, we may well catch at any exquisite passion, or any contribution to knowledge that seems, by a lifted horizon, to set the spirit free for a moment, or any stirring of the senses, strange dyes, strange flowers, and curious odours, or work of the artist's hands, or the face of one's friend. Not to discriminate every moment some passionate attitude in those about us, and in the brilliancy of their gifts some tragic dividing of forces on their ways is, on

---

4 Novalis was the pseudonym of Georg Philipp Friedrich Freiherr von Hardenberg (1772–1801), German Romantic poet and philosopher. The quotation says, 'To philosophize is to cast off inertia, to bring oneself to life.'

this short day of frost and sun, to sleep before evening. With this sense of the splendour of our experience and of its awful brevity, gathering all we are into one desperate effort to see and touch, we shall hardly have time to make theories about the things we see and touch. What we have to do is to be for ever curiously testing new opinions and courting new impressions, never acquiescing in a facile orthodoxy of Comte or of Hegel, or of our own. Theories, religious or philosophical ideas, as points of view, instruments of criticism, may help us to gather up what might otherwise pass unregarded by us. 'Philosophy is the microscope of thought.' The theory, or idea, or system, which requires of us the sacrifice of any part of this experience, in consideration of some interest into which we cannot enter, or some abstract morality we have not identified with ourselves, or what is only conventional, has no real claim upon us.

One of the most beautiful places in the writings of Rousseau is that in the sixth book of the *Confessions*, where he describes the awakening in him of the literary sense.[5] An undefinable taint of death had always clung about him, and now in early manhood he believed himself smitten by mortal disease. He asked himself how he might make as much as possible of the interval that remained; and he was not biased by anything in his previous life when he decided that it must be by intellectual excitement, which he found in the clear, fresh writings of Voltaire.[6] Well, we are all *condamnés*, as Victor Hugo[7] says: we are all under sentence of death but with a sort of indefinite reprieve – *les hommes sont tous condamnés à morte avec des sursis indéfinis*: we have an interval, and then our place knows us no more. Some spend this interval in listlessness, some in high passions, the wisest at least, among 'the children of the world', in art and song. For our one chance lies in expanding that interval, in getting as many pulsations as possible into the given time. Great passions may give us this quickened sense of life, ecstasy and sorrow of love, the various forms of enthusiastic activity, disinterested or otherwise, which come naturally to many of us. Only, be sure it is passion – that it does yield you this fruit of a quickened, multiplied consciousness. Of this wisdom, the poetic passion, the desire of beauty, the love of art for art's sake, has most; for art comes to you professing frankly to give nothing but the highest quality to your moments as they pass, and simply for those moments' sake.

5.10 Francis Herbert Bradley, *Ethical Studies* (London: Henry S. King, 1876)

The son of an evangelical minister and brother to the distinguished Shakespearean critic A. C. Bradley, the Oxford philosopher F. H. Bradley (1846–1924) rejected hedonism (Bentham), rationality (Kant) and historical community (Hegel) respectively as

---

5 Jean-Jacques Rousseau (1712–78), French Enlightenment philosopher and literary figure.

6 Pseudonym of François-Marie Arouet (1694–1778), French Enlightenment philosopher.

7 Victor Hugo, French novelist and poet (1802–85).to bring oneself to life.'

exclusive bases for ethics. Instead, he synthesized British empiricism and German idealism in what he called 'ideal morality'. For Bradley, our 'best self' must arise from our local ideals of family and community, but we must transcend these through our knowledge of other cultures and our own self-critique. The individual must therefore be a 'concrete universal' whose individual life is a unity with others of her kind.

From Essay V. Pleasure for Pleasure's Sake

It is an old story, a theme too worn for the turning of sentences, and yet too living a moral not to find every day a new point and to break a fresh heart, that our lives are wasted in the pursuit of the impalpable, the search for the impossible and the unmeaning. [. . .] And our cry and our desire is for something that will satisfy us, something that we know and do not only think, something that is real and solid, that we can lay hold of and be sure of, and that will not change in our hands. We have said good-bye to our transcendent longings, we have bidden a sad but an eternal farewell to the hopes of our own and of the world's too credulous youth; we have parted for ever from our early loves, from our fancies and aspirations beyond the human. [. . .]

From Essay V. My Station and Its Duties

We have learnt that the self to be realized is not the self as this or that feeling, or as any series of the particular feelings of our own or others' streams or trains of consciousness. It is, in short, not the self to be pleased. The greatest sum of units of pleasure we found to be the idea of a mere collection, whereas, if we wanted morality, it was something like an universal that we wanted. Happiness, as the effort to construct that universal by the addition of particulars, gave us a futile and bastard product, which carried its self-destruction within it, in the continual assertion of its own universality, together with its unceasing actual particularity and finitude; so that happiness was, if we chose, nowhere not realized; or again, if we chose, not anywhere realizable. And passing then to the opposite pole, to the universal as the negative of the particulars, to the supposed pure will or duty for duty's sake, we found that it too was an unreal conception. It was a mere form which, to be will, must give itself a content, and which could give itself a content only at the cost of a self contradiction: we saw, further, that any such content was in addition arbitrarily postulated, and that, even then, the form was either never realized, because real in no particular content, or always and everywhere realized, because equally reconcilable with any content. [. . .]

We have self-realization as the end, the self being so far defined as neither a collection of particular feelings nor as an abstract universal. The self is to be realized as something not simply one or the other; it is to be realized further as will, will not being merely the natural will, or the will as it happens to exist and finds itself here or there, but the will as the *good* will, *i.e.* the will that realizes an end which is above this or that man, superior to them, and capable of confronting them in the shape of a law or an ought. This superior something further, which is a possible law or ought to the individual man, does not depend for its existence on his choice or opinion. Either there is no morality, so says the moral consciousness, or moral duties exist independently of their position of this or that person: my duty may be mine and no other man's, but I do not make it mine. If it is duty, it would be the duty of any person in my case and condition, whether they thought so or not: in a word, duty is 'objective', in the sense of not being contingent on the opinion or choice of this or that subject.

What we have left then (to resume it) is this – the end is the realization of the good will which is superior to ourselves; and again the end is self-realization. Bringing these together, we see the end is the realization of ourselves as the will which is above ourselves. And this will (if morality exists) we saw must be 'objective', because not dependent on 'subjective' liking; and 'universal', because not identifiable with any particular, but standing above all actual and possible particulars. Further, though universal, it is not abstract, since it belongs to its essence that it should be realized, and it has no real existence except in and through its particulars. The good will (for morality) is meaningless, if, whatever else it be, it be not the will of living human beings. It is a concrete universal, because it not only is above but is within and throughout its details, and is so far only as they are. It is the life which can live only in and by them, as they are dead unless within it; it is the whole soul which lives so far as the body lives, which makes the body a living body, and which without the body is as unreal an abstraction as the body without it. It is an organism and a moral organism; and it is conscious self-realization, because only by the will of its self-conscious members can the moral organism give itself reality. It is the self-realization of the whole body, because it is one and the same will which lives and acts in the life and action of each. It is the self-realization of each member, because each member cannot find the function, which makes him himself apart from the whole to which he belongs; to be himself he must go beyond himself, to live his life he must live a life that is not *merely* his own, but which, none the less, but on the contrary all the more, is intensely and emphatically his own individuality. Here and here first, are the contradictions which have beset us solved – here is an universal which can confront our wandering desires with a fixed and stern imperative, but which yet is no unreal form of the mind, but a living soul that penetrates and stands fast in the detail of actual existence. It is real, and real for me. It is in its affirmation that I affirm myself, for I am but as a 'heart-beat in its system'. And I am real in it; for, when I give myself to it, it gives me the fruition of my own personal activity, the accomplished ideal of my life which is happiness. In the realized idea which, superior to me, and yet here and now in and by me, affirms itself in a continuous process, we have found the end, we have found self-realization, duty and happiness in one; – yes, we have found ourselves, when we have found our station and its duties, our function as an organ in the social organism.

5.11 Friedrich Nietzsche, *The Genealogy of Morals* (1887) [trans. Horace B. Samuel, 1910] (Edinburgh: T. N. Foulis, 1913)[8]

Friedrich Nietzsche (1844–1900) was a classically trained philologist who had a brief academic career, a prolonged illness, and a phenomenally productive period from 1878 to 1888 before he collapsed into a madness from which he never recovered. In many ways, he was the philosopher of Decadence, of the fall away from Victorian values and hope for Progress, or at least, like Freud later, he unmasked or 'trans-valued' their ideals. He was for truthfulness rather than one Truth, and his critical methods of perspectivalism and re-evaluation were those of what he called free spirits. His work was influential for both good and ill in the century after his death for its modernity: its breaks with the past, scepticism, perspectivalism, recognition of the manipulations of power, and of humankind's inability to transcend – and even its perverse wilfulness to adhere to – our animal nature.

In the excerpt below Nietzsche asks what kind of creatures humans are and answers that they are unfinished, wilful, desiring, ungrateful, resentful. Whereas Herder's spider and bee were so closely fitted to their environments that they had one sole purpose, to spin or to hive, humans were so inadequate to theirs that they were forced to make many different ways of surviving, according to their cultures and climes. Because they had to, they created choice. Humankind's choice, or freedom, while distinguishing human from non-human animals tied to their specific environments, is also a source of pain. Humankind, in Nietzsche's words, is the diseased animal – 'the great experimenter with himself, the unsatisfied, the insatiate . . . who finds no more any rest from his own aggressive strength'. This insatiability is a pain, and the pain of ceaseless will and choice can sometimes be assuaged by a physiological response: resentment. Knowing that we are free, we feel resentment when, for whatever biological, psychological or sociological reasons, we fail to achieve freedom. Nietzsche understood resentment not just as an individual's destructive path of frustrated desire but as a whole way of life-denying life. Ascetic ideals maintained the status quo by suppressing healthy intruders and diverting the course of resentment. Resentment could tear society apart, but it usually does not because the ascetic priest diverts that resentment back towards the sufferer: you are downcast, you are yourself to blame.

Here Nietzsche criticizes the ascetic who distances himself from life and whose disinterestedness produces false 'objective' knowledge, the latter being merely the perspective of power. The will to Truth, whether a priest's for one God or a scientist's for the facts, oppresses the natural pluralism of the human animal. Nietzsche's idiosyncratic method is often aesthetic, aphoristic and emotive, showing the manifold of human capacities of thinking and feeling.

The reading from the vantage of a distant star of the capital letters of our earthly life, would perchance lead to the conclusion that the earth was the especially

8 Samuel's translation is the earliest held in the British Library, with a 1910 edition by the same publisher. It is part of *The Complete Works of Friedrich Nietzsche*, ed. Dr Oscar Levy.

ascetic Planet, a den of discontented, arrogant, and repulsive creatures, who never got rid of a deep disgust of themselves, of the world, of all life, and did themselves as much hurt as possible out of pleasure in hurting – presumably their one and only pleasure. Let us consider how regularly, how universally, how practically at every single period the ascetic priest puts in his appearance: he belongs to no particular race; he thrives everywhere; he grows out of all classes. Not that he perhaps bred this valuation by heredity and propagated it – the contrary is the case. It must be a necessity of the first order which makes this species, *hostile*, as it is, to *life*, always grow again and always thrive again. – *Life* itself must certainly *have an interest* in the continuance of such a type of self-contradiction. For an ascetic life is a self-contradiction: here rules resentment without parallel, the resentment of an insatiate instinct and ambition, that would be master, not over some element in life, but over life itself, over life's deepest, strongest, innermost conditions; here is an attempt made to utilise power to dam the sources of power; here does the green eye of jealousy turn even against physiological well-being, especially against the expression of such well-being, beauty, joy; while a sense of pleasure is experienced and *sought* in abortion, in decay, in pain, in misfortune, in ugliness, in voluntary punishment, in the exercising, flagellation, and sacrifice of the self. [. . .]

In the same way the very seeing of another vista, the very *wishing* to see another vista, is no little training and preparation of the intellect for its eternal *'Objectivity'* – objectivity being understood not as 'contemplation without interest' (for that is inconceivable and nonsensical), but as the ability to have the pros and cons *in one's power* and to switch them on and off, so as to get to know how to utilise, for the advancement of knowledge, the *difference* in the perspective and in the emotional interpretations. But let us, forsooth, my philosophic colleagues, henceforward guard ourselves more carefully against this mythology of dangerous ancient ideas, which has set up a 'pure, will-less, painless, timeless subject of knowledge'; let us guard ourselves from the tentacles of such contradictory ideas as 'pure reason', 'absolute spirituality', 'knowledge-in-itself': – in these theories an eye that cannot be thought of is required to think, an eye which *ex hypothesi*[9] has no direction at all, an eye in which the active and interpreting functions are cramped, are absent; those functions, I say, by means of which 'abstract' seeing first became seeing something; in these theories consequently the absurd and the nonsensical is always demanded of the eye. There is only a seeing from a perspective, only a 'knowing' from a perspective, and the *more* emotions we express over a thing, the *more* eyes, different eyes, we train on the same thing, the more complete will be our 'idea' of that thing, our 'objectivity'. But the elimination of the will altogether, the switching off of the emotions all and sundry, granted that we could do so, what! would not that be called intellectual *castration*? [. . .]

---

9 In accordance with, or following, from the hypothesis stated.

To put briefly the facts against its being real: *the ascetic ideal springs from the prophylactic and self-preservative instincts which mark a decadent life*, which seeks by every means in its power to maintain its position and fight for its existence; it points to a partial physiological depression and exhaustion, against which the most profound and intact life-instincts fight ceaselessly with new weapons and discoveries. [. . .] What does it come from, this diseased state? For man is more diseased, more uncertain, more changeable, more unstable than any other animal, there is no doubt of it – he is *the* diseased animal: what does it spring from? Certainly he has also dared, innovated, braved more, challenged fate more than all the other animals put together; he, the great experimenter with himself, the unsatisfied, the insatiate, who struggles for the supreme mastery with beast, Nature, and gods, he, the as yet ever uncompelled, the ever future, who finds no more any rest from his own aggressive strength, goaded inexorably on by the spur of the future dug into the flesh of the present: – how should not so brave and rich an animal also be the most endangered, the animal with the longest and deepest sickness among all sick animals? . . . Man is sick of it, oft enough there are whole epidemics of this satiety (as about 1348, the time of the Dance of Death)[10]: but even this very nausea, this tiredness, this disgust with himself, all this is discharged from him with such force that it is immediately made into a new fetter. His 'nay', which he utters to life, brings to light as though by magic an abundance of graceful 'yeas'; even when he *wounds* himself, this master of destruction, of self-destruction, it is subsequently the wound itself that forces him to live.

---

10 The bubonic plague, or 'Black Death'.

6

Art and Aesthetics

Introduction

J. M. W. Turner's *Rain, Steam and Speed* is perhaps the most emblematic painting of the nineteenth century. First exhibited in 1844, at the peak of the railway mania, the painting embraced the nineteenth-century railway revolution at a time when many, including the leading art critic John Ruskin (who was a staunch supporter of Turner), saw the railways as a threat to the countryside. Turner's pictorial conceptualization of Britain's new industrial reality high-lighted a new aesthetic viewpoint. Just as important as the painting's chosen subject – a train speeding in stormy weather through the landscape – was Turner's proto-impressionistic technique. Less interested in reproducing a detailed landscape than in impressing upon the viewer its overall effects, Turner's radical approach succeeded in depicting the mood of the Industrial Revolution and its impact on the landscape.

Turner's artistic conception differed from Ruskin's belief that landscape paint-ing should be a detailed expression of nature. In the introduction to the second edition of his influential *Modern Painters* (published in the same year, 1844) he argued that 'the true ideal of landscape is precisely the same as that of the human form; it is the expression of the specific – not the individual, but the specific – characters of every object, in their perfection.'[1] Turner's and Ruskin's differing views highlight the challenges facing British artists and writers in the nineteenth century. Should literature and the arts engage with Britain's new social, political and industrial reality? What was the role of art and of the artist in the context of capitalism, urbanization and industrialization? How would the new technological and scientific discoveries challenge the art world of the nine-teenth century? Should art depict this new objective reality, this new under-standing of the world? And if so, how? Could new technologies like photography become an art in itself? What was at stake was not just the rela-tionship between art and the world but also the very nature and value of art in a world where science, technology and commodity culture were increasingly dominant.

---

1 John Ruskin, 'Preface to the Second Edition', *Modern Painters*, vol. 1 (London: Smith, Elder & Co., 1844), xxvi.

Some oppositional artists were critical of the conditions of modernity in Britain and many found in the past (most notably the Middle Ages and ancient Hellenism) a new language with which to counterbalance the effects of modernity. Augustus Welby Pugin and John Ruskin, for example, were deeply anxious about the adverse impacts of industrialization; they looked back to the craftsmanship of medieval Gothic architecture in the belief that these were forms of art based on creative rather than alienated, mechanical labour. Medievalism embodied values of community, spirituality and creativity and provided a standpoint from which to critique industrialization. As the extract from Ruskin below demonstrates, his aesthetic critique led him to take up a political stance. Ruskin established the Guild of St George in 1871 to implement his ideas about how society should develop. Ruskin, and followers like William Morris, saw art as a powerful force against industrial capitalism; Morris argued that art needed to maintain its independence from commerce if art was to be of the people, an idea proposed by Richard Wagner as early as 1849 in *The Art Work of the Future*, an extract from which is reproduced below. Wagner asserted the universality of art and its key role in humanity and looked back to the Greeks (the period when, he argued, art was a religion) to create a new art form: the opera-drama.

Wagner's aim was to return art to the status it had had in earlier periods. In the Romantic age, poets were keen to be seen as visionaries, as prophets, because with their poetry they could 'penetrate', as Carlyle put it, 'into the sacred mystery of the Universe'.[2] By the 1830s such a view was in question. John Stuart Mill's essays on poetry, 'What Is Poetry?' and 'Two Kinds of Poetry', show how the crisis created by the emergence of science as the paradigmatic form of knowledge affected the position of poetry in the nineteenth century. One of Mill's arguments was that poetry belonged to the realm of the aesthetic, whose knowledge is based on feeling and bodily experience (unlike science, which is based on objective knowledge). Other writers and artists responded to the growth of science in similar ways, with a shift to the senses and to subjective knowledge. A fascination with visual perception took hold of painters ranging from Turner to James Abbott McNeill Whistler and Walter Sickert. Pre-Raphaelite poets such as D. G. Rossetti and A. C. Swinburne also found in the senses an aesthetic economy that re-evaluated this subjective vision and allowed them to explore subjects beyond the conventional limits of reality and morality (Robert Buchanan's virulent attack on the 'fleshiness' of their poetics provoked one of the most contentious debates on the subject). Extract 6.7 is from Walter Pater's *The Renaissance*, perhaps the most important nineteenth-century manifesto of this aesthetic as he placed the subjective experience of the artist and critic at the centre of art.

Pater's emphasis on subjective knowledge was a provocative challenge to the realist aesthetics that dominated much of the nineteenth century. Andrew

---

2 Thomas Carlyle, *Heroes, Hero-Worship, and the Heroic in History* (London: Chapman and Hall, 1840), 75.

Hemingway has argued that in the nineteenth century 'realism stood for an exact and unedited representation of nature, for truth and contemporaneity. It represented a materialist approach to the world.'[3] But it might be more accurate to speak of nineteenth-century realisms. Ruskin's theory of painting, as we have seen, was based upon the reproduction of detailed idealistic landscape painting but he rejected the Dutch school for its strong emphasis on the minutiae of everyday ordinary life. George Eliot, by contrast, argued that the Dutch school of painting offered a realist aesthetic that could be appropriated as a literary model for the development of the novel. If novels aspired to represent the real world, Eliot argued it should be as close, as faithful to the details and things of daily life, as could possibly be. For some, realism aspired to the condition of photography (Eliot compared Dickens's realism to a photograph, a 'sun picture').[4] For others, realism was an oppositional way of showing uncomfortable truths about the world (as in the 'Condition of England' novel). Whilst the exact nature of 'realism' inevitably remained contested and slippery, the extract below from Eliot exemplifies the creative interaction between different art forms during the nineteenth century.

Towards the end of the Victorian period, we find these two movements, realism and what came to be known as Aestheticism, coexisting but in clear conflict. On the one hand, realism took a new turn in its emphasis on reality. Influenced by French literature, and applying Darwinian principles, Naturalism, as the new movement was called, 'assumed a position of dispassionate scientific observation of social realities'.[5] It painfully described lurid details of working-class life, always depicting its harshness. The best known exponents were the novelists George Moore and George Gissing.

In contrast to the naturalist mode of scientific observation, critics like Pater and Lee, followers of the cult of Beauty and of the art for art's sake movement, saw impressionism as the exemplary modern movement. Modern life appears in their work as something fluid, transitory, always in perpetual flux. Against the fixity of realism's materialist understanding of the real, impressionism was an attempt to capture the intensity of the fleeting moment. If realism and Naturalism aimed at dissecting what was 'real', impressionism was far more interested in suggesting the way in which the subject apprehended the fleeting world. Arthur Symons would redefine impressionism as part of what he called the Decadent movement in literature. Following once again French models, he argued that Decadent literature in English had two branches, impressionism and symbolism. Both sought to find 'la verité vrai', the real truth, but while impres-

---

3 Andrew Hemingway, 'The Realists' Aesthetic in Painting: "Serious and committed, ironic and brutal, sincere and full of poetry"', in *Adventures in Realism*, ed. Matthew Beaumont (Oxford: Blackwell, 2007), 105.

4 See Daniel A. Novak, *Realism, Photography, and Nineteenth-Century Fiction* (Cambridge: Cambridge University Press, 2008), 7.

5 Novak, *Realism, Photography, and Nineteenth-Century Fiction*, 113.

sionism achieved this by showing how this truth was perceived by the senses, symbolism did it through the use of images, dreams and abstract language. Late Victorian aesthetes like Pater and Lee, following the composer Richard Wagner, argued that it was in the abstract language of music that one could find the real truth, hence why all arts aspired to the condition of music.

Oscar Wilde's position in this debate about art's relationship with the world was perhaps the most radical and the wittiest. An aesthete and also a follower of the art for art's sake movement, he rejected altogether the assumption that art was a representation of the real world. Art, he claimed, only represented itself, and famously pointed out that 'life follows art, far more than art follows life'.

6.1 [John Stuart Mill], 'Two Kinds of Poetry' (1833) in 'Poetry and Its Varieties', *Dissertations and Discussions: Political, Philosophical and Historical*, vol. 1 (London: Longmans, Green, Reader and Dyer, 1867)

Though Mill is better known today as a philosopher, political theorist and economist, he was also an important aesthetic writer (see pp. 139–40 for a full biography; see also extracts 3.5, 5.8 and 9.2 as examples of the range of his thought and influence). In 1833 he published in the journal Monthly Repository *two articles on poetry, 'What Is Poetry?' and 'Two Kinds of Poetry'. In these essays, Mill reads aesthetics in the context of science to argue that they belong to two spheres of knowledge, one granted by feelings and bodily experience, and the other granted by scientific, objective methods. In 'Two Kinds of Poetry' he suggests that these two spheres of knowledge create two distinct aesthetics: the poetry of culture (represented by William Wordsworth) and the poetry of nature (Percy Bysshe Shelley). One is the poetry of the intellect and of thought, the other the poetry of feeling. Mill laid the basis for a reading of Victorian poetry in the dialectic expressive emotion and controlled feeling.*

What is poetry, but the thoughts and words in which emotion spontaneously embodies itself? As there are few who are not, at least for some moments and in some situations, capable of some strong feeling, poetry is natural to most persons at some period of their lives. And any one whose feelings are genuine, though but of the average strength, – if he be not diverted by uncongenial thoughts or occupations from the indulgence of them, and if he acquire by culture, as all persons may, the faculty of delineating them correctly, – has it in his power to be a poet, so far as a life passed in writing unquestionable poetry may be considered to confer that title. But ought it to do so? Yes, perhaps, in a collection of 'British Poets'. But 'poet' is the name also of a variety of man, not solely of the author of a particular variety of book: now, to have written whole volumes of real poetry, is possible to almost all kinds of characters, and implies no greater peculiarity of mental construction than to be the author of a history or a novel.

Whom, then, shall we call poets? Those who are so constituted, that emotions are the links of association by which their ideas, both sensuous and spiritual, are connected together. This constitution belongs (within certain limits) to all in whom poetry is a pervading principle. In all others, poetry is something extraneous and superinduced: something out of themselves, foreign to the habitual course of their everyday lives and characters; a world to which they may make occasional visits, but where they are sojourners, not dwellers, and which, when out of it, or even when in it, they think of, peradventure, but as a phantom world, a place of *ignes fatui*[6] and spectral illusions. Those only who have the peculiarity of association which we have mentioned, and which is a natural though not an universal consequence of intense sensibility, instead of seeming not themselves when they are uttering poetry, scarcely seem themselves when uttering anything to which poetry is foreign. Whatever be the thing which they are contemplating, if it be capable of connecting itself with their emotions, the aspect under which it first and most naturally paints itself to them, is its poetic aspect. The poet of culture sees his object in prose, and describes it in poetry; the poet of nature actually sees it in poetry. [. . .]

To the man of science, again, or of business, objects group themselves according to the artificial classifications which the understanding has voluntarily made for the convenience of thought or of practice. But where any of the impressions are vivid and intense, the associations into which these enter are the ruling ones: it being a well-known law of association, that the stronger a feeling is, the more quickly and strongly it associates itself with any other object or feeling. Where, therefore, nature has given strong feelings, and education has not created factitious tendencies stronger than the natural ones, the prevailing associations will be those which connect objects and ideas with emotions, and with each other through the intervention of emotions. Thoughts and images will be linked together, according to the similarity of the feelings which cling to them. A thought will introduce a thought by first introducing a feeling which is allied with it. At the centre of each group of thoughts or images will be found a feeling; and the thoughts or images will be there only because the feeling was there. The combinations which the mind puts together, the pictures which it paints, the wholes which imagination constructs out of the materials supplied by fancy, will be indebted to some dominant feeling, not as in other natures to a dominant thought, for their unity and consistency of character – for what distinguishes them from incoherencies.

The difference, then, between the poetry of a poet, and the poetry of a cultivated but not naturally poetic mind, is that in the latter, with however bright a halo of feeling the thought may be surrounded and glorified, the thought itself is always the conspicuous object; while the poetry of a poet is feeling itself, employing thought only as the medium of its expression. In the one, feeling waits upon thought; in the other, thought upon feeling. The one writer has a

6 Ghostly lights.

distinct aim, common to him with any other didactic author; he desires to convey the thought, and he conveys it clothed in the feelings which it excites in himself, or which he deems most appropriate to it. The other merely pours forth the overflowing of his feelings; and all the thoughts which those feelings suggest are floated promiscuously along the stream.

6.2 A.[ugustus] Welby Pugin, *Contrasts; or, A Parallel Between the Noble Edifices of the Fourteenth and Fifteenth Centuries, and Similar Buildings of the Present Day; Shewing the Present Decay of Taste* (London: Printed for the Author, and published by him at St Marie's Grange, near Salisbury, Wilts., 1836)

Augustus Welby Northmore Pugin (1812–52) is best known for his co-design of Westminster Palace (or Houses of Parliament). He is credited for the building's Gothicness and its sumptuous medieval interiors, as well as the design of the clock tower (known as Big Ben). He was also responsible for the medieval court at the Great Exhibition, as well as numerous churches. The extract below is from the conclusion to Pugin's most important architectural treatise, in which he passionately argues that Catholic Gothic architecture was the only fit style for a Christian country. Medieval ecclesiastical buildings (whose style and unity he claimed to have been defaced by the English Reformation) were far superior to that produced by the Industrial Revolution. Classical architecture was similarly denuded as a 'pagan' style. For Pugin architectural style was an expression and embodiment of the social order; his deep attachment to the Middle Ages was a standpoint to critique and combat nineteenth-century industrial capitalism with its secularism, its profit-driven mentality, and the breakdown of community. Pugin was central to the Gothic revival and his writings influenced John Ruskin and William Morris.

From 'On the Wretched State of Architecture at the Present Day'

PERHAPS there is no theme which is more largely dilated on, in the present day, than the immense superiority of this Century over every other that has preceded it. This great age of improvement and increased intellect, as it is called, is asserted to have produced results which have never been equalled; and, puffed up by their supposed excellence, the generation of the day look back with pity and contempt on all that passed away before them.

In some respects, I am willing to grant, great and important inventions have been brought to perfection: but, it must be remembered, that these are purely of a mechanical nature; and I do not hesitate to say, that as works of this description progressed, works of art and productions of mental vigour have declined in a far greater ratio.

Were I to dilate upon this subject, I feel confident that I could extend this principle throughout all branches of what are termed the fine arts; but as my professed object is to treat on Architecture, I will confine my observations to that point, leaving to some more able hand the task of exposing false colour and superficial style, which has usurped nature of effect and severity of drawing, and of asserting the immense superiority of the etchings of the old schools over the dry and mechanical productions of the steel engravers of our time, whose miserable productions, devoid of soul, sentiment, or feeling, are annually printed by the thousand, and widely circulated, to remain an everlasting disgrace on the era in which they were manufactured.

Let us now, therefore, examine the pretensions of the present Century to a superiority in architectural skill; let us examine the results – that is, the edifices that have been produced: and, I feel confident, we shall not be long in deciding that, so far from excelling past ages, the architectural works of our time are even below par in the scale of real excellence.

Let us look around, and see whether the Architecture of this country is not entirely ruled by whim and caprice. Does locality, destination, or character of a building, form the basis of a design? no; surely not. We have Swiss cottages in a flat country; Italian villas in the coldest situations; a Turkish kremlin for a royal residence; Greek temples in crowded lanes; Egyptian auction rooms; and all kinds of absurdities and incongruities: and not only are separate edifices erected in these inappropriate and unsuitable styles, but we have only to look into those nests of monstrosities, the Regent's Park and Regent Street, where all kinds of styles are jumbled together to make up a mass. [. . .]

This is a serious consideration, for it is true. Where, I ask, are the really fine monuments of the country to be found, but in those edifices erected centuries ago, during the often railed at and despised period of the Middle Ages? What would be the interest of the cities, or even towns and villages, of this country, were they deprived of their ancient gigantic structures, and the remains of their venerable buildings? Why, even in the metropolis itself, the abbey church and hall of Westminster still stand pre-eminent over every other ecclesiastical or regal structure that has since been raised.

No one can look on Buckingham Palace, the National Gallery, Board of Trade, the new buildings at the British Museum, or any of the principal buildings lately erected, but must feel the very existence of such public monuments as a national disgrace.

And if we regard the new castle at Windsor, although the gilding and the show may dazzle the vulgar and the ignorant, the man of refined taste and knowledge must be disgusted with the paucity of ideas and meagre taste which are shown in the decoration; and he will presently discover, that the elongated or extended quatrefoil and never-ending set of six pateras, in the rooms called Gothic, and the vile scroll-work intended for the flowing style of Louis Quatorze,[7] announce it as being the work of the plasterer and the putty presser, instead of the sculptor and the artist.

---

7 Louis Quatorze – Louis XIV, king of France from 1643 to 1715, commonly associated with the art, design and architecture of his reign.

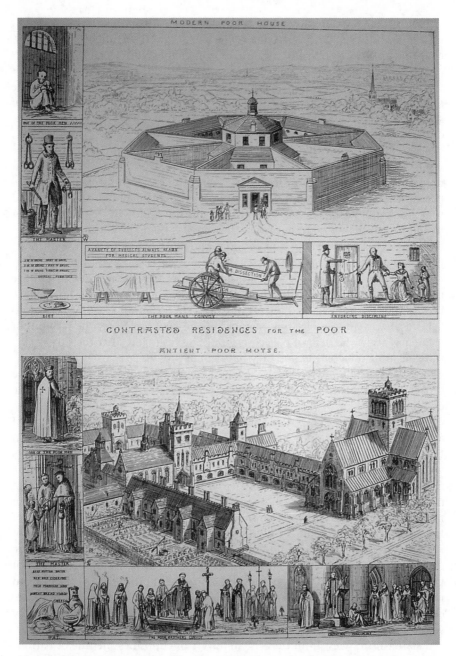

Figure 6.1 Alexander Pugin, *'Contrasted Residences for the Poor'*, *Contrasts: or, a parallel between the noble edifices of the Middle Ages, and corresponding buildings of the present day, shewing the present decay of taste* (1836; London: Charles Dolman, 1841)

Nor is there to be found among the residences of the nobility, either in their own mansions or country seats, lately erected, any of those imposing and characteristic features, or rich and sumptuous ornaments, with which the residences of the Tudor period abounded.

Nor can anything be more contemptible than the frittered appearance of the saloons and galleries, crowded with all sorts of paltry objects, arranged, as if for sale, in every corner, which have replaced the massive silver ornaments, splendid hangings, and furniture of the olden time.

Indeed, I fear that the present general feeling for ancient styles is but the result of the fashion of the day, instead of being based on the solid foundation of real love and feeling for art itself; for, I feel confident, if this were not the case, purchasers could never be found for the host of rubbish annually imported and sold: nor could persons, really acquainted with the beauty of what they profess to admire, mutilate fine things when they possess them, by altering their greatest beauties to suit their own caprice and purposes – a barbarity continually practised in what is called fitting-up old carvings.

Yes, believe me, this goût[8] for antiquities is of too sudden a nature to have proceeded from any real conviction of beauty of those two styles, or to have been produced from other motives but those of whim and fashion; and I do believe that, were some leading member of the *haut ton*[9] to set the fashion for some new style, the herd of collectors would run as madly after their new plaything, as they do after the one they have got at present.

The continual purchase of these things, at extravagant prices, may benefit the broker and the salesman, but does not advance a restoration of such art or style one iota.

Were these people of power and wealth really impressed with a feeling of admiration for the glorious works of ancient days, and anxious for the restoration of the skill and art which produced them, instead of filling their apartments with the stock of a broker's shop, they would establish a museum, where the finest specimens of each style might be found, and from which the sculptor and the artist might school themselves in their principles. They would send forth men to preserve faithful representations of the most interesting monuments of foreign lands, and extend a fostering care for the preservation and repair of those fine remains rapidly falling into decay; and, by encouraging talent where it is to be found, raise up by such a means a race of artists, who, I hesitate not to say, could be found able to conceive and execute things equally fine and masterly as in more ancient days, but who, for want of such support, are compelled to leave the study of what they most admire, and in which they would excel, for some grovelling occupation by which to gain a bare subsistence.

I state this to wrest from these mere buyers of curiosities the title of patrons of art, which has so undeservedly been bestowed upon them. It was under the

---

8 Taste.
9 Fashionable society.

fostering care of the Catholic church,[10] and its noble encouragement, the greatest efforts of art have been achieved; deprived of that, the arts in vain look for an equivalent: for its professors must either starve neglected, or sacrifice the noblest principles and beauties of their art to the caprice and ignorance of their employers.

I could not refrain from making this digression, as I feel that what I have just stated is one of the great causes of the present wretched state of art.

6.3 Richard Wagner, 'The Art-Work of the Future', *Richard Wagner's Prose Works*, trans. William Ashton Ellis, vol. 1 (1849; London: William Reeves, 1895)

The operas of Leipzig-born Richard Wagner (1813–83), for which he wrote the music and libretto, created a storm in Victorian Britain. From Michael Field and Arthur Symons to Walter Pater and Aubrey Beardsley, the British aesthetes of the later part of the nineteenth century saw in his operas the art work of the future. In addition to Wagner's advances in musical language, the themes chosen for his operas were transgressive. Operas such as Tannhauser, *with its emphasis on the mystic union of sacred and profane love,* Tristan und Isolde, *on the ecstatic expression of medieval German romance, and* Der Ring, *with its focus on incest, led writers and artists such as A. C. Swinburne and William Morris to recreate these themes in their work. But perhaps Wagner's most important legacy was his emphasis on the synthesis of his new operatic format, in which drama, music and dance blended together to create a new art form, which he called the 'opera-drama'. Indeed, Walter Pater's much-quoted statement, 'all arts aspire to the condition of music', was inspired by Wagner's understanding of opera-dramas as* Gesamtkunstwerk, *that is, as a synthesis of all the arts. This was the argument of* The Art-Work of the Future, *first published in 1849. It was this type of music drama that Wagner believed was destined to restore Art to the public.*

It is not the lonely spirit, striving by Art for redemption into Nature, that can frame the Art-work of the Future; only the spirit of Fellowship, fulfilled by Life, can bring this work to pass. But yet the lonely one can prefigure it to himself; and the thing that saves his preconception from becoming a mere idle fancy, is the very character of his striving, – his striving after *Nature*. The mind that casts back longing eyes to Nature, and therefore goes a-hungering in the modern Present, sees not alone in Nature's great sum-total, but also in the *human nature* that history lays before it, the types by whose observing it may reconcile itself with life in general. It recognises in this nature a type for all the Future, already shown in narrower bounds; to widen out these bounds to broadest compass, rests on the imaginative faculty of its nature-craving instinct. [. . .]

---

10 Pugin became a Roman Catholic in 1835.

But that *Art* is not an *artificial* product, – that the need of Art is not an arbitrary issue, but an inbred craving of the natural, genuine, and uncorrupted man, – who proves this in more striking manner than just these Peoples? Nay, whence shall our uneasy 'spirit' derive its proofs of Art's necessity, if not from the testimony of this artistic instinct and its glorious fruits afforded by these nature-fostered peoples, by the great *Folk* itself? Before what phenomenon do we stand with more humiliating sense of the impotence of our frivolous culture, than before the art of the *Hellenes*? To this, to the art of the darlings of all-loving Nature, of those fairest children whom the great glad Mother holds up to us before the darksome cloud of modern modish culture, as the triumphant tokens of what she can bring forth, – let us look far hence to glorious Grecian Art, and gather from its inner understanding the outlines for the Art-work of the Future! Nature has done all that she could do, – she has given birth to the Hellenic people, has fed it at her breast and formed it by her mother-wisdom; she sets it now before our gaze with all a mother's pride, and cries to wide mankind with mother-love: 'This have I done for you; now, of your love for one another, do ye that which ye can!'

Thus have we then to turn *Hellenic* art to *Human* art; to loose from it the stipulations by which it was but an *Hellenic* and not a *Universal* art. The *garment of Religion*, in which alone it was the common Art of Greece, and after whose removal it could only, as an egoistic, isolated art-species, fulfil the needs of Luxury – however fair – but no longer those of Fellowship, – this specific garb of the *Hellenic Religion*, we have to stretch it out until its folds embrace the Religion of the Future, the Religion of *Universal Manhood*, and thus to gain already a presage of the Art-work of the Future. But this bond of union, this *Religion of the Future*, we wretched ones shall never clasp the while we still are *lonely units*, howe'er so many be our numbers who feel the spur towards the Art-work of the Future. The Art-work is the living presentation of Religion; – but religions spring not from the artist's brain; their only origin is from the *Folk*. –

Let us then – without a spark of egoistic vanity, without attempting to console ourselves with any kind of self-derived illusion, but honestly and lovingly and hopefully devoted to the Art-work of the Future – content ourselves to-day by testing first the nature of the art-*species* which, in their shattered segregation, make up the general substance of our modern art; let us sharpen our gaze for this examination by glancing at Hellenic art; and thereafter let us draw a bold and confident conclusion anent the *great and universal Art-work of the Future!*

6.4 John Ruskin, 'The Nature of Gothic', in *The Stones of Venice: The Sea Stories*, vol. 2 (London: Smith Elder and Co., 1853)

Ruskin's classic essay, embedded in volume 2 of The Stones of Venice, *is one of the most important prose works of the nineteenth century (see also extract 3.6 for his views on gender). What differentiates Gothic from classical architecture and nineteenth-century industrial production is, according to Ruskin, the labourer's creative craftsmanship. As William Morris put it in an 1892 preface, 'The lesson which Ruskin teaches us is that art is the expression of man's pleasure in labour.' Ruskin found in medieval Gothic a radical aesthetic and political alternative to the alienated character of modern labour. Writing against industrialism, Ruskin argues that invention, authenticity and beauty can only be truly possible if labourers are freed from market economy and from the division of labour. Aesthetic value was an expression of the social conditions of the production of any art or artefact. Ruskin's discussion of Gothic architecture and the value of craftsmanship is still today one of the most important critiques of industrial capitalism.*

VI. I believe, then, that the characteristic or moral elements of Gothic are the following, placed in the order of their importance:

    1. Savageness.
    2. Changefulness.
    3. Naturalism.
    4. Grotesqueness.
    5. Rigidity.
    6. Redundance.

These characters are here expressed as belonging to the building; as belonging to the builder, they would be expressed thus: – 1. Savageness, or Rudeness. 2. Love of Change. 3. Love of Nature. 4. Disturbed Imagination. 5. Obstinacy. 6. Generosity. And I repeat, that the withdrawal of any one, or any two, will not at once destroy the Gothic character of a building, but the removal of a majority of them will. I shall proceed to examine them in their order.

VII. 1. SAVAGENESS. I am not sure when the word 'Gothic' was first generically applied to the architecture of the North; but I presume that, whatever the date of its original usage, it was intended to imply reproach, and express the barbaric character of the nations among whom that architecture arose. It never implied that they were literally of Gothic lineage, far less that their architecture had been originally invented by the Goths themselves; but it did imply that they and their buildings together exhibited a degree of sternness and rudeness, which, in contradistinction to the character of Southern and Eastern nations, appeared like a perpetual reflection of the contrast between the Goth and the Roman in their first encounter. And when that fallen Roman, in the utmost impotence of his luxury, and insolence of his guilt, became the model for the imitation of civilized Europe, at the close of the so-called Dark ages, the word Gothic became a term of unmitigated contempt, not unmixed with aversion. From that contempt, by the exertion of the antiquaries and architects of this century, Gothic architecture has been sufficiently vindicated; and perhaps some among us, in our admiration of the magnificent science of its structure, and sacredness of its expression, might desire that the term of ancient reproach should be withdrawn, and some other, of more apparent honourableness, adopted in its place. There is no chance, as there is no need, of such a substitution. As far as the epithet was used scornfully, it was used falsely; but there is no reproach in the word, rightly understood; on the contrary, there is a profound truth, which the instinct of mankind almost unconsciously recognizes. It is true, greatly and deeply true, that the architecture of the North is rude and wild; but it is not true, that, for this reason, we are to condemn it, or despise. Far otherwise: I believe it is in this very character that it deserves our profoundest reverence. [. . .]

But the modern English mind has this much in common with that of the Greek, that it intensely desires, in all things, the utmost completion or perfection compatible with their nature. This is a noble character in the abstract but becomes ignoble when it causes us to forget the relative dignities of that nature itself and to prefer the perfectness of the lower nature to the imperfection of the higher [. . .] Understand this clearly: You can teach a man to draw a straight line and to cut one; to strike a curved line, and to carve it; and to copy and carve any number of given lines or forms, with admirable speed and perfect precision; and you find his work perfect of its kind: but if you ask him to think about any of those forms, to consider if he cannot find any better in his own head, he stops; his execution becomes hesitating; he thinks, and ten to one he thinks wrong; ten to one he makes a mistake in the first touch he gives to his work as a thinking being. But you have made a man of him for all that. He was only a machine before, an animated tool.

And now, reader, look round this English room of yours, about which you have been proud so often, because the work of it was so good and strong, and the ornaments of it so finished. Examine again all those accurate mouldings, and perfect polishings, and unerring adjustments of the seasoned wood and tempered steel. Many a time you have exulted over them, and thought how great England was, because her slightest work was done so thoroughly. Alas! if read rightly, these perfectnesses are signs of a slavery in our England a thousand times more bitter and more degrading than that of the scourged African, or helot Greek. Men may be beaten, chained, tormented, yoked like cattle, slaughtered like summer flies, and yet remain in one sense, and the best sense, free. But to smother their souls within them, to blight and hew into rotting pollards the suckling branches of their human intelligence, to make the flesh and skin which, after the worm's work on it, is to see God, into leathern thongs to yoke machinery with, – this it is to be slave-masters indeed; and there might be more freedom in England, though her feudal lords' lightest words were worth men's lives, and though the blood of the vexed husbandman dropped in the furrows of her fields, than there is while the animation of her multitudes is sent like fuel to feed the factory smoke, and the strength of them is given daily to be wasted into the fineness of a web, or racked into the exactness of a line.

And, on the other hand, go forth again to gaze upon the old cathedral front, where you have smiled so often at the fantastic ignorance of the old sculptors: examine once more those ugly goblins, and formless monsters, and stern statues, anatomiless and rigid; but do not mock at them, for they are signs of the life and liberty of every workman who struck the stone; a freedom of thought, and rank in scale of being, such as no laws, no charters, no charities can secure; but which it must be the first aim of all Europe at this day to regain for her children. [. . .]

XVI. We have much studied and much perfected, of late, the great civilized invention of the division of labour; only we give it a false name. It is not, truly speaking, the labour that is divided; but the men: – Divided into mere segments of men – broken into small fragments and crumbs of life; so that all the little piece of intelligence that is left in a man is not enough to make a pin, or a nail, but exhausts itself in making the point of a pin, or the head of a nail. Now it is a good and desirable thing, truly, to make many pins in a day; but if we could only see with what crystal sand their points were polished, – sand of human soul, much to be magnified before it can be discerned for what it is, – we should think there might be some loss in it also. And the great cry that rises from all our manufacturing cities, louder than their furnace blast, is all in very deed for this, – that we manufacture everything there except men; we blanch cotton, and strengthen steel, and refine sugar, and shape pottery; but to brighten, to strengthen, to refine, or to form a single living spirit, never enters into our estimate of advantages. And all the evil to which that cry is urging our myriads can be met only in one way: not by teaching nor preaching, for to teach them is but to show them their misery, and to preach to them, if we do nothing more than preach, is to mock at it. It can be met only by a right understanding, on the part of all classes, of what kinds of labour are good for men, raising them, and making them happy; by a determined sacrifice of such convenience, or beauty, or cheapness as is to be got only by the degradation of the workman; and by equally determined demand for the products and results of healthy and ennobling labour.

XVII. And how, it will be asked, are these products to be recognized, and this demand to be regulated? Easily, by the observance of three broad and simple rules:

1. Never encourage the manufacture of any article not absolutely necessary, in the production of which *Invention* has no share.
2. Never demand an exact finish for its own sake, but only for some practical or noble end.
3. Never encourage imitation or copying of any kind, except for the sake of preserving record of great works. [. . .]

XXI. Nay, but the reader interrupts me, – 'If the workman can design beautifully, I would not have him kept at the furnace. Let him be taken away and made a gentleman, and have a studio, and design his glass there, and I will have it cut for him and blown by common workmen, and so I will have my design and my finish too.'

All ideas of this kind are founded upon two mistaken suppositions: the first, that one man's thoughts can be, or ought to be, executed by another man's hands; the second, that manual labour is degradation, when it is governed by intellect.

On a large scale, and in work determinable by line and rule, it is indeed both possible and necessary that the thoughts of one man should be carried out by the labour of others; in this sense I have already defined the best architecture to be the expression of the mind of manhood by the hands of childhood. But on a smaller scale, and in a design which cannot be mathematically defined, one man's thoughts can never be expressed by another: and the difference between the spirit of touch of the man who is inventing, and of the man who is obeying directions, is often all the difference between a great and a common work of art. How wide the separation is between original and second-hand execution, I shall endeavour to show elsewhere; it is not so much to our purpose here as to mark the other and more fatal error of despising manual labour when governed by intellect; for it is no less fatal an error to despise it when thus regulated by intellect, than to value it for its own sake. We are always in these days endeavouring to separate the two; we want one man to be always thinking, and another to be always working, and we call one a gentleman, and the other an operative; whereas the workman ought often to be thinking, and the thinker often to be working, and both should be gentlemen, in the best sense. [. . .]

XXVI. The second mental element above named was CHANGEFULNESS, or Variety.

I have already enforced the allowing independent operation to the inferior workman, simply as a duty *to him*, and as ennobling the architecture by rendering it more Christian. We have now to consider what reward we obtain for the performance of this duty, namely, the perpetual variety of every feature of the building.

Wherever the workman is utterly enslaved, the parts of the building must of course be absolutely like each other; for the perfection of his execution can only be reached by exercising him in doing one thing, and giving him nothing else to do. The degree in which the workman is degraded may be thus known at a glance, by observing whether the several parts of the building are similar or not; and if, as in Greek work, all the capitals are alike, and all the mouldings unvaried, then the degradation is complete; if, as in Egyptian or Ninevite[11] work, though the manner of executing certain figures is always the same, the order of design is perpetually varied, the degradation is less total; if, as in Gothic work, there is perpetual change both in design and execution, the workman must have been altogether set free.

6.5 [Elizabeth Eastlake], 'Photography', *Quarterly Review*, 101 (January & April 1857), 461–5

Elizabeth Eastlake (1809–93) was a central figure in Victorian art criticism. In 1849, she married Charles Eastlake, the would-be director of the National Gallery, who later

---

11 Nineveh was the ancient capital of Assyria.

became also the President of the Royal Academy and the President of the Photographic
Society. Together they entertained one of the most powerful artistic circles of nineteenth-
century London, including J. M. W. Turner, Ruskin, Thackeray, Anna Jameson and
Carlyle. Elizabeth Eastlake was a frequent contributor to the periodical press (and the
first regular female contributor to the Quarterly Review*), and was also author of*
several travel narratives and translations of German art criticism. As photography
developed as a new art form in the nineteenth century, theorists began to examine the
aesthetic possibilities of the new medium: some critics claimed that its mechanical
reproduction of reality precluded it from being considered an art that could ever compete
with established fine arts like painting. In this essay, Eastlake, a photographer herself,
examines photography in relation to science and art.

But let us examine a little more closely those advances which photography owes
to science – we mean in an artistic sense. We turn to the portraits, our *premiers*
amours,[12] now taken under every appliance of facility both for sitter and operator. Far greater detail and precision accordingly appear. Every button is seen –
piles of stratified flounces in most accurate drawing are there, – what was at first
only suggestion is now all careful making out, – but the likeness to Rembrandt
and Reynolds is gone! There is no mystery in this. The first principle in art is that
the most important part of a picture should be best done. Here, on the contrary,
while the dress has been rendered worthy of a fashion-book, the face has
remained, if not so unfinished as before, yet more unfinished in proportion to
the rest. Without referring to M. Claudet's[13] well-known experiment of a falsely
coloured female face, it may be averred that, of all the surfaces of a few inches
square the sun looks upon, none offers more difficulty, artistically speaking, to
the photographer, than a smooth, blooming, clean washed, and carefully
combed human head. The high lights [sic] which gleam on this delicate epider-
mis so spread and magnify themselves, that all sharpness and nicety of model-
ling is obliterated – the fineness of skin peculiar to the under lip reflects so much
light, that in spite of its deep colour it presents a light projection, instead of a
dark one – the spectrum or intense point of light on the eye is magnified to a
thing like a cataract. If the cheek be very brilliant in colour, it is as often as not
represented by a dark stain. If the eye be blue, it turns out as colourless as water;
if the hair be golden or red, it looks as if it had been dyed, if very glossy it is cut
up into lines of light as big as ropes. This is what a fair young girl has to expect
from the tender mercies of photography – the male and the older head, having
less to lose, has less to fear. Strong light and shade will portray character, though
they mar beauty. Rougher skin, less glossy hair, Crimean moustaches and beard
overshadowing the white under lip, and deeper lines, are all so much in favour

12 Literally, first loves.
13 Antoine François Jean Claudet (1797–1867), French photographer and daguerreotypist. In 1853 he
   was appointed Photographer in Ordinary to Queen Victoria. In 1845 he employed the miniaturist
   painter L. Mansion to colour daguerreotypes.

of a picturesque result. Great grandeur of feature too, or beauty of *pose* and senti-ment, will tell as elevated elements of the picturesque in spite of photographic mismanagement. Here and there also a head of fierce and violent contrasts, though taken perhaps from the meekest of mortals, will remind us of the Neapolitan or Spanish school, but, generally speaking, the inspection of a set of faces, subject to the usual conditions of humanity and the camera, leaves us with the impression that a photographic portrait, however valuable to relative or friend, has ceased to remind us of a work of art at all. [. . .]

Here, therefore, the debt of Science for additional clearness, precision, and size may be gratefully acknowledged. What photography can do, is now, with her help, better done than before; what she can but partially achieve is best not brought too elaborately to light. Thus the whole question of success and failure resolves itself into an investigation of the capacities of the machine, and well may we be satisfied with the rich gifts it bestows, without straining it into a competition with art. For everything for which Art, so-called, has hitherto been the means but not the end, photography is the allotted agent – for all that requires mere manual correctness, and mere manual slavery, without any employment of the artistic feeling, she is the proper and therefore the perfect medium. She is made for the present age, in which the desire for art resides in a small minority, but the craving, or rather neces-sity, for cheap, prompt, and correct facts in the public at large. Photography is the purveyor of such knowledge to the world. She is the sworn witness of everything presented to her view. What are her unerring records in the service of mechanics, engineering, geology, and natural history, but facts of the most sterling and stub-born kind? What are her studies of the various stages of insanity – pictures of life unsurpassable in pathetic truth – but facts as well as lessons of the deepest physi-ological interest? What are her representations of the bed of the ocean, and the surface of the moon – of the launch of the *Marlborough*, and of the contents of the Great Exhibition – of Charles Kean's now destroyed scenery of the 'Winter's Tale',[14] and of Prince Albert's now slaughtered prize ox – but facts which are neither the province of art nor of description, but of that new form of communication between man and man – neither letter, message, nor picture – which now happily fills up the space between them? What indeed are nine-tenths of those facial maps called photographic portraits, but accurate landmarks and measurements for loving eyes and memories to deck with beauty and animate with expression, in perfect certainty, that the ground-plan is founded upon fact?

6.6 George Eliot, *Adam Bede* (Edinburgh and London: William Blackwood and Sons, 1859)

This extract from George Eliot's (pseudonym of Marian Evans) first novel, Adam Bede, *is a reflexive summary of her realist aesthetic: it demonstrates the interaction between*

14 A famous Victorian production of Shakespeare's *The Winter's Tale*.

literature and the visual arts, as well as the way that notions of literary realism were indebted to larger philosophical debates between idealism and materialism (see Section 5, pp. 123–4). In the early nineteenth century, the Dutch school of painting was less revered than other genres because of its particular attention to concrete detail and its subject matter: portraits of common people and genre scenes of everyday life. Eliot uses this digression within the novel to argue that this kind of realism, with its emphasis on common tasks and everyday people, is more effective than idealized or sentimental portrayals, because it relates more directly to real life and raises in the observer and reader a sympathetic feeling for the characters. Marian Evans (1819–80), who published under the pseudonym of George Eliot, was one of the leading intellectuals of the day. Her interests were broad and cosmopolitan and she enjoyed a long unmarried partnership with George Henry Lewes (see extracts 8.4 and 10.9).

So I am content to tell my simple story, without trying to make things seem better than they were; dreading nothing, indeed, but falsity, which, in spite of one's best efforts, there is reason to dread. Falsehood is so easy, truth so difficult. The pencil is conscious of a delightful facility in drawing a griffin – the longer the claws, and the larger the wings, the better; but that marvellous facility which we mistook for genius is apt to forsake us when we want to draw a real unexaggerated lion. Examine your words well, and you will find that even when you have no motive to be false, it is a very hard thing to say the exact truth, even about your own immediate feelings – much harder than to say something fine about them which is *not* the exact truth.

It is for this rare, precious quality of truthfulness that I delight in many Dutch paintings, which lofty-minded people despise. I find a source of delicious sympathy in these faithful pictures of a monotonous homely existence, which has been the fate of so many more among my fellow-mortals than a life of pomp or of absolute indigence, of tragic suffering or of world-stirring actions. I turn without shrinking, from cloud-borne angels, from prophets, sibyls, and heroic warriors, to an old woman bending over her flower-pot, or eating her solitary dinner, while the noonday light, softened perhaps by a screen of leaves, falls on her mob-cap, and just touches the rim of her spinning-wheel, and her stone jug, and all those cheap common things which are the precious necessaries of life to her; – or I turn to that village wedding, kept between four brown walls, where an awkward bridegroom opens the dance with a high-shouldered, broad-faced bride, while elderly and middle-aged friends look on, with very irregular noses and lips, and probably with quart-pots in their hands, but with an expression of unmistakeable contentment and goodwill. 'Foh!' says my idealistic friend, 'what vulgar details! What good is there in taking all these pains to give an exact likeness of old women and clowns? What a low phase of life! – what clumsy, ugly people!'

But, bless us, things may be loveable that are not altogether handsome, I hope? I am not at all sure that the majority of the human race have not been ugly, and even among those 'lords of their kind', the British, squat figures, ill-shapen nostrils, and dingy complexions are not startling exceptions. Yet there is a great deal of family love amongst us. I have a friend or two whose class of features is such that the Apollo curl on the summit of their brows would be decidedly trying; yet to my certain knowledge tender hearts have beaten for them, and their miniatures – flattering, but still not lovely – are kissed in secret by motherly lips. I have seen many an excellent matron, who could never in her best days have been handsome, and yet she had a packet of love-letters in a private drawer, and sweet children showered kisses on her sallow cheeks. And I believe there have been plenty of young heroes, of middle stature and feeble beards, who have felt quite sure they could never love anything more insignificant than a Diana, and yet in middle years have found themselves in middle life happily settled with a wife who waddles. Yes! thank God; human feeling is like the mighty rivers that bless the earth: it does not wait for beauty – it flows with resistless force and brings beauty with it.

All honour and reverence to the divine beauty of form! Let us cultivate it to the utmost in men, women, and children – in our gardens and in our houses. But let us love that other beauty too, which lies in no secret of proportion, but in the secret of deep human sympathy. Paint us an angel, if you can, with a floating violet robe, and a face paled by the celestial light; paint us yet oftener a Madonna, turning her mild face upward and opening her arms to welcome the divine glory; but do not impose on us any aesthetic rules which shall banish from the region of Art those old women scraping carrots with their work-worn hands, those heavy clowns taking holiday in a dingy pot-house, those rounded backs and stupid weather-beaten faces that have bent over the spade and done the rough work of the world – those homes with their tin pans, their brown pitchers, their rough curs and their clusters of onions. In this world there are so many of these common, coarse people, who have no picturesque sentimental wretchedness! It is so needful we should remember their existence, else we may happen to leave them quite out of our religion and philosophy, and frame lofty theories which only fit a world of extremes. Therefore let Art always remind us of them; therefore let us always have men ready to give the loving pains of a life to the faithful representing of commonplace things – men who see beauty in these commonplace things, and delight in showing how kindly the light of heaven falls on them. There are few prophets in the world; few sublimely beautiful women; few heroes. I can't afford to give all my love and reverence to such rarities: I want a great deal of those feelings for my everyday fellow-men, especially for the few in the foreground of the great multitude, whose faces I know, whose hands I touch, for whom I have to make way with kindly courtesy. Neither are the picturesque lazzaroni[15] or romantic criminals half so frequent as your common labourer, who gets his own bread, and eats it vulgarly but creditably with his own pocket-knife. It is more needful that I should have a fibre of sympathy connecting me with that vulgar citizen who weighs out my sugar in

---

15 Homeless idlers of Naples.

a vilely assorted cravat and waistcoat, than with the handsomest rascal in red scarf and green feathers; – more needful that my heart should swell with loving admiration at some trait of gentle goodness in the faulty people who sit at the same hearth with me, or in the clergyman of my own parish, who is perhaps rather too corpulent, and in other respects is not an Oberlin[16] or a Tillotson[17], than at the deeds of heroes whom I shall never know except by hearsay, or at the sublimest abstract of all clerical graces that was ever conceived by an able novelist.

6.7 Walter Pater, 'The School of Giorgione', *The Renaissance: Studies in Art and Poetry* (1873; London: Macmillan, 1888)

A primary concern of the Aesthetic Movement was the correlation of the arts. Consider the bewildering number of works that combine more than one art form: for example Wagner's operas (dance, music and drama), Whistler's paintings (with titles such as 'Nocturnes' and 'Harmonies') or ekphrastic works that combined painting and poetry (Michael Field's Sight and Song*). Dante Gabriel Rossetti was both a poet and a painter; William Morris was a poet, a book illustrator and a wallpaper designer. Pater (1839–94) was an Oxford academic with wide interests in European art (see p. 142 for a biographical note). In the late 1860s he began publishing journal articles that led to* Studies in the History of the Renaissance *(1873) (see extract 5.9). In 'The School of Giorgione', first published in the* Fortnightly Review *in October 1877 and added to the retitled third edition* The Renaissance: Studies in Art and Poetry *in 1888, Pater writes about the translatability of any art form. But his most important idea here is that 'all arts aspire to the condition of music'. This is because the aim of any art is abstraction and this abstraction is the most perfect in music, where matter and form are one.*

But although each art has thus its own specific order of impressions, and an untranslatable charm, while a just apprehension of the ultimate differences of the arts is the beginning of æsthetic criticism; yet it is noticeable that, in its special mode of handling its given material, each art may be observed to pass into the condition of some other art, by what German critics term an *Anders-streben* – a partial alienation from its own limitations, by which the arts are able, not indeed to supply the place of each other, but reciprocally to lend each other new forces.

Thus, some of the most delightful music seems to be always approaching to figure, to pictorial definition. Architecture, again, though it has its own laws – laws esoteric enough, as the true architect knows only too well – yet sometimes

---

16 John Frederick Oberlin (1740–1826), cleric of Alsace, who did much to promote the welfare of the people of the Ban de la Roche area, where he ministered for over 50 years.

17 Tillotson (1630–94), archbishop of Canterbury and leading theologian of the latter half of the seventeenth century.

aims at fulfilling the conditions of a picture, as in the *Arena* chapel, or of sculpture, as in the flawless unity of Giotto's tower at Florence; and often finds a true
poetry, as in those strangely twisted staircases of the *châteaux* of the country of
the Loire, as if it were intended that among their odd turnings the actors in a
wild life might pass each other unseen; there being a poetry also of memory and
of the mere effect of time, by which it often profits greatly. Thus, again, sculpture aspires out of the hard limitation of pure form towards colour, or its equivalent; poetry also, in many ways, finding guidance from the other arts, the
analogy between a Greek tragedy and a work of Greek sculpture, between a
sonnet and a relief, of French poetry generally with the art of engraving, being
more than mere figures of speech; and all the arts in common aspiring towards
the principle of music; music being the typical, or ideally consummate art, the
object of the great *Anders-streben* of all art, of all that is artistic, or partakes of
artistic qualities.

All art constantly aspires towards the condition of music. For while in all other
works of art it is possible to distinguish the matter from the form, and the understanding can always make this distinction, yet it is the constant effort of art to
obliterate it. That the mere matter of a poem, for instance – its subject, its given
incidents or situation; that the mere matter of a picture – the actual circumstances of an event, the actual topography of a landscape – should be nothing
without the form, the spirit, of the handling; that this form, this mode of
handling, should become an end in itself, should penetrate every part of the
matter: – this is what all art constantly strives after, and achieves in different
degrees. [. . .]

Poetry, again, works with words addressed in the first instance to the mere
intelligence; and it deals, most often, with a definite subject or situation.
Sometimes it may find a noble and quite legitimate function in the expression
of moral or political aspiration, as often in the poetry of Victor Hugo. In such
instances it is easy enough for the understanding to distinguish between the
matter and the form, however much the matter, the subject, the element which
is addressed to the mere intelligence, has been penetrated by the informing,
artistic spirit. But the ideal types of poetry are those in which this distinction is
reduced to its *minimum*; so that lyrical poetry, precisely because in it we are at
least able to detach the matter from the form, without a deduction of something
from that matter itself, is, at least artistically, the highest and most complete
form of poetry. And the very perfection of such poetry often seems to depend,
in part, on a certain suppression or vagueness of mere subject, so that the meaning reaches us through ways not distinctly traceable by the understanding, as in
some of the most imaginative compositions of William Blake, and often in
Shakespere's [sic] songs, as pre-eminently in that song of Mariana's page in
Measure for Measure, in which the kindling force and poetry of the whole play
seems to pass for a moment into an actual strain of music.

And this principle holds good of all things that partake in any degree of artistic qualities, of the furniture of our houses, and of dress, for instance, of life

itself, of gesture and speech, and the details of daily intercourse; these also, for the wise, being susceptible of a suavity and charm, caught from the way in which they are done, which gives them a worth in themselves; in which, indeed, lies what is valuable and justly attractive, in what is called the fashion of a time, which elevates the trivialities of speech, and manner, and dress, into 'ends in themselves', and gives them a mysterious grace and attractiveness in the doing of them.

Art, then, is thus always striving to be independent of the mere intelligence, to become a matter of pure perception, to get rid of its responsibilities to its subject or material; the ideal examples of poetry and painting being those in which the constituent elements of the composition are so welded together, that the material or subject no longer strikes the intellect only; nor the form, the eye or the ear only; but form and matter, in their union or identity, present one single effect to the 'imaginative reason', that complex faculty for which every thought and feeling is twin-born with its sensible analogue or symbol.

It is the art of music which most completely realises this artistic ideal, this perfect identification of form and matter. In its ideal, consummate moments, the end is not distinct from the means, the form from the matter, the subject from the expression; they inhere in and completely saturate each other; and to it, therefore, to the condition of its perfect moments, all the arts may be supposed constantly to tend and aspire. Music, then, and not poetry, as is so often supposed, is the true type or measure of perfected art. Therefore, although each art has its incommunicable element, its untranslatable order of impressions, its unique mode of reaching the 'imaginative reason', yet the arts may be represented as continually struggling after the law or principle of music, to a condition which music alone completely realises; and one of the chief functions of aesthetic criticism, dealing with the products of art, new or old, is to estimate the degree in which each of those products approaches, in this sense, to musical law.

6.8 Vernon Lee, *Euphorion: Being Studies of the Antique and the Mediæval in the Renaissance* (1884; London: T. Fisher Unwin, 1899)

Vernon Lee (1856–1935), pseudonym of Violet Paget, was a prolific art critic, novelist, short-story writer and aesthete. After the success of her two first critical works, Studies in the Renaissance *(1880) and* Belcaro *(1883), Lee continued to examine aesthetic subjects such as medieval and Renaissance art and literature in* Euphorion *(1884). The volume is particularly important because of its defence of impressionism not only as a new form of aesthetic expression but also, and perhaps more significantly, as a form of knowledge. This interest in impressionism was distinctly different from the realist aesthetics of the mid-Victorian period (George Eliot, for example). Following Walter Pater's view that the aim of the art critic was to 'know one's impression [of an art work] as it really is', Lee argues that impressionism was a more real-*

istic form of artistic expression than realism, because it allowed the critic to show the
real effect of an art work on the observer, offering thus a different kind of knowledge
of the object.

For a period in history is like a more or less extended real landscape: it has, if
you will, actual, chemically defined colours in this and that, if you consider this
and that separate and unaffected by any kind of visual medium; and measura-
ble distances also between this point and the other, if you look down upon it
as from a balloon. But, like a real landscape, it may also be seen from different
points of view, and under different lights; then, according as you stand, the
features of the scene will group themselves – this ridge will disappear behind
that, this valley will open out before you, that other will be closed. Similarly,
according to the light wherein the landscape is seen, the relative scale of
colours and tints of objects, due to pervading light and to distances – what
painters call the values – will alter: the scene will possess one or two predomi-
nant effects, it will produce also one or, at most, two or three (in which case co-
ordinated) impressions. The art which deals with impressions, which tries to
seize the relative values of colours and tints at a given moment, is what you call
new-fangled: its doctrines and works are still subject to the reproach of charla-
tanry. Yet it is the only truly realistic art, and it only, by giving you a thing as
it appears at a given moment, gives it you as it really ever is; all the rest is the
result of cunning abstraction, and representing the scene as it is always, represents it (by striking an average) as it never is at all. I do not pretend that in questions of history we can proceed upon the principles of modern landscape
painting: we do not know what were the elevations which made perspective,
what were the effects of light which created scales of tints, in that far distant
country of the past; and it is safer certainly, and doubtless much more useful,
to strike an average, and represent the past as seen neither from here nor from
there, neither in this light nor that, and let each man imagine his historical
perspective and colour value to the best of his powers. Yet it is nevertheless
certain that the past, to the people who were in it, was not a miraculous map
or other marvellous diagram constructed on the principle of getting at the
actual qualities of things by analysis; that it must have been, to its inhabitants,
but a series of constantly varied perspectives and constantly varied schemes of
colour, according to the position of each individual, and the light in which that
individual viewed it. [. . .]

The following studies are not samples, fragments at which one tries one's
hand, of some large and methodical scheme of work. They are mere impressions developed by means of study: not merely currents of thought and feeling
which I have singled out from the multifold life of the Renaissance; but
currents of thought and feeling in myself, which have found and swept along
with them certain items of Renaissance lore. For the Renaissance has been to
me, in the small measure in which it has been anything, not so much a series
of studies as a series of impressions. I have not mastered the history and litera-

ture of the Renaissance (first-hand or second-hand, perfectly or imperfectly), abstract and exact, and then sought out the places and things which could make that abstraction somewhat more concrete in my mind; I have seen the concrete things, and what I might call the concrete realities of thought and feeling left behind by the Renaissance, and then tried to obtain from books some notion of the original shape and manner of wearing these relics, rags and tatters of a past civilization.

6.9 Oscar Wilde, 'The Decay of Lying: A Dialogue', *Nineteenth Century: A Monthly Review* 25 (January 1889), 35–56

Not only was the flamboyant Oscar Wilde (1854–1900) the aesthete par excellence but his novel The Picture of Dorian Gray *was considered by many to be the Bible of Aestheticism. One of Wilde's most important literary techniques was his epigrammatic use of language, as evidenced in the extract selected here. Wilde used language and form, most notably in this case, the Socratic dialogue (in the manner of Plato), to think about art in a non-referential manner. This essay is perhaps one of the most important texts of the art for art's sake movement. Wilde's witty remarks (for example, 'Art never expresses anything but itself') point to an important shift in the understanding of aesthetics at the end of the nineteenth century. Valuing artifice over naturalness, art over life, Wilde argues that the object of art is not to reproduce or recreate life. Art is its own referent, its own mirror.*

SCENE. – *The Library of a Country House in England.*
PERSONS. – CYRIL *and* VIVIAN.

V. [. . .] But before this comes to pass we must cultivate the lost art of Lying".

C. Then we must certainly cultivate it at once. But in order to avoid making any error I want you to tell me briefly the doctrines of the new aesthetics.

V. Briefly, then, they are these. Art never expresses anything but itself. It has an independent life, just as Thought has, and develops purely on its own lines. It is not necessarily realistic in an age of realism, nor spiritual in an age of faith. So far from being the creation of its time, it is usually in direct opposition to it, and the only history that it preserves for us is the history of its own progress. Sometimes it returns on its own footsteps, and revives some old form, as happened in the archaistic movement of late Greek art, and in the pre-Raphaelite movement of our own day. At other times it entirely antici- pates its age, and produces in one century work that it takes another century to understand, to appreciate, and to enjoy. In no case does it reproduce its age. To pass from the art of a time to the time itself is the great fallacy of all historians.

The second doctrine is this. All bad art comes from returning to life and nature, and elevating them into ideals. Life and nature may sometimes be used as part of art's rough material, but before they are of any real service to art they must be translated into artistic conventions. The moment Art surrenders its imaginative medium it surrenders everything. As a method Realism is a complete failure, and the two things that every artist should avoid are modernity of form and modernity of subject-matter. To us, who live in the nineteenth century, any century is a suitable subject for art except our own. The only beautiful things are things that do not concern us. It is, to have the pleasure of quoting myself, exactly because Hecuba is nothing to us that her sorrows are so suitable a motive for a tragedy.

The third doctrine is that Life imitates Art far more than Art imitates Life. This results not merely from Life's imitative instinct, but from the fact that the desire of Life is simply to find expression, and that Art offers it certain beautiful forms through which it may realise that energy. It is a theory that has never been put forward before, but it is extremely fruitful, and throws an entirely new light on the history of Art.

The last doctrine is that Lying, the telling of beautiful untrue things, is the proper aim of Art. But of this I think I have spoken at sufficient length. And now let us go out on the terrace, where 'the milk-white peacock glimmers like a ghost', while the evening star 'washes the dusk with silver'. At twilight nature becomes a wonderfully suggestive effect and is not without loveliness, though perhaps its chief use is to illustrate quotations from the poets. Come! We have talked long enough.

6.10 Arthur Symons, 'The Decadent Movement in Literature', *Harper's New Monthly Magazine* 87 (November 1893), 858–69

Arthur Symons (1865–1945) was a poet, editor and critic; his first book of verse, Days and Nights *(1889), dedicated to Walter Pater, established him as an urban Decadent poet. This manifesto, published in the American journal* Harper's New Monthly Magazine, *takes forward the Aesthetes' interest in impressionism to argue that the Decadent Movement, which has its roots in European urban literature, has two branches, corresponding to two different epistemological understandings of the world and two aesthetics: impressionism and symbolism. Both branches seek to find 'la verité vrai', the real truth, but while impressionism achieves this in the way in which this truth appears to the senses, symbolism finds truth in abstract language. After the demise of Oscar Wilde in 1895, decadence became a byword for sexual deviancy. When the book version of this article was published in 1899, Symons changed its title to* The Symbolist Movement in Literature. *(See also extract 8.10 for an alternative* fin de siècle *challenge to Victorian literary conventions.)*

The latest movement in European literature has been called by many names, none of them quite exact or comprehensive – Decadence, Symbolism, Impressionism, for instance. It is easy to dispute over words, and we shall find that Verlaine[18] objects to being called a Decadent, Maeterlinck[19] to being called a Symbolist, Huysmans[20] to being called an Impressionist. These terms, as it happens, have been adopted as the badge of little separate cliques, noisy, brain-sick young people who haunt the brasseries of the Boulevard Saint-Michel, and exhaust their ingenuities in theorizing over the works they cannot write. But, taken frankly as epithets which express their own meaning, both Impressionism and Symbolism convey some notion of that new kind of literature which is perhaps more broadly characterized by the word Decadence. The most represen-tative literature of the day – the writing which appeals to, which has done so much to form, the younger generation – is certainly not classic, nor has it any relation with that antithesis of the Classic, the Romantic. After a fashion it is no doubt a decadence; it has all the qualities that mark the end of great periods, the qualities that we find in the Greek, the Latin, decadence: an intense self-consciousness, a restless curiosity in research, an over subtilizing refinement upon refinement, a spiritual and moral perversity. If what we call the classic is indeed the supreme art – those qualities of perfect simplicity, perfect sanity, perfect proportion, the supreme qualities – then this representative literature of to-day, interesting, beautiful, novel as it is, is really a new and beautiful and interesting disease.

Healthy we cannot call it, and healthy it does not wish to be considered. The Goncourts,[21] in their prefaces, in their *Journal*, are always insisting on their own pet malady, *la névrose*. It is in their work, too, that Huysmans notes with delight, 'le style tacheté et faisandé' – high-flavored and spotted with corruption – which he himself possesses in the highest degree. 'Having desire without light, curios-ity without wisdom, seeking God by strange ways, by ways traced by the hands of men, offering rash incense on the high places to an unknown God, who is the God of darkness' – that is how Ernest Hello,[22] in one of his apocalyptic moments, characterizes the nineteenth century. And this unreason of the soul – of which Hello himself is so curious a victim – this unstable equilibrium, which has overbalanced so many brilliant intelligences into one form or another of spiritual confusion, is but another form of the *maladie fin de siècle*. For its very disease of form, this literature is certainly typical of a civilization grown over-luxurious, over-inquiring, too languid for the relief of action, too uncertain for any emphasis in opinion or in conduct. It reflects all the moods, all the manners, of a sophisticated society; its very artificiality is a way of being true to nature, simplicity, sanity, proportion – the classic qualities – how much do we

---

18 Paul Verlaine (1844–96), French poet associated with symbolism.
19 Maurice Maeterlinck (1862–1949), Belgian symbolist writer and poet who received the Nobel Prize for literature in 1911.
20 Joris-Karl Huysmans (1848–1907), French novelist associated with the Decadent Movement.
21 Edmond de Goncourt (1822–96) and Jules de Goncourt (1830–70), naturalist writers and critics who worked in collaboration until the early death of Jules. Their *Journal des Goncourt* is an important record of literary and cultural life in late nineteenth-century Paris.
22 Ernest Hello (1828–85), French scholar and writer who influenced the symbolists.

possess them in our life, our surroundings, that we should look to find them in our literature – so evidently the literature of a decadence?

Taking the word Decadence, then, as most accurately expressing the general sense of the newest movement in literature, we find that the terms Impressionism and Symbolism define correctly enough the two main branches of that movement. Now Impressionist and Symbolist have more in common than either supposes; both are really working on the same hypothesis, applied in different directions. What both seek is not general truth merely, but *la vérité vraie*, the very essence of truth – the truth of appearances to the senses, of the visible world to the eyes that see it; and the truth of spiritual things to the spiritual vision. The Impressionist, in literature as in painting, would flash upon you in a new, sudden way so exact an image of what you have just seen, just as you have seen it, that you may say, as a young American sculptor, a pupil of Rodin,[23] said to me on seeing for the first time a picture of Whistler's,[24] 'Whistler seems to think his picture upon canvas – and there it is!' Or you may find, with Sainte-Beuve,[25] writing of Goncourt, the 'soul of the landscape' – the soul of whatever corner of the visible world has to be realized. The Symbolist, in this new, sudden way, would flash upon you the 'soul' of that which can be apprehended only by the soul – the finer sense of things unseen, the deeper meaning of things evident. And naturally, necessarily, this endeavour after a perfect truth to one's impression, to one's intuition – perhaps an impossible endeavour – has brought with it, in its revolt from ready-made impressions and conclusions, a revolt from the ready-made of language, from the bondage of a traditional form, of a form become rigid. In France, where this movement began and has mainly flourished, it is Goncourt who was the first to invent a style in prose really new, impressionistic, a style which was itself almost sensation. It is Verlaine who has invented such another new style in verse.

---

23 Auguste Rodin (1840–1917), major French sculptor.
24 James Abbott McNeill Whistler (1834–1903), American painter and etcher.
25 Charles Augustin Sainte-Beuve (1804–69), French critic and literary historian.

7

Popular Culture

Introduction

Popular culture is a notoriously multivalent concept. Raymond Williams has suggested that its different meanings include 'well liked by many people', 'inferior kinds of work', 'work deliberately setting out to win favour with the people' and 'culture actually made by the people for themselves'.[1] All of these meanings are evident in this section. During the nineteenth century the term only rarely functioned in a neutral fashion as simply connoting the everyday habits of the broad mass of 'the people'. It more often operated as a synonym for working-class customs; moreover, these were often described by members of the social elite who were, if not looking down on the working class, at least observing them from a safe distance. A question worth asking of all the following pieces is – what ideological relationship do the authors have to their subject? Who is determining or defining the characteristics of Victorian popular culture? Only Thomas Wright, publishing under the pseudonym 'The Journeyman Engineer', writes from an overtly working-class identity, and even this is problematic given that his books were one of the ways he gained access to the cultural elite.

For many, everyday life in the nineteenth-century was dominated by work. Debates around popular culture, however, usually focus on leisure rather than labour, with the increase of the former one of the principal signs of rising living standards. Reductions in working hours and rising incomes meant both free time and the spending power to enjoy it. Industrialization, though, did more than put pennies in pockets. It significantly altered the established rhythms of work and leisure, encouraging a move away from the seasonal pace of rural life to the more regimented tempo of urban living. Greater regulation and standardization of working hours – epitomized by the factory horn calling men and women to and from work – led to the dying out of traditional practices such as 'Saint Monday', whereby workers did not immediately return to work on the Monday morning following their Sunday rest. Such losses were compensated for by benefits such as statutory Bank Holidays, legislation for which was first passed in 1871. No longer would Scrooge warn Bob Cratchit to come in early on Boxing Day.

---

1 Raymond Williams, *Keywords* (London: Fontana, 1983), 287.

The changing pattern of leisure time meant that the traditional calendar of fairs, wakes and holy days was supplemented by many new forms of leisure activity, ranging from music halls and bazaars to amateur photography and cycling clubs. Urbanization created large, increasingly affluent audiences, and a crucial aspect of the changing character of popular leisure was an increase in its scale, organization and commercial character. Theatre, music hall and variety entertainment were enormously successful institutions; the section includes several examples of handbills advertising different types of popular performance. Their variety is intended to demonstrate the range of nightly entertainments found not just in London but in provincial towns and cities throughout Britain. By the end of the century, recreation and entertainment were being provided by a culture industry that operated on a mass scale. Correspondingly, it was no longer possible to conceive of popular culture as something predominantly created by the people, a kind of authentic self-expression, but rather as a commodity produced *for* them, according to an idea of what they desired.

Industrial and technological advances were an important influence upon popular culture. The railways encouraged tourism and travel, while individual devices like the camera, phonograph and stereoscope were enormously popular. The appeal of these devices stemmed, in part, from the way that the mechanical reproduction of sound and image enabled them to captivate ever-larger numbers of consumers. Equally, the procession of new gadgets often thrilled because they were part of the way modernity was refiguring the human sensorium. Thus the article below on the stereoscope focuses on the wonder and novelty of the device in expanding the cultural boundaries of perception.

An anthropological fascination with the everyday life of the working class often went hand in hand with the desire to regulate it. The increasing amount of leisure time led to numerous anxieties over the way it was being utilized. There was constant tension between working-class pleasures and middle- and upper-class attempts to wean them onto more cultured and improving pastimes. Particularly in the period between 1830 and 1880, when fears about class conflict were prevalent, it was a widespread belief that leisure activities offered an important means of building social cohesion. As Matthew Arnold argued in *Culture and Anarchy* – brilliantly codifying many existing assumptions – culture offered a national collective bond that would not only substitute for the decline of institutionalized religion, but would provide an antidote to working-class political agitation and narcissistic bourgeois individualism (see extracts 2.9 and 8.7 for examples of Arnold's cultural agenda).

The extensive provision of leisure activities for the working class by the cultural and social elite is evident in the founding of institutions such as lyceums, temperance halls, mechanics' institutes, athenaeums, museums, reading rooms and church societies. Many of these offered an ongoing programme of lectures, readings, concerts, scientific demonstrations and exhibitions. While appealing to a cross-section of the local community, part of the aim of these institutions was to wean the working class away from the boisterous conviviality of the public house, the immorality of the penny gaff and the saturnalia of the fair (see extracts 7.1, 7.3 and 7.5). An article of faith for these institutions was the belief in 'rational recreation', the notion that leisure time should be used for activities that were improving yet entertaining, educational yet amusing.

It was not only minds that were to be improved though rational recreation but bodies as well. Parks and open spaces were among the facilities created for the urban working class, while greater organization of sports and games created standardized versions of pursuits like football, rugby and lawn tennis. Sport, however, remained a demonstration of the degree to which leisure replicated class hierarchies. Cricket was split between Gentleman amateurs and professional Players, with the former controlling the ethos and rules of the game. Rugby similarly divided into two different codes in 1895: the formation of a Northern Union stemmed from a dispute over the Rugby Football Union's refusal to sanction payment to working-class players as compensation for time off from their jobs.

Athleticism was particularly important to late Victorian Christian manliness, with many public school games believed to propagate an Englishness based on fair play, perseverance and collective endeavour (see extract 4.2). Women, though, were equally beneficiaries of the popularity of physical recreation. The promotion of healthy activity for women and girls was one of the new freedoms they enjoyed as the constraints upon respectable feminine behaviour were challenged. The bicycling New Woman, independent and mobile, was an icon of the 1890s (see extract 7.10). Women, particularly middle- and upper-class women, enjoyed a distinct position vis-à-vis leisure pursuits because it was less likely that the majority of their time was taken up with paid employment. Many women found an outlet for creative self-expression in pastimes such as needlework, water-colour painting, embroidery, music and singing. Not all the pursuits undertaken by genteel women, however, were concerned with making the drawing room a space for family relaxation. The article below from the *English Women's Journal*, 'What Are Women Doing?', includes charity work amongst prevalent pastimes, and, in so doing, reflects the breadth of those activities that come under the rubric of popular culture.

7.1 Charles Dickens, 'Gin-Shops', *Sketches By Boz* (London: John Macrone, 1837)

Conviviality and the consumption of alcohol were central to nineteenth-century social and business life. In response, thriving temperance societies such as the Band of Hope (formed in 1847, with branches across the country) organized large rallies, concerts and lectures to try and wean the working class away from their attachment to the communal life of the public house. The drive for the moral and educational improvement of the working class, of the kind that motivated the foundation of mechanics'

*institutes, often set itself against the insidious effect of the evils of drink. 'Gin-Shops'
was first published on 7 February 1835 in the* Evening Chronicle, *when the 23-year-
old Dickens was working as a journalist and parliamentary reporter. It was first
published in volume form in 1836. As Dickens makes clear, the ostentatious decoration
of gin shops was in deliberately stark contrast to the poverty of many of the people visiting it.*

We will endeavour to sketch the bar of a large gin-shop, and its ordinary
customers, for the edification of such of our readers as may not have had opportunities of observing such scenes; and on the chance of finding one, well suited
to our purpose, we will make for Drury-Lane, through the narrow streets and
dirty courts which divide it from Oxford-street, and that classical spot adjoining the brewery at the bottom of Tottenham-court-road, best known to the
initiated as the 'Rookery'. The filthy and miserable appearance of this part of
London can hardly be imagined by those (and there are many such) who have
not witnessed it. Wretched houses with broken windows patched with rags and
paper, every room let out to a different family, and in many instances to two or
even three [. . .]

You turn the corner. What a change! All is light and brilliancy. The hum of
many voices issues from that splendid gin-shop which forms the commencement of the two streets opposite; and the gay building with the fantastically
ornamented parapet, the illuminated clock, the plate-glass windows
surrounded by stucco rosettes, and its profusion of gas-lights in richly-gilt
burners, is perfectly dazzling when contrasted with the darkness and dirt we
have just left. The interior is even gayer than the exterior. A bar of French-
polished mahogany, elegantly carved, extends the whole width of the place;
and there are two side aisles of great casks, painted green and gold, enclosed
within a light brass rail, and bearing such inscriptions as 'Old Tom, 549';
'Young Tom, 360'; 'Samson, 1421'. Beyond the bar is a lofty and spacious
saloon, full of the same enticing vessels, with a gallery running round it,
equally well furnished. On the counter, in addition to the usual spirit apparatus, are two or three little baskets of cakes and biscuits, which are carefully
secured at top with wicker-work, to prevent their contents being unlawfully
abstracted. Behind it, are two showily-dressed damsels with large necklaces,
dispensing the spirits and 'compounds'. [. . .]

It is growing late, and the throng of men, women, and children, who have
been constantly going in and out, dwindles down to two or three occasional
stragglers – cold, wretched-looking creatures, in the last stage of emaciation and
disease. The knot of Irish labourers at the lower end of the place, who have been
alternately shaking hands with, and threatening the life of, each other for the
last hour, become furious in their disputes; and finding it impossible to silence
one man, who is particularly anxious to adjust the difference, they resort to the
expedient of knocking him down and jumping on him afterwards. The man in
the fur cap, and the potboy rush out; a scene of riot and confusion ensues; half

the Irishmen get shut out, and the other half get shut in; the potboy is knocked among the tubs in no time; the landlord hits every body, and every body hits the landlord; the barmaids scream; in come the police; the rest is a confused mixture of arms, legs, staves, torn coats, shouting, and struggling. Some of the party are borne off to the station-house, and the remainder slink home to beat their wives for complaining, and kick the children for daring to be hungry.

We have sketched this subject very slightly, not only because our limits compel us to do so, but because, if it were pursued farther, it would be painful and repulsive. Well-disposed gentlemen, and charitable ladies, would alike turn with coldness and disgust from a description of the drunken, besotted men, and wretched, broken-down, miserable women, who form no inconsiderable portion of the frequenters of these haunts; forgetting, in the pleasant consciousness of their own high rectitude, the poverty of the one, and the temptation of the other. Gin-drinking is a great vice in England, but poverty is a greater; and until you can cure it, or persuade a half-famished wretch not to seek relief in the temporary oblivion of his own misery, with the pittance which, divided among his family, would just furnish a morsel of bread for each, gin-shops will increase in number and splendour. If Temperance Societies would suggest an antidote against hunger and distress, or could establish dispensaries for the gratuitous distribution of bottles of Lethe-water, gin-palaces would be numbered among the things that were.

7.2 'Directions to Ladies for Shopping', *Punch* 7 (July–December 1844), 142

For those with ample financial means, one of the distinct pleasures of the period was consuming the large number of goods being manufactured, which included fashionable and luxurious items made out of raw materials from disparate parts of the globe. A plenitude of desirable wares combined with rising incomes and an increase in leisure time: the result was that shopping became an enjoyable and distinct leisure activity. Punch, launched in 1841, was the most influential satirical journal of the period, and, as this satire emphasizes, in the 1840s shopping remained a genteel pleasure, oriented towards conspicuous consumption, and conducted in upmarket retail spaces such as bazaars and arcades. It was not until the 1880s and 1890s that a mass consumer culture came to the fore, symbolized by the emergence of the department store as the dominant form of modern retailing.

Shopping is the amusement of spending money at shops. It is to a lady what sporting is to a gentleman; somewhat productive, and very chargeable. Sport, however, involves the payment of one's own shot; shopping may be managed by getting it paid for. Ride all the way till you come to the shopping-ground in a coach, if you can; in an omnibus, if you must; lest you should be tired when you get there. If you are a lady of fashion, do not get out of your carriage; and when you stop before your milliners, particularly if it is a cold, wet day, make one of the young women come out to you, and without a bonnet, in her thin shoes, stand on the kerb-stone in the damp and mud. The best places for shopping are fashionable streets, bazaars, and the like. Street-shopping principally relates to hosiery, drapery, and jewellery of the richer sort. Bazaar and Arcade-shopping, to fancy articles, nick-nacks, and perfumery. In street-shopping walk leisurely along, keeping a sharp look-out on the windows. In bazaar-shopping, beat each stall separately. Many patterns, colours, novelties, conveniences, and other articles will thus strike your eye, which you would otherwise have never wanted or dreamt of. When you have marked down some dress, or riband, for instance, that you would like, go and inquire the price of it; haggle, demur, examine, and, lastly, buy. You will then be asked 'whether there is any other article to-day?' Whether there is or not, let the shopman show you what wares he pleases; you will very likely desire one or more of them. Whatever you think very cheap, that buy, without reference to your need of it; it is a bargain. You will find, too, as you go on, that one thing suggests another; as bonnets – ribands for trimming, or flowers; and handkerchiefs – perfumery. In considering what more you want, try and recollect what your acquaintances have got that you have not; or what you have seen worn by strangers in going along. See if there is anything before you superior in any respect to a similar thing which you have already; if so, get it instantly, not reflecting whether your own will do well enough. You had better finish your streets before you take your bazaars and arcades; for there the shopping, which one might otherwise call cover-shopping, though excellent sport, refers mostly to articles of no manner of use; and it may be as well to reserve toys and superfluities to the last. Married ladies, when they have laid in all they want for themselves, are recommended to show their thoughtfulness by purchasing some little trifle for their husbands, who, of course, will have to pay for it in the end.

7.3 Albert Smith, 'Greenwich Fair', *Gavarni in London: Sketches of Life and Character*, ed. Albert Smith (London: Bogue, 1849), 75–8

Fairs had long formed part of the traditional calendar of popular life, an opportunity for merrymaking during the few holidays enjoyed by most people. As the nineteenth century progressed, fairs lost their original trading function and became more devoted to amusements, consisting of a plethora of travelling shows of the type described here. Greenwich Fair, held in Easter week, was one of the largest traditional fairs, attracting large numbers of Londoners. Like other fairs, it was often subject to censure due to its perceived riotousness and was abolished in 1857. Albert Smith (1816–60), journalist, playwright and periodical editor (he ran his own journal, The Man in the Moon, *1847–9), was also a prominent showman. He fronted one of the most successful panoramic entertainments of the nineteenth century, 'Mr Albert Smith's Ascent of Mont Blanc', which ran for six years from 1852 at the Egyptian Hall, Piccadilly.*

There is not a goodlier day of merry-making, for the regular traditional Monday-keepers, passed in the neighbourhood of London than at Greenwich Fair. The Pool, and the Port, of London are always objects of astonishment to a foreigner; but to see them on Whit-Monday, or at the commencement of a fine Easter week, is the most extraordinary sight he will meet with.

At a very early hour, there is a busy note of preparation sounded at the steamboat piers along the river. The streets are thronged with decently dressed people, the greater part of whom are progressing towards the Thames. [. . .]

The fair begins directly you land. From the Ship Torbay Tavern up to the park gates, the road is bordered on either side with stalls, games, and hand-waggons, containing goods or refreshments of every description. Mr Punch, too, sets up the temple of his illegitimate drama at three or four points of the thoroughfare, at each of which (in our belief that there is but one Punch and that he is ubiquitous), he is pursuing that reckless career of vice and dissipation with which his audience are always so delighted. Snuff-boxes to throw at – refreshments of singularly untempting appearance, which nevertheless find eager purchasers – vendors of spring rattles, who ensure 'the whole fun o' the fair for a penny' – speculators in heavy stocks of Waterloo crackers and detonating balls – proprietors of small percussion guns, to shoot with at targets for nuts – keep increasing, together with the visitors, as we near the park; until the diminished breadth of the street brings them all together in one struggle to get through the gates, like the grains of sand in an egg-glass. [. . .]

There is always the same concourse of people outside the upper park gates, upon Blackheath; but the style of amusement is here varied. Fortune-tellers and donkeys form the chief attraction; and the hirers of the latter continually bestridden and belaboured animals meet with as frequent falls as the runners on the hill, and apparently with as little consequences. The gipsies, also, are driving a brisk trade amongst the credulous, inviting everybody to peep into their own futurity; indeed we are so frequently addressed as 'My pretty gentleman', and hear so many gratifying things for nothing, told in the hope of luring us on to cross the olive hand presented to us with a 'piece of silver', that we began to think our own lot in life was not so miserable after all. [. . .]

The shows, possibly, are our greatest delight, for we love to be harmlessly imposed upon at these wandering exhibitions. The last time we were at Greenwich Fair, we saw one held in a dismantled dwelling-house, where various forms in wax-work, of the true Mrs. Jarley breed, were set up for inspection.[2] In the recess of a window were placed two figures, evidently intended, originally, for Amy Robsart and the Earl of Leicester, but which represented, we were informed, Queen Victoria and Prince Albert, enjoying the retirement of private life, apart from the pomp of royalty.[3] Why they should have chosen to enjoy

---

2 Mrs Jarley is a character in Charles Dickens's *Old Curiosity Shop*, who had a run-down travelling waxwork show.

3 Amy Robsart (1532–60) was the wife of Robert Dudley (1532–88), 1st Earl of Leicester; she died in controversial and unexplained circumstances.

retirement in fancy dresses of the Elizabethan period, those best acquainted with the habits of those august personages can possibly inform us. All the characters of the exhibition were, however, old friends. We fancied that we once knew them in High Holborn, where the organ turned at the door, and the monkey sat on the hot gas-pipe. At all events, if they were not the identical ones, the artist had cast two in the same mould whilst he was about it. [. . .]

In another show were some learned birds. This was also held in an unfinished house. A curtain nailed to the rafters divided the rude interior into two parts; by pushing it aside we saw a flock-bed upon the ground, a mouldering fire, and a tin saucepan: a thin unhappy dog was persuading himself that he was asleep on the bed. In front of the *penetralia* was a dirty breeding-cage, in which five or six poor little ragged canaries were sitting on a perch, huddled up together as if for better self-defence.[4] A man came to the front and said, 'Stand back, gents, and then all can see – the canaries, the performing canaries, brought from the Canary Islands for the Queen.' The birds were then taken out, and had to pull carts and draw water, sit on the end of a trumpet whilst it was played, and fire cannon; the explosion of the gunpowder throwing them into a state of tumbling, chuffing, and sneezing, from which they did not recover by the conclusion of the entertainment.

7.4 Oliver Wendell Holmes, 'The Stereoscope and the Stereograph' (1859), *Soundings from the Atlantic* (Boston: James R. Osgood, 1872)

Optical shows and devices, such as the panorama, magic lantern, stereoscope and peepshow, were ubiquitous forms of public and domestic entertainment. The stereoscope was one of a number of optical devices that first emerged out of investigations into the physiology of vision in the 1820s and 1830s. Its initial function was to demonstrate the role of binocular vision in creating the way that the body perceived three-dimensional space. With the advent of photography though, stereoscopes and stereographs shot to commercial success. The London Stereoscopic Company was set up in 1854 and, by 1858, claimed over 100,000 pictures in its trade catalogue. One slogan of the company was 'Seems Madam, NAY IT IS'. Although best known as an American writer, Wendell Holmes (1809–74) also produced his own design of stereoscope, which was particularly successful in the USA. This essay was first published in the American periodical, the Atlantic Monthly, *in June 1859.*

THE STEREOSCOPE. – This instrument was invented by Professor Wheatstone, and first described by him in 1838.[5] [. . .]

---

4 Penetralia – the innermost recesses or most secret parts of a structure (or, figuratively, of the soul or mind).

A stereoscope is an instrument which makes surfaces look solid. All pictures in which perspective and light and shade are properly managed, have more or less of the effect of solidity; but by this instrument that effect is so heightened as to produce an appearance of reality which cheats the senses with its seeming truth. [. . .]

What is to come of the stereoscope and the photograph we are almost afraid to guess, lest we should seem extravagant. But, premising that we are to give a *colored* stereoscopic mental view of their prospects, we will venture on a few glimpses at a conceivable, if not a possible future.

Form is henceforth divorced from matter. In fact, matter as a visible object is of no great use any longer, except as the mould on which form is shaped. Give us a few negatives of a thing worth seeing, taken from different points of view, and that is all we want of it. Pull it down or burn it up, if you please. We must, perhaps, sacrifice some luxury in the loss of color; but form and light and shade are the great things, and even color can be added, and perhaps by and by may be got direct from Nature.

There is only one Colosseum or Pantheon; but how many millions of potential negatives have they shed, – representatives of billions of pictures – since they were erected! Matter in large masses must always be fixed and dear; form is cheap and transportable. We have got the fruit of creation now, and need not trouble ourselves with the core. Every conceivable object of Nature and Art will soon scale off its surface for us. Men will hunt all curious, beautiful, grand objects, as they hunt the cattle in South America, for their *skins*, and leave the carcasses as of little worth.

The consequence of this will soon be such an enormous collection of forms that they will have to be classified and arranged in vast libraries, as books are now. The time will come when a man who wishes to see any object, natural or artificial, will go to the Imperial, National, or City Stereographic Library and call for its skin or form, as he would for a book at any common library. We do now distinctly propose the creation of a comprehensive and systematic stereographic library, where all men can find the special forms they particularly desire to see as artists, or as scholars, or as mechanics, or in any other capacity. Already a workman has been travelling about the country with stereographic views of furniture, showing his employer's patterns in this way, and taking orders for them. This is a mere hint of what is coming before long.

Again, we must have special stereographic collections, just as we have professional and other special libraries. And as a means of facilitating the formation of public and private stereographic collections, there must be arranged a comprehensive system of exchanges, so that there may grow up something like a

---

5 Charles Wheatstone (1802–75), renowned scientist who made numerous discoveries in optics, acoustics and telegraphy, and who was Professor of Experimental Physics at King's College, London. The stereoscope was first described in a paper given to the Royal Society in 1838.

Figure 7.1 Fold-out wooden stereoscope with glass stereograph, c.1870

universal currency of these bank-notes, or promises to pay in solid substance, which the sun has engraved for the great Bank of Nature.

7.5 Henry Mayhew, 'Of the Penny Gaff', London Labour and the London Poor, vol. 1 (London: Griffith, Bohn, and Co., 1861)

Penny gaffs were downmarket venues providing cheap theatrical entertainment. First coming to the fore in the 1830s, they catered predominantly to the working-class juvenile audiences in large cities, making them one of the products of urbanization. James Grant's Sketches of London *(1838) estimated that there were then 80 to 100 penny gaffs in London. These less than salubrious venues usually provided a diverse entertainment that might include short melodramas and theatrical pieces, music, singing, dancing, and variety turns such as performing animals, panoramas and ventriloquism. Penny gaffs were often attacked as immoral. However, the anxieties they provoked were only in part due to their supposedly licentious fare, particularly their predilection for portraying gruesome crimes, and were as much due to the fact that they encouraged the congregation of large number of youths of both sexes. Henry Mayhew's account is taken from his four-volume,* London Labour and the London Poor, *which was an expanded version of a series of letters describing the state of the urban poor that were published in the* Morning Chronicle *between October 1849 and December 1850. (See p. 56 for a biographical note on Mayhew and for another extract from* London Labour and the London Poor.*)*

In many of the thoroughfares of London there are shops which have been turned into a kind of temporary theatre (admission one penny), where dancing and singing take place every night. Rude pictures of the performers are arranged outside, to give the front a gaudy and attractive look, and at night-time coloured lamps and transparencies are displayed to draw an audience. These places are called by the costers 'Penny Gaffs'; and on a Monday night as many as six performances will take place, each one having its two hundred visitors.

It is impossible to contemplate the ignorance and immorality of so numerous a class as that of the costermongers, without wishing to discover the cause of their degradation. Let any one curious on this point visit one of these penny shows, and he will wonder that *any* trace of virtue and honesty should remain among the people. Here the stage, instead of being the means for illustrating a moral precept, is turned into a platform to teach the cruelest debauchery. The audience is usually composed of children so young, that these dens become the school-rooms where the guiding morals of a life are picked up; and so precocious are the little things, that the girl of nine will, from constant attendance at such places, have learnt to understand the filthiest sayings, and laugh at them as loudly as the grown-up lads around her. What notions can the young female form of marriage and chastity, when the penny theatre rings with applause at the performance of a scene whose sole point turns upon the pantomimic imitation of the un-restrained indulgence of the most corrupt appetites of our nature? How can the lad learn to check his hot passions and think honesty and virtue admirable, when the shouts around him impart a glory to a descriptive song so painfully corrupt, that it can only have been made tolerable by the most habitual excess? The men who preside over these infamous places know too well the failings of their audiences. They know that these poor children require no nicely-turned joke to make the evening pass merrily, and that the filth they utter needs no double meaning to veil its obscenity. The show that will provide the most unrestrained debauchery will have the most crowded benches; and to gain this point, things are acted and spoken that it is criminal even to allude to.

Not wishing to believe in the description which some of the more intelligent of the costermongers had given of these places, it was thought better to visit one of them, so that all exaggeration might be avoided. One of the least offensive of the exhibitions was fixed upon. The 'penny gaff' chosen was situated in a broad street near Smithfield; and for a great distance off, the jingling sound of music was heard, and the gas-light streamed out into the thick night air as from a dark lantern, glittering on the windows of the houses opposite, and lighting up the faces of the mob in the road, as on an illumination night. The front of a large shop had been entirely removed, and the entrance was decorated with paintings

Figure 7.2 Phiz, 'Pantomime Night', *Illustrated London News* (8 January 1848), 8

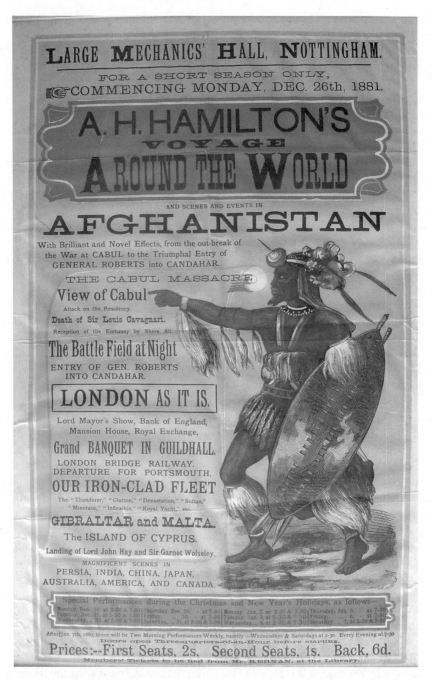

Figure 7.3 'A. W. Hamilton's Voyage Around the World', Large Mechanics' Hall, Nottingham (1881)

of the 'comic singers', in their most humourous attitudes. On a table against the wall was perched the band, playing what the costers call 'dancing tunes' with great effect, for the hole at the money-taker's box was blocked up with hands tendering the penny. [. . .]

After waiting in the lobby some considerable time, the performance inside was concluded, and the audience came pouring out through the canvass door. As they had to pass singly, I noticed them particularly. Above three-fourths of them were women and girls, the rest consisting chiefly of mere boys – for out of about two hundred persons I counted only eighteen men. [. . .]

Singing and dancing formed the whole of the hours' performance, and, of the two, the singing was preferred. [. . .]

When I had left, I spoke to a better class costermonger on this saddening subject. 'Well, sir, it is frightful,' he said, 'but the boys *will* have their amuse-ments. If their amusements is bad they don't care; they only wants to laugh, and this here kind of work does it. Give 'em better singing and better dancing, and they'd go, if the price was as cheap as this is. I've seen, when a decent concert was given at a penny, as many as four thousand costers present, behaving them-selves as quietly and decently as possible. Their wives and children was with 'em, and no audience was better conducted. It's all stuff talking about them preferring this sort of thing. Give 'em good things at the same price, and I *know* they will like the good, better than the bad.'

My own experience with this neglected class goes to prove, that if we would really lift them out of the moral mire in which they are wallowing, the first step must be to provide them with *wholesome* amusements. The misfortune, however, is, that when we seek to elevate the character of the people, we give them such mere dry abstract truths and dogmas to digest, that the uneducated mind turns with abhorrence from them. We forget how we ourselves were originally won by our *emotions* to the consideration of such subjects. We do not remember how our own tastes have been formed, nor do we, in our zeal, stay to reflect how the tastes of a people generally are created; and, consequently, we cannot perceive that a habit of enjoying any matter whatsoever can only be induced in the mind by linking with it some æsthetic affection. The heart is the mainspring of the intellect, and the feelings the real educers and educators of the thoughts. As games with the young destroy the fatigue of muscular exercise, so do the sympa-thies stir the mind to action without any sense of effort. It is because 'serious' people generally object to enlist the emotions in the education of the poor, and look upon the delight which arises in the mind from the mere perception of the beauty of sound, motion, form, and colour – or from the apt association of harmonious or incongruous ideas – or from the sympathetic operation of the affections; it is because, I say, the zealous portion of society look upon these matters as *'vanity'*, that the amusements of the working-classes are left to venal traders to provide. [. . .] It is folly to fancy that the mind, spent with the irksome-ness of compelled labour, and depressed, perhaps, with the struggle to live by that labour after all, will not, when the work is over, seek out some place where

ALHAMBRA THEATRE,

LEICESTER SQUARE LONDON. Telephone No. 35065.

General Manager ... ... Mr. ALFRED MOUL.

Business Manager—Mr. DOUGLAS COX. Secretary and Treasurer—Mr. H. WOODFORD.
Stage Manager—Mr. A. G. FORDE. Maitre de Ballet—Signor C. COPPI.
Musical Director—Mons. G. JACOBI.

Programme

For the Week commencing MONDAY, AUGUST 3rd, 1896.

(1) Overture ... ... " Si j'etais Roi " ... ... *Adam*

(2) THE MUSICAL KORRIES.

(3) A NEW AND ORIGINAL IRISH DIVERTISSEMENT, entitled—
"DONNYBROOK,"
Invented and Produced by Signor CARLO COPPI. The Music by Mons. GEORGES JACOBI.

CHARACTERS:

PATRICK 'Chief of the Whiteboys) Miss JULIE SEALE | PADDY LEARY ... (a Farmer) ... Mr. G. ALMONTI
MICKY DUNN ... (a Spy) ... Mr. E. ALMONTI | MOLLY ... ... (his Wife) ... Miss E. AUDUS
FATHER FLAHERTY (a Priest) ... Mr. LYTTON GREY | EILY ... their Daughter Miss J. CASABONI
O'CALLIGHAN (Sergeant of Constabulary) | CHIEF OF THE GYPSIES ... ... Mr. MARRA
Mr. FRED STOREY | THE VILLAGE FIDDLER ... Mr. BERNARD LEYTON
ENGLISH OFFICER ... ... Miss ETHEL BRAND | THE CONJUROR ... ... Professor HERMANN
Soldiers, Police, Whiteboys, Villagers, etc., by the full strength of the ALHAMBRA CORPS DE BALLET.
PERIOD 1830.

(4) EMMY'S TROUPE OF TRAINED TOY TERRIERS.
Exclusively Engaged.

(5) THE LUPPUS,
In their Great Quadruple Bar Act. First appearance in England.
Exclusively Engaged.

(6) THE NEWSKY ROUSSOTINE TROUPE,
Russian Singers and Dancers. Exclusively Engaged.

(7) Selection ... ... "Romeo and Juliet" ... ... *Gounod*
Conducted by Mons. G. JACOBI.

(8) THE
ANIMATOGRAPHE,
THE PHOTO-ELECTRIC SENSATION OF THE DAY,
Exhibited by this marvellous mechanism under the personal superintendence of the Inventor,
Mr. R. W. PAUL, M.I.E.E.

(9) Mr. MORRIS CRONIN, Club Manipulator.
Exclusively Engaged.

(10) A NEW GRAND DRAMATIC BALLET IN FIVE TABLEAUX, entitled—
"RIP VAN WINKLE."
The Scenario compiled and the Ballet invented by Signor CARLO COPPI, upon the old Legend familiarised by WASHINGTON IRVING'S celebrated work, " Rip Van Winkle."
The Music by Mons. ROBERT PLANQUETTE.
The Scenery by Mr. T. E. RYAN. The Costumes by Mons. and Madame ALIAS (from designs by HOWELL RUSSELL). Wigs by GUSTAVE. Machinist, Mr. F. FOX. Property Master, Mr. FINLAY. Limelight by Mr. STONE. Gas and Electrical Effects by Mr. F. W. HENTON. Orchestra of 60 Performers, Conductor—Mons. GEORGES JACOBI.

CHARACTERS:

RIP VAN WINKLE ... ... Mr. FRED STOREY | THE BURGOMASTER ... ... Mr. G. ALMONTI
FRAU VAN WINKLE (his Wife) } Miss JULIE SEALE | DERRICK ... ... Mr. E. ALMONTI
In Scenes I. and II. } | THE VILLAGE PRIEST ... ... Mr. W. ALMONTI
RIP'S SON { In Scene I. ... ... Miss SKELLY | THE SCHOOLMASTER { Scenes I., II., III., Mr. VANARA
{ In Scene V. ... Mr. VANARA | { Scene V. ... Mr. HERMANN
RIP'S DAUGHTER { Scenes I and II. Miss BUSHLAG | FIRST CITIZEN ... ... Mr. MARRA
{ Scene V. Miss JULIE SEALE | SECOND CITIZEN ... ... Mr. KALLIERE
NICK VEDDER (the Innkeeper) } Mr. LYTTON GREY | THE ENGLISH CAPTAIN ... Miss ETHEL BRAND
Scenes I. and II. } | THE GOBLIN STEWARD Sig. LAURENTINI GOBBO
YOUNG NICK VEDDER, Scene V. } | THE MOUNTAIN FAY ... Signorina CAMPANA
FRAU VEDDER ... ... Miss AUDUS | (Première Danseuse)
GRETCHEN (Waitress at the Inn) ... Miss CASABONI
Villagers, Peasants, Soldiers, Election Agents, Politicians, Gnomes, Phantoms, &c., &c., by the ALHAMBRA CORPS DE BALLET.

(11) MONS. FARINI, Juggler.

Figure 7.4 Alhambra Theatre programme, Leicester Square, London, 3 August 1896

at least it can forget its troubles or fatigues in the temporary pleasure begotten by some mental or physical stimulant. It is because we exact too much of the poor – because we, as it were, strive to make true knowledge and true beauty as forbidding as possible to the uneducated and unrefined, that they fly to their penny gaffs, their twopenny-hops, their beer-shops, and their gambling-grounds for pleasures which we deny them, and which we, in our arrogance, believe it is possible for them to do without.

The experiment so successfully tried at Liverpool of furnishing music of an enlivening and yet elevating character at the same price as the concerts of the lowest grade, shows that the people may be won to delight in beauty instead of beastiality, and teaches us again that it is *our* fault to allow them to be as they are and not their's to remain so. All men are compound animals, with many inlets of pleasure to their brains, and if one avenue be closed against them, why it but forces them to seek delight through another. So far from the perception of beauty inducing habits of gross enjoyment as 'serious' people generally imagine, a moment's reflection will tell us that these very habits are only the necessary consequences of the non-development of the æsthetic faculty; for the two assuredly cannot co-exist. To cultivate the sense of the beautiful is necessarily to inculcate a detestation of the sensual.

7.6 'What Are Women Doing?' *English Woman's Journal* 7 (1 March 1861), 51–3

Women's relationship to leisure was defined by their class as well as their gender; as this article makes clear, the range of popular activities undertaken by genteel women developed due to their predominantly domestic role and lack of opportunities for professional employment. Dancing, singing and needlework were promoted as refined feminine pursuits. The English Woman's Journal *(1858–64) was a monthly publication founded by Barbara Leigh Smith (from 1857 Barbara Leigh Smith Bodichon) and Bessie Rayner Parkes, who came from dissenting families steeped in radical politics. Its low circulation belies its importance as a journal which was run by women, which published material by women, and which was generally devoted to promoting both their interests and furthering their legal, social and political rights. Between 1860 and 1863 it was published by Emily Faithfull's Victoria Press, which employed female compositors in a demonstration of the different employments women could fulfil. The* English Woman's Journal's *belief in the importance of paid occupations for women (particularly middle-class women who were its principal readers) is reflected in this article's rather equivocal attitude to the leisured occupations of some upper-class women, of which it provides an excellent summary. See also extracts 2.7, 3.2, 7.10 and 8.3, which discuss the issue of women's work and leisure.*

At the present moment we hear it asked on all sides, – What can women do? What may they do? Why do they attempt this? How is it that they have not turned their attention to that? Beside all these questions arises another, not without interest – What are women doing? [. . .]

Let us begin with what may be called the upper middle-class, including under this general denomination, all those who are not dependent on their own exertions for maintenance. Among these, a few pursue either art or litera- ture as a vocation. A larger proportion devote most of their time to religious and philanthropic work. They are occupied in the management of societies and of schools; in the superintendence of Bible-women and mothers' meetings; in district visiting and tract distributing, and in working for bazaars. Whether their well-meant zeal does not sometimes defeat its own object is perhaps an invidious question. Another large division might be described as people who do a little of everything. They play a little, sing a little, dance a little – they draw a little, and paint a little in water-colors – they read a little read French and a little German, to keep up their languages – they read the magazines, too, and can talk a little about most of the new books, which they have seen noticed in the reviews. They visit the poor a little, they keep up a little friendly intercourse with their neighbours, and they take a little interest in what is going on in the world.

No one can say that they are not busy; but with what aim and what result are they working? We will leave them to answer for themselves and turn to another section, including, I fear, a larger number than either of the former. I refer to those who make 'society' their business. The arts they cultivate are those which 'tell' at an evening party; namely, dress, talking, and a certain brilliant style of musical performance. During the season, their nights are spent in party-going, their days in 'great labors' of the needle, in the exchange of morning calls and in attendance upon milliners and dressmakers, varied by the occasional excite- ment of a wedding, a bazaar or a flower-show. Their few hours of relaxation are given to novel-reading. At the close of the season, a visit to a fashionable water- ing-place restores in some measure their exhausted energies, and in due time they are ready to begin again the weary round.

7.7 Report from the Select Committee on Theatrical Licenses and Regulations (London: House of Commons, 1866), 259–63

Music halls came to prominence in the 1850s, and subsequently enjoyed enormous success as one of the most popular forms of working-class entertainment. As this extract demonstrates, the origins of music hall performance owed much to licensing laws restricting what different venues could perform. Only theatres were licensed for full dramatic performances, so-called legitimate drama (effectively plays without music). Of necessity, music halls offered a mixture of songs, ballet, dancing, opera, comic turns and speciality acts. Licensing laws were a continual source of friction between music halls and the theatre, with theatres prosecuting perceived infringements and music halls devising creative ways around the legal restrictions. Although some-

times criticized by genteel critics for their dubious character, by the late nineteenth century music halls were metamorphosing into large, commercially organized, respectable variety theatres.

Mr Daniel Saunders, called in; and examined.

7377. *Mr. Locke.*] I believe that you are the manager of Day's Music Hall, at Birmingham? – Yes.

7378. How long have you been manager of that house? – About three years and a half.

7379. How many persons is it capable of accommodating? – 2,500.

7380. How are you licensed? – By the magistrates.

7381. What license have you? – A music and dancing license. [. . .]

7397. Have you a stage and scenery there? – Yes.

7398. How many performers have you engaged there? – Probably 120.

7399. Will you inform the committee what is the description of your perform-ance? – The best thing I can do, I think, is to give you a programme of an evening's entertainment (*handing in a specimen programme*).

7400. 'Day's Crystal Palace Concert Hall, Smallbrook-street, Birmingham; Sole Proprietor, Mr. James Day. Thursday, May 10th 1866.' You begin with a concert, I see? – Yes.

7401. 'During which will be exhibited an Act Drop, "The New Street Station"'? – Yes.

7402. Does that come in the middle of the concert? – Yes; in the middle of the concert, while the overture is being played.

7403. 'Grand Garland Divertissement, supported by Miss Fanny Lauri and a New London Corps de Ballet; scenery by Messrs E. Day and J. Watson;' what was that ballet? – That was a ballet of the usual kind, with appropriate scenery; the scenery in this case was a scene by moonlight.

7404. Did that ballet tell a story? – No; it told no story.

7405. 'Grand Selection from Bellini's favourite opera "Norma,"' and several other pieces? – Yes.

7406. Did those singers sing in character? – No; in evening dress.

7407. Now I see here, 'Comic Entertainment, by Mr J. G. Forde;' what is that? – He is what is called a patter-comic singer, after the style of Mr Charles Matthews.[6]

7408. Then there is a gymnastic entertainment by the Brothers Ridley, 'Reading – Mr Reuben Roe; Waltz (Gungl) Orchestra;' that is merely music given by the orchestra, I suppose? – Just so.

7409. Then you had a pantomimic ballet, called 'The Adventures of Lord Dundreary, supported by the celebrated Lauri family; Comic Song; and Ethiopian Entertainment.' You had this pantomimic ballet, the 'Adventures of

---

6 Charles Mathews (1803–78), an actor renowned for his comic style.

Lord Dundreary;' did that come within the provisions of the 6 & 7 Victoria?[7] – According to my interpretation of it, it does. [. . .]

7433. What is the average admission fee at you hall? – I do not think it would amount to more than 6d.

7434. Would you be good enough to inform the Committee the exact prices? – Admission, 1s. front stalls; 6d. side stalls; 6d. for the floor, with 3d. returned in refreshments; 7d. or 8d. would be the average.

7435. Threepence is returned in refreshments on the floor? – Yes, 3d. is returned by check.

7436. Now, what class of people compose the bulk of the audience? – Our audiences are generally composed of a very superior class of people, manufacturers and their wives, artisans and their wives, and on special occasions, and sometimes without special occasion, the magistrates visit us; and ever since the hall has been opened the magistrates are very well satisfied with the way in which it has been conducted [. . .]

7440. Now, with regard to the entertainments that you find it necessary to give at the music halls, will you state to the Committee what description of performance you find it necessary to give, in order to make the place attractive? – It is necessary to give a variety; it is necessary to perform ballets; it is necessary to perform good music in the shape of operatic selections; and that pantomimic selections should be given, it is necessary to make up a programme and to change it; it would be necessary, in fact, to have greater privileges than we have.

7441. What privileges would you desire to have in addition to what you have at present, though indeed I do not know that you have any? – We have none at present; I should like to play pantomimes, and to perform ballets and burlesques.

7442. Do you think it would be an advantage to you to have the privilege of playing a light vaudeville? – I do.

7443. Or such a piece as 'Box and Cox,' for instance?[8] – Anything lasting more than three quarters of an hour in a concert hall would be against the interests of the establishment; they like continual change.

7444. If you had the same privileges as the theatres, do you think it would answer your purpose to give any kind of acting beyond a very light piece indeed of one act? – I do not think so.

7445. But you do think it would be an advantage? – It would. [. . .]

7524. *Mr. Powell.*] How many spectators have you room for in your music hall at one time? – It would be full with 2,500 people. [. . .]

7529. Do you take any steps to exclude improper characters? – Yes, we have an officer always at the entrance, and it is his duty, if he is of opinion that a person is an improper character to be admitted, to refuse him admittance.

---

7 6 & 7 Victoria refers to the Theatres Act of 1843, which defined the licensing of drama in the UK, hence governing what music halls could perform.

8 John Maddison Morton's *Box and Cox* was a popular farce first performed at the Royal Lyceum, London, in 1847.

7530. If there was a reason to suppose that a woman of improper character was coming to your hall in pursuit of her unhappy vocation, it would be the officer's duty to exclude her, would it? – Yes, we do not admit them at all if we know it.

7531. If a woman came frequently alone, for example, or if there was any circumstance of that kind, such as to indicate her vocation, would you exclude her? – No, I do not think I should; so long as she conducted herself properly she would have as much right to be there as any one else, in my opinion. [. . .]

7.8 The Journeyman Engineer [Thomas Wright], *Some Habits and Customs of the Working Classes* (London: Tinsley Brothers, 1867)

Penny readings formed part of an ensemble of improving and respectable events, including lectures, concerts, magic lantern shows, panoramas and scientific demonstrations, which constituted a significant proportion of the evening leisure activities in cities and provincial towns. Often seeking to counter the influence of the public house, these events were underpinned by a belief of the cultural and educational 'improvement' of the working classes. Penny readings and the like were often organized by local literary societies, athenaeums and mechanics' institutes (see extract 8.2 on the development of these institutions). Thomas Wright (1839–1909) was apprenticed as an engineer, but a dedicated course of self-education allowed him to become a school inspector from 1872, an occupation he fulfilled for the rest of his life. He published numerous articles on working-class life and social habits under the pseudonym 'The Journeyman Engineer'. Wright's belief in the importance of social and educational improvement is reflected in his attitude to penny readings.

Now when my energetic old friend Smith, president of the Boughtborough Histrionic Club, chairman of the local Mechanics' Institution, and the great promoter of all intellectual amusements in the borough, established the Penny Readings, and subsequently saluted me whenever we met, with, 'You should come and hear me read,' I, while replying, 'I shall come and hear you some of these odd times,' mentally put it down as another case of Bishop of Batterseaism.[9] But as I began to hear upon all hands that the Penny Readings were 'jolly things', and were 'drawing immensely', I determined to attend one of the Boughtborough Penny Readings to hear my friend Smith read. Accordingly one Saturday night I wended my way to the Boughtborough music hall, a little before eight o'clock, at which hour the doors of the hall were to be opened. The hall was capable of holding fifteen hundred persons, and when I arrived in front of it, there was, so far as I was able to judge, more than that number of persons waiting outside. [. . .]

---

9 'The Bishop of Battersea' was a comical character from a popular entertainment, who would exclaim 'Hear me preach! Hear me preach!' as a prelude to drunken conversation.

Those of the audience who had no one with whom to enter into conversation, and of this section I was one, fell to consulting the programme of the evening's entertainments, which was as follows:–

Pianoforte Solo ....Mr. Crotchet.
Reading............'The Trial Scene from the Merchant of Venice'......Mr. O. Rater
(Shakespeare)

Song ....'The Gleaner'........................Mr D. Robinson.
Recitation...........'The Combat' from 'The Lady of the Lake'......Mr S. Poulter.
(Sir Walter Scott.)

Flute Solo ....Airs from 'The Rose of Castile'......................Mr Potts.
Reading.......'Mr. Pickwick and the Lady with Yellow Curl Papers'...Mr. Smith.
(Dickens.)

Glee....................................'Hail, Smiling Morn'...................Members of the
Boughtborough
Glee Union.
Recitation ....'Lord Tom Noddy'............................Mr Brown.
(Barham.)

Song..'Madoline' ....Miss Arline
Crotchet.
Reading ....'The Rioters at the Maypole' ....Mr Tomkins.
(Dickens.)

Part Song...........................'The Red Cross Knight' ....Members of the
Boughtborough
Glee Union.

Precisely at eight o'clock, the chairman for the evening, who was no less a person than the proprietor and editor of the *Boughtborough Chronicle*, was introduced, and after he had made a few of the usual formal observations respecting his pride and pleasure at being called upon to preside over so numerous and respectable an audience, the entertainments of the evening commenced with Crotchet's performance of the pianoforte solo set down for him. [. . .]

But the great feature of the evening was Smith's reading – the reading to hear which was the chief cause of my being present upon that occasion. The announcement that the next reading would be by Mr. Smith was received by a tremendous burst of cheering, and cries from the *habitués* of the readings of 'Pickwick! Pickwick!' a name which it appeared they had bestowed upon Smith in token of their admiration of the series of readings descriptive of the adventures of that immortal hero which he had given. And as he came upon the platform, his stout comfortable figure, and broad good-humoured face – although such an idea had never occurred to me before – now seemed to me to be the perfect realization of Pickwick in the flesh; and when he had adjusted his gold-mounted spectacles, I involuntarily began to try and select a representative – Sam Weller, or at least a Mr. Snodgrass – from among the gentlemen assembled on the platform, and felt quite disappointed at not being able to do so.[10] [. . .]

From that hour I became an ardent admirer of penny readings. In the course of the pilgrimages which in the pursuit of my profession I am compelled to take, I have attended them in all parts of England, and more especially in the manufacturing districts, and I am glad to find that they are exceedingly popular all over the country. Of the many plans that have been devised for providing the working classes with that amusement of which, it is admitted upon all hands, they stand in need, the penny readings, considered upon the principle of judging a tree by its fruits, are the best. The many thousands of working men and boys who frequent them give unmistakable evidence of their appreciation of them; and, apart from this consideration, I know, from constantly mingling with the working men of the densely populated manufacturing towns, that the penny readings are immensely popular with them. [. . .]

Independently of the attraction which lies in their cheapness, and the absence from them of oppressive patronage, the 'Penny Readings' are peculiarly well calculated to draw large audiences of all classes of working-men, save that now fast decreasing section of them whose only amusement is to be found in the pot-house. Thanks to the vastness and variety of English literature, age cannot wither, or custom stale the infinite variety of the selections which may be given at these readings; and the amateur musician has a world before him where to choose, almost as varied. [. . .]

The pieces given at a penny reading should as a rule be of a light and popular character. Rhymed verse of a dramatic or narrative kind seems to 'take' best, and after that comic or satiric prose gives the most satisfaction; but poetic prose, or purely picturesque or philosophic blank verse, as yet finds little favour in the ears of the penny-headed multitude. I have frequently heard compositions of that class, even when given by good readers, coughed down, and always listened to impatiently.

But the readings given at these entertainments are only part of the evening's amusements: vocal and instrumental music now invariably form a considerable portion of the programme, and in this department more uniform excellence of execution is obtainable than in the reading. For moderately good, or at least mechanically accurate, amateur pianists, and performers upon the flute and cornet-à-piston, willing and anxious to discourse sweet music to their fellow-townsmen, are always to be found in abundance, and the glee and other musical associations now established in almost every town and village in England, furnish trained singers of fair ability.

---

10 Characters from Dickens's *The Pickwick Papers* (1836–7).

7.9 William Stanley Jevons, 'Amusements of the People', *Contemporary Review* 33 (October 1878), 498–513

The purpose of popular leisure was a fraught and much debated question during the period. This essay articulates a widespread anxiety over the development of new forms of working-class amusement such as the music hall, and the belief, most commonly asserted by members of the civic and cultural elite, that their influence needed to be countered through the provision of improving activities such as concerts, museums, art galleries, exhibitions and parks. Underpinning this agenda was a belief in 'rational recreation', the notion that amusement should be not be an end in itself but a means of furthering moral and cultural reform. William Stanley Jevons (1835–82) was an influential British economist (he became Professor of Political Economy at UCL in 1876), while the Contemporary Review *was a leading monthly journal.*

It is obvious, of course, that in any single article it is impossible to treat of more than one Method of Social Reform. In selecting, for the subject of the present article Public Amusements, I must not be supposed to attribute to it any exclusive or disproportionate weight. Nevertheless, there is hardly any other Method, taken separately, to which greater importance should be attributed than to the providing of good moral public amusements, especially musical entertainments. Up to quite recent years, the English people have, in this respect, been woefully backward, as compared with the more cultured Continental nations. There are still large parts of the manufacturing and more thickly populated districts of the kingdom where pure and rational recreation for the poorer classes can hardly be said to exist at all. The richer classes do not suffer much from this lack of local amusement. They take care to enjoy themselves in periodic visits to London, in tours abroad, or in residence at watering-places, where entertainments are provided. Their amusements on their own estates chiefly consist in shooting, and other forms of sport, in the prosecution of which they are led to exclude the mass of the people even from the natural enjoyments of the air and the sun. It is hardly too much to say that the right to dwell freely in a grimy street, to drink freely in the neighbouring public-house, and to walk freely between the high-walled parks and the jealously preserved estates of our landowners, is all that the just and equal laws of England secure to the mass of the population.

England is traditionally called 'Merrie England;' but there has always seemed to me to be something absurdly incongruous in the name at present. It is a case of anachronism, if not of sarcasm. England may have been merry in the days when the village green and the neighbouring common were still unenclosed; when the Maypole was set up, and the village fiddler and the old English sports were really existing institutions. But all that sort of thing is a matter of history. Popular festivals, fairs, wakes, and the like, have fallen into disuse or contempt, and have to a great extent been suppressed by the magistrates, on the ground of the riotous and vicious assemblages which they occasioned. [. . .]

But, if old amusements are by degrees to be suppressed, and no new ones originated, England must indeed be a dull England. Such it has, in fact, been for a length of time. Taking it on the average, England is as devoid of amusements as a country of such wealth can be. The people seem actually to have forgotten how to amuse themselves, so that when they do escape by an excursion train from their depressing alleys, there is no provision of music, no harmless games, nor other occupation for the vacant time. The unusual elevation of spirits which the fresh air occasions vents itself in horse-play and senseless vulgarity; and, in the absence of any counter-attraction, it is not surprising that the refreshment-bar and the nearest tap-room are the chief objects of attention.

I quite allow that when our English masses try to amuse themselves, they do it in such a clumsy and vulgar way as to disgust one with the very name of amusement. Witness the Bank Holidays on Hampstead Heath, where the best fun of the young men and women consists in squirting at each other with those detestable metal pipes which some base genius has invented. Then, again, what can be worse than the common run of London music-halls, where we have a nightly exhibition of all that is degraded in taste? [. . .]

Now I believe that this want of culture greatly arises from the fact that the amusements of the masses, instead of being cultivated, and multiplied, and refined, have been frowned upon and condemned, and eventually suppressed, by a dominant aristocracy. Amusement has been regarded as in itself almost sinful, and at the best as a necessary evil. Accordingly, villages and towns have grown up in the more populous parts of the kingdom absolutely devoid of any provision whatever for recreation. It seems to be thought that the end of life is accomplished if there be bread and beef to eat, beer to drink, beds to sleep in, and chapels and churches to attend on Sundays. The idea that the mass of the people might have their refined, and yet popular amusements, is only just dawning. [. . .]

Among the means towards a higher civilisation, I unhesitatingly assert that the deliberate cultivation of public amusement is a principal one. Surely we may accept as an axiom that the average man or woman requires an average amount of recreation. At least it is not for our richer classes to say nay. The life of a young man or a young woman in aristocratic circles is one continuous round of varied amusements. Are we to allow that what is to them the perfection of existence is to have no counterpart whatever among the poor drudges of the farm or factory? Is it not all the more requisite that when there are few hours in the week to spare for recreation, those hours should be sweetened in the most wholesome and agreeable way? And as, by the progress of science and invention, those vacant hours are gradually prolonged, it becomes more and more requisite that provision should be made for their harmless occupation. The old idea of keeping people moral by keeping their noses to the grindstone must be abandoned. As things are going, people will, and, what is more, they ought to have all possible means of healthy recreation. The question is, the Free Library and the News-room *versus* the Public-house; and, as my more immediate subject, the well-conducted Concert *versus* the inane and vulgar Music-hall.

There is, indeed, a brighter side to this question than I have yet mentioned. All that I have been saying was more true of our population twenty or thirty years ago than it is now. What I shall advocate is mainly suggested by things already accomplished in one part of the country or another. [. . .]

Already it has dawned upon people that a town is incomplete without its public park, and a few wealthy men have made the noble present of a park to the borough with which they are connected. Manchester has been foremost in providing a series of parks at the cost of the ratepayers. But I hold that a public park should be considered incomplete without its winter garden and music pavilion, and naturally the music pavilion is incomplete without the music. It is well to have places where people may take the air; but it is better still to attract them every summer evening into the healthy, airy park by the strains of music.

There are many modes by which recreation and culture may be brought within the reach of the multitude; but it is my present purpose to point out that the most practicable and immediately efficacious mode is the cultivation of pure music. I have no wish to disparage Theatres, Art Galleries, Museums, Public Libraries, Science Lectures, and various other social institutions, the value and true uses of which I may perhaps attempt to estimate on some other occasions; but I am certain that music is the best means of popular recreation. It fulfils all the requirements. In the first place, it involves no bodily fatigue, since it can best be enjoyed sitting down. To inspect a picture gallery or a museum is always a tiring work, neither exercise nor repose; the standing or stooping posture, the twisting of the neck, and the straining of the eyes, tend to produce, after a few hours, a state approaching nervous and muscular exhaustion. This is not the way to recreate the wearied mechanic, or the overworked clerk or man of business. [. . .]

7.10 [Benjamin Ward Richardson], 'On Recreation for Girls', *Girl's Own Paper* 15 (2 June 1894), 545–7

Exercise and sport had long been popular activities, but they took on an increasingly organized and codified character during the nineteenth century (notable examples being the founding of the Football Association in 1863, the Rugby Football Union in 1872 and the Cricket County Championship in 1890). Sport and exercise played an important ideological role in late Victorian culture due to its perceived role in disciplining and regulating the body, particularly those of the young. Sport helped train them to be efficient workers, soldiers and mothers – or instil in them the values of fair play in the case of public schools. Compared with the physical and social restrictions previously placed upon them, women, though, as this article demonstrates, enjoyed the benefits of this emphasis on physical recreation. An active, more mobile lifestyle was part of the iconography of the New Woman. Sir Benjamin Ward Richardson (1828–96) was a renowned physician, whose work was often concerned with public health issues. Elected a fellow of the Royal College of Physicians in 1865, and of the Royal Society in 1867, he was an early advocate of the benefits of cycling. The Girl's Own Paper *(1880–1927) was a pioneering girl's magazine, published by the Religious Tract Society to accompany their* Boy's Own Paper; *both journals tended to focus on the provision of rational recreation, which included organized sport and healthy exercise.*

The day is fast passing away when the common belief existed that women were, by nature, consigned to the monotony of indoor life and domestic care. [. . .] Within a very short space of time, within my own recollection, certainly, a change has been effected in respect to the cultivation of physical exercise amongst women that is historical in its character. My old and able teacher of anatomy, when I was a student, was persistent in his lesson that women were not capable of cultivation, physically, like men. He did not pretend that their ribs differed in number from those of men, indeed, from two fine skeletons, one of a woman, another of a man, he demonstrated that the sexes were alike, strictly, in respect to ribs, but in the matter of muscles he held that they were not alike; a women could not throw a cricket ball as a man did; she could 'chuck' it by an 'underhand movement', but she could not fling it or pitch it. The muscles were not formed for the work. We know better now, for have we not a ladies' team, and does not the team do credit to the old English game?

Of course the argument of the old school men was based on a fundamental error. They simply witnessed the phenomenon of deficient development from deficient exercise, and they mistook cause for effect. Except under special circumstances women are just as able as men to take part in recreative pursuits; they are as much benefited by such pursuits, and, if yielding wisely and judiciously to circumstances, they moderate their zeal so as not to show too competitive a spirit in any contests in which they may be engaged, they add greatly and gracefully to the science of health and to the usefulness of life, by their new efforts.

This general fact admitted, and there are, amongst scholars who have studied the subject carefully, very few, I think, who would question the matter; the points to be considered are those of detail respecting recreative exercise for women. It is to this inquiry I shall devote attention, collecting my material from the information obtained from a fairly long period of observation of experience.

Before entering into these details I would beg permission to remark that there are certain general principles relating to recreation for women which, in a degree, stand alone, that is to say, while they apply to some extent to both sexes, they especially apply to the female sex.

First and foremost, those recreations are best adapted for women which do not interfere with duties and functions especially belonging to the women, duties and functions which cannot possibly be performed by men. One of the great dangers at the present time is that women, in their great anxiety to compete in various recreative exercises, are given to forget the fact that, *nolens volens*,[11] they are born to do what men never can do; that if the race is to progress they must some day become mothers, that they must undertake special maternal duties, and that for home to be home they must, within the sphere of home, display domestic talents, and do domestic work which comes exclusively under their control. They must remember, moreover, without thinking of giving up recreative pleasures and exercises as matters of necessity, that every attempt to pass in recreation beyond a certain bound of natural womanly duties is to pass into a sphere with which such duties are utterly incompatible. In other words, extreme physical strength and power of resistance to natural forces, with skill to surmount great obstacles, with craft to overcome great difficulties, with courage to carry everything that may come in the way, with dispositions, in plain words, to fight and make level all that is in opposition, means a state of body and mind which could not be in harmony with those gentler traits, attributes, and affections belonging to the birth and the care of the young and feeble. Mind and body go together in action, are attuned one to the other when a mere strength of physical organisation is fully developed. The mental qualities of resolution and conflict are joined to the physical qualities which sustain strength, resolution, and conflict, and it were something worse than crushing a fly on the wheel of a locomotive, to see the representative of pure manly attributes engaged systematically in the nursery.

Secondly, those recreations are best for women which, according with the more refined spirit of the woman, do not vulgarise. All qualities that vulgarise make the woman not only objectionable generally but objectionable specifically when they unfit her for the instruction and training of children, male or female. Too often necessity makes mothers and women vulgar in their nature. Brought up in schools where rudeness and vulgarity of habit are dominant, they reflect upon young and susceptible minds their own nature, and we look with pity if we are merciful, with disgust if we are not merciful, on the mixed products of nature and imitation which follow on the rude patterns we would avoid in recreative pursuits.

Thirdly, the best recreations for women are those which cause the body to be equally developed, and to be, in development, as perfect as possible. This is another way of saying that recreations should lead to beauty, and, if I am correct in my view, every recreation should have this tendency. A man may say this without being supposed to flatter the opposite sex, for beauty is a virtue as commendable to men as to women. What is more, it is a tribute which being much sought after, is one that should render recreations for women specially agreeable to their tastes and inclinations, for women more than men love, naturally, beauty not only when they see it, but beauty as they know it in their own persons. [. . .]

TYPICAL RECREATIONS
The recreations of the English life open to women at the present time, and coinciding with the principles above narrated, is the question that now concerns us.

---

11 Whether willing or unwilling.

In answering it as briefly as possible, I shall refer to a few forms of recreation most likely to be attractive.

Walking is naturally the first exercise, and carried out correctly is, perhaps, the best of all, though it may be the most monotonous. Good walking is an art to be learned; it does not consist in moving with rapidity; neither man nor woman is destined to walk more than four miles per hour, and the woman who achieves three and a half miles does well. [. . .]

Swimming should be cultivated not only as a recreation but as a useful practice. No recreation brings a larger number of muscles into play than swimming, and barring accidents, I know of no exercise that more equally develops the body or gives freer play to the respiration [. . .]

Dancing properly carried out is one of the happiest and healthiest of recreations. Unfortunately, it has of late dropped into an absurd fashion of overwork and overstrain, in late hours, and in unwholesome atmospheres. Dancing should be cultivated as an outdoor exercise as it was in the olden time, and should consist, more than it does, of individual dancing than in couples, as in the waltz. [. . .]

Lawn tennis, which has become so essentially an English game, stands well on the roll of recreations for women, in so far as healthy movement is concerned. [. . .]

Cycling is unquestionably a good exercise for women, but it has its disadvantages in that it does not equalise muscular movement. Carried too far, in fact, it leads to an unbalanced development of the lower limbs, and may produce a certain measure of deformity in the lower limbs. The exercise of cycling greatly increases the circulation, the heart increasing in its beat to an unnatural degree. Extreme competition even by powerful women has been shown in my experience to be detrimental to the health, and I particularly warn riders against efforts in climbing hills and against prolonged extreme efforts [. . .]

Cricket is an excellent game for women; it calls into play great groups of muscles, it teaches measurement of distance, it causes precision of movement of the hands guided by sight, and it produces good active running movements of the body.

8

Literary Production and Reception

Introduction

Nineteenth-century industrialization often conjures up images of grimy cities, factories full of toiling machinery, or the engineering of ships, bridges and railways. Yet the steam power utilized by the railways and cotton mills played an equally important role in the development of the publishing industry: new steam printing presses produced books, magazines and newspapers in unprecedented numbers (the first edition of *The Times* to be printed on a steam press appeared in November 1814). The railways that carried people all over the country also transported books and newspapers, distributing an unprecedented volume and variety of reading matter. Publishing and printing were major beneficiaries of the Industrial Revolution. Industrialization helped to make cheap print media possible. Between 1840 and 1870, the British population rose by 40 per cent, yet the number of books published annually rose by about 400 per cent.[1]

The enormous expansion in the production of books, newspapers, journals and periodicals was matched and encouraged by the advent of the first genuinely mass reading public. Economic, educational and demographic changes all played their part in creating a large market of potential readers. The increase in living standards produced by industrialization gave a rapidly expanding population more disposable income and extended leisure time. In particular, it was the growth of the urban working and middle class that constituted a new readership for the flood of cheap fiction and periodicals. At the same time, educational reforms led to an increase in literacy levels. A national report of 1840, based simply on an ability to sign the marriage register, found that 67 per cent of males and 51 per cent of females were literate. These percentages rose slowly but steadily over the century and the gender differential also closed: by 1871, 81 per cent of men and 73 per cent of women were literate.[2] Increasing numbers of readers created economies of scale for publishers, which overall favoured lower prices and more production, which attracted more readers, and so on and so forth in a continuous cycle of growth (see extract 8.1).

---

1 Philip Davis, *The Oxford English Literary History*, Volume 8: *1830–1880, The Victorians* (Oxford: Oxford University Press, 2002), 202.
2 Davis, *The Oxford English Literary History*, vol. 8, 103.

The expansion of the literary marketplace played an instrumental role in the success of most major nineteenth-century novelists, for it was those who wrote in prose – novelists, essayists and reviewers – that benefited most from the expansion of print media. One crucial reason they did so was the development of the periodical press, with many journals and magazines publishing serial fiction alongside a miscellany of articles. The periodical press played a central role in the development of nineteenth-century literary culture, and indeed society as a whole (the articles below by Wilkie Collins, G. H. Lewes and Thomas Hardy describe different characteristics of the periodical press). In 1859, E. S. Dallas proclaimed that 'The rise of the periodical press is the great event of modern history [. . .] it represents the triumph of moral over physical force; it gives every one of us a new sense – a sort of omniscience, as well as a new power – a sort of ubiquity.'[3] In 1864, the *Newspaper Press Directory* listed 1,764 periodical titles being published in Britain; by 1887 it listed 3,597, and by 1901, there were 4,914 periodicals being published in Britain.[4]

The periodical press provided a forum for critical discussion of literary, political, social, scientific and historical issues. It was where many of the distinguished intellectuals and writers of the day, including Harriet Martineau, Thomas Carlyle, Matthew Arnold, Herbert Spencer and Francis Galton, published their work. Intellectual exchange took place through the public forum of the periodical press. Indeed, its importance is reflected in the number of pieces in this section that were initially published in journals or magazines.

The growth of the periodical press impacted upon the lives and careers of many Victorian novelists in that, almost for the first time, it allowed authors – both male and female – to live by their pens. Those writers whom we tend to think of as novelists were almost invariably involved in multiple activities for the periodical press. The career of Charles Dickens typifies this: before making his name as a novelist with the *Pickwick Papers*, he worked as a journalist and parliamentary reporter. Following the success of his novels, he set up and edited two journals of his own, *Household Words* (1850–9) and *All the Year Round*, which he edited from 1859 until his death in 1870. Novelists such as Mary Elizabeth Braddon, George Eliot, William Thackeray, Anthony Trollope and Ellen Wood all worked as journal editors.

The fortunes of novelists and the periodical press were also conjoined by the dominance of serialization as a mode of publication. Fiction was published in individual weekly, fortnightly or monthly issues, and was also included as a principal feature of many periodicals. The advantage of serial publication was that many more readers could buy a weekly or monthly issue of a novel than could afford the relatively expensive price of a whole novel. As a mode of publi-

---

3 [E. S. Dallas], 'Popular Literature – the Periodical Press (No. 1)', *Blackwood's Edinburgh Magazine* 85 (1859), 101.

4 Simon Eliot, *Some Patterns and Trends in British Publishing, 1800–1919* (London: The Bibliographical Society, 1993), 148.

cation, serialization dramatically increased the potential readership of fiction. Serial fiction was enthusiastically taken up by the growing number of cheap penny journals in the 1840s, which sold hundreds of thousands of parts per week. The success of penny fiction weeklies led to numerous attempts to wrestle with the conundrum of a marketplace that was ostensibly being newly divided between the 'popular' and the 'literary', of which the piece below by Wilkie Collins, 'The Unknown Public', is one well-known example. As the century progressed, however, there were a growing number of attacks on the dominance of the literary marketplace and the restraints it imposed upon those writers who wished to challenge aesthetic and moral norms. Thomas Hardy's essay from 1890 (extract 8.10) argues that, thanks in part to the influence of the periodical press, literature was increasingly caught between the incompatible demands of art and commercialism.

The expansion of print media invariably raised hopes and fears about the influence of novels, periodicals and newspapers. Many liberals firmly believed that its spread was part of the onward march of progress, improvement and civilization, that it had the potential to raise the mental level of the nation. This widespread belief in the improving value of literature and journals is important and led to many libraries and mechanics' institutes being set up to disseminate wholesome reading matter to the newly literate working classes, exemplified in this section by Robert Peel's address at the opening of the Tamworth Library and Reading Room (extract 8.2). The increase in the variety of reading spaces played an important role in making books accessible to the reading public.

Print media was part of the period's grand narrative of progress; however, both because and in spite of this, there were also recurrent fears about its influence, particularly upon women, children and the working classes. Mechanics' institutes, libraries and literary societies often regulated what material was read, excluding controversial works of fiction, politics or religion. Yet *how* texts were read could also be an important means of controlling their interpretation; for example, our excerpt by Sarah Stickney Ellis argues that reading aloud within the family circle was a means of promoting family harmony and of tempering the potentially dangerous imaginative freedom of solitary reading. The variety of ways of reading, when taken alongside the influence of publication formats such as serialization, demonstrates the key role that the production, dissemination and reception of texts played in the function and impact of Victorian literature.

8.1 [Charles Knight], 'The Commercial History of a Penny Magazine', *Penny Magazine* 2 (1833), 377–84

Charles Knight (1791–1873) was a pioneering publisher of the 1830s and 1840s; his prominence stemmed from his position as publisher for the Society for Diffusion of Useful Knowledge, and, more particularly, from his role in the launch of the Penny Magazine *in 1832. The* Penny Magazine – *whose title advertised its cheapness – was a landmark*

in the provision of inexpensive print media. It was claimed that the first issue of the
Penny Magazine *sold 213,241 copies, a vast number at the time. Knight's enormous*
publishing output also included the Penny Cyclopaedia, Pictorial Shakespeare *and*
Pictorial Bible. *He was regularly praised as one of the principal initiators of the dissem-*
ination of cheap, improving literature. The article below demonstrates the way techno-
logical advances impacted upon the economics of publishing and helped to facilitate the
publication of cheap books and journals. It also exemplifies Knight's belief in the way
that a free market for literature could further social and political enlightenment.

The process of printing, when compared with that of writing, is unquestionably
a cheap process; provided a sufficient number of copies of any particular book
are printed, so as to render the proportion of the first expense upon a single
copy inconsiderable. If, for example, it were required, even at the present time,
to print a single copy, or even three or four copies, only of any production, the
cost of printing would be greater than the cost of transcribing. It is when
hundreds, and especially thousands, of the same work are demanded that the
great value of the printing press in making knowledge cheap, is particularly
shown. [. . .] For some years after the invention of printing, many of the ingenious, learned, and enterprising men who devoted themselves to the new art
which was to change the face of society, were ruined, because they could not sell
cheaply unless they printed a considerable number of a book; and there were
not readers enough to take off the stock which they thus accumulated. In time,
however, as the facilities for acquiring knowledge which printing afforded
created many readers, the trade of printing books became one of less general
risk; and dealers in literature could afford more and more to dispense with individual patronage, and rely upon the public demand. [. . .]

It has been said, that 'the bent of civilization is to make good things cheap'.
There can be no doubt whatever, that in all the processes in which science is
applied the article produced is not only made better but cheaper; and the more
'the bent of civilization' leads to an extension of demand, the more will scientific knowledge, and the division of labour be called into employment. But this
is peculiarly the case in all *copying* processes, among which printing is the foremost. [. . .] The cost of authorship, of designs for wood-cuts, and of the wood-
cuts themselves, of the 'Penny Magazine', for example, required to produce a
yearly volume, amounts, in round numbers, to 3,000*l.*, or 60,000 shillings. If
120,000 copies are sold, that expense is sixpence upon each volume; if 60,000,
one shilling; if 10,000, six shillings; if 3,000, one pound. The purchasers, therefore, of a twelvemonths' numbers of the 'Penny Magazine', for which less than
four shillings is paid to the publisher, buy not only sixty-four sheets of printed
paper, but as much labour of literature and art as would cost a pound if only
3,000 copies were sold, and six shillings if only 10,000 were sold. Those, therefore, who attempt to persuade the public that cheap books must *essentially* be
bad books, are very shallow, or very prejudiced reasoners. The complete reverse
is the truth. The cheapness ensures a very large number of purchasers; and the

Figure 8.1 '"The Times" Office. New Printing Machine', *The Ladies' Treasury* 4 (1860), 149

larger the number the greater the power of commercially realizing the means for liberal outlay upon those matters in which the excellence of a book chiefly consists, – its text, and its illustrations.

8.2 Robert Peel, *An Inaugural Address, Delivered by the Right Hon. Sir Robert Peel, Bart. M.P., President of the Tamworth Library and Reading Room, on Tuesday, 19th January, 1841* (London: James Bain, 1841)

The creation of reading spaces that allowed for the sharing of texts was, for many people, a principal means of gaining access to a wide range of books and periodicals, the cost of which would have been too expensive for them to buy. Texts were shared through the development of circulating and public libraries, schools, coffee houses and mechanics' institutes. The inauguration of the Tamworth Library and Reading Room, described below, is exemplary of the way that, although such institutes sought to encourage popular reading, the motivation for their development often stemmed from a utilitarian belief in the 'improving' value of literature. Robert Peel (1788–1850) was Tory Prime Minister for the periods 1834–5 and 1841–6; he served as MP for Tamworth from 1830 until his death. His address provoked a series of critical letters in The Times *from John Henry Newman (see extract 4.6), under the pseudonym 'Catholicus', in which Newman attacked the secular and utilitarian bias of Peel's promotion of useful knowledge.* (See also extract 7.8 for the activities of such institutions.)

It has been usual on the foundation of Institutions similar to that which it has been proposed to establish in this Town – to open the proceedings with an Inaugural Lecture or Address, explanatory of the principles on which such Institutions have been founded, and of the objects which they have in view. In conformity with that practice, and from a desire faithfully to discharge the functions of the appointment to which I have been recently elected, I have willingly undertaken a duty which is generally ascribed to the office of President. [. . .]

It is proposed to establish a Reading Room and Library. The Reading Room to be open for a portion of every day, (sundays and certain holidays excepted) with permission to the members of the Society, to have for perusal at their homes, the Books of the Library, under such Rules as may hereafter be established by the Committee of Management. If the funds of the Institution will permit, plain and popular Lectures will be given upon such subjects as Astronomy – as Chemistry – as Botany – upon recent improvements in Arts and Manufactures; and upon the application of Scientific Discoveries, and of the successful experiments of practical observers, to Agriculture, and to those Trades and occupations which chiefly engross the labour and thoughts of this district of the country.

All persons above the age of fourteen years, without distinction of political or religious opinions, may become entitled to the privileges of this Institution upon the payment of so trifling sum, as one shilling quarterly in advance.

It is open to the female as well as the male population of the district, for we should have considered it a gross injustice to the well-educated and virtuous Women of this town and neighbourhood, to presume that they are less capable than their husbands or their brothers of profiting by the opportunities of acquiring knowledge; or that they were less interested in promoting the cause of rational recreation, and intellectual improvement. We willingly give to them in the control and management of this Institution, equal power and equal influence with others; well assured as we are, that that power and influence will be exerted, if their exertion should be necessary, in favour of whatever is sound and profitable in respect to knowledge, and decorous and exemplary in respect to conduct. [. . .]

There may I trust be occasional access at some hour in the day-time, to the Globes and Maps, or Books of Reference, in the Reading Room, and parents may thus be enabled to make the stores of knowledge there accumulated, available for the instruction and improvement of children below the age of fourteen years. I trust that it is not too sanguine a hope that those stores may accumulate from other sources, than the funds of the Institution, and that we may be now founding a treasury of knowledge, richer and more various than our printed Regulations contemplate. For instance: in a district not deficient itself in mineral productions, and bordering on one which is pregnant with iron and coal, the great incentives to human skill and industry – a collection of Mineral specimens may perhaps gradually be formed, most interesting to the inquisitive mind, and facilitating the comprehension of written treatises, or of Lectures on Mineralogy and kindred subjects [. . .]

I beg to call your attention to the constitution of the Book Committee, because I understand that the rule of the Institution, which has been principally objected to, is that which places on the Book Committee the Vicar and one of the Curates of Tamworth named by the Vicar, as members, ex-officio, of this Book Committee. I do not feel the force of that objection. In founding a Literary and Scientific Institution, it seems to me a just and reasonable proposal, that Ministers of the Established Church, whose office is a permanent and responsible one – who cannot hold that office without a previous course of study, and without literary acquirements – who have duties assigned to them by the State, immediately connected with the *moral* condition and *moral* improvement of the people – who receive a public endowment for the purpose of performing those duties – it seems to me a just and reasonable proposal that they should be invited, nay, *required*, to give their assistance towards affecting that which we avow to be a main object of the Society, namely the exclusion of works of a frivolous, or immoral, or evil tendency, from the Library of the Society. [. . .]

The examples I have been referring to are of knowledge immediately profitable, with reference to the daily occupation and the present condition of man. There will be other knowledge connected with history, with the various improvements in Art, and discoveries in Science. And let me make an earnest and affectionate appeal to you – to you, for whose especial benefit this Institution is intended – not to neglect the opportunity of occasionally combining relaxation from the active pursuits in which you are engaged, with mental improvement. Heed not the sneers, the foolish sarcasms against learning, of those who would keep you depressed, and are unwilling that you should rise above the level of their own contented ignorance. Do not believe that you have not time for acquiring knowledge. It is the idle man who wants time for everything. The industrious man is the man who knows the value of the economy of time, and can find leisure for rational recreation and mental improvement. Do not believe that the acquisition of knowledge, of such knowledge as we shall offer, will obstruct your worldly prosperity, or that it is inconsistent with your worldly pursuits. You cannot sharpen your intellectual faculties, you cannot widen the range of your knowledge, without becoming more skilful in the business or employment that occupies you. And be assured of this, that there is a spirit of enquiry aboard, a spirit of enterprise, an extent and activity of competition which will make success impossible, if you remain in the rear of intelligent rivals. All the increased facilities of intercourse – every steam boat that cuts the waters, every railway carriage that shoots along the levelled line, are operating as bounties upon Mechanical skill and knowledge. They are shortening, nay, they are effacing, the interval between the producer and the consumer; and destroying the preferences which old habits and neighbourhood, and local connections, might heretofore have secured, for comparative inferiority. [. . .]

It seems to me, that by bringing into immediate contact, the intelligent minds of various classes and various conditions of life – by uniting (as we have united) in the Committee of Management of this Institution, the Gentleman of ancient family and great landed possessions, with the most skilful and intelligent of our Mechanics that we are harmonizing the gradations of society, and establishing a bond of connection which will derive no common strength from the motives that influence us, and the cause in which we are engaged.

8.3 Mrs [Sarah Stickney] Ellis, *The Young Ladies' Reader; or, Extracts from Modern Authors, adapted for Educational or Family Use* (London: Grant & Griffith, 1845)

The Young Ladies' Reader *was an offshoot of a series of conduct books published by Stickney Ellis (1812–72) in the late 1830s and 1840s, including* The Women of England *(1838) and* The Daughters of England *(1842). (For a biographical note on Ellis see p. 74.) Ellis's promotion of reading aloud within the home exemplifies the prevalence of oral reading during the period: the practice offered a way of transmitting texts to the many people who were unable to read or who were semi-literate. As the extract suggests, reading aloud creates a different encounter with the text, one that is collective rather than solitary; interpretation and meaning can be created through dialogue or controlled through the power dynamic between reader and listener. Ellis's piece, however, also typifies the ideological anxiety around the figure of the solitary woman reader. There was an oft-expressed desire to regulate women's reading, both for her sake and because she was often the conduit for passing on knowledge to her children through reading to them.*

From 'The Art of Reading Well, as Connected with Social Improvement'
If in our ideas of the *fine arts*, we include all those embellishments of civilized life, which combine in a high degree the gratification of a refined taste, with the exercise of an enlightened intellect; then must reading aloud hold a prominent place amongst those arts which impart a charm to social intercourse, at the same time that they elevate and purify the associations of ordinary life.

The art of reading aloud, and in reading *well*, is thus entitled to our serious consideration, inasmuch as it may be made a highly influential means of imparting a zest, and an interest, to domestic associations; and of investing with the charm of perpetual freshness the conversation of the family circle, the intercourse of friendship, and the communion of 'mutual minds' [. . .]

The hurried manner in which most persons are now spending their lives, tends, perhaps more than any other cause, to destroy the interest and the advantage that might be derived from reading aloud. Mere snatches of time are all which the generality of people believe they can afford to give to a book; and thus, each volume of the vast number circulated by our libraries and book-societies, is snatched at by each separate member of a family, and supposed to be read as far as time will allow.

[. . .] Suppose a family to consist of ten members, each of whom indulges at intervals in an hour's silent and exclusive reading of any given book, and it must be a small book indeed which can be thoroughly read in an hour. According to this plan, ten separate hours must be consumed in order to enable each individual to say they have read the book at all, and that without the benefit of each other's impressions or remarks, and without those lively outbursts of thought and feeling which tend so much to render all such impressions forcible and lasting, – as regards the young, too, without the great advantage of the observations of age, and experience, to correct their sentiments and opinions.

Ten uninterrupted hours of social and family reading! What a sum of intellectual enjoyment might be gathered into that space of time! But then it must be *good* reading, or the enjoyment is exchanged for the unspeakable annoyance [. . .]

As music is to the ear, and to the passions, so is reading aloud to the ear, and to the mind. Yet, how amazing is the difference in the amount of time bestowed upon the one, and upon the other! It is no mean recommendation to the accomplishment of reading well, that it tends to promote family union and concord. A good book is like the conversation of an intelligent friend, and ought to be treated with the same respect. It forms, in fact, a safe rallying point, around which different tempers, feelings, and constitutions, can meet without jarring or discord; and in a far higher degree than music, it tends to draw each mind out of its petty cares and perplexities, to meet with other minds on common ground, where a wider extent of interest, and often a nobler range of thought, have the effect of shewing, by contrast, how trivial and unimportant are the little things of self in the great aggregate of human happiness and misery.

[. . .] On the other hand, the habit of silent and solitary reading has the inevitable effect, in a family, of opening different trains of thought and feelings, which tend rather to separate than unite, and which naturally induce habits of exclusive, selfish, and unprofitable musing. [. . .]

The habit of reading aloud, and well, is most especially important to women, because of the amount of time usually occupied by them in quiet and sedentary employments. Mind has so very little to do with the vast proportion of these employments, that for idle and unprofitable thoughts, for vague and endless musing, they are almost worse than nothing. [. . .]

The two principal errors into which young readers are apt to fall, – that of attaching too much importance to whatever affects the feelings and the passions, and too little to what belongs to the reasoning faculties, are equally likely to be corrected by the habit of reading aloud in families, and especially in the presence of intelligent and right-judging parents. [. . .] It is the free access to circulating libraries, the solitary and indiscriminate devouring of novels merely as such, and because they beguile the restless craving of a diseased imagination, which combine to constitute one of the greatest evils to which youth is liable. [. . .]

For the moral causes which operate on the well-being of nations, I am convinced we look too much to legislature, and too little to individual duty. We seek a panacea for the evils around us in the opinions of a new party, of the doctrines of some new sect; and persuading ourselves that some one great thing demands our exclusive attention, we overlook the many small things that make up the sum of life. But as a simultaneous effort throughout our land to render homes in general more attractive would do more towards keeping families united than the establishment of a new police for forcing fathers, husbands, and brothers to remain within their own doors; so any single object of attainment which has this tendency is richly worth our best endeavours; and to a highly improved method of reading aloud, I am sanguine enough to look for one amongst the many means of promoting social feeling, which ought not on any consideration to be neglected.

8.4 [George Henry Lewes], 'The Condition of Authors in England, Germany and France', *Fraser's Magazine for Town and Country* 35 (1847), 285–95

The expansion of the periodical press played a key role in encouraging the professionalization of authorship. The advent of a large number of journals, reviews and magazines provided writers with extensive remunerative opportunities, allowing them to live by their pens. Significantly, writers of all kind benefited because most journals consisted of a miscellany of articles, covering any and all subjects. In keeping with the claims of this article, George Henry Lewes (1817–78) was a distinguished journalist, critic and intellectual, who supported himself through a wide range of literary activity. As well as articles on philosophy, science, drama and literature, in 1847 his already published work included a novel, Ranthorpe *(1847), and* A Biographical Dictionary of Philosophy *(1845–6). (See extract 10.9 for a biographical note on Lewes and an example of the range of his work.)*

Literature has become a profession. It is a means of subsistence, almost as certain as the bar or the church. The number of aspirants increases daily, and daily the circle of readers grows wider. That there are some evils inherent in such a state of things it would be folly to deny; but still greater folly would it be to see nothing beyond these evil. Bad or good, there is no evading the 'great fact', now that it is so firmly established. We may deplore, but we cannot alter it. Declamation in such a cause is, therefore, worse than idle.

Some inquiry into the respective conditions of literature in England, Germany, and France, may not be without interest; and in the course of that inquiry we shall, perhaps, meet with some suggestions towards bettering the condition of English writers, which may be worth considering.

If we reflect upon the great aims of literature, we shall easily perceive how important it is that the lay teachers of the people should be men of an unmistakeable vocation. Literature should be a profession, not a trade. It should be a profession, just lucrative enough to furnish a decent subsistence to its members, but in no way lucrative enough to tempt speculators. As soon as its rewards are high enough to tempt men to enter the lists for the sake of the reward, and parents think of it as an opening for their sons, from that moment it becomes vitiated. Then will the ranks, already so numerous, be swelled by an innumerable host of hungry pretenders. It will be – and, indeed, is, now fast approaching that state – like the army of Xerxes, swelled and encumbered by women, children, and the ill-trained troops.[5] It should be a Macedonian phalanx, chosen, compact, and irresistible.

Let this not be thought chimerical. By a calculation made some time ago, the authors of England amounted to many thousands. These, of course, included barristers with scarce briefs, physicians with few patients, clergymen on small livings, idle women, rich men, and a large crop of aspiring noodles; the professional authors formed but a small item in the sum total. Yet we have only to suppose the rewards of literature secure, and the pursuit lucrative, and we have then the far greater proportion of this number quitting their own professions, and taking seriously to that of literature. [. . .]

In money payments to literary men England far surpasses either France or Germany. The booksellers are far more generous in England; abroad, the governments. In making this assumption, we purposely exclude such exceptional cases as those of Dickens, Eugène Sue, and Thiers;[6] the extraordinary success of their works warrants extraordinary payments. Yet, even here the advantage is greatly on the side of England; Dickens received 3000*l.* for one of his tiny Christmas stories, whereas Eugène Sue only received 4000*l.* for the ten volumes of *Juif Errant.*[7] [. . .]

It may reasonably excite some surprise, how two such very literary countries as France and Germany should suffer literature to remain in so miserable a condition; whilst in England affairs look far more encouraging. It cannot be our greater wealth which makes the difference, because if our wealth be greater, our expenses are also heavier; because, moreover, our wealth, only a few years ago, did not operate at all in that way; our authors were as beggarly as those of our neighbours. The real cause we take to be the excellence and abundance of periodical literature. It is by our reviews, magazines, and journals, that the vast majority of professional authors earn their bread; and the astonishing mass of talent and energy which is thus thrown into periodical literature is not only quite unexampled abroad, but is, of course, owing to the certainty of moderate yet, on the whole, sufficient remuneration.

We are not deaf to the loud wailings set up (by periodical writers, too!) against periodical literature. We have heard – not patiently, indeed, but silently

---

5 Xerxes I (486–465 BC), Persian king, used a massive army in an attempt to invade Greece in 480 BC.

6 Eugène Sue (1804–57), French novelist best known as the author of *Les Mystères de Paris* (1842–3). Adolphe Thiers (1797–1877), French statesman, historian and journalist, founded the newspaper *Le National*.

7 Sue was actually given 100,000 francs for his daily serial *Le Juif Errant* (*The Wandering Jew*, 1844–5) by the newspaper *Le Constitutionnel* – an unprecedented sum. According to Lewes, 100 francs were worth 4*l.*

– the declamation uttered against this so-called disease of our age; how it fosters superficiality – how it ruins all earnestness – how it substitutes brilliancy for solidity, and wantonly sacrifices truth to effect; we have listened to so much eloquence, and read so much disquisition on the subject, that, were we only half as anxious to sacrifice truth to effect as are the eloquent declaimers whom we here oppose, we might round a period, or produce an essay on the evils of periodical literature, which (to speak it with the downcast eyes of modesty) should call forth the approbation of all those serious men who view with sorrow the squandered ability of our age. Why should we not? It would be far easier than to look calmly, closely into the matter. It is always a cheap thing this declamation. It covers a multitude of deficiencies. It is paid for as highly as honest labour in inquiry, and saves so much time! In the present instance, it could be done with so little fatigue, and would fall in so softly with the commonplaces of every reader, and would flatter the 'seriousness' of magazine readers, to whom such works are 'sacred', – men who scorn 'cheap literature', and read no other. [. . .]

Periodical literature is a great thing. It is a potent instrument for the education of a people. It is the only decisive means of rescuing authorship from the badge of servility. Those who talk so magniloquently about serious works, who despise the essay-like fragmentary nature of periodical literature, forget that while there are many men who can produce a good essay, there has at all times been a scarcity of those who can produce good works. A brilliant essay, or a thoughtful fragment, is not the less brilliant, is not the less thoughtful, because it is brief, because it does not exhaust the subject.

8.5 [Wilkie Collins], 'The Unknown Public', *Household Words* 18 (21 August 1858), 217–22

The 1840s and 1850s saw the emergence of penny periodicals whose principal attraction was their serial fiction. They sold in their hundreds of thousands. Wilkie Collins's article, a quasi-sociological exploration of the growth of mass-market reading tastes by a member of the literary elite, is replete with corresponding assumptions concerning its attractions and deficiencies. At the time of writing, Collins (1824–84) was already a close friend of Dickens; he had been contributing fiction and non-fiction pieces to Household Words *for several years. In spite of its generalizations, this article also originally functioned as a defence of Mark Lemon, a friend of Dickens and Collins, who had been appointed editor of the enormously successful penny publication, the* London Journal, *by the publishers, Bradley and Evans, after they had purchased it in 1857. Lemon was editor of* Punch, *which was published by Bradley and Evans (who also published Charles Dickens's* Household Words). *Lemon's editorship of the* London Journal *attempted to raise its literary tone using tactics akin to those described by Collins; its circulation, however, fell dramatically.*

Do the subscribers to this journal, the customers at the eminent publishing houses, the members of book-clubs and circulating libraries, and the purchasers and borrowers of newspapers and reviews, compose altogether the great bulk of the reading public of England? There was a time when, if anybody had put this question to me, I, for one, should certainly have answered, Yes.

I know better now. I know that that the public just now mentioned, viewed as an audience for literature, is nothing more than a minority.

This discovery (which I venture to consider equally new and surprising) dawned upon me gradually. I made my first approaches towards it, in walking about London, more especially in the second and third rate neighbourhoods. At such times, whenever I passed a small stationer's or small tobacconist's shop, I became conscious, mechanically as it were, of certain publications which invariably occupied the windows. These publications all appeared to be of the same small quarto size; they seemed to consist merely of a few unbound pages; each one of them had a picture on the upper half of the front leaf, and a quantity of small print on the under. I noticed just as much as this, for some time, and no more. None of the gentlemen who profess to guide my taste in literary matters had ever directed my attention toward these mysterious publications. My favourite Review is, as I firmly believe, at this very day, unconscious of their existence. My enterprising librarian who forces all sorts of books on my attention that I don't want to read, because he has bought whole editions of them at a great bargain, has never yet tried me with the limp unbound picture quarto of the small shops. Day after day, and week after week, the mysterious publications haunted my walks, go where I might; and, still, I was too inconceivably careless to stop and notice them in detail. I left London and travelled about England. The neglected publications followed me. There they were in every town, large or small. I saw them in fruit-shops, in oyster-shops, in cigar-shops, in lollypop-shops. Villages even – picturesque, strong-smelling villages – were not free from them. Wherever the speculative daring of one man could open a shop, and the human appetites and necessities of his fellow-mortals could keep it from shutting up again, there, as it appeared to me, the unbound picture-quarto instantly entered, set itself up obtrusively in the window, and insisted on being looked at by everybody. 'Buy me, borrow me, stare at me, steal me – do anything, O inattentive stranger, except contemptuously pass me by!'

Under this sort of compulsion, it was not long before I began to stop at shop-windows and look attentively at these all-pervading specimens of what was to me a new species of literary production. I made acquaintance with one of them among the deserts of West Cornwall; with another in a populous thoroughfare of Whitechapel; with a third in a dreary little lost town at the north of Scotland. I went into a lovely county of South Wales; the modest railway had not penetrated to it, but the audacious picture-quarto had found it out. Who could resist this perpetual, this inevitable, this magnificently unlimited appeal to notice and patronage? From looking in at the windows of the shops, I got on to entering the shops themselves, to buying specimens of this locust-flight of small publica-

THE

LONDON JOURNAL:

And Weekly Record of Literature, Science, and Art.

No. 412.—Vol. XVI.   FOR THE WEEK ENDING JANUARY 15, 1853.   [Price One Penny.

[ELLEN DE VERE AND THE AYAH IN THE PICTURE GALLERY.]

THE WILL AND THE WAY.

BY THE AUTHOR OF
THE JESUIT," "THE PRELATE," "MINNIGREY," ETC.

CHAPTER XL.

The strongest resolutions oft are wrung
From the heart's weakness; passion's voice
Drowning weak conscience's whisperings.
OLD PLAY.

Although still weak, and suffering from his wound, Meeran Hafaz no longer kept his couch—despite the remonstrances of his medical attendants and the entreaties of the Khan, he persisted in leaving it: the physical pain he endured was nothing weighed in the scale against the mental torture to which his forced inactivity had condemned him. With the young Indian, life was action; he was a being of impulse—a creature to whom excitement and emotion were as necessary as the fulcrum to the lever, or the main-spring to the watch; his mental enjoyments proceeded rather from that quick sensibility which admires the beautiful in art and nature, than the intellectual analysis and appreciation of it. Thus, without being a sensualist in taste, he was a materialist: fine as the line of demarcation is, it is perfectly possible to draw it.

The first feeling of consolation he experienced since the morning of the duel, was from the visit of the ayah, who came to inform him that his rival had actually departed on his journey to Italy. The intelligence appeared to afford him mingled satisfaction and regret: satisfaction, that he was no longer basking in the light of Ellen's beauty, breathing his heart's young hope, impassioned vows, into her willing ear—riveting yet closer the delicious bonds which knit them like one soul together; regret, that he had escaped him—for on his couch of agony—compared to which Ixion's wheel must have been a bed of roses—he

had sworn a fearful oath to have the life of Henry Ashton.

"'Tis well!" he said, a faint smile illuminating his pale features, like a fading sunbeam resting on a corse. "I can breathe more freely now I know that seas divide them! Never, never, must they meet again!" Zara—who, as usual, had seated herself upon the ground—gazed for an instant upon her foster-son with a cold, mocking expression of contempt.

"Seas divide them!" she repeated; "resolution, long ere this, would have placed a grave between your rival and yourself! This land of gloom and shadows has broken the temper of your soul, Meeran, or you would never prate of seas—they may be crossed! The grave," she continued, lowering her voice, "is narrower than the sea—its depths are less profound—but *they are impassable!* When before did one of your race receive an insult, and let the insulter live?"

The countenance of Meeran became darkly shadowed: the words of the temptress had roused all that was evil in his nature, and recalled the scene of his humiliation so vividly before him, that again he saw the flashing eye of his insulting rival, the curl of his scornful lip, as, in the presence of Ellen and her friends, he crushed his pride and trampled on his pretensions, by reminding him of the charity extended by the Ashtons to his father.

"He *shall* die!" he muttered between his clenched teeth; "but not yet—not yet! It would be envy, not revenge, to slay him in his dream of happiness, his trusting confidence in the bright future; for what is death?—a momentary pang—oblivion—rest! No," he added, "he must *awaken* first—when, one by one, I have stripped life of its illusions—when I have wrung his heart till the strained nerves are dead to every sense of agony—when hope and feeling are alike extinct —then, and not till then, will I place my heel upon his neck, and crush the reptile! I can no longer torture—I must humble ere I destroy!"

"Words!" replied the ayah, "words! Long ere this I had mixed for him the draught, which in our own land rids love and ambition of their rival—hate, of its victim—but for the fear that Ellen's lips might taste it!"

It had frequently been in the power of the speaker to perpetrate the crime she meditated; for since her arrival at the abbey she had daily made coffee for the drawing-room: her foster-child preferred it after the manner of the East, and Zara had prepared it for her from childhood.

"Thank heaven," exclaimed Meeran, whose very heart trembled at the thought of risk to Ellen, "you did not attempt it!"

Their further conversation was interrupted by the Khan, who came to announce the visit of the warrener to his young charge: there was a degree of sadness in the tone in which the old man spoke to him—for he felt that confidence no longer existed between them, and that the estrangement was becoming wider every hour.

"Admit him!" exclaimed Meeran, impatiently; and the next moment, Will Sideler, who had followed closely on the steps of his conductor, entered the apartment, which the renegade quitted: he did not wish to be directed a second time to wait in the antechamber, under the insulting pretext of preventing intrusion.

"Well," demanded his employer, impatiently, "have you succeeded?"

"I had succeeded, when——"

"Pshaw!" interrupted Meeran—who, in his contempt for the sordidness of the instrument he was merely trying employ, imagined that the warrener was merely trying to extort more gold from him, by some well fabricated tale—"I am no niggard, to drive a huckster's bargain with a thing like thee! Name thy price, man, and give me the packet!"

Figure 8.2 'Ellen De Vere and the Ayah in the Picture Gallery', *The London Journal: A Weekly Record of Literature, Science and Art* 16 (15 January 1853), 289

tions, to making strict examination of them from the first page to the last, and finally, to instituting inquiries about them in all sorts of well-informed quarters. The result – the astonishing result – has been the discovery of an Unknown Public; a public to be counted by millions; the mysterious, the unfathomable, the universal public of the penny-novel Journals.[8]

I have five of these journals now before me, represented by one sample copy, bought hap-hazard, of each. There are many more; but these five represent the successful and well-established members of the literary family. The eldest of them is a stout lad of fifteen years standing. The youngest is an infant of three months old. All five are sold at the same price of one penny; all five are published regularly once a week; all five contain about the same quantity of matter. The weekly circulation of the most successful of the five is now publicly advertised (and, as I am informed, without exaggeration) at half a Million. Taking the other four as attaining altogether to a circulation of another half-million (which is probably much under the right estimate) we have a sale of a Million weekly for five penny journals. Reckoning only three readers to each copy sold, the result is *a public of three millions* – a public unknown to the literary world; unknown, as disciples, to the whole body of professed critics; unknown, as customers, at the great libraries and the great publishing houses; unknown, as an audience, to the distinguished English writers of our own time. A reading public of three millions which lies right out of the pale of literary civilization is a phenomenon worth examining – a mystery which the sharpest man among us may not find it easy to solve.

In the first place, who are the three million – the Unknown Public – as I have ventured to call them? The known reading public – the minority already referred to – are easily discovered and classified. There is the religious public, with book-sellers and literature of its own, which includes reviews and newspapers as well as books. There is the public which reads for information, and devotes itself to Histories, Biographies, Essays, Treatises, Voyages and Travels. There is the public which reads for amusement, and patronizes the Circulating Libraries and the railway book-stalls. There is, lastly, the public which reads nothing but newspapers. We all know where to lay our hands on the people who represent these various classes. We see the books they like on their tables. We meet them out at dinner, and hear them talk of their favourite authors. We know, if we are at all conversant with literary matters, even the very districts of London in which certain classes of people live who are to be depended upon beforehand as the picked readers for certain kinds of books. But what do we know of the enormous outlawed majority – of the lost literary tribes – of the prodigious, the over-whelming three millions? Absolutely nothing. [. . .]

In the absence, therefore, of any positive information on the subject, it is

---

8 *Original Note:* It may be as well to explain that I use this awkward compound word in order to mark the distinction between a penny journal and a penny newspaper. The 'journal' is what I am now writing about. The 'newspaper' is an entirely different subject, with which this article has no connection.

only possible to pursue the investigation which occupies these pages by accept-
ing such negative evidence as may help us to guess with more or less accuracy,
at the social position, the habits, the tastes, and the average intelligence of the
Unknown Public. Arguing carefully by inference, we may hope, in this matter,
to arrive, by a circuitous road, at something like a safe, if not a satisfactory,
conclusion.

To begin with, it may be fairly assumed – seeing that the staple commodity
of each one of the five journals before me is composed of Stories – that the
Unknown Public reads for its amusement more than for its information. [. . .]

[. . .] To the serial story, therefore, we may fairly devote our chief attention,
because it is clearly regarded as the chief attraction of these very singular publications.

Two of my specimen copies contain, respectively, the first chapters of new
stories. In the case of the other three, I found the stories in various stages of
progress. The first thing that struck me, after reading the separate weekly
portions of all five, was their extraordinary sameness. Each portion purported to
be written (and no doubt was written) by a different author, and yet all five
might have been produced by the same man. [. . .]

And this sort of writing appeals to a monster audience of at least three
millions! Has a better sort ever been tried? It has. The former proprietor of one
of these penny journals commissioned a thoroughly competent person to
translate The Count of Monte Christo, for his periodical.[9] He knew that there
was hardly a language in the civilized world into which that consummate specimen of the rare and difficult art of storytelling had not been translated. In
France, in England, in America, in Russia, in Germany, in Italy, in Spain,
Alexandre Dumas had held hundreds of thousands of readers breathless. The
proprietor of the penny journal naturally thought that he could do as much
with the Unknown Public. Strange to say, the result of this apparently certain
experiment was a failure. The circulation of the journal in question seriously
decreased from the time when the first of living story-tellers became a contributor to it! [. . .]

How is this to be accounted for? [. . .]

Plainly this, as I believe. The Unknown Public is, in a literary sense, hardly
beginning, as yet, to learn to read. The members of it are evidently, in the mass,
from no fault of theirs, still ignorant of almost everything which is generally
known and understood among readers whom circumstances have placed,
socially and intellectually, in the rank above them. [. . .] An immense public has
been discovered; the next thing to be done is, in a literary sense, to teach that
public how to read. [. . .]

Meanwhile, it is perhaps hardly too much to say that the future of English
fiction may rest with this Unknown Public, which is now waiting to be taught
the difference between a good book and a bad. It is probably a question of time

---

9 Alexandre Dumas, *The Count of Monte Cristo* (1844–5).

only. The largest audience for periodical literature, in this age of periodicals, must obey the universal law of progress, and must, sooner or later, learn to discriminate. When that period comes, the readers who rank by millions, will be the readers who give the widest reputations, who return the richest rewards, and who will, therefore, command the service of the best writers of their time. A great, an unparalleled prospect awaits, perhaps, the coming generation of English novelists. To the penny journals of the present time belongs the credit of having discovered a new public. When that public shall discover its need of a great writer, the great writer will have such an audience as has never yet been known.

8.6 [Andrew Wynter], 'Our Modern Mercury', *Once a Week* 4 (2 February 1861), 160–3

The spread of the railways, both as a form of communication and as a source of leisure, enjoyed an almost symbiotic relationship with the growth of print media. As Andrew Wynter's article recounts, W. H. Smith and Son took advantage of the railway network for the selling and circulation of books, journals and newspapers. It was the principal firm to organize newspaper distribution via the railways, and, in November 1848, they also opened their first bookstall at Euston station. These soon became ubiquitous, the firm even running a successful circulating library enabling borrowers to pick up a book at one station and drop it off at another. Andrew Wynter (1819–76), physician and author, devoted much of his career to the study of the insane. He published articles in the Edinburgh Review *and* Quarterly Review, *as well as short entertaining sketches of contemporary life in the periodical* Once a Week.

It is impossible to calculate the fruits which spring indirectly from any new discovery. Who would have imagined that the introduction of railways would be a powerful and direct means of increasing a thousand-fold the influence of Belles Lettres, and of scattering throughout the country the literary treasures that find their birth as a natural consequence in great capitals? The institution of railway libraries by Messrs. Smith is, we think, one of the most remarkable features of the present day. On the first establishment of railways, the porters were allowed to keep book-stalls for their own emolument. Low-class intellects, of course, could only appreciate low-class literature, consequently these stalls at last became disseminators of literary trash and rubbish, and were quite a nuisance. It was evident that the note of public taste had been struck a whole octave too low. At this juncture, the stalls of nearly all the railway stations fell into the hands of Mr. W. H. Smith; and a book for the journey speedily became as a great a necessity as a railway rug or cap. Our readers must have observed that a certain class of literature was called into existence to fill the new want. The shilling series of Routledge were the true offspring of the railway libraries.[10] Even their highly-embellished covers were of the rapid school of design, calculated to ensnare the eye of the passing traveller. It cannot be denied that this new style of literature had its evil as well as its good side, and had a tendency to deteriorate our current literature with a certain slang and fast element which boded anything but good for the future. It was speedily discovered that higher priced books, such as are published by Messrs. Murray and Longman, seldom found a sale at these stalls, and the circulating population would feed on no literary food but that which was of an exciting, stimulating character. In this country, however, things have a tendency to work straight, and it occurred to Mr. W. H. Smith that every book stall could be turned into a circulating library, fed by the central depôt in London. Listen to this, young ladies in remote villages, eaten out by *ennui*, and pining to read the last new novel! Imagine one of the largest booksellers in the metropolis proposing to pour without stint all the resources of his establishment into your remote Stoke Pogis, and you will find this unheard-of proposition is now an actual and accomplished fact. At the present moment almost every railway in Great Britain and Ireland, with the exception of the Great Western, is in literary possession of Mr W. H. Smith. At two hundred stations, metropolitan, suburban, and provincial, a great circulating library is opened, which can command the whole resources of an unlimited supply of first-class books: and to appreciate this fact we must remember the state of things it displaces. In the country village the circulating library is generally an appendage to the general shop. A couple of hundred thumbed volumes, mostly of the Edgeworth, Hannah More, or Sir Charles Grandison class, form the chief stock-in-trade.[11] If by any chance a new novel loses its way down into one of these villages, in a couple of months' time a resident may have a chance of reading it. But all this is now changed. In Mr W. H. Smith's circulating library the reader may have any book he may choose to order down by the next morning train, regardless of its value. Imagine Southey living in this age, and whilst he enjoyed his lovely Cumberland Lake, having a stream of new books down from London fresh and fresh, at an annual cost of a little more than one volume would have cost him in his day![12] The subscriber to the railway library simply has to present his ticket to the book-stall keeper, wherever he may be, to get the book he wants, if it be in stock; if not, a requisition is forwarded to the house in the Strand, and he gets it by the next day. He can get the book he wants with a great deal more certainty, and almost as quickly even in the North of England, than he could by sending to the next country town. If he is travelling he may exchange his books at any station where he may happen to be.

10 George Routledge's shilling Railway Library was one of the most prominent series of cheap reprints and was launched in 1848.

11 Maria Edgeworth (1767–1849); Hannah More (1745–1833); Samuel Richardson published *Sir Charles Grandison* in 1753–4; all three figures would have been very dated by the 1860s.

12 Robert Southey (1774–1843), Romantic poet who lived for most of his life at Greta Hall, Keswick, Cumberland.

8.7 Matthew Arnold, 'The Function of Criticism at the Present Time', *Essays in Criticism* (London: Macmillan and Co., 1865)

For a biographical note on Arnold see p. 65. This famous essay forms part of Arnold's mission to imbue criticism with a far-reaching cultural and social importance, and, in so doing, to overturn the parochialism and political bias of much existing English literary criticism. Published initially in the National Review *in 1864, the essay was then republished as the opening piece in his groundbreaking* Essays in Criticism *(1865). Its key argument was that criticism should not be regarded as the poor relation of creative endeavour because it played an instrumental role in facilitating the greatness of a nation's literary culture. Some of the ideas introduced in the essay, particularly that of disinterestedness, were highly influential in the establishment of English Literature as an academic discipline.*

Many objections have been made to a proposition which, in some remarks of mine on translating Homer, I ventured to put forth; a proposition about criticism, and its importance at the present day. I said: 'Of the literature of France and Germany, as of the intellect of Europe in general, the main effort, for now many years, has been a critical effort; the endeavour, in all branches of knowledge, theology, philosophy, history, art, science, to see the object as in itself it really is.' I added, that owing to the operation in English literature of certain causes, 'almost the last thing for which one would come to English literature is just that very thing which now Europe most desires – criticism'; and that the power and value of English literature was thereby impaired. More than one rejoinder declared that the importance I here assigned to criticism was excessive, and asserted the inherent superiority of the creative effort of the human spirit over its critical effort. [. . .]

The critical power is of lower rank than the creative. True; but in assenting to this proposition, one or two things are to be kept in mind. It is undeniable that the exercise of a creative power, that a free creative activity, is the true function of man; it is proved to be so by man's finding in it his true happiness. But it is undeniable, also, that men may have the sense of exercising this free creative activity in other ways than in producing great works of literature or art; if it were not so, all but a very few men would be shut out from the true happiness of all men. They may have it in well-doing, they may have it in learning, they may have it even in criticising. This is one thing to be kept in mind. Another is, that the exercise of the creative power in the production of great works of literature or art, however high this exercise of it may rank, is not at all epochs and under all conditions possible; and that therefore labour may be vainly spent in attempting it, which might with more fruit be used in preparing for it, in rendering it possible. [. . .] This is why great creative epochs in literature are so rare; this is why there is so much that is unsatisfactory in the productions of many men of real genius; because for the creation of a master-work of literature two powers must concur, the power of the man and the power of the moment, and the man is not enough without the moment; the creative power has, for its happy exercise, appointed elements, and those elements are not in its own control.

Nay, they are more within the control of the critical power. It is the business of the critical power, as I said in the words already quoted, 'in all branches of knowledge, theology, philosophy, history, art, science, to see the object as in itself it really is'. Thus it tends, at last, to make an intellectual situation of which the creative power can profitably avail itself. It tends to establish an order of ideas, if not absolutely true, yet true by comparison with that which it displaces; to make the best ideas prevail. Presently these new ideas reach society, the touch of truth is the touch of life, and there is stir and growth everywhere; out of this stir and growth come the creative epochs of literature. [. . .]

At first sight it seems strange that out of the immense stir of the French Revolution and its age should not have come a crop of works of genius equal to that which came out of the stir of the great productive time of Greece, or out of that of the Renascence [sic], with its powerful episode the Reformation. But the truth is that the stir of the French Revolution took a character which essentially distinguished it from such movements as these. These were, in the main, disinterestedly intellectual and spiritual movements; movements in which the human spirit looked for its satisfaction in itself and in the increased play of its own activity. The French Revolution took a political, practical character. [. . .]

The Englishman has been called a political animal, and he values what is political and practical so much that ideas easily become objects of dislike in his eyes, and thinkers 'miscreants', because ideas and thinkers have rashly meddled with politics and practice. This would be all very well if the dislike and neglect confined themselves to ideas transported out of their own sphere, and meddling rashly with practice; but they are inevitably extended to ideas as such, and to the whole life of intelligence; practice is everything, a free play of the mind is nothing. The notion of the free play of the mind upon all subjects being a pleasure in itself, being an object of desire, being an essential provider of elements without which a nation's spirit, whatever compensations it may have for them, must, in the long run, die of inanition, hardly enters into an Englishman's thoughts. It is noticeable that the word *curiosity*, which in other languages is used in a good sense, to mean, as a high and fine quality of man's nature, just this disinterested love of a free play of the mind on all subjects, for its own sake, – it is noticeable, I say, that this word has in our language no sense of the kind, no sense but a rather bad and disparaging one. But criticism, real criticism, is essentially the exercise of this very quality. It obeys an instinct prompting it to try to know the best that is known and thought in the world, irrespectively of practice, politics, and everything of the kind; and to value knowledge and thought as they approach this best, without the intrusion of any other considerations whatever. [. . .]

It is of the last importance that English criticism should clearly discern what rule for its course, in order to avail itself of the field now opening to it, and to produce fruit for the future, it ought to take. The rule may be summed up in one word, – *disinterestedness*. And how is criticism to show disinterestedness? By keeping aloof from what is called 'the practical view of things'; by resolutely following the law of its own nature, which is to be a free play of the mind on all subjects which it touches; by steadily refusing to lend itself to any of those ulterior, political, practical considerations about ideas which plenty of people will be sure to attach to them, which perhaps ought often to be attached to them, which in this country at any rate are certain to be attached to them quite sufficiently, but which criticism has really nothing to do with. Its business is, as I have said, simply to know the best that is known and thought in the world, and by in its turn making this known, to create a current of true and fresh ideas. [. . .] For what is at present the bane of criticism in this country? It is that practical considerations cling to it and stifle it. It subserves interests not its own. Our organs of criticism are organs of men and parties having practical ends to serve, and with them those practical ends are the first thing and the play of mind the second; so much play of mind as is compatible with the prosecution of those practical ends is all that is wanted.

8.8 Thomas Cooper, *The Life of Thomas Cooper. Written by Himself* (London: Hodder & Stoughton, 1872)

The working-class reader thirsting for knowledge and self-improvement was sometimes an idealized product of the imaginings of the nineteenth-century literary and intellectual elite. Nonetheless, autodidacts flourished, often playing an active role in radical politics. Although many desired to prove the untapped potential of both themselves and their class, this aspiration, as this piece suggests, was necessarily achieved by mimicking the perceived trappings of 'high' culture. Cooper (1805–92), the illegitimate son of a dyer, was an autodidact poet, political activist and novelist. From his early years he followed a programme of rigorous reading and worked for a time as a schoolteacher; however, his involvement in Chartist riots led to a two-year imprisonment in 1843–5. Much of his subsequent life was spent as an itinerant religious lecturer. Cooper's autobiography is fascinating not only for his account of Chartism but for the details of his self-education and reading practices. In the passage below he is 19, an apprentice shoemaker in Gainsborough, Lincolnshire. He has just joined a cheap private circulating library and started borrowing from a free one.

From Chapter VI. Student-Life: Its Enjoyments: 1824–1828

How rich I was, with ten shillings per week, to buy food and clothes – now all this intellectual food was glutting me on every side! And how resolute I was on becoming solitary, and also on becoming a scholar! [. . .]

I said in my heart, if one man can teach himself a language, another can. But there seemed such a wealth of means of learning now around me, that I felt as if I must attempt to accomplish a broader triumph of self-education than Lee accomplished. I must try if I could not combine the study of languages with that of mathematics; complete a full course of reading in ancient and modern history, and get an accurate and ample acquaintance with the literature of the day. [. . .]

I thought it possible that by the time I reached the age of twenty-four I might be able to master the elements of Latin, Greek, Hebrew, and French; might get well through Euclid, and through a course of Algebra; might commit the entire 'Paradise Lost', and seven of the best plays of Shakespeare, to memory; and might read a large and solid course of history, and of religious evidences; and be well acquainted also with the current literature of the day.

I failed considerably, but I sped on joyfully while health and strength lasted. I was between nineteen and twenty when I began to commit Ruddiman's Rudiments to memory – thinking it was better of [sic] begin to learn Latin with the book that Lee used – though I found afterwards I might have done better. I committed almost the entire volume to memory – notes and all. Afterwards, I found Israel Lyon's small Hebrew Grammar, on a stall, bought it for a shilling, and practised Hebrew *writing* as the surest means of beginning to learn, every Sunday evening. I got hold of a Greek Grammar about a year after; but did not master it earnestly, because I thought it better to keep close to the Latin for some time. I also picked up a small French Grammar; but *that* seemed so easy, that I thought I could master it without care or trouble.

On Sunday mornings, whether I walked, or had to stay indoors on account of the weather, my first task was to commit a portion of the 'Paradise Lost' to memory. I usually spent the remainder of Sunday, save the evening, whether I walked or remained at home, in reading something that bore on the Evidences.[13] [. . .]

Historical reading, or the grammar of some language, or translation, was my first employment on week-day mornings, whether I rose at three or four, until seven o'clock, when I sat down to the stall.

A book or a periodical in my hand while I breakfasted, gave me another half-hour's reading. I had another half-hour, and sometimes an hour's reading, or study of language, at from one to two o'clock, the time of dinner – usually eating my food with a spoon, after I had cut it in pieces, and having my eyes on a book all the time.

I sat at work till eight, and sometimes nine, at night; and, then, either read or walked about our little room and committed 'Hamlet' to memory, or the rhymes of some modern poet, until compelled to go to bed from sheer exhaustion – for it must be remembered that I was repeating something, audibly, as I sat at work, the greater part of the day – either declensions and conjugations, or rules of syntax, or propositions of Euclid, or the 'Paradise Lost', or 'Hamlet', or poetry of some modern or living author.

---

13 The 'Evidences' for the truth of Christianity had been a subject of study for Cooper.

8.9 'Literature Regarded as a Profession', *Work and Leisure: The Englishwoman's Advertiser, Reporter, and Gazette* n.s. 2 (1881), 40–3

Women authors and readers played a key role in the development of nineteenth-century literary culture, and of fiction in particular. Given that it could be carried out within the home, writing was often seen as an occupation that could be undertaken by women without compromising their femininity. As the century progressed, increasing numbers of women worked as professional reviewers, novelists and journalists (the Society of Women Journalists was formed in 1893, for example). Work and Leisure: The Englishwoman's Advertiser, Reporter, and Gazette *(1880–93) was a pioneering, monthly London-based journal, edited by Louisa Hubbard, a campaigner for women's employment and founder of a teacher training college for women. The aim of* Work and Leisure *was to provide advice and practical information on the employment opportunities available for genteel women. (See also extracts 2.7, 3.2 and 7.6 for debates about women's occupations and lack of them.)*

Of all the occupations or professions open to women in the present day, it appears that Literature is the favourite, if one may judge by the number of candidates there are for literary distinction. For a long time writing was considered to be as much the province of men as medicine or law, and the first women who made their way into the arena wrote as much in the style of men as possible. Even in our own day some of our greatest writers deemed it advisable to adopt a masculine *nom de plume*, as Georges Sand and George Eliot.[14]

Looking at the matter from a purely practical point of view, I do not think that the literary profession offers such a very brilliant opening for women as many of them seem to believe, and I think it is often adopted without due or careful consideration. To women who have some half-formed, hazy idea of using their pens as *a means of support* a few words on the subject might not be uninteresting.

In no calling or profession by which a woman may earn her bread is there so much need for the motto, 'Work and Wait', as in literature. There is bread to be won, and bread buttered on both sides too, no one, I think, will deny; but that the battle is easy, the labour light, and the victory sure, is a very common mistake.

Given a woman of good education, average intellect, and a talent for writing (for the ability to write *well*, *is* a talent just as the power to sing, play, act, or paint well, is), who has to stand entirely on her own merits, front the world, and earn her daily bread as best she can, what are her prospects? What are her chances of success from a worldly point of view? Without hesitation, I reply, Poor enough; poorer than from any other occupation or profession to which she would bring the same education, intellect, and perseverance. The prizes in the literary profession are few, the blanks many; and such success as she may

---

14 George Sand (1804–76) was the pseudonym for Amandine Aurore Lucile Dupin, French writer and feminist; George Eliot was the pseudonym for Marian (Mary Ann) Evans (1819–80).

command depends, to a very great extent, upon herself. Not on her education, not on her intellect, not on her love for literature, taste, or culture, but on her force of character, her irrepressibility, her industry, and a dogged determination to succeed. Any woman who has not largely developed that quality which Sterne says is called perseverance in a good cause, obstinacy in a bad, had better never take a pen in her fingers, if she means to earn her bread by it. She must be prepared to look at literature from a commercial point of view, and take failure philosophically. Very good business people fail sometimes. Just at first she will be disappointed, disheartened, perhaps disgusted, for there is no sentimental side to literature now-a-days; everything is prosaic and practical to the last degree. Take *Magazinism*, for instance, and what aspiring young author does not look to that as a stepping-stone to *fame*? An editor says, the public require certain things; can you supply them, *not as well*, but *better*, than any one else? For there is fierce competition, and more people are writing for their daily bread than the world is aware of. A young beginner *can't* write what she likes; she *must* write what the public wants; no matter how singular that taste may appear, no matter how uncongenial the subject, if she is to get on at all, and I greatly question the average woman's capacity for that versatility which is the actual soul and secret of success. She may write well on one subject, but that is insufficient, as 'specialists' are not so successful in literature as in medicine.

Then there are disappointments innumerable. MSS. are frequently 'declined' without the customary, though not very consolatory, thanks, or accepted and laid aside for months and months, till circumstances create an opportunity for using them. [. . .]

Three-volume novels are not much more successful. A story wants to be of something more than ordinary merit or interest to induce a publisher to bring it out, except on 'mutual terms'; unless, indeed, it is by a popular author. A woman working hard for her bread has no money to speculate with, and, in the majority of cases, a three-volume novel is a speculation, and usually a losing one to a young author.

Indeed, there seems to be a very inaccurate idea floating about as to the publication of books, which is a much more difficult matter to arrange than at first appears. There are several methods. First, best, and rarest, the publisher purchasing the MSS. outright, or the copyright of an edition, or number of editions, and producing them in good style; as, of course, he will do, seeing it is his capital that is invested. Next, and much more common (I am writing of first books by unknown writers), is the arrangement whereby the author pays *half* the expenses, about 100*l*, of a first edition, about 500 copies, and receives in return, *after all expenses are paid*, three-fourths, or five sixths, of the profit, *if there is any*. [. . .]

But some one will exclaim impatiently, 'Look at all the well-known authors there are – women rich, famous, popular, who are always before the public, whose names are "familiar in our mouths as household words!"' I say, Granted; there are some brilliant successes! *But who can tell all the failures?* And I will venture to say, that of all the successful ones not ten per cent were ever really and truly without resource and entirely dependent on literature for their daily bread, forced to find all the necessities of life from the guineas received from editors and publishers. And a woman who can exist by her pen (and the case is exceptional) has, after all, much to endure, much to contend with; she feels she is wasting the best years of her life in poverty and obscurity [. . .]

But in spite of all the drawbacks, disappoints, and discouragements, there is an attractive side to the literary profession. There is a sort of independence about it; that is, a woman serves many masters instead of one, and so does not seem to feel the servitude. And she is to a great extent her own mistress; she can go in and out as she likes, live where and how she likes, read, write, or idle as she seems disposed; and to many natures that sort of freedom possesses a rare charm. Existence is of necessity a little solitary and Bohemian, for there is neither time nor money for social enjoyment; but what of that when a woman is working, waiting, and hoping? And if life is solitary now, it will be all the brighter by-and-by.

But I think I am safe in saying, that there are very few women who could endure, much less enjoy, such an existence; fewer still who would enter it from pure choice, if they saw it at all clearly mapped out. No woman would continue it longer than she could help, unless there was *some* warped thread in her nature, for it is a morbid, unhealthy, unnatural life; and work that separates the worker from actual daily intercourse with the world loses half its charm.

8.10 Thomas Hardy, 'Candour in English Fiction', *New Review* 2 (January 1890), 15–21

Many progressive late Victorian authors were concerned that the commercialism of the literary marketplace was having a repressive and stifling effect on the development of fiction. One oft-cited cause was the censorious influence exerted by circulating libraries and the periodical press. The commercial power of the circulating libraries (they purchased the majority of new three-volume novels) was such that they were able to influence what was produced by publishers. Their conservative tastes placed an over-bearing pressure on novelists. Authors who desired to challenge the social and aesthetic conventionalities of the novel found their creative efforts stifled, and the literary marketplace was seemingly becoming increasingly split between popular and avant-garde writing (see also extracts 6.9 and 6.10). Thomas Hardy (1840–1928) was often the victim of the moral strictures that his article describes. Novels such as Tess of the D'Ubervilles *(1891) were either initially rejected outright by journals, or modified by editors in order to tone down their controversial treatment of sexual themes. Hardy's article was one of three short pieces on 'Candour in English Fiction' for the* New Review *(the other two were by Eliza Lynn Linton [see extract 3.4] and Walter Besant[15]).*

---

15 Walter Besant (1836–1901), novelist and philanthropist. Best known today for his writings about London's East End.

But when observers and critics remark, as they often do remark, that the great bulk of English fiction of the present day is characterised by its lack of sincerity, they usually omit to trace this serious defect to external, or even eccentric, causes. They connect it with an assumption that the attributes of insight, conceptive power, imaginative emotion, are distinctly weaker nowadays than at particular epochs of earlier date. This may or may not be the case to some degree; but, on considering the conditions under which our popular fiction is produced, imaginative deterioration can hardly be deemed the sole or even the chief explanation why such an undue proportion of this sort of literature is in England a literature of quackery.

By a sincere school of Fiction we may understand a Fiction that expresses truly the views of life prevalent in its time, by means of a selected chain of action best suited for their exhibition. [. . .]

Anyhow, conscientious fiction alone it is which can excite a reflective and abiding interest in the minds of thoughtful readers of mature age; who are weary of puerile inventions and famishing for accuracy; who consider that, in representations of the world, the passions ought to be proportioned as in the world itself. This is the interest which was excited in the minds of the Athenians by their immortal tragedies, and in the minds of Londoners at the first performance of the finer plays of three hundred years ago. They reflected life, revealed life, criticised life. Life being a physiological fact, its honest portrayal must be largely concerned with, for one thing, the relations of the sexes, and the substitution for such catastrophes as favour the false colouring best expressed by the regulation finish that 'they married and were happy ever after', of catastrophes based upon sexual relations as it is. To this expansion English society opposes a well-nigh insuperable bar.

The popular vehicles for the introduction of a novel to the public have grown to be, from one cause and another, the magazine and the circulating library; and the object of the magazine and the circulating library is not upward advance but lateral advance; to suit themselves to what is called household reading, which means, or is made to mean, the reading either of the majority in a household or of the household collectively. The number of adults, even in a large household, being normally two, and these being the members which, as a rule, have least time on their hands to bestow on current literature, the taste of the majority can hardly be, and seldom is, tempered by the ripe judgement which desires fidelity. However, the immature members of a household often keep an open mind, and they might, and no doubt would, take sincere fiction with the rest but for another condition, almost generally co-existent: which is that adults who would desire true views for their own reading insist, for a plausible but questionable reason, upon false views for the reading of their young people.

As a consequence, the magazine in particular and the circulating library in general do not foster the growth of the novel which reflects and reveals life. They directly tend to exterminate it by monopolising all literary space. Cause and effect were never more clearly conjoined, though commentators upon the result, both French and English, seem seldom if ever to trace their connection. A sincere and comprehensive sequence of the ruling passions, however moral in its ultimate bearings, must not be put on paper as the foundation of imaginative works, which have to claim notice through the above-named channels, though it is extensively welcomed in the form of newspaper reports. That the magazine and library have arrogated to themselves in the dispensation of fiction is not the fault of the authors, but of the circumstances over which they, as representatives of Grub Street, have no control.

What this practically amounts to is that the patrons of literature – no longer Peers with a taste – acting under the censorship of prudery, rigorously exclude from the pages they regulate subjects that have been made, by general approval of the best judges, the bases of the finest imaginative compositions since litera-ture rose to the dignity of an art. [. . .]

To say that few of the old dramatic masterpieces, if newly published as a novel (the form which, experts tell us, they would have taken in modern condi-tions), would be tolerated in English magazines and libraries is a ludicrous understatement. Fancy a brazen young Shakespeare of our time – *Othello*, *Hamlet*, or *Anthony and Cleopatra* never having yet appeared – sending up one of those creations in narrative form to the editor of a London magazine, with the author's compliments, and his hope that the story will be found acceptable to the editor's pages; suppose him, further, to have the temerity to ask for the candid remarks of the accomplished editor upon the manuscript. One can imag-ine the answer that young William would get from his mad supposition of such fitness from any one of the gentlemen who so correctly conduct that branch of the periodical Press.[16] [. . .]

There remain three courses by which the adult may find deliverance. The first would be a system of publication under which books could be bought and not borrowed, when they would naturally resolve themselves into classes instead of being, as now, made to wear a common livery in style and subject, enforced by their supposed necessities in addressing indiscriminately a general audience.

But it is scarcely likely to be convenient to either authors or publishers that the periodical form of publication for the candid story should be entirely forbid-den, and in retaining the old system thus far, yet ensuring that the old emanci-pated serial novel should meet the eyes of those for whom it is intended, the

---

16 *Original Note*: It is indeed curious to consider what great works of the past the notions of the present day would aim to exclude from circulation, if not from publication, if they were issued as new fiction. In addition to those mentioned, think of the *King Œdipus* of Sophocles, the *Agamemnon* of Æschylus, Goethe's *Faust* and *Wilhelm Meister*, the *Prometheus* of Æschylus, Milton's *Paradise Lost*. The 'unpleasant subjects' of the two first-named compositions, the 'unsuitableness' of the next two, would be deemed equalled only by the profanity of the two last; for Milton, as it is hardly necessary to remind the reader, handles as his puppets the Christian divinities and fiends quite as freely as the Pagan divinities were handled by the Greek and Latin imaginative authors.

plan of publication as a *feuilleton* in newspapers read mainly by adults might be more generally followed, as in France. In default of this, or co-existent with it, there might be adopted what, upon the whole, would perhaps find more favour than any with those who have artistic interests at heart, and that is, magazines for adults; exclusively for adults, if necessary. As an offshoot there might be at least one magazine for the middle-aged and old.

9

Empire and Race

Introduction

By the time of Queen Victoria's death Britain would rule directly over a quarter of the world's population and nearly one quarter of its land surface. This section demonstrates the historical circumstances and ideological issues which under-pinned Victorian notions of Britain's global sovereignty, and which fed into this period of unparalleled overseas expansion. But in so doing it foregrounds the various and manifold problems, disputes and controversies which characterized debates over how the British should best conceive of their nation's imperial status, and how they should think about the way in which their programmes of overseas expansion would affect those peoples they considered – for differing reasons and to differing extents – racially inferior.

Imperialism is a complex and contested term. Broadly speaking it can be understood to refer to a process featuring a power which comes to dominate and control peoples and territories it considers as peripheral adjuncts to its own metropolitan ambitions, whether these ambitions are economic, political and/or cultural. It is important to note that imperialism does not necessitate colonization, which refers to the takeover and occupation of a particular terri-tory by administrators and/or settlers. When Queen Victoria came to the throne Britain possessed different types of colonies, including Australia, Canada, British India, Ireland and West Indian colonies. But there was a pronounced feeling that these possessions acted as a drain on the nation's resources, that 'empire' was associated with the pride and fall of Napoleonic France, and that Britain would be better off in economic terms if it traded freely with the entire world rather than protecting colonial trade. Notwithstanding this feeling, the early to mid-Victorian period saw Britain extending its formal empire (including New Zealand, parts of South Africa, and Hong Kong). Moreover, empowered as it was by the unrivalled prowess of the Royal Navy, which enabled it to pursue effec-tive, coercive and often violent acts of 'gunboat diplomacy', Britain excelled at 'free trade imperialism', which informally 'opened up' territories (including China, Japan and parts of South America) on advantageous trading terms.

From around the 1870s onwards, though, and associated with the advance of Britain's industrializing rivals, there can be traced a shift in political and popular opinion away from free trade and informal imperialism towards the idea that

Britain needed to pursue far more actively its colonial ambitions. This drive to secure formally parts of the world in order to shore up geopolitical ambition became known as the New Imperialism, and was best exemplified in the 'Scramble for Africa', which began in the 1880s. With the advent of the New Imperialism, Britain's expansionist endeavours were increasingly celebrated by popular events, narratives and practices. Disraeli's bestowal of the title 'Empress of India' upon Queen Victoria in 1877 is symptomatic of a pronounced concern to represent through pageant and ritual Britain's imperial status and authority. While literature produced throughout the Victorian period can be understood with regard to Britain's overseas activities and enterprises, imperial themes and issues became more pronounced during this latter period. The term 'imperial romance' is often used to group together a wide variety of differently accented novels and short stories, by authors including Joseph Conrad, H. Rider Haggard and Robert Louis Stevenson, that were published around this time. Many imperial romances can be read with regard to Victorian jingoism and racial chauvinism. But in common with much fiction from across the period, Britain's imperial relations were often figured ambivalently; such tales generate doubt and anxiety as well as confidence and conviction.

Although Victorian imperialism was characterized by numerous kinds of economic and political relationships, one consequence of Britain undergoing key financial and industrial revolutions earlier than other European powers was that it headed up the nineteenth-century process which *The Communist Manifesto* described as the bourgeois drive to 'establish connexions everywhere'. The extracts below from Marx and Morris both critique the fact that, whether via formal or informal imperial methods, Britain penetrated parts of the world (principally non-European) in ways which attempted to open them up as markets for British manufactures, sites for British capital investment, and suppliers of raw materials to British factories. Such imperialism was energized by the feeling that new communication technologies – particularly the train, the electric telegraph and the steamship – rendered the commercial compression of the planet economically viable on a hitherto unforeseen scale. It was authorized by the conviction that particular 'backward', 'barbaric' or 'savage' global communities had failed to make the most of what Nature – or Providence – had given them. Thus Victorian commentators consistently highlighted the failure of these peoples to mix their labour with their land in the same rational, progressive and God-fearing manner which had seen the British scale such civilized heights. (Ruskin's piece below is an example of this point of view.) But more than this, they often claimed that the natives' previously wasted land and lives would be redeemed as a result of Britain's capacity to investigate scientifically their indigenous resources, allied with the capacity of British manufacturers to buy up the raw materials these lands could produce. According to this potent combination of market economics and missionary zeal – which the explorer and missionary David Livingstone championed in terms of a symbiotic relationship between the three 'Cs': commerce, Christianity and civilization – imperial intervention might necessitate violence, but it led to mutual benefits: the metropolis gained trading partners; savage peoples entered into a dependent but dynamic relationship that allowed them to prosper in moral and religious as well as material terms (on religion and imperialism see extract 4.7).

This inspiring vision of Britain's civilizing imperial mission was, however, troubled and compromised throughout the period by racial discourse. The idea of race was an important field of knowledge and power in the nineteenth century, codifying and promoting not just difference but inequality between global peoples. Understood as a scientifically verifiable marker of biological and/or cultural difference, race became a topic increasingly investigated from the 1840s by new disciplines such as anthropology and ethnology. However, race was a variously employed and highly contested category: the articles below from Carlyle and Mill, in which Mill uses the same journal as Carlyle to repudiate his claims, typify the opposing attitudes played out in books, lectures and periodicals. In the early Victorian period a significant debate took place between monogenetic thinkers (who believed all humans were of the same species) and polygenetic thinkers (who held that different races constituted different species). The publication of Darwin's *On the Origin of Species* (1859) changed the debate because it proposed that species were not fixed but mutable. What remained constant within these debates, however, were efforts to use race as a category which could explain at once why some global communities were superior to others, as well as why this state of affairs was or was not set to continue.

Whilst they were often complacent in assuming that they inhabited the intellectual, moral and religious high ground, it is important to stress that many Victorians were genuinely committed – in line with Christian doctrine – to the notion of essential human similitude, and thus to the idea that forms of imperial stewardship would allow them to raise up after their own image those 'childlike' peoples in their charge. But even when it allowed for such development, racial thinking worked to complicate matters. In a succinct summary of the way in which racial discourse fed into ideas about the kinds of historical divisions it was claimed separated advanced from backward peoples, Cora Kaplan notes the way in which race disturbed the idea of generic human progress, thus problematizing the efficacy of the civilizing mission:

> theories of racial hierarchy and difference before and after Darwin used the metaphor of human development from infant to adult to discriminate between racial types and also between the stages of civilisation that native peoples were assumed to have reached. Non-Europeans (and sometimes women) were often thought to be fixed in a perpetual childhood – monumental in the sense that it remained undeveloped. Even when non-European cultures or non-white peoples were thought to be able to achieve 'civilised' status through education and acculturation, they were imagined as developing within a different, and slower, temporality, their 'catching up' with Europeans often measured vaguely in centuries rather than decades or generations. The

idea that racial types were fixed, but also capable of improvement, were therefore formally in conflict, and fiercely debated by ethnologists and social and
political thinkers. Popular opinion often entertained the two ideas at once.[1]

So although race was a debated category, ideologies concerning arrested or slug-
gish development constituted a way of understanding human existence that not
only justified imperial intervention, but could also explain the sustained exploitation, subjugation and violence which followed. At the same time, ideas about race
allowed for regression as well as progress: by the 1890s anxieties circulated
amongst commentators concerned that British national identity – and British
imperial standing – was threatened by the racial degeneration of its population.
    While the majority of the section is given over to British commentators, it is
of course important to recognize that the legitimacy and effects of Victorian
expansionism were widely debated and challenged by various global communities. Concerned specifically with Ireland – England's oldest colony – the extract
from Douglas Hyde's 1892 lecture is also more broadly illustrative of the way in
which struggles against British imperialism would take shape throughout the
world in the twentieth century.

9.1 [Thomas Carlyle], 'Occasional Discourse on the Negro Question', *Fraser's Magazine for Town and Country* 40 (December 1849), 670–9

*Slavery was officially abolished throughout the British Empire in 1833. However,
continuing exploitative practices by British plantation owners, coupled with the fact
that slavery was both sanctioned and widely practised throughout the world by other
nations (most notably the United States), meant that the anti-slavery lobby remained
a powerful force. Attacking this lobby, and bemoaning its negative impact, Carlyle's
essay (which he republished in 1853 with the deliberately more offensive title,
'Occasional Discourse on the Nigger Question') poured scorn upon the combination of
Christian philanthropy and free trade economics that characterized anti-slavery arguments. Carlyle's defence of slavery was influenced by racist ideology that contrasted the
historical energies (bound up with an aptitude for work) of particular peoples with the
failure of others to utilize properly natural resources, and which sanctioned the notion
that some racial groups had a right to control those felt to be inferior. (See p. 50 for a
biographical note on Carlyle.)*

West-Indian affairs, as we all know, and some of us know to our cost, are in a
rather troublous condition this good while. In regard to West Indian affairs,
however, Lord John Russell[2] is able to comfort us with one fact, indisputable

---

1 Cora Kaplan, *Victoriana – Histories, Fictions, Criticisms* (Edinburgh: Edinburgh University Press, 2007),
   143–4.
2 Russell was the Liberal Prime Minister, 1846–52.

where so many are dubious, that the negroes are all very happy and doing well. A fact very comfortable indeed. West Indian Whites, it is admitted, are far enough from happy; West Indian colonies not unlike sinking wholly into ruin: at home, too, the British Whites are rather badly off – several millions of them hanging on the verge of continual famine[3] [. . .]

Where a Black man, by working half an hour a-day (such is the calculation), can supply himself, by aid of sun and soil, with as much pumpkin as will suffice, he is likely to be a little stiff to raise into hard work! Supply and demand, which, science says, should be brought to bear on him, have an uphill task of it with such a man. Strong sun supplies itself gratis – rich soil, in those unpeopled or half-peopled regions, almost gratis; these are *his* 'supply'; and half an hour a day, directed upon these, will produce pumpkin, which is his 'demand'. The fortunate Black man, very swiftly does he settle *his* account with supply and demand: – not so swiftly the less fortunate white man of these tropical localities. He himself cannot work; and his black neighbour, rich in pumpkin, is in no haste to help him. Sunk to the ears in pumpkin, imbibing saccharine juices, and much at his ease in the creation, he can listen to the less fortunate white man's 'demand', and take his own time in supplying it. Higher wages, massa; higher, for your cane-crop cannot wait; still higher, – till no conceivable opulence of cane crop will cover such wages! [. . .]

Truly, my philanthropic friends, Exeter Hall[4] Philanthropy is wonderful; and the Social Science – not a 'gay science', but a rueful – which finds the secret of this universe in 'supply-and-demand', and reduces the duty of human governors to that of letting men alone, is also wonderful. Not a 'gay science', I should say, like some we have heard of; no, a dreary, desolate and, indeed, quite abject and distressing one; what we might call, by way of eminence, the *dismal science*.[5] These two, Exeter Hall Philanthropy and the Dismal Science, led by any sacred cause of Black Emancipation, or the like, to fall in love and make a wedding of it, – will give birth to progenies and prodigies; dark extensive moon-calves, unnameable abortions, wide-coiled monstrosities, such as the world has not seen hitherto! [. . .]

To do competent work, to labour honestly according to the ability given them; for that and for no other purpose was each one of us sent into this world [. . .] Whatsoever prohibits or prevents a man from this, his sacred appointment, to labour while he lives on earth, – that, I say, is the man's deadliest enemy; and all men are called upon to do what is in their power, or opportunity, towards delivering him from it. If it be his own indolence that prevents and prohibits him, then his own indolence is the enemy he must be delivered from: and the

---

3 An allusion to famine in Ireland, but also to deprivation in England.

4 A building on the Strand, in central London, which hosted religious and philanthropic meetings. Meetings of the Anti-Slavery Society were held there; the venue's name thus became synonymous with the anti-slavery lobby.

5 A jibe, originally Disraeli's, at political economy.

first 'right' he has, – poor indolent blockhead, black or white, is, That every *un*prohibited man, whatsoever wiser, more industrious person may be passing that way, shall endeavor to 'emancipate' him from his indolence, and, by some wise means, as I said, compel him to do the work he is fit for. [. . .]

Up to this time, it is the Saxon British mainly; they hitherto have cultivated with some manfulness: [. . .] it was not Black Quashee,[6] or those he represents, that made those West India Islands what they are, or can, by any hypothesis, be considered to have the right of growing pumpkins there. For countless ages, since they first mounted oozy, on the back of earthquakes, from their dark bed in the Ocean deeps, and reeking saluted the tropical Sun, and ever onwards, till the European white man first saw them some three short centuries ago, those islands had produced mere jungle, savagery, poison-reptiles and swamp-malaria: till the white European first saw them, they were as if not yet created, – their noble elements of cinnamon, sugar, coffee, pepper black and grey, lying all asleep, waiting the white Enchanter, who should say to them, Awake! Till the end of human history and the sounding of the Trump of Doom, they might have lain so, had Quashee and the like of him been the only artists in the game. [. . .]

No; the gods wish, besides pumpkins, that spices and valuable products be grown in their West Indies; thus much they have declared in so making the West Indies: – infinitely more they wish, that manful, industrious men occupy their West Indies, not indolent two-legged cattle, however 'happy' over their abundant pumpkins! Both these things, we may be assured, the immortal gods have decided upon, passed their eternal act of parliament for: and both of them, though all terrestrial parliaments and entities oppose it to the death, shall be done. Quashee, if he will not help in bringing out the spices, will get himself made a slave again (which state will be a little less ugly than his present one), and with beneficent whip, since other methods avail not, will be compelled to work.

9.2 [John Stuart Mill], 'The Negro Question', *Fraser's Magazine for Town and Country* 41 (January 1850), 25–31

John Stuart Mill's impassioned and eloquent response to his one-time friend Carlyle's 'Occasional Discourse on the Negro Question' (see previous extract), bears powerful witness to the fact that debate not consensus often dominated Victorian responses to matters of empire and race. Refusing the kind of biological racism which posited that particular peoples were inherently superior to others, Mill argued it was environment not nature which explained differences between global communities, and attacked the self-serving nature of Carlyle's position. Mill's universalist commitment was bound up with his belief in the capacity of free trade to peacefully and progressively unite all

---

6 Plantation workers in the West Indies often gave their children African-derived names based on the days of the week; 'Quashee' meant 'Sunday'.

peoples. This belief in the power of the market over the power of the whip represents precisely the kind of liberal philosophy against which Carlyle stood. (For a biographical note on Mill, see p. 139.)

SIR, – Your last month's number contains a speech against the 'rights of Negroes', the doctrines and spirit of which ought not to pass without remonstrance. The author issues his opinions, or rather ordinances, under imposing auspices no less than those of the 'immortal gods'. [. . .] This so-called 'eternal act of parliament' is no new law, but the old law of the strongest – a law against which the great teachers of mankind have in all ages protested – it is the law of force and cunning; the law that whoever is more powerful than an other, is 'born lord' of that other, the other being born his 'servant', who must be 'compelled to work' for him by 'beneficent whip', if 'other methods avail not'. I see nothing divine in this injunction. If 'the gods' will this, it is the first duty of human beings to resist such gods. [. . .]

He entirely misunderstands the great national revolt of the conscience of this country against slavery and the slave-trade if he supposes it to have been an affair of sentiment. [. . .] It triumphed because it was the cause of justice; and, in the estimation of the great majority of its supporters, of religion. Its originators and leaders were persons of a stern sense of moral obligation, who, in the spirit of the religion of their time, seldom spoke much of benevolence and philanthropy, but often of duty, crime, and sin. For nearly two centuries had negroes, many thousands annually, been seized by force or treachery and carried off to the West Indies to be worked to death, literally to death; for it was the received maxim, the acknowledged dictate of good economy, to wear them out quickly and import more. [. . .] And the motive on the part of the slave-owners was the love of gold; or, to speak more truly, of vulgar and puerile ostentation. I have yet to learn that anything more detestable than this has been done by human beings towards human beings in any part of the earth. [. . .]

After fifty years of toil and sacrifice, the object was accomplished, and the negroes, freed from the despotism of their fellow-beings, were left to themselves [. . .] These chances proved favourable to them, and, for the last ten years, they afford the unusual spectacle of a labouring class whose labour bears so high a price that they can exist in comfort on the wages of a comparatively small quantity of work. This, to the ex-slave-owners, is an inconvenience; but I have not yet heard that any of them has been reduced to beg his bread, or even to dig for it, as the negro, however scandalously he enjoys himself, still must [. . .]

According to him [Carlyle], the whole West Indies belong to the whites [. . .] 'It was not Black Quashee, or those he represents, that made those West India islands what they are.' I submit, that those who furnished the thews and sinews really had something to do with the matter. 'Under the soil of Jamaica the bones of many thousand British men' – 'brave Colonel Fortescue, brave Colonel Sedgwick, brave Colonel Brayne', and divers others, 'had to be laid'. How many hundred thousand African men laid their bones there, after having had their lives pressed out by slow or fierce torture? [. . .] Not only they did not, but it seems they *could* not, have cultivated those islands. 'Never by art of his' (the negro) 'could one pumpkin have grown there to solace any human throat.' They grow pumpkins, however, and more than pumpkins, in a very similar country, their native Africa. [. . .]

'You will have to be servants,' he tells the negroes, 'to those that are born wiser than you, that are born lords of you – servants to the whites, if they are (as what mortal can doubt that they are?) born wiser than you.' [. . .] By 'born wiser', I will suppose him to mean, born more capable of wisdom: a proposition which, he says, no mortal can doubt, but which, I will make bold to say, that a full moiety of all thinking persons, who have attended to the subject, either doubt or positively deny. Among the things for which your contributor professes entire disrespect, is the analytical examination of human nature. It is by analytical examination that we have learned whatever we know of the laws of external nature; and if he had not disdained to apply the same mode of investigation to the laws of the formation of character, he would have escaped the vulgar error of imputing every difference which he finds among human beings to an original difference of nature. As well might it be said, that of two trees, sprung from the same stock one cannot be taller than another but from greater vigour in the original seedling. Is nothing to be attributed to soil, nothing to climate, nothing to difference of exposure [. . .] Human beings are subject to an infinitely greater variety of accidents and external influences than trees, and have infinitely more operation in impairing the growth of one another; since those who begin by being strongest, have almost always hitherto used their strength to keep the others weak. [. . .] But I again renounce all advantage from facts: were the whites born ever so superior in intelligence to the blacks, and competent by nature to instruct and advise them, it would not be the less monstrous to assert that they had therefore a right either to subdue them by force, or circumvent them by superior skill [. . .]

9.3 [Charles Dickens], 'The Noble Savage', *Household Words* 11 June 1853, 141–8

Dickens's essay 'The Noble Savage' was in part inspired by the display of a troupe of live Ojibbeway Indians from America at London's Egyptian Hall by the American traveller, painter, writer and showman George Catlin in 1843. Catlin had intended that his show portray Native Americans in a positive light; however, ethnographic exhibitions of 'exotic' peoples, of which there were many, often served to enforce popular assumptions of British national and racial superiority. Stridently refusing the romanticized notion of the Noble Savage associated with Jean-Jacques Rousseau, which held that primitive peoples existed in an enviable state of grace, Dickens (1812–70) was nevertheless careful to note that violence towards savages was illegitimate. But his virulent insistence that they should be 'civilised off the face of the earth' can be associated with race scientists such as Robert Knox, who proposed, in The Races of Men *(1850), that European expansion would lead to the disappearance of humanity's 'dark races'.*

To come to the point at once, I beg to say that I have not the least belief in the Noble Savage. I consider him a prodigious nuisance, and an enormous superstition. His calling rum fire-water, and me a pale face, wholly fail to reconcile me to him. I don't care what he calls me. I call him a savage, and I call a savage a something highly desirable to be civilised off the face of the earth. I think a mere gent (which I take to be the lowest form of civilisation) better than a howling, whistling, clucking, stamping, jumping, tearing savage. It is all one to me, whether he sticks a fish-bone through his visage, or bits of trees through the lobes of his ears, or bird's feathers in his head; whether he flattens his hair between two boards, or spreads his nose over the breadth of his face, or drags his lower lip down by great weights, or blackens his teeth, or knocks them out, or paints one cheek red and the other blue, or tattoos himself, or oils himself, or rubs his body with fat, or crimps it with knives. Yielding to whichsoever of these agreeable eccentricities, he is a savage – cruel, false, thievish, murderous; addicted more or less to grease, entrails, and beastly customs; a wild animal with the questionable gift of boasting; a conceited, tiresome, bloodthirsty, monotonous humbug.

Yet it is extraordinary to observe how some people will talk about him, as they talk about the good old times; how they will regret his disappearance, in the course of this world's development, from such and such lands where his absence is a blessed relief and an indispensable preparation for the sowing of the very first seeds of any influence that can exalt humanity; how, even with the evidence of himself before them, they will either be determined to believe, or will suffer themselves to be persuaded into believing, that he is something which their five senses tell them he is not.

There was Mr Catlin, some few years ago, with his Ojibbeway Indians. Mr Catlin was an energetic, earnest man, who had lived among more tribes of Indians than I need reckon up here, and who had written a picturesque and glowing book about them. With his party of Indians squatting and spitting on the table before him, or dancing their miserable jigs after their own dreary manner, he called, in all good faith, upon his civilised audience to take notice of their symmetry and grace, their perfect limbs, and the exquisite expression of their pantomime; and his civilised audience, in all good faith, complied and admired. Whereas, as mere animals, they were wretched creatures, very low in the scale and very poorly formed; and as men and women possessing any power of truthful dramatic expression by means of action, they were no better than the chorus at an Italian Opera in England – and would have been worse if such a thing were possible. [. . .]

To conclude as I began. My position is, that if we have anything to learn from the Noble Savage, it is what to avoid. His virtues are a fable; his happiness is a delusion; his nobility, nonsense.

We have no greater justification for being cruel to the miserable object, than for being cruel to a WILLIAM SHAKESPEARE or an ISAAC NEWTON; but he passes away before an immeasurably better and higher power than ever ran wild in any earthly woods, and the world will be all the better when his place knows him no more.

9.4 Karl Marx, 'The Future Results of British Rule in India', *New York Daily Tribune*, 8 August 1853

As the first half of the nineteenth century developed, India's trading relationship with Britain changed: no longer primarily an exporter of luxury goods, the subcontinent became increasingly significant as a supplier to, and market for, metropolitan manufacturers. This article is Marx's response to the twin-pronged British programme to deindustrialize India (particularly its textile industry), and to open the subcontinent up to British manufacturers through a modern transport infrastructure. Marx signals the exploitative intentions behind these imperial ambitions, which fell under the administrative auspices of Britain's East India Company, but he was clear, here and elsewhere in his writing, that such bourgeois greed would unintentionally effect a world-wide socialist revolution. Although Marx was outraged by the violence which characterized imperialism (he was particularly scathing in his attack of the British response to the Indian 'Mutiny' of 1857), and although he did not subscribe to racist ideologies concerning the inability of non-European peoples to progress, he had little regard for the passivity, stagnancy and barbarism he associated with non-European life. So while Marx did not share the faith expressed by many British imperialists in the capacity of capitalism to bring about universal social prosperity, he did share the Eurocentric beliefs which allowed that the bourgeois penetration of non-Europe could be couched in terms of a civilizing mission. See also extract 1.8 for an account of the Indian 'Mutiny'.

London, Friday, July 22, 1853

Indian society has no history at all, at least no known history. What we call its history is but the history of successive intruders who founded their empires on the passive basis of that unresisting and unchanging society. [. . .]

England has to fulfill a double mission in India: one destructive, the other regenerating the annihilation of old Asiatic society, and the laying the material foundations of Western society in Asia.

Arabs, Turks, Tartars, Moguls, who had successively overrun India, soon became Hindooized, the barbarian conquerors being, by an eternal law of history, conquered themselves by the superior civilization of their subjects. The British were the first conquerors superior, and therefore, inaccessible to Hindoo civilization. They destroyed it by breaking up the native communities, by uprooting the native industry, and by levelling all that was great and elevated in the native society. The historic pages of their rule in India report hardly anything beyond that destruction. The work of regeneration hardly transpires through a heap of ruins. Nevertheless it has begun. [. . .]

The ruling classes of Great Britain have had, till now, but an accidental, transitory and exceptional interest in the progress of India. The aristocracy wanted to conquer it, the moneyocracy to plunder it, and the millocracy to undersell it. But now the tables are turned. The millocracy have discovered that the transformation of India into a reproductive country has become of vital importance to them, and that, to that end, it is necessary, above all, to gift her with means of irrigation and of internal communication. They intend now drawing a net of railroads over India. And they will do it. The results must be inappreciable. [. . .]

I know that the English millocracy intend to endow India with railways with the exclusive view of extracting at diminished expenses the cotton and other raw materials for their manufactures. But when you have once introduced machinery into the locomotion of a country, which possesses iron and coals, you are unable to withhold it from its fabrication. You cannot maintain a net of railways over an immense country without introducing all those industrial processes necessary to meet the immediate and current wants of railway locomotion, and out of which there must grow the application of machinery to those branches of industry not immediately connected with railways. The railway-system will therefore become, in India, truly the forerunner of modern industry. This is the more certain as the Hindoos are allowed by British authorities themselves to possess particular aptitude for accommodating themselves to entirely new labor, and acquiring the requisite knowledge of machinery. [. . .]

The Indians will not reap the fruits of the new elements of society scattered among them by the British bourgeoisie, till in Great Britain itself the now ruling classes shall have been supplanted by the industrial proletariat, or till the Hindoos themselves shall have grown strong enough to throw off the English yoke altogether.

[. . .]

The bourgeois period of history has to create the material basis of the new world – on the one hand universal intercourse founded upon the mutual dependency of mankind, and the means of that intercourse; on the other hand the development of the productive powers of man and the transformation of material production into a scientific domination of natural agencies. Bourgeois industry and commerce create these material conditions of a new world in the same way as geological revolutions have created the surface of the earth. When a great social revolution shall have mastered the results of the bourgeois epoch, the market of the world and the modern powers of production, and subjected them to the common control of the most advanced peoples, then only will human progress cease to resemble that hideous, pagan idol, who would not drink the nectar but from the skulls of the slain.

9.5 Francis Galton, 'Hereditary Talent and Character. Second Paper', *Macmillan's Magazine* 12 (1865), 318–27

Francis Galton (1822–1911) was an anthropologist, traveller, meteorologist, statistician and biologist, as well as being Darwin's first cousin. In 1883, he coined the term 'eugenics', which he defined as 'the science of improving stock'. But Galton's work in this field had begun much earlier, influenced as it was by the way in which On the Origin of Species *could be applied socially ('practical Darwinism' for Galton) in order to protect civilized society from what he saw as the degenerative tendencies encouraged by a mode of life that worked against Darwinian principles, allowing the weak to survive. He argued that the very characteristics which distinguished the Anglo-Saxon race were now threatened by the progress these qualities had brought about. Important too is the fact that although Galton's was primarily a class-based analysis, interested in the state of the nation, ideas about foreign races were prominent in his work. Galton's fears haunted* fin de siècle *social theorists concerned that degeneracy would render Britain unfit for imperial enterprise; nonetheless, his writing did much to justify imperial conquest (conceived as racial competition), as well as warning against inter-racial breeding.*

The idea of investigating the subject of hereditary genius occurred to me during the course of a purely ethnological enquiry, into the mental peculiarities of different races. [. . .]

The Hindu, the Mongol, the Teuton, and very many more, have each of them their peculiar characters. We have not space to analyse them on this occasion; but, whatever they are, they are transmitted, generation after generation, as truly as their physical forms.

What is true for the entire race is equally true for its varieties. If we were to select persons who were born with a type of character that we desired to intensify, – suppose it was one that approached to some ideal standard of perfection – and if we compelled marriage within the limits of the society so selected, generation after generation; there can be no doubt that the offspring would ultimately be born with the qualities we sought, as surely as if we had been breeding for physical features, and not for intellect or disposition. [. . .]

The most notable quality that the requirements of civilization have hitherto bred in us, living as we do in a rigorous climate and on a naturally barren soil, is the instinct of continuous steady labour. This is alone possessed by civilized races, and it is possessed in a far greater degree by the feeblest individuals among them than by the most able-bodied savages. Unless a man can work hard and regularly in England, he becomes an outcast. If he only works by fits and starts he has not a chance of competition with steady workmen. An artizan who has variable impulses, and wayward moods, is almost sure to end in intemperance and ruin. In short, men who are born with wild and irregular dispositions, even though they contain much that is truly noble, are alien to the spirit of a civilized country, and they and their breed are eliminated from it by the law of selection.

On the other hand, a wild, untameable, restlessness is innate with savages. I have collected numerous instances where children of a low race have been separated at an early age from their parents, and reared as part of a settler's family, quite apart from their own people. Yet, after years of civilized ways, in some fit of passion, or under some craving, like that of a bird about to emigrate, they have abandoned their home, flung away their dress, and sought their countrymen in the bush, among whom they have subsequently been found living in contented barbarism, without a vestige of their gentle nurture. This is eminently the case with the Australians, and I have heard of many others in South Africa. There are also numerous instances in England where the restless nature of gipsy half-blood asserts itself with irresistible force.

Another difference, which may either be due to natural selection or to original difference of race, is the fact that savages seem incapable of progress after the first few years of their life. The average children of all races are much on a par. Occasionally, those of the lower races are more precocious than the Anglo-Saxons; as a brute beast of a few weeks old is certainly more apt and forward than a child of the same age. But, as the years go by, the higher races continue to progress, while the lower ones gradually stop. They remain children in mind, with the passions of grown men. [. . .]

Besides these three points of difference – endurance of steady labour, tameness of disposition, and prolonged development – I know of none that very markedly distinguishes the nature of the lower classes of civilized man from that of barbarians. In the excitement of a pillaged town the English soldier is just as brutal as the savage. Gentle manners seem, under those circumstances, to have been a mere gloss thrown by education over a barbarous nature. One of the effects of civilization is to diminish the rigour of the application of the law of natural selection. It preserves weakly lives, that would have perished in barbarous lands. The sickly children of a wealthy family have a better chance of living and rearing offspring than the stalwart children of a poor one. As with the body, so with the mind. Poverty is more adverse to early marriages than is natural bad temper, or inferiority of intellect. In civilized society, money interposes her aegis between the law of natural selection and very many of its rightful victims. Scrofula[7] and madness are naturalised among us by wealth; short-sightedness is becoming so. There seems no limit to the morbific tendencies of body or mind that might accumulate in a land where the law of primogeniture was general, and where riches were more esteemed than personal qualities. Neither is there any known limit to the intellectual and moral grandeur of nature that might be introduced into aristocratical families, if their representatives, who have such rare privilege in winning wives that please them best, should invariably, generation after generation, marry with a view of transmitting those noble qualities to their descendants. Inferior blood in the representative of a family might be eliminated from it in a few generations.

---

7 A disease of the skin, now recognized as a form of tuberculosis.

9.6 John Ruskin, *Lectures on Art: delivered before the University of Oxford in Hilary term, 1870* (Oxford: Clarendon Press, 1870)

It might seem strange that in the conclusion to his inaugural lecture as Slade Professor of Fine Art at Oxford, given on 8 February 1870, Ruskin (1819–1900) turned to champion imperialism, yet the move can be understood in terms of his concern with the alienating, enervating impact of industrial capitalism (for a biographical note on Ruskin, see p. 85). So whilst the extract below extols the advances of science and technology, it is noticeable that Victorian expansion is associated with the traditional virtues of the English race (including hard work, agricultural productivity, patriotic duty, religious rectitude, and a commitment to the hierarchical organization of the nation). Ruskin shared with many commentators – perhaps most notably Thomas Carlyle – the belief that the imperial conquest of supposedly 'wasted' yet fecund parts of the globe constituted a way of combating the pernicious effects of metropolitan modernity. He was also quite prepared to sanction the suppression of those indigenous inhabitants who stood in the way of such endeavour. Thus when Governor Eyre's brutal response to the 1865 Jamaica Insurrection prompted figures such as John Stuart Mill, Thomas Huxley, Charles Darwin and Herbert Spencer to protest against the widespread executions and floggings, Ruskin joined those such as Carlyle, Charles Dickens and Alfred Tennyson who were prepared to defend Eyre's actions.

From Lecture I. Inaugural Lecture

There is a destiny now possible to us – the highest ever set before a nation to be accepted or refused. We are still undegenerate in race; a race mingled of the best northern blood. We are not yet dissolute in temper, but still have the firmness to govern, and the grace to obey. We have been taught a religion of pure mercy, which we must either now betray, or learn to defend by fulfilling. And we are rich in an inheritance of honour, bequeathed to us through a thousand years of noble history, which it should be our daily thirst to increase with splendid avarice, so that Englishmen, if it be a sin to covet honour, should be the most offending souls alive. Within the last few years we have had the laws of natural science opened to us with a rapidity which has been blinding by its brightness; and means of transit and communication given to us, which have made but one kingdom of the habitable globe. One kingdom; – but who is to be its king? Is there to be no king in it, think you, and every man to do that which is right in his own eyes? Or only kings of terror, and the obscene empires of Mammon and Belial?[8] Or will you, youths of England, make your country again a royal throne of kings; a sceptred isle, for all the world a source of light, a centre of peace; mistress of Learning and of the Arts; – faithful guardian of great memories in the midst of irreverent and ephemeral visions; – faithful servant of time-tried principles, under temptation from fond experiments and licentious desires;

---

8 Biblical figures of evil. The false god Mammon represents avarice and the loves of material riches. Belial, a fallen angel, stands for lust and confusion.

and amidst the cruel and clamorous jealousies of the nations, worshipped in her strange valour of goodwill towards men? [. . .]

And this is what she must either do, or perish: she must found colonies as fast and as far as she is able, formed of her most energetic and worthiest men; – seizing every piece of fruitful waste ground she can set her foot on, and there teaching her colonists that their chief virtue is to be fidelity to their country, and that their first aim is to be to advance the power of England by land and sea: and that, though they live on a distant plot of ground, they are no more to consider themselves therefore disenfranchised from their native land, than the sailors of her fleets do, because they float on distant waves. So that literally, these colonies must be fastened fleets; and every man of them must be under authority of captains and officers, whose better command is to be over fields and streets instead of ships of the line; and England, in these her motionless navies (or, in the true and mightiest sense, motionless *churches*, ruled by pilots of the Galilean lake of all the world), is to 'expect every man to do his duty'; recognizing that duty is indeed possible no less in peace than war, and if we can get men, for little pay, to cast themselves against cannon-mouths for love of England, we may find men also who will plough and sow for her, who will behave kindly and righteously for her, who will bring up their children to love her, and who will gladden themselves in the brightness of her glory, more than in all the light of tropic skies.

But that they may be able to do this, she must make her own majesty stainless; she must give them thoughts of their home of which they can be proud. The England who is to be mistress of half the earth, cannot remain herself a heap of cinders, trampled by contending and miserable crowds; she must yet again become the England she was once, and in all beautiful ways, – more: so happy, so secluded, and so pure, that in her sky – polluted by no unholy clouds – she may be able to spell rightly of every star that heaven doth show; and in her fields, ordered wide and fair, of every herb that sips the dew; and under the green avenues of her enchanted garden, a sacred Circe,[9] true Daughter of the Sun, she must guide the human arts, and gather the divine knowledge, of distant nations, transformed from savageness to manhood, and redeemed from despairing into peace.

9.7 Charles Darwin, *The Descent of Man, and Selection in Relation to Sex* (London: John Murray, 1871)

Following the emphasis of On the Origin of Species *upon evolution as a process characterized by variation and mutability, the thrust of* The Descent of Man *was concerned to demonstrate that humans had evolved from other animals. Given this focus, it is unsurprising that Darwin rejected the idea that differences between human groups could be comprehended with relation to racial essence or purity. Since the entire*

---

9 In Greek mythology, an enchantress who lived on the island of Aeaea.

Victorian period witnessed a tremendous amount of energy and authority invested in establishing racial categories in just such fixed, stable terms, this commitment was significant. However, whilst Darwin countered polygenetic arguments, which proposed humanity comprised of distinct (and sexually incompatible) species, and whilst he contended that it was possible through environmental or cultural conditioning to civilize savages, the final two paragraphs of the extract make apparent that, in the struggle for life, particular races or sub-species of the human family were far better equipped than others. If this racialized conception of the 'survival of the fittest' (Herbert Spencer's phrase) spoke brutally to the idea of some humans progressing at the expense of others, Darwin's theories allowed for decline and fall as well as ascendancy and domination. It was the fact that The Descent of Man – *like* On the Origin of Species – *stressed that evolution was not inherently progressive which led social Darwinism to emphasize that with miscegenation came racial contamination and degeneration. (See extracts 3.7 and 10.7 for further examples of the impact of Darwin's thinking.)*

From 'On the Races of Man'

We have now seen that a naturalist might feel himself fully justified in ranking the races of man as distinct species; for he has found that they are distinguished by many differences in structure and constitution, some being of importance. These differences have, also, remained nearly constant for very long periods of time. He will have been in some degree influenced by the enormous range of man, which is a great anomaly in the class of mammals, if mankind be viewed a single species. He will have been struck with the distribution of the several so-called races, in accordance with that of other undoubtedly distinct species of mammals. Finally he might urge that the mutual fertility of all the races has not as yet been fully proved; and even if proved would not be an absolute proof of their specific identity.

On the other side of the question, if our supposed naturalist were to enquire whether the forms of man kept distinct like ordinary species, when mingled together in large numbers in the same country, he would immediately discover that this was by no means the case. In Brazil he would behold an immense mongrel population of Negroes and Portugese; in Chiloe [*sic*] and other parts of South America, he would behold the population consisting of Indians and Spaniards blended in various degrees. In many parts of the same continent he would meet with the most complex crosses between Negroes, Indians, and Europeans; and such triple crosses afford the severest test, judging from the vegetable kingdom, of the mutual fertility of the parent-forms. In one island of the Pacific he would find a small population of mingled Polynesian and English blood [. . .]

Although the existing races of man differ in many respects, as in colour, hair, shape of skull, proportions of the body, &c., yet if their whole organisation be taken into consideration they are found to resemble each other closely in a multitude of points. Many of these points are of so unimportant or of so singular a nature, that it is extremely improbable that they should have been independently acquired by aboriginally distinct species or races. The same remark holds good with equal or greater force with respect to the numerous points of mental similarity between the most distinct races of man. The American aborigines, Negroes and Europeans differ as much from each other in mind as any three races that can be named; yet I was incessantly struck, whilst living with the Fuegians[10] on board the 'Beagle', with the many little traits of character, shewing how similar their minds were to ours; and so it was with a full-blooded negro with whom I happened once to be intimate. [. . .]

On the Extinction of the Races of Man. – The partial and complete extinction of many races and sub-races of man are historically known events. [. . .]

When civilised nations come into contact with barbarians the struggle is short, except where a deadly climate gives its aid to the native race. Of the causes which lead to the victory of civilised nations, some are plain and some very obscure. We can see that the cultivation of the land will be fatal in many ways to savages, for they cannot, or will not, change their habits. New diseases and vices are highly destructive; and it appears that in every nation a new disease causes much death, until those who are most susceptible to its destructive influence are gradually weeded out; and so it may be with the evil effects from spirituous liquors, as well as with the unconquerably strong taste for them shewn by so many savages. It further appears, mysterious as is the fact, that the first meeting of distinct and separated people generates disease. [. . .]

The grade of civilisation seems a most important element in the success of nations which come in competition. A few centuries ago Europe feared the inroads of Eastern barbarians; now, any such fear would be ridiculous. It is a more curious fact, that savages did not formerly waste away, as Mr Bagehot[11] has remarked, before the classical nations, as they now do before modern civilized nations; had they done so, the old moralists would have mused over the event; but there is no lament in any writer of that period over the perishing barbarians.

9.8 John Seeley, *The Expansion of England* (London: Macmillan, 1883)

In a famous speech delivered in 1872, Benjamin Disraeli, the Conservative Party leader, suggested that Britain faced a stark choice. The nation could continue with its liberal or 'continental principles' which were supposedly at odds with imperial endeavour, thus meeting 'an inevitable fate'. Alternatively, it could secure its position as 'a great country, – an imperial country'. Eleven years later the historian John Seeley (1834–95) proposed something very similar in The Expansion of England, *for although he memorably argued Britain had 'conquered and peopled half the world in a fit of absence of mind' (a comment which really referred to the haphazard way Britain's*

---

10 Indigenous inhabitants of the island of Tierra del Fuego.
11 Walter Bagehot (1826–77), the noted essayist and editor of the *Economist* (see p. 63 for additional information).

empire had developed historically), he also indicated that the nation was set to lose its world-leading status if it did not work to promote imperial union and expansion. Whilst both Disraeli and Seeley are associated with New Imperialism, the former envisioned a strong British Empire building upon Indian conquests, whereas Seeley desired a federation of settler colonies – a kind of Greater Britain the inhabitants of which were English by 'blood', not conquest.

There is something very characteristic in the indifference which we show toward this mighty phenomenon of the diffusion of our race and the expansion of our state. We seem, as it were, to have conquered and peopled half the world in a fit of absence of mind. While we were doing it, that is in the eighteenth century, we did not allow it to affect our imaginations or in any degree to change our ways of thinking; nor have we even now ceased to think of ourselves as simply a race inhabiting an island off the northern coast of the Continent of Europe. We constantly betray by our modes of speech that we do not reckon our colonies as really belonging to us; thus if we are asked what the English population is, it does not occur to us to reckon-in the population of Canada and Australia. [. . .]

[. . .] Let us consider what this Greater Britain at the present day precisely is.

Excluding certain small possessions, which are chiefly of the nature of naval or military stations, it consists besides the United Kingdom of four great groups of territory, inhabited either chiefly or to a large extent by Englishmen and subject to the Crown, and a fifth great territory also subject to the Crown and ruled by English officials, but inhabited by a completely foreign race. The first four are the Dominion of Canada, the West Indian Islands, among which I include some territories on the continent of Central and Southern America, the mass of South African possessions of which Cape Colony is the most considerable, and fourthly the Australian group, to which, simply for convenience, I must here add New Zealand. The dependency is India. [. . .]

But of course it strikes us at once that this enormous Indian population does not make part of Greater Britain in the same sense as those tens of millions of Englishmen who live outside of the British Islands. The latter are of our own blood, and are therefore united with us by the strongest tie. The former are of alien race and religion, and are bound to us only by the tie of conquest. It may be fairly questioned whether the possession of India does or ever can increase our power or our security, while there is no doubt that it vastly increases our dangers and responsibilities. Our colonial Empire stands on quite a different footing; it has some of the fundamental conditions of stability. There are in general three ties by which states are held together, community of race, community of religion, community of interest. By the first two our colonies are evidently bound to us, and this fact by itself makes the connexion strong. It will grow indissolubly firm if we come to recognise also that interest bids us maintain the connexion, and this conviction seems to gain ground. When we inquire then into the Greater Britain of the future we ought to think much more of our Colonial than of our Indian Empire. [. . .]

I point out that two alternatives are before us, and that the question, incomparably the greatest question which we can discuss, refers to the choice between them. The four groups of colonies may become four independent states, and in that case two of them, the Dominion of Canada and the West Indian group, will have to consider the question whether admission into the United States will not be better for them than independence. In any case the English name and English institutions will have a vast predominance in the New World, and the separation may be so managed that the mother-country may continue always to be regarded with friendly feelings. Such a separation would leave England on the same level as the states nearest to us on the Continent, populous, but less so than Germany and scarcely equal to France. But two states, Russia and United States would be on an altogether higher scale of magnitude, Russia having at once, and the United States perhaps before very long, twice our population. Our trade too would be exposed to wholly new risks.

The other alternative is, that England may prove able to do what the United States does so easily, that is, hold together in a federal union countries very remote from each other. In that case England will take rank with Russia and the United States in the first rank of state, measured by population and area, and in a higher rank than the states of the Continent. We ought by no means to take for granted that this is desirable. Bigness is not necessarily greatness; if by remaining in the second rank of magnitude we can hold the first rank morally and intellectually, let us sacrifice mere material magnitude. But though we must not prejudge the question whether we ought to retain our Empire, we may fairly assume that is desirable after due consideration to judge it.

9.9 William Morris, *News from Nowhere, or, an Epoch of Rest: being some chapters from a utopian romance* (London: Reeves and Turner, 1891)

William Morris's News from Nowhere *was first published as a serial in the socialist journal* Commonweal *in 1890; it was revised and republished in book form in 1891 (see p. 67 for biographical note on Morris). Although the extract below expresses a critique of imperial expansion through the character of Hammond, the knowledgeable old socialist, it ventriloquizes Morris's own hostility to the industrial capitalist penetration of non-Europe by European powers, particularly Britain. Written at a time when many of Morris's countrymen and women were busy championing British imperialism, the passage provides powerful historical testament to David Harvey's contention that in the nineteenth century 'the world's spaces were deterritorialized, stripped of their preceding significations, and then reterritorialized according to the convenience of colonial and imperial administration'.[12] Morris's recognition of the role fulfilled by*

12 David Harvey, *The Condition of Postmodernity: An Enquiry into the Origins of Cultural Change* (Oxford: Blackwell, 1990), 264.

'hypocrisy and cant' in such imperial exploitation would be memorably underscored later in the decade by Joseph Conrad's Heart Of Darkness *(1899).*

Said he, settling himself in his chair again for a long talk: 'It is clear from all that we hear and read, that in the last age of civilisation men had got into a vicious circle in the matter of production of wares. They had reached a wonderful facility of production, and in order to make the most of that facility they had gradually created (or allowed to grow, rather) a most elaborate system of buying and selling, which has been called the World-Market; and that World-Market, once set a-going, forced them to go on making more and more of these wares, whether they needed them or not. So that while (of course) they could not free themselves from the toil of making real necessaries, they created in a never-ending series sham or artificial necessaries, which became, under the iron rule of the afore-said World-Market, of equal importance to them with the real necessaries which supported life. By all this they burdened themselves with a prodigious mass of work merely for the sake of keeping their wretched system going.'
[. . .]
'The appetite of the World-Market grew with what it fed on: the countries within the ring of "civilisation" (that is, organised misery) were glutted with the abortions of the market, and force and fraud were used unsparingly to "open up" countries *outside* that pale. This process of "opening up" is a strange one to those who have read the professions of the men of that period and do not understand their practice; and perhaps shows us at its worst the great vice of the nineteenth century, the use of hypocrisy and cant to evade the responsibility of vicarious ferocity. When the civilised World-Market coveted a country not yet in its clutches, some transparent pretext was found – the suppression of a slavery different from and not so cruel as that of commerce; the pushing of a religion no longer believed in by its promoters; the "rescue" of some desperado or homicidal madman whose misdeeds had got him into trouble amongst the natives of the "barbarous" country – any stick, in short, which would beat the dog at all. Then some bold, unprincipled, ignorant adventurer was found (no difficult task in the days of competition), and was bribed to "create a market" by breaking up whatever traditional society there might be in the doomed country, and by destroying whatever leisure or pleasure he found there. He forced wares on the natives which they did not want, and took their natural products in "exchange", as this new form of robbery was called, and thereby he "created new wants", to supply which (that is, to be allowed to live by their new masters) the hapless, helpless people had to sell themselves into the slavery of hopeless toil so that they might have something wherewith to purchase the nullities of "civilisation".'

9.10 Douglas Hyde, 'The Necessity for De-Anglicising Ireland', in Sir Charles Garvan Duffy, George Sigerson and Douglas Hyde, *The Revival of Irish Literature* (London: T. Fisher Unwin, 1894), 117–61

Douglas Hyde (1860–1949), the writer who would serve as Eire's first president from 1938 to 1945, delivered 'The Necessity for De-Anglicising Ireland' to Dublin's newly founded National Literary Society on 25 November 1892. At a time when political agitation for increased independence from British rule (most prominently with the Irish Home Rule campaign) was gathering momentum, Hyde's speech drew attention to the importance of Irish culture as a way of combating the damaging impact of British imperialism and of uniting nationalist sentiment. Arguing that as Ireland had become Anglicized so too the significance of its glorious Gaelic past had been greatly diminished, Hyde advocated a return to Gaelic custom, traditions and history, with the Irish language figuring prominently as the means with which to sustain and enrich Irish national identity (he went on to found the Gaelic League in 1893). While Hyde's address became monumentally important to the Irish nationalist struggle, the extract here can also be read in relation to the way in which cultural nationalism has inspired and energized battles against imperialism across all quarters of the globe.

When we speak of 'The Necessity for De-Anglicising the Irish Nation', we mean it, not as a protest against imitating what is *best* in the English people, for that would be absurd, but rather to show the folly of neglecting what is Irish, and hastening to adopt, pell-mell, and indiscriminatingly, everything that is English, simply because it *is* English. [. . .]

But you ask, why should we wish to make Ireland more Celtic than it is – why should we de-Anglicise it at all?

I answer because the Irish race is at present in a most anomalous position, imitating England and yet apparently hating it. How can it produce anything good in literature, art or institutions as long as it is actuated by motives so contradictory? Besides, I believe it is our Gaelic past which, though the Irish race does not recognise it just at present, is really at the bottom of the Irish heart, and prevents us becoming citizens of the Empire, as, I think, can be easily proved.

To say that Ireland has not prospered under English rule is simply a truism; all the world admits it, England does not deny it. You have not prospered they say, because you would not settle down contentedly, like the Scotch, and form part of the Empire. 'Twenty years of good, resolute, grand-fatherly government,' said a well-known Englishman, will solve the Irish question. He possibly made the period too short, but let us suppose this. Let us suppose for a moment – which is impossible – that there were to arise a series of Cromwells in England for the space of one hundred years, able administrators of the Empire, careful rulers of Ireland, developing to the utmost our national resources, while they unremittingly stamped out every spark of national feeling, making Ireland a land of wealth and factories, whilst they extinguished every thought and every idea that was Irish, and left us, at last, after a hundred years of good government, fat, wealthy and populous, but with all our characteristics gone, with every external that at present differentiates us from the English lost or dropped; all our Irish names of places and people turned into English names; the Irish language completely extinct; the O's and the Macs dropped; our Irish intonation changed, as far as possible by English schoolmasters into something English; our history no longer remembered or taught; the names of our rebels and martyrs blotted out; our battlefields and traditions forgotten; the fact that we were not of Saxon origin dropped out of sight and memory, and let me now put the question – How many Irishmen are there who would purchase material prosperity at such a price? It is exactly such a question as this and the answer to it which shows the difference between the English and the Irish race. Nine Englishmen out of ten would jump to make the exchange, and I as firmly believe that nine Irishmen out of ten would indignantly refuse it.

And yet this awful idea of complete Anglicisation which I have here put before you in all its crudity is, and has been, making silent inroads upon us for nearly a century. [. . .]

We have at last broken the continuity of Irish life, and just at the moment when the Celtic race is presumably about to largely recover possession of its own country, it finds itself deprived and stript of its Celtic characteristics, cut off from the past, yet scarcely in touch with the present. It has lost since the beginning of this century almost all that connected it with the era of Cuchullain and of Ossian, that connected it with Brian Boru and the heroes of Clontarf, with the O'Neills and the O'Donnells, with Rory O'More, with the Wild Geese, and even to some extent with the men of '98.[13] It has lost all that they had – language, traditions, music, genius, and ideas. Just when we should be starting to build up anew the Irish race and the Gaelic nation – as within our own recollection Greece has been built up anew – we find ourselves despoiled of the bricks of nationality.

9.11 Mary Kingsley, *Travels in West Africa: Congo Français, Corisco and the Cameroons* (London: Macmillan, 1897)

With time on her hands, and 'feeling like a boy with a new half-crown', Mary Kingsley (1862–1900) introduced Travels in West Africa *by detailing the disembodied instruction which prompted her explorations: '"Go and learn your tropics," said Science.' The exhortation speaks to the Victorian sense of a world opened up to British individuals as well as British state expansion, a fact reflected by the wide array of travel writing produced by adventurers, cartographers, explorers, missionaries and naturalists amongst others throughout the period. But, as Kingsley's revealing introduction regis-*

---

13 Hyde here refers to warriors and kings of Ireland's past, with the addition of Ossian (an ancient poet of doubtful authenticity), the Wild Geese (an Irish army who fought for the Jacobite cause against William III) and the Irish uprising against English rule in 1798.

ters, this work was dominated by men – most famously by the popular writings of the explorer and missionary David Livingstone. Although Victorian travel writing often described apparently innocent scientific or philanthropic projects, such works can be understood to have encoded imperial authority and encouraged imperial exploitation. Travels in West Africa – which became a bestseller, profiting on the authority and celebrity Kingsley's adventures earned her – borrows from the 'monarchic male discourse of domination and intervention' with which Mary Louise Pratt associates much of this writing. However, as Pratt argues, and as the extract shows, Kingsley's was 'a monarchic female voice that asserts its own kind of mastery even as it denies domination and parodies power'.[14]

When we got into the cool forest beyond it was delightful; particularly if it happened to be one of those lovely stretches of forest, gloomy down below, but giving hints that far away above us was a world of bloom and scent and beauty which we saw as much of as earth-worms in a flower-bed. Here and there the ground was strewn with great cast blossoms, thick, wax-like, glorious cups of orange and crimson and pure white, each one of which was in itself a handful, and which told us that some of the trees around us were showing a glory of colour to heaven alone. Sprinkled among them were bunches of pure stephan-otis-like flowers, which said that the gaunt bush-ropes were rubber vines that had burst into flower when they had seen the sun. These flowers we came across in nearly every type of forest all the way, for rubber abounds here.

I will weary you no longer with the different kinds of forest and only tell you I have let you off several. The natives have separate names for seven different kinds, and these might, I think, be easily run up to nine.

A certain sort of friendship soon arose between the Fans and me.[15] We each recognised that we belonged to that same section of the human race with whom it is better to drink than to fight. We knew we would each have killed the other, if sufficient inducement were offered, and so we took a certain amount of care that the inducement should not arise. Gray Shirt and Pagan also, their trade friends, the Fans treated with an independent sort of courtesy; but Silence, Singlet, the Passenger, and above all Ngouta, they openly did not care a row of pins for, and I have small doubt that had it not been for us other three they would have killed and eaten these very amiable gentlemen with as much compunction as an English sportsman would kill as many rabbits. They on their part hated the Fan, and never lost an opportunity of telling me 'these Fan be bad man too much'. I must not forget to mention the other member of our party, a Fan gentleman with the manners of a duke and the habits of a dustbin. He came with us, quite uninvited by me, and never asked for any pay; I think he only wanted to see the fun, and drop in for a fight if there was one going on, and to pick up the pieces generally. He was evidently a man of some importance, from

14 Mary Louise Pratt, *Imperial Eyes: Travel Writing and Transculturation* (London: Routledge, 1992), 213.
15 The Fan were a tribe Kingsley met while journeying in Africa.

the way the others treated him; and moreover he had a splendid gun, with a gorilla skin sheath for its lock, and ornamented all over its stock with brass nails. His costume consisted of a small piece of dirty rag round his loins; and whenever we were going through dense undergrowth, or wading a swamp, he wore that filament tucked up scandalously short. Whenever we were sitting down in the forest having one of our nondescript meals, he always sat next to me and appropriated the tin. Then he would fill his pipe, and turning to me with the easy grace of aristocracy, would say what may be translated as 'My dear Princess, could you favour me with a Lucifer?'

I used to say, 'My dear Duke, charmed, I'm sure,' and give him one ready lit. [. . .]

The first day in the forest we came across a snake[16] – a beauty with a new red-brown and yellow-patterned velvety skin, about three feet six inches long and as thick as a man's thigh. Ngouta met it, hanging from a bough, and shot backwards like a lobster, Ngouta having among his many weaknesses a rooted horror of snakes. [. . .]

The Duke stepped forward and with one blow flattened its head against the tree with his gun butt, and then folded the snake up and got as much of it as possible into the bag, while the rest hung dangling out. [. . .] We had the snake for supper, that is to say the Fan and I; the others would not touch it, although a good snake, properly cooked, is one of the best meats one gets out here, far and away better than the African fowl.

---

16 *Original Note*: Vipera nasicornis; M'pongwe, Ompenle.

10

Science and Technology

Introduction

The extracts in this section fit into three groups. The first consists of passages by William Paley, Humphrey Davy and G. H. Lewes, and deals with general issues of scientific method and value. The second concentrates on the physical and life sciences, with passages by Charles Lyell, Charles Darwin, T. H. Huxley and William James. The last consists of Ada Lovelace, Charles Dickens and Charles Babbage and focuses on applied science and the impacts of technology, dealing especially with transport, communication and industrial manufacture. However, numerous themes run across all of them and offer a glimpse of the main preoccupations of Victorian scientists, and the writers who responded to their work. Of those dealing with general scientific issues, for example, Davy debates the relationship between pure and applied science, and Lewes discusses the ethics of vivisection, then as now a particular talking point in the debate about scientific processes. These issues, dealing with the general purposes of science and matters of social benefit, have a direct bearing on the responses to scientific and technological development to be found in the next part.

If one had to pick a key thread in the overall development of Victorian scientific thinking, one might point to the following. In the first passage, by the Reverend William Paley, one finds an account of nature that is reassuring and above all coherently simple. Paley's view – which had enormous influence – is that the works of nature, no matter how complex, are the product of deliberate design by God and thereby confirm His existence as well as benignity. They are integrated, rational and consistent and belong to a stable and hierarchical universe in which mankind enjoys a position at the pinnacle of Creation. (The argument has direct connection with the modern anti-Darwinian, pro-Christian position known, especially in the USA, as Intelligent Design.)

One might see Natural Theology as the background belief against which Victorian natural science undertook its work. A key word to focus on is 'complexity'. Armed with new methods of data gathering, and the possibilities of new observational technologies such as microscopes and telescopes, as well as by exposure to new environments through global travel (many of these writers travelled extensively and both Darwin and Huxley undertook lengthy round-the-world scientific voyages), these thinkers embarked on crucial conceptual as well as empirical discoveries which cumulatively pictured the world as complex, risky, dangerous and uncertain. Probability replaced certainty; induction replaced deduction in terms of method; and observation replaced belief. But it would be misleading to over-simplify this as atheist science challenging Christian faith. To be sure, some of these writers (Lewes, Darwin and Lyell for example) were religious sceptics or held even stronger views: Huxley – who coined the term 'agnostic' in the same year, 1869, as he wrote the essay excerpted here – pugnaciously maintained that issues of faith had no business in analytical science. Others, however, such as Michael Faraday and John Herschel, found no contradiction between Christian belief and scientific investigation. The real issue, they often argued, concerned how one explains the rich, functioning complexity of nature, and it could be said that such discoveries were themselves a religious duty. For some on both sides, the metaphysical perspectives that might (or might not) lie behind such investigations were, like the social impacts of science's activities, matters of separate discussion.

Nonetheless, Victorian science inevitably produced sharp conflicts. The quarrel over Darwinian biology is the best known and took multiple forms. If nature was a battlefield fought over by competing species, and by individuals within the same species, what happens to morality, let alone faith? And what happens to one's conception of the environment that surrounds and enables us to live, which many of the previous 'Romantic' generation had idealized as a living principle? For some Victorians, such as the Poet Laureate Alfred Tennyson in *In Memoriam* (1850), the benign, reassuring world of Paley's Natural Theology seemed an uncrossable distance away: Nature was now 'red in tooth and claw'. In response, Darwin and Huxley argued that, in such a world, ethical behaviour and cooperative endeavour were actually even more important for human purposes. Further, far from emptying nature of significance, they maintained that their investigations enriched it. There is a 'grandeur in this view of life', Darwin insists at the end of *On the Origin of Species*, because of the awe it inspires at nature's inexhaustible beauty, intricacy and diversity. But there was ample room for speculation either way: Victorian science swung between a fascination with the minute and the detailed on the one hand, and, on the other, with the operations of vast forces in space and time in the vistas opened by astronomy, geology and biological evolution over millennia.

But the crisis in morals and beliefs provoked by scientific discovery was accompanied by other anxieties. The spectre of Frankensteinian meddling in nature, and catastrophic interventions in its processes, haunted much Victorian science both theoretical and applied. At the same time, the issue of the extent to which human beings could themselves be analysed by scientific methods troubled Victorian theory in psychology and human biology. Could humans be accounted for in terms of their biological descent, a topic tackled by Darwin in *The Descent of Man*? And could the human mind, the most intimate and precious space of all, be explained by the functioning of the animal body? If so, what happens to those special capacities of humans that are traditionally claimed to distinguish us from brutes: conscience, reverence, creativity and love, for example? This was a matter of bitter dispute throughout the century. In the controversial essay by Huxley extracted here, he combatively insists that the mind must be understood in terms of its physiological machinery. But how then does one account for the subtlety of consciousness and thought, or the apparent miracle by which a scientific theory might be developed or a great poem written? The work of William James, by contrast, comes a little later in the period when the polemical sharpness of such exchanges had begun to settle. James celebrates the importance of neurophysiology, but asks how we should therefore reconsider our understanding of the development and organization of consciousness, equally a fact of nature.

Finally, in an important sense what we now call 'science' is a retrospective construction. For it was not until around the time of Queen Victoria's death in 1901 that words like 'science' and, especially, 'scientist' were used with quite their modern flavour. By then the word 'scientist' had begun to refer to men (rather than women, usually) working in iconic white coats, in a special place called a laboratory, and communicating research in increasingly specialist journals which bypass the general public. The scientist, the technocrat, the professional expert – a familiar figure in modern iconography – was established. But for most literate and intellectually curious Victorian people, knowledge was not like this. When they felt they needed to make distinctions, they tended to refer to 'natural philosophers' and not to 'scientists', and although papers at the technical end of things were, then as now, demanding for non-specialists (especially in mathematics), writers on scientific subjects remained committed to what we would now call the 'public understanding of science'. Many were inspiring lecturers whose appearances pulled in huge crowds.

But it was largely through the medium of the major periodicals such as the *Quarterly Review, Edinburgh Review, Cornhill Magazine* and legion others that they communicated their ideas to the broader public. It is the eclectic nature of these journals that is now so striking. Typically, pieces on cutting-edge science were printed alongside pieces of fiction, poetry, travel writing, memoir, history, political reflection, theology, and so forth. It constituted what has been called a rich 'common culture' that was profoundly interdisciplinary. Understanding this goes a long way towards explaining why scientific ideas had such an impact on literary writing, and why literary writing in turn fed back into informed general debate. James Clerk Maxwell, the most influential physicist of his generation, was a poet; G. H. Lewes was a novelist, dramatist and critic before he became one of the period's more distinguished psycho-physiologists. His partner was the novelist George Eliot and her fiction, in turn, is steeped in scientific ideas and language. Among the many things for which the Victorian intellectual world is so remarkable is this interpenetration of what we now, with regret, still call the 'two cultures' of science and art.

10.1 William Paley, *Natural Theology, or, evidences of the existence and attributes of the deity, collected from the appearances of nature* (London: R. Faulder, 1802)

William Paley (1743–1805) was the son of a clergyman and headmaster who himself had enjoyed a distinguished career as a churchman and as an academic at Cambridge where he taught mathematics and moral philosophy. Eventually Archdeacon of Carlisle, he was a successful author whose clarity and accessibility in defence of tradi-tionalist Anglicanism was widely praised. Natural Theology *was his most successful work, though its enormous influence was largely posthumous. First published in 1802, it became the classic defence of the orthodox Christian position on the natural world. Many times reprinted, it became a major reference point in all debates about science and religion, as well as influencing the intellectual development of scientists like Darwin who later challenged its fundamental tenets.* Natural Theology *argues that the beauty, elegance and functionality of the natural world are evidence of God's Creation. It insists that nothing so perfectly formed and fit for purpose as, for instance, the human hand or eye could have arrived by accident. It begins by imagining the chance discovery of a watch by someone unaware of what a watch is; that person, Paley argues, could only infer that the watch had been designed even though its purpose may be unclear. Thus are humans situated in relation to the natural world, whose eloquent efficiency exemplifies not only God's Creation but also His goodness. In terms of scientific explanation, its authority for Victorian thinkers lay in its reassurance, its accommodation of the unknown, and the elegance of its explanations. It is a key start-ing point for understanding the Victorian scientist's ventures into increasing complexity and doubt.*

[T]he division of organized substances into animals and vegetables, and the distribution and sub-distribution of each into genera and species, which distri-bution is not an arbitrary act of the mind, but is founded in the order which prevails in external nature, appear to me to contradict the supposition of the present world being the remains of an indefinite variety of existences; of a vari-ety which rejects all plan. The hypothesis teaches, that every possible variety of being hath, at one time or other, found its way into existence (by what cause or in what manner is not said), and that those which were badly formed, perished: but how or why those which survived should be cast, as we see that plants and animals are cast, into regular classes, the hypothesis does not explain; or rather the hypothesis is inconsistent with this phænomenon.

The hypothesis, indeed, is hardly deserving of the consideration which we have given to it. What should we think of a man, who, because we had never ourselves seen watches, telescopes, stocking-mills, steam-engines, etc. made; knew not how they were made; or could prove by testimony when they were made, or by whom; – would have us believe that these machines, instead of deriving their curious structures from the thought and design of their inventors and contrivers, in truth derive them from no other origin than this; that, a mass of metals and other materials having run when melted into all possible figures, and combined themselves in all possible forms and shapes and proportions, these things which we see, are what were left from the accident, as best worth preserving; and, as such, are become the remaining stock of a magazine, which, at one time or other, has, by this means, contained every mechanism, useful and useless, convenient and inconvenient, into which such like materials could be thrown? I cannot distinguish the hypothesis as applied to the works of nature, from this solution, which no one would accept, as applied to a collection of machines. [. . .]

Were there no example in the world of contrivance except that of the *eye*, it would be alone sufficient to support the conclusion which we draw from it, as to the necessity of an intelligent Creator. It could never be got rid of: because it could not be accounted for by any other supposition, which did not contradict all the principles we possess of knowledge; the principles according to which, things do, as often as they can be brought to the test of experience, turn out to be true or false. Its coats and humours, constructed, as the lenses of a telescope are constructed, for the refraction of rays of light to a point, which forms the proper action of the organ; the provision in its muscular tendons for turning its pupil to the object, similar to that which is given to the telescope by screws, and upon which power of direction in the eye, the exercise of its office as an optical instrument depends; the further provision for its defence, for its constant lubricity and moisture, which we see in its socket and its lids, in its gland for the secretion of the matter of tears, its outlet or communication with the nose for carrying off the liquid after the eye is washed with it; these provisions compose altogether an apparatus, a system of parts, a preparation of means, so manifest in their design, so exquisite in their contrivance, so successful in their issue, so precious and so infinitely beneficial in their use, as, in my opinion, to bear down all doubt that can be raised upon the subject. And what I wish, under the title of the present chapter, to observe, is, that, if other parts of nature were inaccessible to our enquiries, or even if other parts of nature presented nothing to our examination but disorder and confusion, the validity of this example would remain the same. If there were but one watch in the world, it would not be less certain that it had a maker. If we had never in our lives seen any but one single kind of hydraulic machine; yet, if of that one kind we understood the mechanism and use, we should be as perfectly assured that it proceeded from the hand, and thought, and skill of a workman, as if we visited a museum of the arts, and saw collected there twenty different kinds of machines for drawing water, or a thousand different kinds for other purposes. Of this point each machine is a proof, independently of all the rest. So it is with the evidences of a divine agency. The proof is not a conclusion, which lies at the end of a chain of reasoning, of which chain each instance of contrivance is only a link, and of which, if one link fail, the whole falls; but it is an argument separately supplied by every separate example. An error in stating an example affects only that example. The argument is cumulative in the fullest sense of that term. The eye proves it without the ear; the ear without the eye. The proof in each example is complete; for when the design of the part, and the conduciveness of its structure to that design, is shewn, the mind may set itself at rest: no future consideration can detract any thing from the force of the example. [. . .]

[I]n a *moral view*, I shall not, I believe, be contradicted when I say, that, if one train of thinking be more desirable than another, it is that which regards the phænomena of nature with a constant reference to a supreme intelligent Author. To have made this the ruling, the habitual sentiment of our minds, is to have laid the foundation of every thing which is religious. The world from thenceforth becomes a temple, and life itself one continued act of adoration. The change is no less than this, that, whereas formerly God was seldom in our thoughts, we can now scarcely look upon any thing without perceiving its relation to him. Every organized natural body, in the provisions which it contains for its sustentation and propagation, testifies a care on the part of the Creator expressly directed to these purposes. We are on all sides surrounded by such bodies; examined in their parts, wonderfully curious; compared with one another, no less wonderfully diversified. So that the mind, as well as the eye, may either expatiate in variety and multitude, or fix itself down to the investigation of particular divisions of the science. And in either case it will rise up from its occupation, possessed by the subject, in a very different manner, and with a very different degree of influence, from what a mere assent to any verbal proposition which can be formed concerning the existence of the Deity, at least that merely complying assent with which those about us are satisfied, and with which we are too apt to satisfy ourselves, can or will produce upon the thoughts. More especially may this difference be perceived, in the degree of admiration and of awe, with which the Divinity is regarded, when represented to the understanding by its own remarks, its own reflections, and its own reasonings, compared with what is excited by any language that can be used by others. The works of nature want only to be contemplated. When contemplated, they have every thing in them which can astonish by their greatness; for, of the vast scale of operation, through which our discoveries carry us, at one end we see an intelligent Power arranging planetary systems, fixing, for instance, the trajectory of *Saturn*, or constructing a ring of a hundred thousand miles diameter, to surround his body, and be suspended like a magnificent arch over the heads of his inhabitants; and, at the other, bending a hooked tooth, concerting and providing an appropriate mechanism, for the clasping and reclasping of the filaments of the feather of a humming bird.

10.2 Sir Humphrey Davy, *Consolations in Travel, or The Last Days of a Philosopher*, ed. John Davy (London: John Murray, 1830)

Hailing from modest circumstances in Cornwall, Humphrey Davy (later Lord Davy 1778–1829) was one of his generation's most distinguished and influential scientists. Primarily a chemist, working originally on gases, he made major contributions to both theoretical and applied science. He is perhaps best known as the inventor of the 'Davy Lamp', a device designed, in the days before electricity, to enable naked-flame lamps to be used in mines, thus avoiding explosions from 'firedamp' (naturally occurring methane gas). Its importance for the safety of miners, and also for the productivity of Britain's coal industry, cannot be underestimated. Davy declined to take out a patent on his lamp on grounds that its utility was too great to restrict its use. He turned his back on a fortune, no doubt (though success elsewhere, and a prosperous marriage, left him far from deprived). But his philanthropy illustrates his own conviction about the public benefits of science outlined in the following passages. Consolations in Travel *(1830) was written at the close of his life while suffering from a fatal heart condition and published posthumously. It is in many ways an unusual book: partly about the benefits of travel and recreational fishing, partly a set of philosophical ruminations, partly fantasy of a kind we would now call science fiction (including intergalactic travel by comet). In the following extracts, set in the form of visionary philosophical dialogues between various characters, Davy debates important issues including the relationship between pure and applied science. The characters are, in order of appearance here, The Genius (a sort of surrogate for scientific enquiry), Eubathes, a travelling companion, and The Unknown, whose name refers to his mysterious appearance rather than to any philosophical or metaphysical principle.*

GENIUS. – The practical results of the progress of physics, chemistry and mechanics, are of the most marvellous kind, and to make them all distinct would require a comparison of ancient and modern states: ships that were moved by human labour in the ancient world are transported by the winds; and a piece of steel, touched by the magnet, points to the mariner his unerring course from the old to the new world; and by the exertions of one man of genius, aided by the resources of chemistry, a power which, by the old philosophers could hardly have been imagined, has been generated and applied to almost all the machinery of active life; the steam-engine performs not only the labour of horses, but of man, by combinations which appear almost possessed of intelligence; waggons are moved by it, constructions made, vessels caused to perform voyages in opposition to wind and tide, and a power placed in human hands which seems almost unlimited. To these novel and still extending improvements may be added others, which, though of a secondary kind, yet materially affect the comforts of life, the collecting from fossil materials the elements of combustion, and applying them so as to illuminate, by a single operation, houses, streets, and even cities. If you look to the results of chemical arts, you will find new substances of the most extraordinary nature applied to various novel purposes; you will find a few experiments in electricity leading to the marvellous result of disarming the thunder-cloud of its terrors, and you will see new instruments created by human ingenuity, possessing the same powers as the electrical organs of living animals. To whatever part of the vision of modern times you cast your eyes you will find marks of superiority and improvement, and I wish to impress upon you the conviction, that the results of intellectual labour, or of scientific genius, are permanent and incapable of being lost. Monarchs change their plans, governments their objects, a fleet or an army effect their purpose and then pass away; but a piece of steel touched by the magnet, preserves its character for ever, and secures to man the dominion of the trackless ocean. A new period of society may send armies from the shores of the Baltic to those of the Euxine,[1] and the empire of the followers of Mahomet may be broken in pieces by a northern people, and the dominion of the Britons in Asia may share the fate of that of Tamerlane or Zengiskhan[2]; but the steamboat which ascends the Delaware or the St. Lawrence will continue to be used, and will carry the civilization of an improved people into the deserts of North America and into the wilds of Canada. [. . .]

EUB. – We will allow that you have shown in many cases the utility of scientific investigations, as connected with the progress of the useful arts. But, in general, both the principles of chemistry are followed, and series of experiments performed without any view to utility; and, a great noise is made if a new metal or a new substance is discovered, or, if some abstracted law is made known relating to the phenomena of nature; yet, amongst the variety of new substances, few have been applied to any *trifling* use even, and the greater number have had no application at all; and, with respect to the general views of the science, it would be difficult to show that any real good had resulted from the discovery or extension of them. It does not add much to the dignity of a pursuit that those who have followed it for profit, have really been most useful; and that the mere artizan or chemical manufacturer has done more for society than the chemical philosopher. [. . .]

THE UNKNOWN. – I deny in toto the accuracy of what you are advancing. I have already shown that real philosophers, not labouring for profit, have done much by their own inventions for the useful arts; and, amongst the new substances discovered, many have had immediate and very important applications. The chlorine, or oxymuriatic gas of Scheele was scarcely known before it was applied by Berthollet to bleaching; scarcely was muriatic acid gas discovered by Priestley, when Guyton de Morveau used it for destroying contagion.[3] Consider the varied and diversified applications of platinum, which has owed its existence as a useful metal entirely to the labours of an illustrious chemical philosopher; look at the beautiful yellow afforded by one of the new metals, chrome; consider the medical effects of iodine, in some of the most painful and disgusting maladies belonging to human nature, and remember how short a time

---

1 Another name for the Black Sea of south-eastern Europe (properly, the name of an abyssal plain in its centre); from the Greek *Euxeinos Pontos*.

2 Zengiskhan: after Genghis Khan (*c*.1155–1227), founder of the Mongol Empire. Tamerlane: like 'Tamburlane', a Western name for Timur (1335–1405), Turko-Mongol founder of the Timurid Empire and Timurid Dynasty.

3 Louis-Bernard Guyton de Morveau (1737–1816), French chemist and educator. Joseph Priestley (1733–1804), English clergyman and scientist. Claude-Louis Berthollet (1748–1822), French chemist. Carl Wilhelm Scheele (1742–86), German Swedish chemist.

investigations have been made for applying the new substances. Besides, the mechanical or chemical manufacturer has rarely discovered any thing; he has merely applied what the philosopher has made known, he has merely worked upon the materials furnished to him. We have no history of the manner in which iron was rendered malleable; but we know that platinum could only have been worked by a person of the most refined chemical resources, who made multiplied experiments upon it after the most ingenious and profound views. But, waving all common utility, all vulgar applications; there is something in knowing and understanding the operation of nature, some pleasure in contemplating the order and harmony of the arrangements belonging to the terrestrial system of things. There is no absolute utility in poetry; but it gives pleasure, refines and exalts the mind. Philosophic pursuits have likewise a noble and independent use of this kind; and there is a double reason offered for pursuing them, for, whilst in their sublime speculations they reach to the heavens, in their application they belong to the earth; whilst they exalt the intellect, they provide food for our common wants and likewise minister to the noblest appetites and most exalted views belonging to our nature. [. . .] It is surely a pure delight to know, how and by what processes this earth is clothed with verdure and life, how the clouds, mists and rain are formed, what causes all the changes of this terrestrial system of things, and by what divine laws order is preserved amidst apparent confusion. It is a sublime occupation to investigate the cause of the tempest and the volcano, and to point out their use in the economy of things, – to bring the lightning from the clouds and make it subservient to our experiments, – to produce as it were a microcosm in the laboratory of art, and to measure and weigh those invisible atoms, which, by their motions and changes according to laws impressed upon them by the Divine Intelligence, constitute the universe of things. The true chemical philosopher sees good in all the diversified forms of the external world. Whilst he investigates the operations of infinite power guided by infinite wisdom, all low prejudices, all mean superstitions disappear from his mind. He sees man an atom amidst atoms fixed upon a point in space; and yet modifying the laws that are around him by understanding them; and gaining, as it were, a kind of dominion over time, and an empire in material space, and exerting on a scale infinitely small a power seeming a sort of shadow or reflection of a creative energy, and which entitles him to the distinction of being made in the image of God and animated by a spark of the divine mind.

10.3 Sir Charles Lyell, *Principles of Geology, being an attempt to explain the former changes of the earth's surface, by reference to causes now in operation* (London: John Murray, 1830–3)

From a well-to-do family (his father was a botanist), Charles Lyell (1797–1875) was a pioneer of modern geology. Training first in law he came gradually to science with a particular interest in systematic exposition aimed at a general as well as professional audience. Like Darwin, whom he influenced, Lyell had an omnivorous curiosity and a strong belief in fieldwork and data collection, often from international sources. Principles of Geology (1830–3) is a large work, running to 1,400 pages. It covers all elements of geological processes from movements of the earth and seas to the actions of climate and plants. It is detailed and thorough, and makes a powerful argument that the earth is formed by continuous, gradual processes. Lyell also insists that geological knowledge must be evidenced and detailed, and that what we understand of past processes must be extrapolated from what we observe in the present. In emphasizing the importance of time, and the cumulative, haphazard impacts of multiple causes – in the parlance of the day he was a 'uniformitarian' rather than a 'catastrophist' – Lyell's views threatened Creation and Design, two key tenets of Natural Theology. He argued against catastrophe accounts of the formation of the earth such as the biblical flood. But, on balance, Lyell was probably more radical in impact (which was considerable) than intention and was an early opponent of evolutionary theory (though he converted later). As the passages below illustrate, he was concerned to integrate his views with more traditional opinion.

But it would be idle to controvert, by reference to modern analogies, the conjectures of those who think they can ascend in their retrospect to the origin of our system. Let us, therefore, consider what changes the crust of the globe suffered after the consolidation of that ancient series of rocks to which we have adverted. Now, there is evidence that, before our secondary strata were formed, those of older date (from the old red sandstone to the coal inclusive) were fractured and contorted, and often thrown into vertical positions. We cannot enter here into the geological details by which it is demonstrable, that at an epoch extremely remote, some parts of the carboniferous series were lifted above the level of the sea, others sunk to greater depths beneath it, and the former, being no longer protected by a covering of water, were partially destroyed by torrents and the waves of the sea, and supplied matter for newer horizontal beds. These were arranged on the truncated edges of the submarine portions of the more ancient series, and the fragments included in the more modern conglomerates still retain their fossil shells and corals, so as to enable us to determine the parent rocks from whence they were derived. By such remodelling of the surface the small islands of the first period increased in size, and new land was introduced into northern regions, consisting partly of primary and volcanic rocks and partly of the newly raised carboniferous strata. Among other proofs that earthquakes were then governed by the same laws which now regulate the subterranean forces, we find that they were restrained within limited areas, so that the site of Germany was not agitated, while that of some parts of England was convulsed. The older rocks, therefore, remained in some cases undisturbed at the bottom of the ancient ocean, and in this case the strata of the succeeding epoch were deposited upon them in conformable position. By reference to groups largely developed on the continent, but which are some of them entirely wanting, and others feebly represented in our own country, we find that the apparent interruption in the chain of events between the formation of our coal and the lias arises merely from local deficiency in the suite of geological monuments. During the great interval which separated the formation of these groups, new species of animals and plants made their appearance, and in their turn became extinct; volcanos broke out, and were at length exhausted; rocks were destroyed in one region, and others accumulated elsewhere, while, in the mean time, the geographical condition of the northern hemisphere suffered material modifications. Yet the sea still extended over the greater part of the area now occupied by the lands which we inhabit, and was even of considerable depth in many localities where our highest mountain-chains now rise. The vegetation, during a part at least of this new period (from the lias to the chalk inclusive), appears to have approached to that of the larger islands of the equatorial zone. These islands appear to have been drained by rivers of considerable size, which were inhabited by crocodiles and gigantic oviparous reptiles, both herbivorous and carnivorous, belonging for the most part to extinct genera. Of the contemporary inhabitants of the land we have as yet acquired but scanty information, but we know that there were flying reptiles, insects, and small insectivorous mammifera,[4] allied to the opossum. In farther confirmation of the opinion that countries of considerable extent now rose above the sea in the temperate zone, we may mention the discovery of a large estuary formation in the south-west of England of higher antiquity than the chalk, containing terrestrial plants and fresh-water testacea,[5] tortoises, and large reptiles, – in a word, such an assemblage as the delta of the Ganges, or a large river in a hot climate might be expected to produce. [. . .]

The geologist who yields implicit assent to the truth of these principles, will deem it incumbent on him to examine with minute attention all the changes now in progress on the earth, and will regard every fact collected respecting the causes in diurnal action, as affording him a key to the interpretation of some mystery in the archives of remote ages. Our estimate, indeed, of the value of all geological evidence, and the interest derived from the investigation of the earth's history, must depend entirely on the degree of confidence which we feel in regard to the permanency of the laws of nature. Their immutable constancy alone can enable us to reason from analogy, by the strict rules of induction, respecting the events of former ages, or, by a comparison of the state of things at two distinct geological epochs, to arrive at the knowledge of general principles in the economy of our terrestrial system.

The uniformity of the plan being once assumed, events which have occurred at the most distant periods in the animate and inanimate world will be acknowledged to throw light on each other, and the deficiency of our information respecting some of the most obscure parts of the present creation will be removed. For as by studying the external configuration of the existing land and

---

4 Mammalia (mammals).
5 A name for various groups of invertebrate animals having shells (excluding Crustacea).

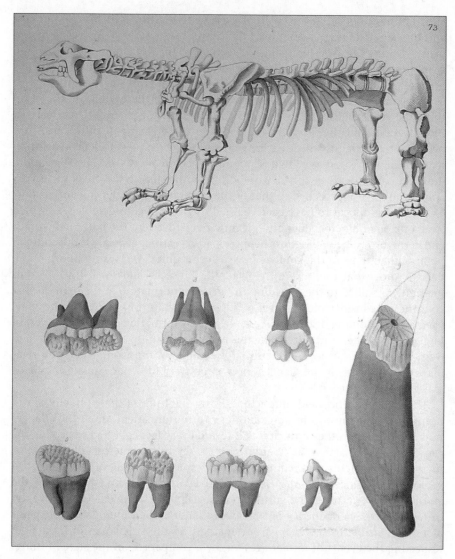

73

Figure 10.1 Gideon Mantell, 'Fossil Teeth of Mammalia', *A Pictorial Atlas of Fossil Remains* (London: H. G. Bohn, 1850)

its inhabitants, we may restore in imagination the appearance of the ancient continents which have passed away, so may we obtain from the deposits of ancient seas and lakes an insight into the nature of the subaqueous processes now in operation, and of many forms of organic life, which, though now existing, are veiled from our sight. Rocks, also produced by subterranean fire in former ages at great depths in the bowels of the earth, present us, when upraised by gradual movements, and exposed to the light of heaven, with an image of those changes which the deep-seated volcano may now occasion in the nether regions. Thus, although we are mere sojourners on the surface of the planet, chained to a mere point in space, enduring but for a moment of time, the human mind is not only enabled to number worlds beyond the unassisted ken of mortal eye, but to trace the events of indefinite ages before the creation of our race, and is not even withheld from penetrating into the dark secrets of the ocean, or the interior of the solid globe; free, like the spirit which the poet described as animating the universe,

> Thro' Heavn'n, and Earth, and Oceans depth he throws
> His Influence round, and kindles as he goes.[6] [. . .]

When we consider attentively the changes brought about by earthquakes during the last century, and reflect on the light which they already throw on the ancient history of the globe, we cannot but regret that investigations into the effects of this powerful cause have hitherto been prosecuted with so little zeal. The disregard of this important subject may be attributed to the general persuasion, that former revolutions of the earth were not brought about by causes now in operation, – a theory which, if true, would fully justify a geologist in neglecting the study of such phenomena. [. . .]

In vain do we aspire to assign limits to the works of creation in *space*, whether we examine the starry heavens, or that world of minute animalcules which is revealed to us by the microscope. We are prepared, therefore, to find that in *time* also, the confines of the universe lie beyond the reach of mortal ken. But in whatever direction we pursue our researches, whether in time or space, we discover everywhere the clear proofs of a Creative Intelligence, and of His foresight, wisdom, and power.

As geologists, we learn that it is not only the present condition of the globe that has been suited to the accommodation of myriads of living creatures, but that many former states also have been equally adapted to the organization and habits of prior races of beings. The disposition of the seas, continents, and islands, and the climates have varied; so it appears that the species have been changed, and yet they have all been so modelled, on types analogous to those of existing plants and animals, as to indicate throughout a perfect harmony of design and unity of purpose. To assume that the evidence of the beginning or end of so vast a scheme lies within the reach of our philosophical inquiries, or even of our speculations, appears to us inconsistent with a just estimate of the relations which subsist between the finite powers of man and the attributes of an Infinite and Eternal Being.

---

6 Book IV, lines 325–6 from the 1697 translation of Virgil's *Georgics* by English poet and dramatist John Dryden (1631–1700).

10.4 Charles Babbage, *On the Economy of Machinery and Manufactures* (London: Charles Knight, 1832)

Charles Babbage (1791–1871) was the son of a banker who left a substantial fortune. Babbage is now best known as the father of the modern computer for his work on an 'analytical engine' which could perform mathematical calculations. A major mathematician (he was Lucasian Professor of Mathematics at Cambridge in the 1830s), he was instrumental in the development of mathematical education in Britain, especially in calculus. But his interests were wide and applied. He spent many partially successful, but frequently frustrating years building prototypes of his calculating machines, agitating unsuccessfully for government support for the development of such projects. A powerful voice in the development of pro-science opinion, he also co-founded the British Association for the Advancement of Science. On the Economy of Machinery and Manufactures *is a treatise on manufacturing technology and its social benefits. In the extract here, Babbage looks far-sightedly at modes of transport and communication to come.*

The conveyance of letters is another case, in which the importance of saving time would allow of great expense in any new machinery for its accomplishment [. . .]

(336.) Let us imagine a series of high pillars erected at frequent intervals, perhaps every hundred feet, and as nearly as possible in a straight line between two post towns. An iron or steel wire must be stretched over proper supports, fixed on each of these pillars, and terminating at the end of every three or five miles, as may be found expedient, in a very strong support, by which it may be stretched. At each of these latter points a man ought to reside in a small station-house. A narrow cylindrical tin case, to contain the letters, might be suspended by two wheels rolling upon this wire; the cases being so constructed as to enable the wheels to pass unimpeded by the fixed supports of the wire. An endless wire of much smaller size must pass over two drums, one at each end of the station. This wire should be supported on rollers, fixed to the supports of the great wire, and at a short distance below it. There would thus be two branches of the smaller wire always accompanying the larger one; and the attendant at either station, by turning the drum, might cause them to move with great velocity in opposite directions. In order to convey the cylinder which contains the letters, it would only be necessary to attach it by a string, or by a catch, to either of the branches of the endless wire. Thus it would be conveyed speedily to the next station, where it would be removed by the attendant to the commencement of the next wire, and so forwarded. It is unnecessary to enter into the details which this, or any similar plan, would require. The difficulties are obvious; but if these could be overcome, it would present many advantages besides velocity; for if an attendant resided at each station, the additional expense of having two or three deliveries of letters every day, and even of sending expresses at any moment, would be comparatively trifling; nor is it impossible that the stretched wire might itself be available for a species of telegraphic communication yet more rapid.

Perhaps if the steeples of churches, properly selected, were made use of, connecting them by a few intermediate stations with some great central building, as, for instance, with the top of St Paul's; and if a similar apparatus were placed on the top of each steeple, with a man to work it during the day, it might be possible to diminish the expense of the two-penny post, and make deliveries every half hour over the greater part of the metropolis.

(337.) The power of steam, however, bids fair almost to rival the velocity of these contrivances; and the fitness of its application to the purposes of conveyance, particularly where great rapidity is required, begins now to be generally admitted. The following extract from the Report of the Committee of the House of Commons on steam-carriages, explains clearly its various advantages:

> Perhaps one of the principal advantages resulting from the use of steam, will be, that it may be employed as cheaply at a quick as at a slow rate; 'this is one of the advantages over horse labour, which becomes more and more expensive as the speed is increased. There is every reason to expect, that in the end the rate of travelling by steam will be much quicker than the utmost speed of travelling by horses; in short, the safety to travellers will become the limit to speed.' [. . .]

(338.) Another instance may be mentioned in which the object to be obtained is so important, that although it might be rarely wanted, yet machinery for that purpose would justify considerable expense. A vessel to contain men, and to be navigated at some distance below the surface of the sea, would, in many circumstances, be almost invaluable.

10.5 Ada Lovelace, 'Notes By the Translator', for L. F. Menabrea, 'Sketch of the Analytical Engine Invented by Charles Babbage, Esq', *Scientific Memoirs* 3 (1843), 666–731

Augusta Ada Byron King, Lady Lovelace (1815–52) was the daughter of Lord Byron and Anne Isabella Milbanke. A talented mathematician, Lovelace was described by Charles Babbage as the 'enchantress of numbers', and it is for her contribution to development of Babbage's Analytical Engine that she is best known. Lovelace met and began to correspond with Babbage in 1833, when she was just 17. Babbage was already renowned as the inventor of the Difference Engine, a calculating machine (for more on Babbage see extract 10.4). The Analytical Engine was a logical development of this principle. Where the Difference Engine had been capable of calculating a result according to a fixed set of parameters, the Analytical Engine was designed to allow its operator to vary – or program – the parameters of calculation by means of punched cards.

Lovelace is remembered particularly for her translation of an article on the Analytical Engine by Italian mathematician Luigi Menabrea and for the production of a set of accompanying notes. Amongst these extended notes Lovelace describes a sequence of operations for the Analytical Engine. This sequence, it has been suggested, constitutes the very first computer program. The extract below is taken from Lovelace's notes and, in addition to describing the fundamental distinction between the Difference Engine and the Analytical Engine, indicates some of the potential applications of mechanical computation.

The operating mechanism can even be thrown into action independently of any object to operate upon (although of course no result could then be developed). Again, it might act upon other things besides number, were objects found whose mutual fundamental relations could be expressed by those of the abstract science of operations, and which should be also susceptible of adaptations to the action of the operating notation and mechanism of the engine. Supposing, for instance, that the fundamental relations of pitched sounds in the science of harmony and of musical composition were susceptible of such expression and adaptations, the engine might compose elaborate and scientific pieces of music of any degree of complexity or extent.

The Analytical Engine is an embodying of the science of operations, constructed with peculiar reference to abstract number as the subject of those operations [. . .]

Those who view mathematical science, not merely as a vast body of abstract and immutable truths, whose intrinsic beauty, symmetry and logical completeness, when regarded in their connexion together as a whole, entitle them to a prominent place in the interest of all profound and logical minds, but as possessing a yet deeper interest for the human race, when it is remembered that this science constitutes the language through which alone we can adequately express the great facts of the natural world, and those unceasing changes of mutual relationship which, visibly or invisibly, consciously or unconsciously to our immediate physical perceptions, are interminably going on in the agencies of the creation we live amidst: those who thus think on mathematical truth as the instrument through which the weak mind of man can most effectually read his Creator's works, will regard with especial interest all that can tend to facilitate the translation of its principles into explicit practical forms.

The distinctive characteristic of the Analytical Engine, and that which has rendered it possible to endow mechanism with such extensive faculties as bid fair to make this engine the executive right-hand of abstract algebra, is the introduction into it of the principle which Jacquard devised for regulating, by means of punched cards, the most complicated patterns in the fabrication of brocaded stuffs.[7] It is in this that the distinction between the two engines lies. Nothing of

---

7 Invented in 1801 by Joseph Marie Jacquard, the Jacquard loom used punched cards to control an automatic sequence of operations in order to produce complex woven patterns.

the sort exists in the Difference Engine. We may say most aptly, that the Analytical Engine weaves algebraical patterns just as the Jacquard-loom weaves flowers and leaves. Here, it seems to us, resides much more of originality than the Difference Engine can be fairly entitled to claim. We do not wish to deny to this latter all such claims. We believe that it is the only proposal or attempt ever made to construct a calculating machine founded on the principle of successive orders of differences, and capable of printing off its own results; and that this engine surpasses its predecessors, both in the extent of the calculations which it can perform, in the facility, certainty and accuracy with which it can effect them, and in the absence of all necessity for the intervention of human intelligence during the performance of its calculations. Its nature is, however, limited to the strictly arithmetical, and it is far from being the first or only scheme for constructing arithmetical calculating machines with more or less of success.

The bounds of arithmetic were however outstepped the moment the idea of applying the cards had occurred; and the Analytical Engine does not occupy common ground with mere 'calculating machines'. It holds a position wholly its own; and the considerations it suggests are most interesting in their nature. In enabling mechanism to combine together general symbols in successions of unlimited variety and extent, a uniting link is established between the operations of matter and the abstract mental processes of the most abstract branch of mathematical science. A new, a vast, and a powerful language is developed for the future use of analysis, in which to wield its truths so that these may become of more speedy and accurate practical application for the purposes of mankind than the means hitherto in our possession have rendered possible. Thus not only the mental and the material, but the theoretical and the practical in the mathematical world, are brought into more intimate and effective connexion with each other. We are not aware of its being on record that anything partaking in the nature of what is so well designated the Analytical Engine has been hitherto proposed, or even thought of, as a practical possibility, any more than the idea of a thinking or of a reasoning machine.

10.6 Charles Dickens, *Dombey and Son* (London: Bradbury and Evans, 1848)

As one of the most successful writers of his or any age, Dickens barely needs introducing except to note that his talents extended beyond fiction into topical and campaigning journalism. He took a lively interest in science and technology and was a keen observer of new ideas and the impact of new inventions. Recognizing the brilliance of Faraday's lectures, for instance, his journal Household Worlds *featured a vivid, semi-fictional account in which a nephew, who has attended the lectures, explains the wonders of the new chemistry to his uncle.* Dombey and Son *(serialized 1846–8), the novel from which this extract is taken, follows a different line in its concern at the impact of new, devastating technologies on communities and neighbourhoods. Though Dickens was*

Figure 10.2 'The Two Giants of the Time (steam and electricity)', *Punch* 33 (1857), 132

exhilarated by speed and novelty (something of this can be glimpsed even in this passage), Dombey and Son, *written at the height of the railway boom, remains sceptical about the social consequences of applied technology on this scale.*

The first shock of a great earthquake had, just at that period, rent the whole neighbourhood to its centre. Traces of its course were visible on every side. Houses were knocked down; streets broken through and stopped; deep pits and trenches dug in the ground; enormous heaps of earth and clay thrown up; buildings that were undermined and shaking, propped by great beams of wood. Here, a chaos of carts, overthrown and jumbled together, lay topsy-turvy at the bottom of a steep unnatural hill; there, confused treasures of iron soaked and rusted in something that had accidentally become a pond. Everywhere were bridges that led nowhere; thoroughfares that were wholly impassable; Babel towers of chimneys, wanting half their height; temporary wooden houses and enclosures, in the most unlikely situations; carcases of ragged tenements, and fragments of unfinished walls and arches, and piles of scaffolding, and wildernesses of bricks, and giant forms of cranes, and tripods straddling above nothing. There were a hundred thousand shapes and substances of incompleteness, wildly mingled out of their places, upside down, burrowing in the earth, aspiring in the air, mouldering in the water, and unintelligible as any dream. Hot springs and fiery eruptions, the usual attendants upon earthquakes, lent their contributions of confusion to the scene. Boiling water hissed and heaved within dilapidated walls; whence, also, the glare and roar of flames came issuing forth; and mounds of ashes blocked up rights of way, and wholly changed the law and custom of the neighbourhood.

In short, the yet unfinished and unopened Railroad was in progress; and, from the very core of all this dire disorder, trailed smoothly away, upon its mighty course of civilisation and improvement.

10.7 Charles Darwin, *On the Origin of Species by means of Natural Selection, or the Preservation of Favoured Races in the Struggle for Life* (London: John Murray, 1859)

Charles Darwin (1809–82) was one of the most powerful and influential scientific minds of the century, who changed entirely the modern understanding of nature. From a gentry background in the West Midlands, which included a celebrated family circle of scientists and intellectuals, and educated in Edinburgh and Cambridge, Darwin gave his name to a world-view that remains current, even though some of its more sloganistic versions were actually the work of opponents and commentators: 'nature red in tooth and claw' (Tennyson), 'the survival of the fittest' (Herbert Spencer). After a heady, five-year globetrotting expedition aboard the survey ship HMS Beagle, in which he contemplated the range and astonishing profusion of nature, especially in South America, he returned to Britain in 1836 to ponder and describe his findings. After much anxious delay he published On the Origin of Species *in 1859. The core idea of* On the Origin *is powerfully simple. Species propagate; as they do so, nature being imperfect, they produce random variations. Of these, many will die, the variation being harmful, but some will actually be better adapted to their circumstances and will flourish, taking a larger share of the available resources; as they do so, they will breed, and what was originally a mutated strain will become dominant. Thus, over centuries, species evolve. It is easy to see how different this world-view is from the orthodoxies of William Paley. Nature is no longer designed but fundamentally chancy. It is unstable and changes radically over time; it is neither benign nor sufficient in resources; the death of some is crucial to the life of others; it does not exempt humans from special treatment for they too are subject to want and change; the moral and the biological orders are not identical. In scientific terms, the causes and mechanisms of things are neither simple nor predictable. In the passages that follow one can note the effort in language to render complexity and multiplicity of cause and effect in metaphor, image and example.*

Darwin, of course, struggled with his theory and its implications, dismayed by the challenge it posed not only to orthodoxy but to human values in general. Its logic was inescapable; yet it was equally true that humans live in environments in which actions are determined by value choices as well as by natural mechanisms. Though often characterized, especially by shocked contemporaries, as an abandonment of values, it is more correct to see Darwin's work as an enquiry into why humans have the values they do, and why it is that these give advantage in what is undoubtedly a struggle for life. (See also extracts 3.7 and 9.7 for Darwin's theories on sexual relations and racial groupings.)

From 'Natural Selection'

If during the long course of ages and under varying conditions of life, organic beings vary at all in the several parts of their organisation, and I think this cannot be disputed; if there be, owing to the high geometrical ratio of increase of each species, a severe struggle for life at some age, season, or year, and this certainly cannot be disputed; then, considering the infinite complexity of the relations of all organic beings to each other and to their conditions of existence, causing an infinite diversity in structure, constitution, and habits, to be advantageous to them, I think it would be a most extraordinary fact if no variation ever had occurred useful to each being's own welfare, in the same manner as so many variations have occurred useful to man. But if variations useful to any organic being do occur, assuredly individuals thus characterised will have the best chance of being preserved in the struggle for life; and from the strong principle of inheritance they will tend to produce offspring similarly characterised. This principle of preservation, I have called, for the sake of brevity, Natural Selection; and it leads to the improvement of each creature in relation to its organic and inorganic conditions of life.

Natural selection, on the principle of qualities being inherited at corresponding ages, can modify the egg, seed, or young, as easily as the adult. Amongst many animals, sexual selection will give its aid to ordinary selection, by assuring to the most vigorous and best adapted males the greatest number of offspring. Sexual selection will also give characters useful to the males alone, in their struggles with other males.

Whether natural selection has really thus acted in nature, in modifying and adapting the various forms of life to their several conditions and stations, must be judged of by the general tenor and balance of evidence given in the following chapters. But we already see how it entails extinction; and how largely extinction has acted in the world's history, geology plainly declares. Natural selection, also, leads to divergence of character; for more living beings can be supported on the same area the more they diverge in structure, habits, and constitution, of which we see proof by looking to the inhabitants of any small spot or to naturalised productions. Therefore during the modification of the descendants of any one species, and during the incessant struggle of all species to increase in numbers, the more diversified these descendants become, the better will be their chance of succeeding in the battle for life. Thus the small differences distinguishing varieties of the same species, steadily tend to increase till they come to equal the greater differences between species of the same genus, or even of distinct genera.

We have seen that it is the common, the widely-diffused, and widely-ranging species, belonging to the larger genera, which vary most; and these tend to transmit to their modified offspring that superiority which now makes them dominant in their own countries. Natural selection, as has just been remarked, leads to divergence of character and to much extinction of the less improved and intermediate forms of life. On these principles, I believe, the nature of the affinities of all organic beings may be explained. It is a truly wonderful fact – the wonder of which we are apt to overlook from familiarity – that all animals and all plants throughout all time and space should be related to each other in group subordinate to group, in the manner which we everywhere behold – namely, varieties of the same species most closely related together, species of the same genus less closely and unequally related together, forming sections and sub-genera, species of distinct genera much less closely related, and genera related in different degrees, forming sub-families, families, orders, sub-classes, and classes. The several subordinate groups in any class cannot be ranked in a single file, but seem rather to be clustered round points, and these round other points, and so on in almost endless cycles. On the view that each species has been independently created, I can see no explanation of this great fact in the classification of all organic beings; but, to the best of my judgment, it is explained through inheritance and the complex action of natural selection, entailing extinction and divergence of character, as we have seen illustrated in the diagram.

The affinities of all the beings of the same class have sometimes been represented by a great tree. I believe this simile largely speaks the truth. The green and budding twigs may represent existing species; and those produced during each former year may represent the long succession of extinct species. At each period of growth all the growing twigs have tried to branch out on all sides, and to overtop and kill the surrounding twigs and branches, in the same manner as species and groups of species have tried to overmaster other species in the great battle for life. The limbs divided into great branches, and these into lesser and lesser branches, were themselves once, when the tree was small, budding twigs; and this connection of the former and present buds by ramifying branches may well represent the classification of all extinct and living species in groups subordinate to groups. Of the many twigs which flourished when the tree was a mere bush, only two or three, now grown into great branches, yet survive and bear all the other branches; so with the species which lived during long-past geological periods, very few now have living and modified descendants. From the first growth of the tree, many a limb and branch have decayed and dropped off; and these lost branches of various sizes may represent those whole orders, families, and genera which have now no living representatives, and which are known to us only from having been found in a fossil state. As we here and there see a thin straggling branch springing from a fork low down in a tree, and which by some chance has been favoured and is still alive on its summit, so we occasionally see an animal like the Ornithorhynchus or Lepidosiren, which in some small degree connects by its affinities two large branches of life, and which has apparently been saved from fatal competition by having inhabited a protected station. As buds give rise by growth to fresh buds, and these, if vigorous, branch out and overtop on all sides many a feebler branch, so by generation I believe it has been with the great Tree of Life, which fills with its dead and broken branches the crust of the earth, and covers the surface with its ever branching and beautiful ramifications.

From 'Recapitulation and Conclusion'

Authors of the highest eminence seem to be fully satisfied with the view that each species has been independently created. To my mind it accords better with what we know of the laws impressed on matter by the Creator, that the production and extinction of the past and present inhabitants of the world should have been due to secondary causes, like those determining the birth and death of the individual. When I view all beings not as special creations, but as the lineal descendants of some few beings which lived long before the first bed of the Silurian system was deposited, they seem to me to become ennobled. Judging from the past, we may safely infer that not one living species will transmit its unaltered likeness to a distant futurity. And of the species now living very few will transmit progeny of any kind to a far distant futurity; for the manner in which all organic beings are grouped, shows that the greater number of species of each genus, and all the species of many genera, have left no descendants, but have become utterly extinct. We can so far take a prophetic glance into futurity as to foretell that it will be the common and widely-spread species, belonging to the larger and dominant groups, which will ultimately prevail and procreate new and dominant species. As all the living forms of life are the lineal descendants of those which lived long before the Silurian epoch,[8] we may feel certain that the ordinary succession by generation has never once been broken, and that no cataclysm has desolated the whole world. Hence we may look with some confidence to a secure future of equally inappreciable length. And as natural selection works solely by and for the good of each being, all corporeal and mental endowments will tend to progress towards perfection.

---

8 Third period of the Palaeozoic Era; 443.7–416 million years ago.automatic sequence of operations in order to produce complex woven patterns.

It is interesting to contemplate an entangled bank, clothed with many plants of many kinds, with birds singing on the bushes, with various insects flitting about, and with worms crawling through the damp earth, and to reflect that these elaborately constructed forms, so different from each other, and dependent on each other in so complex a manner, have all been produced by laws acting around us. These laws, taken in the largest sense, being Growth with Reproduction; Inheritance, which is almost implied by reproduction; Variability, from the indirect and direct action of the external conditions of life, and from use and disuse; a Ratio of Increase so high as to lead to a Struggle for Life, and as a consequence to Natural Selection, entailing Divergence of Character and the Extinction of less-improved forms. Thus, from the war with nature, from famine and death, the most exalted object which we are capable of conceiving, namely, the production of the higher animals, directly follows. There is grandeur in this view of life, with its several powers, having been originally breathed by the Creator into a few forms or into one; and that, whilst this planet has gone cycling on according to the fixed law of gravity, from so simple a beginning endless forms most beautiful and most wonderful have been, and are being, evolved.

10.8 T. H. Huxley, 'On the Physical Basis of Life', *Fortnightly Review* n.s. 5 (1 February 1869), 129–45

T[homas] H[enry] Huxley (1825–95) was the son of a schoolteacher. He trained as a physician and served as ship's doctor on HMS Rattlesnake *which, like Darwin on the* Beagle, *allowed him to travel extensively for scientific research, in his case to Australia. On his return, he made his name as a physiologist but eventually settled into a life of crusading advocacy for science and scientific education, spearheading in particular the cause of Darwinian evolution (he became known as 'Darwin's bulldog') and becoming in the process one of Christian orthodoxy's most aggressive opponents. He wrote as prolifically and successfully as he campaigned, and was a star public lecturer and strong advocate for popular education, including education for women. 'On the Physical Basis of Life', which is extracted here, provoked a major controversy in 1869, and the journal in which it appeared was reprinted no less than seven times that year, reminding us that Victorian science was polemical as well as investigatory. The essay bluntly contemplates the prospect that life is fundamentally organic chemistry, though equally bluntly Huxley rejects the idea that he is a mere materialist. For him, materialism is no better than its opposite, spiritualism. Both positions are anti-scientific in reducing complex issues to simple slogans. Nonetheless, Huxley was himself never afraid of the polemical advantage gained by stark plain speaking, uncompromising imagery and pugnacious questioning. Here he challenges his reader to consider whether human beings are like machines given that our lives are so determined by physical forces and processes. Such a provocation requires us weigh up the ways in which we perceive, analyse and categorize the external and internal worlds.*

I suppose that, to many, the idea that there is such a thing as a physical basis, or matter, of life, may be novel – so widely spread is the conception of life as a something which works through matter, but is independent of it; and even those who are aware that matter and life are inseparably connected, may not be prepared for the conclusion plainly suggested by the phrase, '*the* physical basis or matter of life', that there is some one kind of matter which is common to all living beings, and that their endless diversities are bound together by a physical, as well as an ideal, unity. In fact, when first apprehended, such a doctrine as this appears almost shocking to common sense.

What, truly, can seem to be more obviously different from one another in faculty, in form, and in substance, than the various kinds of living beings? What community of faculty can there be between the brightly-coloured lichen, which so nearly resembles a mere mineral incrustation of the bare rock on which it grows, and the painter, to whom it is instinct with beauty, or the botanist, whom it feeds with knowledge? [. . .]

Such objections as these must, I think, arise in the mind of every one who ponders, for the first time, upon the conception of a single physical basis of life underlying all the diversities of vital existence; but I propose to demonstrate to you that, notwithstanding these apparent difficulties, a threefold unity – namely, a unity of power, or faculty, a unity of form, and a unity of substantial composition – does pervade the whole living world. [. . .]

In physiological language this means, that all the multifarious and compli-cated activities of man are comprehensible under three categories. Either they are immediately directed towards the maintenance and development of the body, or they effect transitory changes in the relative positions of parts of the body, or they tend towards the continuance of the species. Even those manifes-tations of intellect, of feeling, and of will, which we rightly name the higher faculties, are not excluded from this classification, inasmuch as to every one but the subject of them, they are known only as transitory changes in the relative positions of parts of the body. Speech, gesture, and every other form of human action are, in the long run, resolvable into muscular contraction, and muscular contraction is but a transitory change in the relative positions of the parts of a muscle. But the scheme which is large enough to embrace the activities of the highest form of life, covers all those of the lower creatures. The lowest plant, or animalcule, feeds, grows, and reproduces its kind. In addition, all animals mani-fest those transitory changes of form which we class under irritability and contractility; and, it is more than probable, that when the vegetable world is thoroughly explored, we shall find all plants in possession of the same powers, at one time or other of their existence. [. . .]

The spectacle afforded by the wonderful energies prisoned within the compass of the microscopic hair of a plant, which we commonly regard as a merely passive organism, is not easily forgotten by one who has watched its display, continued hour after hour, without pause or sign of weakening. The possible complexity of many other organic forms, seemingly as simple as the protoplasm of the nettle, dawns upon one; and the comparison of such a protoplasm to a body with an internal circulation, which has been put forward by an eminent physiologist, loses much of its startling character. Currents similar to those of the hairs of the nettle have been observed in a great multitude of very different plants, and weighty authorities have suggested that they probably occur, in more or less perfection, in all young vegetable cells. If such be the case, the wonderful noonday silence of a tropical forest is, after all, due only to the dulness of our hearing; and could our ears catch the murmur of these tiny Maelstroms, as they whirl in the innumerable myriads of living cells which constitute each tree, we should be stunned, as with the roar of a great city. [. . .]

Thus a nucleated mass of protoplasm turns out to be what may be termed the structural unit of the human body. As a matter of fact, the body, in its earliest state, is a mere multiple of such units; and, in its perfect condition, it is a multiple of such units, variously modified.

But does the formula which expresses the essential structural character of the highest animal cover all the rest, as the statement of its powers and faculties covered that of all others? Very nearly. Beast and fowl, reptile and fish, mollusk, worm, and polype, are all composed of structural units of the same character, namely, masses of protoplasm, with a nucleus. There are sundry very low animals, each of which, structurally, is a mere colourless blood-corpuscle, leading an independent life. But, at the very bottom of the animal scale, even this simplicity becomes simplified, and all the phenomena of life are manifested by a particle of protoplasm without a nucleus. Nor are such organisms insignificant by reason of their want of complexity. It is a fair question whether the protoplasm of those simplest forms of life, which people an immense extent of the bottom of the sea, would not outweigh that of all the higher living beings which inhabit the land put together. And in ancient times, no less than at the present day, such living beings as these have been the greatest of rock builders. [. . .]

Protoplasm, simple or nucleated, is the formal basis of all life. It is the clay of the potter: which, bake it and paint it as he will, remains clay, separated by artifice, and not by nature, from the commonest brick or sun-dried clod.

Thus it becomes clear that all living powers are cognate, and that all living forms are fundamentally of one character. The researches of the chemist have revealed a no less striking uniformity of material composition in living matter. [. . .]

And now, what is the ultimate fate, and what the origin, of the matter of life?

Is it, as some of the older naturalists proposed, diffused throughout the universe in molecules, which are indestructible and unchangeable in themselves; but, in endless transmigration, unite in innumerable permutations, into the diversified forms of life we know? Or, is the matter of life composed of ordinary matter, differing from it only in the manner in which its atoms are aggregated. [sic] Is it built up of ordinary matter, and again resolved into ordinary matter when its work is done?

Modern science does not hesitate a moment between these alternatives. Physiology writes over the portals of life –

'Debemur morti nos nostraque',[9]

with a profounder meaning than the Roman poet attached to that melancholy line. Under whatever disguise it takes refuge, whether fungus or oak, worm or man, the living protoplasm not only ultimately dies and is resolved into its mineral and lifeless constituents, but is always dying, and, strange as the paradox may sound, could not live unless it died. [. . .]

Past experience leads me to be tolerably certain that, when the propositions I have just placed before you are accessible to public comment and criticism, they will be condemned by many zealous persons, and perhaps by some few of the wise and thoughtful. I should not wonder if 'gross and brutal materialism' were the mildest phrase applied to them in certain quarters. And most undoubtedly the terms of the propositions are distinctly materialistic. Nevertheless two things are certain: the one, that I hold the statements to be substantially true; the other, that I, individually, am no materialist, but, on the contrary, believe materialism to involve grave philosophical error. [. . .]

Let us suppose that knowledge is absolute, and not relative, and therefore, that our conception of matter represents that which it really is. Let us suppose, further, that we do know more of cause and effect than a certain definite order of succession among facts, and that we have a knowledge of the necessity of that succession – and hence, of necessary laws – and I, for my part, do not see what escape there is from utter materialism and necessarianism. For it is obvious that our knowledge of what we call the material world is, to begin with, at least as certain and definite as that of the spiritual world, and that our acquaintance with law is of as old a date as our knowledge of spontaneity. Further, I take it to be demonstrable that it is utterly impossible to prove that anything whatever may not be the effect of a material and necessary cause, and that human logic is equally incompetent to prove that any act is really spontaneous. A really spontaneous act is one which, by the assumption, has no cause; and the attempt to prove such a negative as this is, on the face of the matter, absurd. And while it is thus a philosophical impossibility to demonstrate that any given phenomenon is not the effect of a material cause, any one who is acquainted with the history of science will admit, that its progress has, in all ages, meant, and now, more than ever, means, the extension of the province of what we call matter and causation, and the concomitant gradual banishment from all regions of human thought of what we call spirit and spontaneity. [. . .]

Thus there can be little doubt that the further science advances the more extensively and consistently will all the phenomena of nature be represented by materialistic formulæ and symbols.

But the man of science, who, forgetting the limits of philosophical inquiry, slides from these formulæ and symbols into what is commonly understood by

9 'Ourselves and all that's ours, to death are due'. Horace, *Ars Poetica*.

materialism, seems to me to place himself on a level with the mathematician, who should mistake the *x*'s and *y*'s, with which he works his problems, for real entities – and with this further disadvantage, as compared with the mathematician, that the blunders of the latter are of no practical consequence, while the errors of systematic materialism may paralyse the energies and destroy the beauty of a life.

10.9 G. H. Lewes, 'On the Dread and Dislike of Science', *Fortnightly Review* n.s. 23 (1 June 1878), 805–15

G[eorge] H[enry] Lewes (1817–78) was a polymath of a distinctively Victorian kind. Lewes came from an undistinguished social background (his father was an itinerant actor). He first trained as a doctor (though he never qualified), before becoming a leading figure in radical journalism and a great success as a freelance writer and intellectual. Lewes was by turns a journalist, novelist, playwright, actor, critic, biographer and historian of philosophy (see also extract 8.4 as an example of the range of his work). An accomplished linguist, he had ready access to major European thought in ways often denied to his contemporaries. He shared with his partner, the novelist George Eliot (Marian Evans), a powerful sense of the intellectual's responsibilities towards the general public, and Lewes became one of the most highly regarded popular communicators of new, demanding ideas in science and philosophy. Later, in the most substantial part of his career, he became one of the period's most innovative psychologists, influencing, among others, William James. He worked on the relations between mind and body, as well as between mind and society, and was a pioneer in the study of physiological psychology. A founder and first Chairman of the Physiological Society, Lewes was a major mid-Victorian commentator on scientific and intellectual issues including, as here, vivisection. He was a prominent witness to the Royal Commission on Vivisection in 1875. In this article he sets out his position as a defender of vivisection, and by extension scientific research in other areas, though he argued strongly for increased regulation of its more flagrant cruelties.

No better illustration can be given of the general suspicion and dislike of Science as Science than the great stress which is laid on the 'iniquity of Vivisection', *because* experiments on animals are pursued for purely scientific purposes. The animating impulse of an effort to awaken a due sympathy with animal suffering and check an inconsiderate affliction of it is one which so entirely commands my esteem, that I would willingly overlook the flagrant contradiction of people tolerating without a murmur the fact that yearly *millions* of creatures are mutilated and tortured to give a few men pleasure, to make food more palatable, and domestic animals more tractable, yet are roused to fury by the fact that a few *score* creatures are mutilated (a smaller number tortured) to discover remedial agents and scientific truths. All the pain inflicted for sport or other pleasure is condoned; the pain inflicted for scientific ends is pronounced diabolical. Is it, therefore, not on account of the suffering inflicted, but on account of the scientific purpose, that Vivisection is to be reprobated? Ten thousand times the amount of suffering is disregarded if only its purpose be *not* that of acquiring knowledge. And that this is so, is manifest in another case. For suffering may be also inflicted on human beings, and on a large scale, without exciting any outcry, if the motive be commercial advantage. Not to mention wars undertaken to push commerce, let us only consider some industrial experiment which will certainly drive hundreds of families from their employment with starvation as the consequence; yet the sufferings thus occasioned, if they excite pity, weigh so little against the prospect of the general good, that if the starving workmen revolt and destroy the machinery, the philanthropist is ready to enforce on them the utmost rigour of the law. Here the social benefit is allowed to override the individual injury. That is to say, an experiment which has the prospect of enlarging *wealth* may inflict suffering on men, women, and children; but an experiment which has only the prospect of enlarging *knowledge* must be forbidden if it inflict suffering on animals! Obviously such a contradiction could not be upheld if Science were recognised as a social benefit. It is not so recognised. And one indication of this is the frequent accusation that physiologists are actuated by the 'selfish motive of acquiring reputation', not by the unselfish motive of benefiting mankind. I will not pause to discuss the question of motives, nor how far the selfish motive may further a social advantage; I will only ask whether the motive of the industrial experimenter is less selfish? Unless Science were a social benefit, no one would ardently desire a scientific reputation.

10.10 William James, *The Principles of Psychology* (London: Macmillan & Co. Ltd, 1890)

Though an American, William James (1842–1910), like his brother, the novelist Henry James, was thoroughly engaged with British and European intellectual and scientific life. His career illustrates the increasing internationalization of intellectual and scientific life towards the end of the century. Like many of the figures in this book, James was a man of wide interests: a major philosopher in the distinctively American tradition of Pragmatism, an influential writer on the study of religion, and, of course, one of the key figures in the development of modern psychology where, with Freud, he is often credited with establishing a distinctively 'modernist' approach to the study of consciousness and the mind. But, like Freud, James owed much to nineteenth-century investigations to a degree not often unappreciated. (His most famous concept, the 'stream of consciousness', was coined not by him but by G. H. Lewes in the 1860s.) James's achievement was nonetheless considerable. Younger than major contemporaries like Huxley and Lewes, and also distanced by virtue of being American from the fraught, local quarrels in which these men engaged over whether the mind was to be understood as a spiritual or a material entity, James was able to reconsider the integration of these perspectives. His 1,000-page masterwork, The Principles of Psychology

(1890), from which this extract is taken, offers a major remodelling of the way consciousness is understood in the context of its neuro-physiological determinants. No longer a rigid entity, it is a 'theatre of simultaneous possibilities', and the second part of this passage illustrates his creative effort to capture its chameleon, pluralistic nature: determined but changeable; specific and various; material and mental; emotional and rational. It is similar to Darwin's attempt, in his writing, to capture the complexity and profusion of the biological world.

Once more take a look at the brain. We believe the brain to be an organ whose internal equilibrium is always in a state of change, – the change affecting every part. The pulses of change are doubtless more violent in one place than in another, their rhythm more rapid at this time than at that. As in a kaleidoscope revolving at a uniform rate, although the figures are always rearranging themselves, there are instants during which the transformation seems minute and interstitial and almost absent, followed by others when it shoots with magical rapidity, relatively stable forms thus alternating with forms we should not distinguish if seen again; so in the brain the perpetual rearrangement must result in some forms of tension lingering relatively long, whilst others simply come and pass. But if consciousness corresponds to the fact of rearrangement itself, why, if the rearrangement stop not, should the consciousness ever cease? And if a lingering rearrangement brings with it one kind of consciousness, why should not a swift rearrangement bring another kind of consciousness as peculiar as the rearrangement itself? The lingering consciousnesses, if of simple objects, we call 'sensations' or 'images,' according as they are vivid or faint; if of complex objects, we call them 'percepts' when vivid, 'concepts' or 'thoughts' when faint. For the swift consciousnesses we have only those names of 'transitive states,' or 'feelings of relation,' which we have used. As the brain-changes are continuous, so do all these consciousnesses melt into each other like dissolving views. Properly they are but one protracted consciousness, one unbroken stream. [. . .]

Looking back, then, over this review, we see that the mind is at every stage a theatre of simultaneous possibilities. Consciousness consists in the comparison of these with each other, the selection of some, and the suppression of the rest by the reinforcing and inhibiting agency of attention. The highest and most elaborated mental products are filtered from the data chosen by the faculty next beneath, out of the mass offered by the faculty below that, which mass in turn was sifted from a still larger amount of yet simpler material, and so on. The mind, in short, works on the data it receives very much as a sculptor works on his block of stone. In a sense the statue stood there from eternity. But there were a thousand different ones beside it, and the sculptor alone is to thank for having extricated this one from the rest. Just so the world of each of us, howsoever different our several views of it may be, all lay embedded in the primordial chaos of sensations, which gave the mere *matter* to the thought of all of us indifferently. We may, if we like, by our reasonings unwind things back to that black and jointless continuity of space and moving clouds of swarming atoms which science calls the only real world. But all the while the world *we* feel and live in will be that which our ancestors and we, by slowly cumulative strokes of choice, have extricated out of this, like sculptors, by simply rejecting certain portions of the given stuff. Other sculptors, other statues from the same stone! Other minds, other worlds from the same monotonous and inexpressive chaos! My world is but one in a million alike embedded, alike real to those who may abstract them. How different must be the worlds in the consciousness of ant, cuttle-fish, or crab!

Further Reading

General Works

Adams, James Eli. *A History of Victorian Literature*. Malden, MA and Oxford: Wiley-Blackwell, 2009.

Altick, Richard. *Victorian People and Ideas*. London: Dent, 1974.

Armstrong, Isobel. *Victorian Poetry: Poetry, Poetics and Politics*. New York and London: Routledge, 1993.

Armstrong, Isobel. *Victorian Glassworlds: Glass Culture and the Imagination 1830–1880*. Oxford: Oxford University Press, 2008.

Birch, Dinah. *Our Victorian Education*. Oxford: Wiley-Blackwell, 2008.

Boyd, Kelly, and Rohan McWilliam (eds). *The Victorian Studies Reader*. London: Routledge, 2007.

Brantlinger, Patrick, and William B. Thesing (eds). *A Companion to the Victorian Novel*. Oxford: Blackwell, 2002.

Davis, Philip. *The Oxford English Literary History*. Vol. 8: *The Victorians*. Oxford: Oxford University Press, 2002.

Davis, Philip. *Why Victorian Literature Still Matters*. Chichester: Wiley-Blackwell, 2008.

Ermarth, Elizabeth Deeds. *Realism and Consensus in the English Novel: Time, Space and Narrative*. Edinburgh: Edinburgh University Press, 1998.

Gilmour, Robin. *The Victorian Period: The Intellectual and Cultural Context of English Literature, 1830–1890*. London and New York: Longman, 1993.

Ledger, Sally, and Roger Luckhurst (eds). *The Fin de Siècle: A Reader in Cultural History, c.1880–1900*. Oxford: Oxford University Press, 2000.

Levine, George (ed.). *How to Read the Victorian Novel*. Oxford: Wiley-Blackwell, 2008.

MacKenzie, John M. (ed.). *The Victorian Vision: Inventing New Britain*. London: V&A Publications, 2001.

Plunkett, John. *Queen Victoria: First Media Monarch*. Oxford: Oxford University Press, 2003.

Poovey, Mary. *Making a Social Body: British Cultural Formation, 1830–1864*. Chicago and London: University of Chicago Press, 1995.

Shattock, Joanne (ed.). *The Cambridge Companion to English Literature, 1830–1914*. Cambridge: Cambridge University Press, 2010.

Web Sources

NINES (Networked Infrastructure for Nineteenth-Century Electronic Scholarship): www.nines.org/. A site devoted to encouraging online nineteenth-century scholarship.

Victoria Research Web: www.victorianresearch.org/ . A site on conducting research into the nineteenth century, complete with comprehensive listings of major reference and archival sources.

The Victorian Web: www.victorianweb.org/index.html. An invaluable site offering an overview of the period alongside selected scholarly essays and articles.

Voice of the Shuttle: Victorian: http://vos.ucsb.edu/browse.asp?id=2751. A major gateway listing many useful sites.

Key Historical Events

Best, Geoffrey. *Mid-Victorian Britain 1851–1875*. London: Fontana, 1985.

Briggs, Asa. *Victorian Cities*. Harmondsworth: Penguin, 1971.

Chakravarty, Gautam. *The Indian Rebellion in the British Imagination*. Cambridge: Cambridge University Press, 2004.

Chase, Malcolm. *Chartism: A New History*. Manchester: Manchester University Press, 2007.

Fegan, Melissa. *Literature and the Irish Famine 1845–1919*. Oxford: Clarendon Press, 2002.

Ferguson, Niall. *Empire: How Britain Made the Modern World*. London: Penguin, 2004.

Freeman, Michael. *Railways and the Victorian Imagination*. New Haven and London: Yale University Press, 1999.

Harris, José. *Private Lives, Public Spirit: A Social History of Britain, 1870–1914*. Oxford: Oxford University Press, 1993.

Hobsbawm, Eric. *The Age of Revolution: Europe 1789–1848*. London: Phoenix, 2000.

Hobsbawm, Eric. *The Age of Capital: 1848–1875*. London: Weidenfeld and Nicholson, 1995.

Hobsbawm, Eric. *The Age of Empire: 1875–1914*. London: Abacus, 1994.

Porter, Andrew (ed.). *The Nineteenth Century. The Oxford History of the British Empire*. Oxford: Oxford University Press, 1999.

Royle, Trevor. *Crimea: The Great Crimean War, 1854–1856*. London: Abacus, 2000.

Young, Paul. *Globalization and the Great Exhibition: The Victorian New World Order*. Basingstoke: Palgrave Macmillan, 2009.

Society, Politics and Class

Barringer, Tim. *Men at Work: Art and Labour in Victorian Britain*. New Haven: Yale University Press, 2005.

Cannadine, David. *The Decline and Fall of the British Aristocracy*. New Haven: Yale University Press, 1990.

Gagnier, Regenia. *Individualism, Decadence and Globalization: On the Relationship of Part to Whole, 1859–1920*. Basingstoke: Palgrave Macmillan, 2010.

Gallagher, Catherine. *The Industrial Reformation of English Fiction: Social Discourse and Narrative Form, 1832–1867*. Chicago: University of Chicago Press, 1985.

Gallagher, Catherine. *The Body Economic: Life, Death and Sensation in Political Economy and the Victorian Novel*. Princeton: Princeton University Press, 2006.

Hall, Catherine, Keith McClelland and Jane Rendall. *Defining the Victorian Nation: Class, Race, Gender and the Reform Act of 1867*. Cambridge: Cambridge University Press, 2000.

Humphreys, Anne. *Travels into the Poor Man's Country: The Work of Henry Mayhew*. Athens: University of Georgia Press, 1977.

Jones, Gareth Stedman. *Languages of Class: Studies in Working-Class History, 1832–1982*. Cambridge: Cambridge University Press, 1983.

Joyce, Patrick. *Visions of the People: Industrial England and the Question of Class, 1840–1914*. Cambridge: Cambridge University Press, 1991.

Joyce, Patrick. *Democratic Subjects: The Self and the Social in Nineteenth-Century England*. Cambridge: Cambridge University Press 1994.

McWilliam, Rohan. *Popular Politics in Nineteenth-Century England*. London: Routledge, 1998.

O'Brien, Patrick K., and Roland Quinault. *The Industrial Revolution and British Society*. Cambridge: Cambridge University Press, 1993.

Gender and Sexuality

Adams, James Eli. *Dandies and Desert Saints: Styles of Victorian Masculinity*. Ithaca: Cornell University Press, 1995.

Auerbach, Nina. *Woman and the Demon: The Life of a Victorian Myth*. Cambridge, MA: Harvard University Press, 1982.

Caine, Barbara. *Victorian Feminists*. Oxford: Oxford University Press, 1992.

David, Deirdre. *Rule Britannia: Women, Empire and Victorian Writing*. Ithaca and London: Cornell University Press, 1995.

Davidoff, Leonore, and Hall, Catherine. *Family Fortunes: Men and Women of the English Middle Class, 1780–1850*. Rev. edn. London: Routledge, 2002.

Dellamora, Richard (ed.). *Victorian Sexual Dissidence*. Chicago and London: University of Chicago Press, 1999.

Gallagher, Catherine, and Thomas Lacquer (eds). *The Making of the Modern Body: Sexuality and Society in the Nineteenth Century*. Berkeley: University of California Press, 1987.

Gilbert, Sandra, and Susan Gubar. *The Madwoman in the Attic: The Woman Writer and the Nineteenth-Century Literary Imagination*. New Haven: Yale University Press, 2000.

Girouard, Mark. *The Return to Camelot: Chivalry and the English Gentleman*. New Haven: Yale University Press, 1981.

Hadjiafxendi, Kyriaki and Patricia Zakreski, eds. *What is a Woman to Do? A Reader on Women, Work, and Art, c.1830–1890*. Bern: Peter Lang, 2011.

Langland, Elizabeth. *Nobody's Angels: Middle-Class Women and Domestic Ideology in Victorian Culture*. Ithaca and London: Cornell University Press, 1995.

Ledger, Sally. *The New Woman: Fiction and Feminism at the Fin de Siecle*. Manchester: Manchester University Press, 1997.

Nead, Lynda. *Myths of Sexuality: Representations of Women in Victorian Britain*. Oxford: Basil Blackwell, 1988.

Poovey, Mary. *Uneven Developments: The Ideological Work of Gender in Mid-Victorian England*. London: Virago, 1989.

Richardson, Angelique. *Love and Eugenics in the Late Nineteenth Century: Rational Reproduction and the New Woman*. Oxford: Oxford University Press, 2003.

Russett, Cynthia Eagle. *Sexual Science: The Victorian Construction of Womanhood*. Cambridge, MA and London: Harvard University Press, 1989.

Showalter, Elaine. *Sexual Anarchy: Gender and Culture at the Fin de Siècle*. London: Virago, 1992.

Tosh, John. *A Man's Place: Masculinity and the Middle Class Home in Victorian England*. New Haven and London: Yale University Press, 2007.

Religion and Belief

Brooks, Chris, and Andrew Saint (eds). *The Victorian Church: Architecture and Society*. Manchester: Manchester University Press, 1995.

Chadwick, Owen. *The Victorian Church*. 3rd edn. London: SCM, 1987.

Feldman, David. *Englishmen and Jews: Social Relations and Political Culture 1840–1914*. New Haven and London: Yale University Press, 1994.

Fraser, Hilary. *Beauty and Belief: Aesthetics and Religion in Victorian Literature*. Cambridge: Cambridge University Press, 1986.

Griffin, Susan M. *Anti-Catholicism and Nineteenth Century Fiction*. Cambridge: Cambridge University Press, 2004.

Herring, George. *What Was the Oxford Movement?* London: Continuum, 2002.

Jay, Elisabeth. *The Religion of the Heart: Anglican Evangelicalism and the Nineteenth Century Novel*. Oxford: Clarendon Press, 1979.

Jay, Elisabeth. *Faith and Doubt in Victorian Britain*. Basingstoke: Palgrave Macmillan, 1986.

Johnston, A. *Missionary Writing and Empire, 1800–1860*. Cambridge: Cambridge University Press, 2003.

Knight, Mark, and Emma Mason. *Nineteenth Century Religion and Literature: An Introduction*. Oxford: Oxford University Press, 2006.

McLeod, H. *Religion and Society in England, 1850–1914*. Basingstoke: Palgrave Macmillan, 1996.

Oppenheim, Janet. *The Other World: Spiritualism and Psychical Research in England, 1850–191*. Cambridge: Cambridge University Press, 1985.

Snell, K. D. M., and Paul S. Ell. *Rival Jerusalems: The Geography of Victorian Religion*. Cambridge: Cambridge University Press, 2000.

Walker, Pamela J. *Pulling the Devil's Kingdom Down: The Salvation Army in Victorian Britain*. Berkeley: University of California Press, 2001.

Wheeler, M. *Heaven, Hell, and the Victorians*. Cambridge: Cambridge University Press, 1994.

Philosophy and Ideas

Ashton, Rosemary. *The German Idea: Four British Writers and the Reception of German Thought, 1800–1860*. Cambridge: Cambridge University Press, 1980.

Blake, Kathleen. *The Pleasures of Benthamism: Victorian Literature, Utility, Political Economy*. Oxford: Oxford University Press, 2009.

Brake, Laurel. *Walter Pater*. Plymouth: Northcote House, 1994.

Collini, Stefan. *Public Moralists: Political Thought and Intellectual Life in Britain 1850–1930*. Oxford: Oxford University Press, 1993.

Daunton, Martin (ed.). *The Organisation of Knowledge in Victorian Britain*. Oxford: Oxford University Press, 2005.

Francis, Mark. *Herbert Spencer and the Invention of Modern Life*. Chesham: Acumen, 2007.

Gagnier, Regenia. *The Insatiability of Human Wants: Economics and Aesthetics in Market Society*. Chicago: University of Chicago Press, 2000.

Jay, Elisabeth, and Richard Jay (eds). *Critics of Capitalism: Victorian Reactions to 'Political Economy'*. Cambridge: Cambridge University Press, 1986.

Kern, Stephen. *The Culture of Time and Space, 1880–1918*. Cambridge, MA and London: Harvard University Press, 2003.

Scarre, Geoffrey. *Utilitarianism*. London: Routledge, 1996.

Scorupsci, John. *Why Read Mill Today?* London: Routledge, 2006.

Snyder, Laura J. *Reforming Philosophy: A Victorian Debate on Science and Society*. Chicago and London: University of Chicago Press, 2006.

Arts and Aesthetics

Barringer, Tim. *The Pre-Raphaelites: Reading the Image*. London: Weidenfeld and Nicholson, 1998.

Bendiner, Kenneth. *An Introduction to Victorian Painting*. New Haven: Yale University Press, 1985.

Blakesley, Rosalind P. *The Arts and Crafts Movement*. London: Phaidon, 2006.

Brooks, Chris. *The Gothic Revival*. London: Phaidon, 1999.

Bullen, J. B. *The Pre-Raphaelite Body: Fear and Desire in Painting, Poetry and Criticism*. Oxford: Clarendon Press, 1998.

Byerly, Alison. *Realism, Representation and the Arts in Nineteenth Century Literature*. Cambridge: Cambridge University Press, 1997.

Collini, Stefan. *Matthew Arnold: A Critical Portrait*. Oxford: Clarendon Press, 1994.

Flint, Kate. *The Victorians and the Visual Imagination*. Cambridge: Cambridge University Press, 2000.

Gagnier, Regenia. *Idylls of the Marketplace: Oscar Wilde and the Victorian Public*. Stanford: Stanford University Press, 1986.

Hewison, Robert, Ian Warrell and Stephen Wildman. *Ruskin, Turner and the Pre-Raphaelites*. London: Tate Gallery, 2000.

Hill, Rosemary. *God's Architect: Pugin and the Building of Romantic Britain*. London:Allen Lane, 2007.

Lambourne, Lionel. *The Aesthetic Movement*. London: Phaidon, 1996.

Parejo Vadillo, Ana. *Women Poets and Urban Aestheticism: Passengers of Modernity*. Basingstoke: Palgrave Mamillan, 2005.

Prettejohn, Elizabeth. *Art for Art's Sake: Aestheticism in Victorian Painting*. New Haven: Yale University Press, 2008.

Read, Benedict. *Victorian Sculpture*. New Haven: Yale University Press, 1982.

Schaffer, Talia. *The Forgotten Female Aesthetes: Literary Culture in Late-Victorian England*. Charlottesville: University Press of Virginia, 2000.

Yeazell, Ruth Bernard. *Art of the Everyday: Dutch Painting and the Realist Novel*. Princeton: Princeton University Press, 2008.

Popular Culture

Altick, Richard. *The Shows of London*. Cambridge, MA and London: Harvard University Press, 1978.

Bailey, Peter. *Leisure and Class in Victorian England: Rational Recreation and the Quest for Control, 1830–1885*. London: Methuen, 1987.

Bailey, Peter. *Popular Culture and Performance in the Victorian City*. Cambridge: Cambridge University Press, 1998.

Black, Barbara J. *On Exhibit: Victorians and Their Museums*. Charlottesville: University Press of Virginia, 2000.

Booth, Michael R. *Theatre in the Victorian Age*. Cambridge: Cambridge University Press, 1991.

Faulk, Barry J. *Music Hall and Modernity: The Late Victorian Discovery of Popular Culture*. Athens, Ohio: Ohio University Press, 2004.

Harrison, Brian Howard. *Drink and the Victorians: The Temperance Question in England, 1815–1872*. 2nd edn. Keele: Keele University Press, 1994.

Huggins, Mike. *The Victorians and Sport*. London: Hambledon, 2004.

Rappaport, Erika Diane. *Shopping for Pleasure: Women in the Making of London's West End*. Princeton, NJ: Princeton University Press, 2000.

Rauch, Alan. *Useful Knowledge: The Victorians, Morality, and the March of Intellect*. Durham, NC: Duke University Press, 2001.

Literary Production and Reception

Altick, Richard. *The English Common Reader: A Social History of the Mass Reading Public, 1800–1900*. Chicago: University of Chicago Press, 1957.

Brantlinger, Patrick. *The Reading Lesson: The Threat of Mass Literacy in Nineteenth Century British Fiction*. Bloomington: Indiana University Press, 1998.

Flint, Kate. *The Woman Reader 1837–1914*. Oxford: Clarendon Press, 1993.

Fraser, Hilary, Stephanie Green and Judith Johnston. *Gender and the Victorian Periodical*. Cambridge: Cambridge University Press, 2003.

Haywood, Ian. *The Revolution in Popular Literature: Print, Politics and the People 1790–1860*. Cambridge: Cambridge University Press, 2004.

Hughes, Linda, and Michael Lund. *The Victorian Serial*. Charlottesville and London: University Press of Virginia, 1991.

Jordan, John O., and Robert L. Patten (eds). *Literature in the Marketplace: Nineteenth-Century British Publishing and the Circulation of Books*. Cambridge: Cambridge University Press, 1995.

Keating, Peter. *The Haunted Study: A Social History of the English Novel 1875–1914*. London: Fontana Press, 1991.

King, Andrew, and John Plunkett (eds). *Victorian Print Media: A Reader*. Oxford: Oxford University Press, 2005.

Law, Graham. *Serializing Fiction in the Victorian Press*. Basingstoke: Palgrave Macmillan, 2000.

Onslow, Barbara. *Women of the Press in Nineteenth Century Britain*. Basingstoke: Palgrave Macmillan, 2001.

Peterson, Linda H. *Becoming a Woman of Letters: Myths of Authorship, Facts of the Victorian Market.* Princeton: Princeton University Press, 2009.

Rose, Jonathan. *The Intellectual Life of the British Working Classes.* New Haven and London: Yale University Press, 2001.

Shattock, Joanne, and Michael Woolf (eds). *The Victorian Periodical Press: Samplings and Soundings.* Leicester: Leicester University Press, 1982.

Vincent, David. *Literacy and Popular Culture: England, 1750–1914.* Cambridge: Cambridge University Press, 1989.

Empire and Race

Belich, James. *Replenishing the Earth: The Settler Revolution and the Rise of the Angloworld, 1783–1939.* Oxford: Oxford University Press, 1999.

Boehmer, Elleke (ed.). *Empire Writing: An Anthology of Colonial Literature, 1870–1918.* Oxford: Oxford University Press, 1998.

Brantlinger, Patrick. *Rule of Darkness: British Literature and Imperialism 1830–1914.* Ithaca: Cornell University Press, 1988.

Cain, P. J., and A. G. Hopkins. *British Imperialism, 1688–2000.* 2nd edn. Harlow: Longman, 2002.

Cannadine, David. *Ornamentalism: How the British Saw Their Empire.* London: Penguin, 2002.

Davis, Mike. *Late Victorian Holocausts: El Nino Famines and the Making of the Third World.* London and New York: Verso, 2001.

Hall, Catherine. *Cultures of Empire: Civilizing Subjects: Metropole and Colony in the English Imagination, 1830–1867.* Chicago: University of Chicago Press, 2002.

Hall, Catherine (ed.). *Cultures of Empire: Colonisers in Britain and the Empire of the Nineteenth and Twentieth Centuries: A Reader.* Manchester: Manchester University Press, 2000.

MacKenzie, John M. (ed.). *Imperialism and Popular Culture.* Manchester: Manchester University Press, 1986.

Pakenham, Thomas. *The Scramble For Africa 1876–191.* London: Weidenfeld and Nicolson, 1991.

Porter, Andrew, ed. *The Oxford History of the British Empire. Volume II. The Nineteenth Century.* Oxford: Oxford University Press, 1999.

Porter, Bernard. *The Absent-Minded Imperialists: Empire, Society and Culture in Britain.* Oxford: Oxford University Press, 2004.

Porter, Bernard. *The Lion's Share: A Short History of British Imperialism.* 4th edn. Harlow: Longman, 2004.

Pratt, Mary Louise. *Imperial Eyes: Travel Writing and Transculturation.* 2nd edn. London: Routledge, 2008.

Said, Edward. *Culture and Imperialism.* New York: Vintage Books, 1994.

Suleri, Sara. *The Rhetoric of English India.* Chicago: University of Chicago Press, 1992.

Science and Technology

Beer, Gillian. *Darwin's Plots: Evolutionary Narrative in Darwin, George Eliot and Nineteenth-Century Fiction.* 3rd edn. Cambridge: Cambridge University Press, 2009.

Beer, Gillian. *Open Fields: Science in Cultural Encounter*. Oxford: Oxford University Press, 1996.

Bourne Taylor, Jenny, and Sally Shuttleworth (eds). *Embodied Selves: An Anthology of Psychological Texts, 1830–1890*. Oxford: Clarendon Press, 1998.

Bowler, Peter. *Evolution: The History of an Idea*. 3rd edn. Berkeley and London: University of California Press, 1983.

Levine, George. *Darwin and the Novelists: Patterns of Science in Victorian Fiction*. Cambridge, MA: Harvard University Press, 1988.

Levine, George. *Dying to Know: Scientific Epistemology and Narrative in Victorian England*. Chicago: University of Chicago Press, 2002.

Levine, George. *Darwin Loves You: Natural Selection and the Re-Enchantment of the World*. Princeton and Oxford: Oxford University Press, 2006.

Lightman, Bernard. *Victorian Popularizers of Science: Designing Nature for New Audiences*. Chicago: University of Chicago Press, 2007.

Otis, Laura (ed.). *Literature and Science in the Nineteenth Century: An Anthology*. Oxford: Oxford University Press, 2002.

Rylance, Rick. *Victorian Psychology and British Culture, 1850–1880*. Oxford: Oxford University Press, 2000.

Weber, A. S. (ed.). *Nineteenth Century Science: A Selection of Original Texts*. Peterborough, Ontario: Broadview, 2000.

Index

Note: cross references in **bold** refer to whole chapters.